MEMORY AND LEARNING
The Ebbinghaus Centennial Conference

HERMANN EBBINGHAUS
(1850-1909)

Photograph courtesy of the National Library of Medicine,
Bethesda, Maryland

MEMORY AND LEARNING

The Ebbinghaus Centennial Conference

edited by

DAVID S. GORFEIN
ROBERT R. HOFFMAN
Adelphi University

IEA LAWRENCE ERLBAUM ASSOCIATES, PUBLISHERS

1987   Hillsdale, New Jersey   Hove and London

Lawrence Erlbaum Associates, Inc., Publishers
365 Broadway
Hillsdale, New Jersey 07642

Library of Congress Cataloging-in-Publication Data

Ebbinghaus Centennial Conference (1985 : Adelphi University)
Memory and learning.

Bibliography: p.
Includes indexes.
1. Memory—Congresses. 2. Learning, Psychology of—
Congresses. I. Gorfein, David S. II. Hoffman, Robert R.
III. Title.
BF370.E23 1985   153.1   86-24195
ISBN 0-89859-653-X
Printed in the United States of America
10 9 8 7 6 5 4 3 2 1

For Arthur Melton
D.S.G.

For Richard Honeck
R.R.H.

Contents

Preface

This volume should be of interest to experimental psychologists, especially those whose work relates to verbal memory. This volume would be appropriate for reading not only by experimental psychologists, but also by educational psychologists, cognitive scientists, and others whose interests intersect with the problem of verbal memory. This book would make for good reading in a seminar on memory, learning, or cognition. A number of the chapters should be of interest to historians of psychology.

Its focus on *verbal* memory entails the idea that the chapters refer to such topics as the representation of word meaning, word comprehension, and language. Its focus on verbal *memory* entails that the chapters refer to various memory phenomena and hypothetical explanations for them. Although the contributors discuss many specific aspects of memory research and many specific phenomena, the volume is broad in scope—including surveys and discussions of the history of psychology as well as summaries of basic research findings about various memory phenomena.

WHERE THIS VOLUME CAME FROM

Those phenomena, such as the effects of types of practice on memory, the recency effect, and others, were all investigated or were of interest to one Hermann Ebbinghaus, who is regarded as a founder of the field of the experimental psychology of "higher mental processes." For the centennial celebration of the publication of his pioneering work on memory, a group of experimental psychologists gathered to assess the state of the art, and this volume represents the proceedings of that conference.

The moment we reminded ourselves that 1985 would mark the 100th anniversary of the publication of Ebbinghaus' research, *On Memory* (1885), it occurred to us that it might be an appropriate time for experimental psychologists to convene for a discussion of what we've accomplished these past 100 years by all our studies of learning and memory. We were surprised to find that no one in the U.S. was planning such a meeting, and so we immediately went to work making phone calls, writing letters, and trying to drum up some support.

We subsequently learned of the plans of psychologists at Passau University to hold a conference, one that would focus on the history of psychology. The International Hermann Ebbinghaus Symposium was held at the *Institut für Geschichte der Neueren Psychologie* at Passau University May 30–June 2, 1985. We hoped it would be helpful to the field of psychology for us to design a conference that focused on research: (a) The overall results of the past 100 years of research, (b) modern research that follows in the Ebbinhaus tradition, and (c) modern research that appears to challenge that tradition. The plan was to span the gaps between the traditions established by Ebbinghaus, by associationism, the work of the 1950s on verbal behavior, and modern work in the tradition of cognitive science.

Although attempts were made to obtain federal and private grant support for the comparatively modest cost of the conference, we were unable to do so. A global overview of the state of the art was not deemed fundable by some of our peers who reviewed proposals. Other peers had their own nominations for those persons that should be invited, and found it inexplicable that our list did not include Professor ''X.'' We should note that most of those ''Xs'' actually had been invited, but had declined for a variety of good reasons. Those who came to the conference gave a good account of our field.

Awareness of the slim potential for access to outside funding saved us considerable effort, actually. In our initial contacts with colleagues we found there to be considerable interest in holding an ''Ebbinghaus Centennial'' conference, even with everyone knowing that we would be hard-pressed to obtain much in the way of funding.

SOME ACKNOWLEDGMENTS

Our colleagues' support for the idea of a conference enabled us to approach the officers of Adelphi University and make a case for arranging a meeting. Due to its proximity to New York City, travel is easy to arrange. We have had some measure of success with our annual Adelphi Conference on Applied Experimental Psychology, a meeting that attracts people mostly from the northeastern U.S. We felt confident that we could hold a major conference with only a little support (relatively speaking).

We managed to obtain Adelphi funds that enabled us to provide our participants with some reimbursement for their transportation, lodging, and meals. We would like to thank the College of Arts and Sciences and Adelphi University for their support. Without it, the conference would not have been possible.

It is an excellent testament to the spirit of experimental psychology that the participants were eager to come, even though the budget would be slim. When many experimental psychologists find themselves drained and doubtful of their lot in life, and find themselves asking the question "Why am I doing what I'm doing?", they find themselves answering, "Because my work is exciting!". It is gratifying to see how much can be accomplished when a measure of interest is mixed in with a slim budget. It is because of this excitement that conferences like ours can work, despite the economic situation. We thank all of our participants.

For all of us, the real excitement and gratification comes from discussing ideas and research findings. We hope that all of our participants were rewarded by such feelings, whether during the conference itself, during a casual chat in the hotel lobby, or over a plate of Long Island seafood. There were many interesting discussions and debates at the meeting, and we feel that our job as organizers and editors has been amply rewarding.

The effect of the motivational variable was also manifested in another aspect of the conference. A number of our undergraduate psychology majors at Adelphi are very excited, enthused young researchers. Through their efforts, the Psychology Club chipped in and helped sponsor some of the more social aspects of the meeting. We thank President Elizabeth Tierny and all the members of the club for their support. In return, they were able to see a number of major psychologists "in action." In a like manner, many of our graduate students chipped in by volunteering for airport pickup duty, gathering guests from the Long Island Railroad, getting the participants from the hotel to the University, and, in short, being "go-fers." We acknowledge them in alphabetical order: David Balser, Andrea Bubka, Rochelle Geshgoren, Jane O'Brien, Andrea Spata, Marianne Walters, and Megan Willis.

We arranged a modest display of historical memorabilia, and this turned out to be one of the highlights of the conference. We thank Thom Verhave for bringing a number of the rare books he owns, and also thank Michael Pallak, Executive Director of the A.P.A., for allowing us to display the copy of *Über das Gedächtnis* which is in the A.P.A. archives and which contains a signed dedication from Ebbinghaus to T. G. Fechner.

We thank the staff of the Adelphi Computer Center for the help they gave us in loading authors' manuscripts from diskettes onto our PRIME computer, on which most of the editing was done. We also thank Eleanor Shaw, Patricia Carey, Karen Thompson, and especially Ruth Meshijian, all secretaries in the Department of Psychology, for their help with word processing. We are grateful to Robin Akerstrom, of the Department of Psychology at Brandeis University, for her help in preparing the subject index. Finally, we would like to thank Jack Burton and Art Lizza of LEA for their help and smiles.

David S. Gorfein
Robert R. Hoffman

INTRODUCTION

1 Introduction

David S. Gorfein and Robert R. Hoffman
Adelphi University

The moment we reminded ourselves that 1985 would mark the 100th anniversary of the experimental psychology of learning and memory, as dated from the publication of Ebbinghaus' research *On Memory* (1885), it occurred to us that it might be an appropriate time for experimental psychologists to convene for a discussion of the accomplishments to date of research on learning and memory.

We subsequently learned of the plans of psychologists at Passau University to hold a conference to focus on the history of psychology. The International Hermann Ebbinghaus Symposium was held at the Institut für Geschichte der Neueren Psychologie at Passau University May 30–June 2, 1985.

We were surprised to find that no one in the United States was planning such a meeting, and so we immediately went to work. In this volume we present the proceedings of a conference held on April 19 and 20, 1985, at Adelphi University. Our goal was to assemble leading researchers, not so much for the purpose of discussing historical matters as for the purpose of assessing the state of the art in terms of research methods and findings: (a) The overall results of the past 100 years of research, (b) modern research that follows in the Ebbinghaus tradition, and (c) modern research that appears to challenge that tradition. The plan was to span the gaps between the traditions established by Ebbinghaus, by associationism, the work of the 1950s on verbal behavior, and modern work in the tradition of "cognitive science." In summarizing the accomplishments of the past 100 years of research, we also wanted our contributors to describe their own new research.

Looking back on the project, we believe we have met our goals. Although the conference included a few eye-opening discussions of the history of psychology, and Ebbinghaus in particular, it consisted primarily of intensive reviews of

3

research. The chapters in this volume survey a great deal of research, work on theoretical and mathematical models, and new research as well.

The chapters in this volume appear in roughly the same order as the presentations at the conference, which were organized topically beginning with discussions of history and philosophy, proceeding to discussions of modern research.

HISTORICAL BACKGROUND

As the chapters in the opening section reveal, much of what has been written in history of psychology texts is incomplete as far as the psychology of learning is concerned, and much of what has been written about Ebbinghaus is both incomplete and inaccurate. The chapter by William K. Estes, which opens the book, is a broad survey of theories of memory from the inception of the psychology of learning to modern times. Estes' purpose is a difficult one to satisfy: to make some overall assessment of the progress made in our theorizing about memory and learning processes.

The chapter by Chaffin and Herrmann presents a survey of scholarship on learning prior to Ebbinghaus, beginning with the ancients. Chaffin and Herrmann introduce a theme that occurs more than once in the volume: the lament of the state of scholarship in experimental psychology. They point to the benefits of having a solid knowledge of the history of one's field, such as avoiding the effort taken by "rediscoveries." Verhave and Van Hoorn, in their chapter, take this theme further and illustrate some of the misperceptions modern psychologists have about historical facts and about the novelty of their theoretical ideas.

The chapter by Hoffman, Bringmann, Bamberg, and Klein focuses on Ebbinghaus himself, his life and times. Their chapter corrects much of what has been said about Ebbinghaus in history of psychology texts written in English. It also serves as a foundation for many of the chapters that follow, in that it includes a description of each of the actual experiments that Ebbinghaus conducted on learning.

The chapter by Slater Newman focuses on research that was conducted in America in the years following the publication of Ebbinghaus' work. Thus, Newman assesses the ways that Ebbinghaus influenced the development of the experimental psychology of learning in the U.S. in terms of its topics and research methods.

CONTEXT AND MEMORY

Since Ebbinghaus conducted his research on memory, experimental psychology has gone through a number of changes. Much of what was said in Ebbinghaus' day (about the process of learning and association) became assimilated, in America, into the tradition of "verbal behavior" and lost its original mentalistic flavor. The cognitive revolution came to pass, and scores of studies were conducted that relate to one or another type of information-processing model.

In a recent review of the field of research on human memory, Horton and Mills (1984) suggest that the prevailing theme in current research is the focus on one or another aspect of the experimental context. It seems, therefore, an appropriate reflection of the *Zeitgeist* that a major portion of the conference dealt with that topic. In his chapter, Slamecka, in the Ebbinghaus tradition, argues that frequency of exposure is a primary determinant of memory, in contrast to attempts to minimize its impact or subsume it under the rubric of contextual and encoding variability. He presents some new research evidence for the view that the law of frequency is robust under wide variation of experimental manipulation. In his discussion of Slamecka's chapter, Glanzer raises some doubts as to the strength of the case for frequency, that is, perhaps it is overstated by Slamecka.

Wickens' contribution clarifies the meanings of the term "context" as used in the literature. He argues that there are two distinct meanings, and suggests that unless these are clarified by an appropriate modifier, we will be misled in our research and theorizing. Gorfein, in his chapter on a theory of short-term memory, makes use of Wickens' distinction between two types of context, and shows that both contribute to performance in the short-term memory distractor task. Glenberg, long a proponent of contextual fluctuation as an explanation of the "recency" effect in free recall, makes an apparent break with his past theorizing in emphasizing temporal discrimination and not contextual fluctuation as the basis for the recency effect.

In his discussion of the three chapters on context, Crowder and Greene support Glenberg's view but suggest that the "battle appears to have been joined." It will be interesting to see what the future will bring with respect to the issue of context effects in memory and their explanation.

SEMANTIC MEMORY

A major trend in recent psychological research has been the inquiry into the nature of the meanings that underlie the words and concepts that get learned and remembered. In her chapter, Lynne Reder contrasts the approaches of Ebbinghaus and Bartlett in an attempt to explicate the apparent contradictions between them. The contradiction she focuses on deals with the fluency of expert knowledge and the phenomena reported by investigators of the "fan effect." This chapter, like the one by Roediger and Blaxton, involves a focus on the processes of knowledge utilization.

Of all the chapters in this volume, that by Chaffin and Herrmann is most direct in dealing with the problem of meaning as it relates to memory. Chaffin and Herrmann review research on peoples' judgments of semantic relations such as similarity (e.g., antonymy, synonymy), case relations (e.g., agent–action), part–whole (e.g., perception versus action classes). People can sort words on the basis of such relations and are able to identify related families of relations. New research reported by Chaffin and Herrmann shows how the relations underlie analogistic reasoning and latency effects in semantic decisions. Chaffin and Herrmann offer an account that differs from the associative hypothesis in which each relation is regarded as simply an associative link or marker. They postulate that relations can be decomposed into "relational elements."

In his review of the chapters on semantic memory, Glucksberg points to the possibility of alternative explanations of the phenomena that Reder and Chaffin & Herrmann describe, and suggests some cautions in going too far beyond the data. This was a recurrent theme in the conference, as reflected in Bahrick's conference summary.

The chapter by Baars makes for a very interesting contribution to this volume. As a classically trained scholar, Ebbinghaus was familiar with all aspects of psychology and philosophy of mind. It is not widely known that Ebbinghaus' early work in psychology and philosophy (his *Habilitationschrift*) was a treatise on theories of the unconscious. Baars' chapter reflects this side of Ebbinghaus' work and interests. Ebbinghaus would no doubt have been extremely pleased to see how modern psychologists have devised ways to explore experimentally the relations of unconscious intentions to action. Baars' research on speech errors involves the testing of contrasting hypotheses, yielding a model of intention. That, too, would please Ebbinghaus. Although Baars' model is couched in the language of modern information processing, it is compatible with the formulations generated by Herbart, Ebbinghaus, James, and others of their generation.

In his comments on the chapter by Baars, Richard Dolinsky points to a commonality of Baars' work with that reported in the chapter by John Ceraso—a focus on what error data can tell us about the relation of memory, consciousness, and performance. Dolinsky cites parallels between the modern work and earlier theorizing by Vygotsky about the "semantic peculiarities of inner speech." Dolinsky points also to the need for further hypothesis testing of large-scale models such as Baars' "global workspace" model.

TOPICS IN MEMORY RESEARCH

The fifth section of the volume consists of chapters on various topics of modern research on learning and memory. Murdock presents a summary of his recent research and theorizing on memory storage, in an attempt to demonstrate that a distributed memory model can account for a variety of phenomena. Specifically, the model can be fitted to such phenomena as performance improvement across trials, serial position effects, and release from proactive interference in short-term memory. Although broad in scope on a theoretical level, the formulations offered by Murdock are specific and mathematical. Appropriate to our theme on Ebbinghaus, Murdock's model hearkens back to Ebbinghaus' ideas about associations forming "webs" (rather than simple "links").

In her comments on Murdock's paper, Snodgrass points out that although Murdock proposes a model for memory that employs "convolution" and "correlation" operators to describe storage and retrieval, the model itself seems to make assumptions of other storage and retrieval processes as well.

John Ceraso contributed a chapter on generic recall, the name given to the recall that occurs when the item to be recalled is only imperfectly remembered. He presents data that suggest that memory loss mimics the process of storage.

Herman Buschke describes memory from the perspective of a researcher who is interested in assessing deficits in memory and verbal learning, and in relating the deficits to neurological problems. His discussion points out the assumptions that are made in the claim that a person has a memory deficit (e.g., that there are types of memory, that the problem is in memory rather than in learning or acquisition processes). By treating the memory test as an experiment, Buschke is able to establish criteria for the design of memory tests, tests that would be able to identify deficits.

The final major chapter in this section, by Roediger and Blaxton, focuses on "dissociation" in memory, in which performance on recall tasks follows different patterns than performance on fragment completion tasks, when encoding operations are manipulated. They argue for a memory utilization interpretation of dissociation, as opposed to a memory storage approach. In his comments on their chapter, Gorfein points to the importance of dissociation to theories of memory, and urges caution in rejecting theories on the basis of the observed dissociations.

OVERVIEW

In the final section of the volume, Bahrick presents some comments in the way of an overview of the conference and the contributions to it. He alerts us to the dangers of postulating intervening states and urges attention to the implementation of functionalist principles. In many ways, Bahrick's concluding chapter brings us back to where we began, in the section on historical perspectives, with some fundamental questions about memory and about research methods.

II HISTORICAL BACKGROUND

2 One Hundred Years of Memory Theory

William K. Estes
Harvard University

This anniversary of the experimental study of memory is a good time to take stock of the results of the intervening century of research and theorizing. An assessment must be done in relation to some frame of reference, however, and several alternatives are conspicuous in the recent literature on memory.

Romantic. The romantics identify progress with the solution of big, practical problems.

Baconian. In this tradition, the prime task is to accumulate facts, classify them, and look for generalizations.

Newtonian. Progress is measured by the construction and organization of increasingly powerful theories that yield understanding of phenomena at an abstract level.

When we look back over the histories of sciences with many more centuries of experience than ours, the achievements that seem notable are mainly the theories and models that have survived grueling empirical testing—also some facts, to be sure, but facts as interpreted by theories. Occasionally the record shows solutions of major practical problems, generally achieved by application or extension of the experimental and formal methods evolved in the Baconian and Newtonian traditions rather than by direct attacks based on the common sense and intuition of the scientifically unsophisticated. It also seems frivolous to me to suppose that matters will be different when our century of research is looked back on from a longer time perspective. Thus my frame of reference for an attempt at evaluation will probably appear to be about three parts Newtonian to one part Baconian, with just a pinch of Romanticism thrown in.

How does the output of 100 years of research on memory stack up when scaled in these coordinates?

THE GROWTH OF MEMORY THEORY

In Fig. 2.1, I present my own picture of the climb of memory theory from the pre-experimental period (that is to say, pre-Ebbinghaus) to the recent past. The graph itself is a representation of progress on some almost fanciful scale of theoretical achievement, with the plotted points denoting my nominations for advances that mark milestones along the path.

Even the doggedly monotone upward course of the path of memory theory as I reconstruct it is by no means beyond dispute. A similar effort by Tulving (1983), which I recalled after composing mine, exhibits wave-like variation around a distinctly shallow upward trend, a modest peak at the time of Ebbinghaus and James being followed by a decline through the dark ages of behaviorism, and finally recovery to a current plateau barely above the level of 1900. The very different appearances of Tulving's schematization and mine may, however, owe partly to the fact that mine is intended to represent cumulative progress whereas Tulving's evidently indexes the levels of significant activity at different times.

Before discussing some of the evolutionary trends that are implicit in Fig. 2.1,

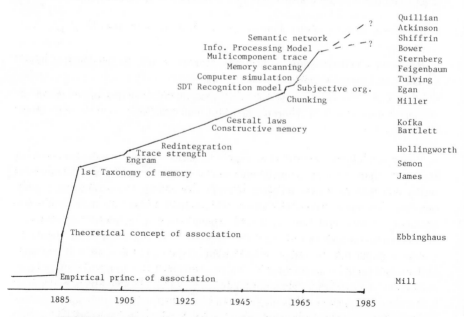

FIGURE 2.1. The growth of memory theory in terms of the appearance of significant concepts, marked along the graph, and investigators associated with them, indicated in the column at the right.

I will explicate briefly the contributions marked along the graph and associated with the investigators listed on the right. Though I could, like Tulving, have started earlier, I chose for purposes of this conference to mark the initial rise of memory theory with Ebbinghaus's formulation of the first genuine theoretical principle of association. Only a few years later, there appeared the beginnings of a theoretically significant taxonomy of memory, in William James's distinction between primary and secondary memory (*Principles of Psychology*, 1890).

The next cluster of advances dealt with the concept of a memory trace. Semon (1906/1921) is credited with introducing the term *engram*, referring both to the representation of an experienced event in memory and its neural substrate (Tulving, 1983). Hollingworth (1913) developed a notion corresponding to the current hypothesis of trace strength, and applied it to the analysis of recognition. Hamilton (1859) and Hollingworth (1928) introduced the concept of *redintegration*, the reinstatement of a memory trace on presentation of a stimulus corresponding to some constituent or fragment of the situation that originally produced the trace.

A new tradition of experimentation on memory in relatively natural settings was initiated by Bartlett (1932), in research designed to bring out the role of imagery and the constructive aspects of recall. Gestalt theory became a conspicuous element in the study of perception from around 1930 but did not exert much direct effect on the growth of memory theory except for its emphasis on dynamic and configural aspects of the memory trace (Koffka, 1935), which influenced some of the "neoassociationistic" theories that began to appear decades later (Anderson & Bower, 1973).

A lengthy period during which research on memory was largely conducted in the framework of functionalism and simple associationism began to shade into a new era marked by the emergence of cognitive psychology as a distinct discipline during the 1950s. Thus, ideas concerning organizational aspects of memory appeared, manifested in the concepts of chunking (Miller, 1956), computer simulated networks (Feigenbaum, 1963), and subjective organization (Tulving, 1968). This line of theorizing continued, with the conceptions of multicomponent memory traces (Bower, 1967) and semantic networks (Quillian, 1967). More or less concurrent with these last developments was the application of signal detectability theory to recognition (Egan, 1958), the flourishing of theoretically driven research on short-term memory scanning (beginning with Sternberg, 1966), and the formulation of the first widely influential model of memory based on information-processing ideas (Atkinson & Shiffrin, 1968).

MODELS OF MEMORY IN CROSS-SECTION

There has assuredly been a great escalation of activity along the path illustrated in Fig. 2.1, but what does it add up to? A common lamentation among students as well as investigators of memory is the lack of cumulative progress toward a generally accepted theory that provides a framework and direction for research. As a convenient starting point for an attempt to assess the judiciousness of this complaint, I turned to the collection of theoretical efforts assembled by Norman (1970) at the height of the wave of mathematical and computer models of memory that gushed forth during the decade following the inception of the information-processing approach to cognition. In that collection, a dozen investigators (in some instances pairs), recognizable as being among the most visible and influential contributors to the flourishing of models of memory in the 1960s, presented their current theories. At first glance, the most conspicuous attribute of the collection is its diversity—apparently quite in support of the claim of a lack of a convergence on any common or generally accepted theory.

Contrary to what one might have expected, and what would probably be true of a similar collection today, the diversity does not stem primarily from heterogeneity of the empirical bases of the theories. A cluster analysis of the empirical studies cited would show not only a great deal of overlap across chapters, but also a distinct concentration of attention on a few research categories. With the exception of the chapter by Feigenbaum, nearly all of the presentations draw heavily on studies of short-term recognition memory, combined in various patterns with short-term recall, free recall, and paired-associate learning. It is the forms of the models that present dazzling variation, ranging from basically deterministic mathematical models of classical form, through probabilistic Markovian models, to network models implemented wholly in computer simulations. Differences in scope are almost as conspicuous. Norman and Rumelhart presented a broad framework, capable in principle of encompassing much of the range of empirical work of the period. A number of other contributors (Wickelgren, Bernbach, Kintsch, Morton, and Feigenbaum) offered alternative approaches with much the same potential scope, though at the time worked out in detail for more limited subareas. A few models were specific to short-term memory (Reitman, Sperling & Speelman, and Murdock), and a still smaller subgroup focused on aspects of memory having to do with information retrieval and rehearsal (Shiffrin, Bjork).

For my present enterprise, however, the prime question is whether the diversity of the models assembled in 1970 reflects the deep structure or only the surface structure, to use a linguistic analogy. An objective answer is not easy to come by, owing to wide variation in terminology and styles of formalization, but I think some important commonalities are discernible. Perhaps the most conspicuous is the assumption of a small number of stages or levels of processing information in memory. It seemed almost universally agreed that the first stage in a learning experience is the registration of patterned sensory information in very short-term, modality-specific, memory systems, or "buffers." This process would free the sensory systems to deal with new input, the buffers holding information long enough for the relatively slow mechanisms associated with cognitive operations to come into play. The second processing stage is the selection of a subset of information from the sensory buffers for passage into limited-capacity, short-term memory system ("active memory," "acquisition memory," or "working memory" in different formulations) where it is maintainable by rehearsal for periods of the order of minutes and is subject to cognitive operations such as scanning, comparison, and recoding. The final stage is the entry of informational units, formed by the selection, combination, or abstraction from the contents of short-term memory into a long-term system, which is organized for retrieval.

As far as I can discern, there were no material differences among the 1970 theorists regarding this basic sequence of processing stages, and indeed none has developed since then, except perhaps on the secondary issue of discreteness of the stages. In the system of Atkinson and Shiffrin (1968), which set the pattern for the treatments in many of the 1970 models, the processing of each item of information follows the same sequence of stages, and this view seems to be implicit, at least, in most work on memory in the information-processing tradition.

There is a core of agreement but also some sharp differences with regard to the outputs of the processing stages. It is universally assumed that the sequence of stages transforms information progressively into forms that are less modality-specific, more abstract, and more highly organized for retrieval. In the Atkinson and Shiffrin system and its variants, the sensory, short-term, and long-term systems comprise distinct memory stores, the major structural components of memory, within which cognitive processes operate. Some theorists who were less influenced by information-processing ideas (e.g., Wickelgren) acknowledged the progressive recoding of information during processing, but preferred a representation in terms of the strengths of very short-term, short-term, and long-term memory traces. In a quite different direction, investigators whose concern was primarily with memory as a constituent of computer-simulation models for information processing viewed short- and long-term memory stores not as structural components of the memory system a learner brings to a task, but rather as components of a dynamic organization generated by the learner in response to task demands. This view seems implicit in Feigenbaum's summary of his EPAM model in the 1970 collection and was developed much more explicitly by Newell (1973).

On the central issue of the form of memory representations, the 1970 review shows less of a consensus than on processing stages. Under the influence of the new information-processing orientation, a majority of the theorists formulated models in terms of the storage and retrieval of units of information, whether as simple as single-letter presentations or as complex as paired associates or verbal concepts. In only a few instances (Norman & Rumelhart, Morton) do we find explicit statements of the assumption that memory representations take the form of vectors of features or attribute values—a characterization that has, I believe, since become the most generally accepted view of representation.

A perennial problem in this field is the interpretation of recognition and recall, the two most common means of assessing memory. The modal view in 1970 was that recognition is based on the comparison of a test stimulus pattern with a stored memory trace, the degree of matching being converted to a recognition judgment by the mechanisms postulated by signal detectability theory. Recall was assumed to require a process of memory search, successful searches eventuating in recognition of a partial match between a stored representation and information incorporated in the cue for recall. Thus, recognition was conceived to be a subprocess of recall.

On some traditional theoretical issues, agreement among the 1970 theorists is much less in evidence. Comparison of the various models shows little consensus on the relation between the concepts of association, memory trace, and units of information storage. Each of the models in the 1970 assemblage is based on one of these three conceptions of what is remembered from a learning experience. The modal view seemed to be that characterizations in terms of the storage and retrieval of items of information had become the most convenient, but the relation of the new information-processing vocabulary to the more traditional one of trace and association received little consideration. It seems likely, however, that few would have disagreed with Greeno's argument that the long-dominant concept of association could best be superseded by the notion of a configured memory trace, even in the case of paired associates, and that operations on memory traces could, in turn, be translated without loss into the vocabulary of item storage and retrieval. Other unresolved issues had to do with the role of strength versus multiplicity of memory traces and the decay versus interference interpretation of forgetting.

A limitation of the 1970 review for our purposes is that a number of currently influential concepts and issues were not represented. Among these are the episodic-semantic memory distinction (Tulving, 1968); the notion of levels of processing as distinguished from memory stores (Craik & Lockhart, 1972); and the distinctions between verbatim and gist recall and between analog and propositional representations (Anderson, 1976). To fill out our picture of overall trends in memory theory over the century since 1885, I propose now to look back from the 1970 cross-section, to trace the development of some of the central concepts, then forward to the present, to see how far we have come toward resolving issues that were open a decade and a half ago.

As displayed along the graph in Fig. 2.1, the significant steps in the development of memory theory often seem to follow one another with no obvious continuity. The reason is to be found mainly in the fact that most of the milestones are associated with one or the other of a few research themes that have been intertwined from the time of Ebbinghaus to the present. I take two of these for review: One deals with the evolution and elaboration of the concept of association, the other with the interpretation of retention and forgetting.

Levels of Association Concepts

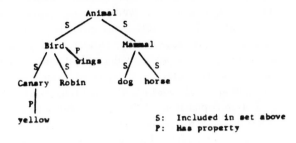

Semantic net

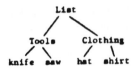

S: Included in set above
P: Has property

Hierarchies

```
                List
              /      \
          Tools       Clothing
          /  \         /   \
      knife  saw     hat   shirt
```

Parallel associations

```
             List
           /   |   \
       knife  hat   table
```

Remote associations   5 - 6 - 2   9 - 6 - 7

Chain associations   VOX - GAF - MEV

FIGURE 2.2.   Levels of concepts in association theory. The ordering from bottom to top also indicates the chronology of the theoretical developments.

THE CONCEPT OF ASSOCIATION

Several stages in the evolution of the concept of association are illustrated in Fig. 2.2. The concept was long familiar by 1885, but it had no real theoretical content, being little more than a label for the observed tendency for one item to lead to recall of another. Ebbinghaus showed that both the existence and the strength of an association could be inferred from independent, converging lines of empirical evidence. Immediately after one has observed the successive occurrence of items A and B, the formation of an association is presumed if presentation of A leads to recall of B. But what if recall fails on a later test? Should we say that the association no longer exists? That it still exists but in a weakened state? These questions had no answers in the earlier, qualitative theories of association. Ebbinghaus, however, demonstrated that variation in the strength of an association could be predicted under specifiable conditions and could be measured by the "savings" in the number of repetitions of the sequence A–B needed to restore recallability. Further, Ebbinghaus recognized that memory for a list or sequence would be vulnerable if supported only by associations between successive members, for the loss or even temporary weakening of any one association could cause recall of the remainder of the sequence to fail.

For an explanation of the actual robustness of many learned sequences, Ebbinghaus proposed an interpretation in terms of remote associations (line 4 of Fig. 2.2) and supported this idea with some ingenious experiments on the transfer of learning from original lists to "derived" lists in which items that were adjacent in the new list had been separated by one, two, or more items in the original list. Positive transfer, in comparison to a random control condition, provided evidence for remote, or indirect associations between nonadjacent items.

The concept of remote associations has had a somewhat checkered history. First, the evidence Ebbinghaus himself was able to adduce does not look terribly robust. Later investigators who tried to replicate Ebbinghaus's findings on savings for derived lists that should benefit from remote associations have reported mixed results (Crowder, 1976; Young, 1968). My own impression is that the idea of remote associations is soundly conceived and that, as I note later, there are good theoretical reasons for expecting mixed results from the kinds of experiments that have been done to test the concept. More importantly, the notions of direct and remote associations together do not suffice to handle all the interesting problems of simple list learning.

Consider my problem when, on moving to Cambridge, I had to learn the prefixes to my home and office telephone numbers, which proved to be 492 and 495, respectively. If the only mechanism available were simple, interitem associations, I could not have learned the two numbers, for the digit 9 would be linked to 5 in one of the phone numbers and to 2 in the other. Remote associations would not help, for the same would be true of the remote linkages of 4 to 5 in one number and 4 to 2 in the other. Meditating on this problem some years ago, I was led to the conclusion that difficulties of the kind illustrated require the assumption that memory for any material taking the form of a list (a phone number, a sequence of letters making up a word, a shopping list, or whatever) is built around a control element—the analog of "list marker" in the models of Anderson and Bower (1972, 1973)—which is associated with all of the items of the list, yielding a structure like the one illustrated in Fig. 2.3. Here, the control element for the phone number 495 is associated with each of the three digits, each of the digits is associated with its neighbor, and also the initial digit, 4, is associated with the terminal digit, 5. The model that I formulated goes further in distinguishing two qualitative types of associations: those leading from the con-

Office   Home

495   492

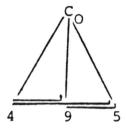   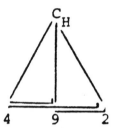

4   9   5   4   9   2

FIGURE 2.3. Memory representations for prefixes of telephone numbers in terms of control elements (C_O and C_H) and excitatory (vertical)
and inhibitory (horizontal) associations.

trol element to the individual items being excitatory and those from one item to
another being inhibitory (Estes, 1972). Thus, when the control element for the
office phone number is activated, it sends excitation to all three of the digits but
the digits 9 and 5 are inhibited by their connections to 4 until the response
corresponding to the first digit is activated and releases its inhibitory effect on the
other allowing 9 to occur next and then 5.

For a preliminary test of the model, I looked at its predictions for grouping
effects in list learning. The nature of the predictions can be illustrated in terms of
an unpublished experiment conducted in my laboratory in which subjects learned
strings of 12 unrelated letters to a criterion of perfect recall. Five conditions
differed in the way the letters were grouped when simultaneously presented to
the subject: In one condition they were presented as a single list of 12, in another
condition two lists of 6, in another three lists of 4, in another four lists of 3, and
in the fifth condition six lists of 2. On the assumption that the different kinds of
associations were formed with equal probabilities on each learning trial, the
model implies that the relationship between trials to learn and the size of subgroups should be as illustrated in Fig. 2.4, with a maximum for list length 12 and
a minimum when the items are grouped into triads. The data for our subjects
follow the predicted pattern, lending some support to the model. However, the
model is still in a very incomplete state of development, not yet able to account
for many details of the learning of even such simple lists. To my knowledge there
is, in fact, no extant model that can provide a reasonable quantitative account of

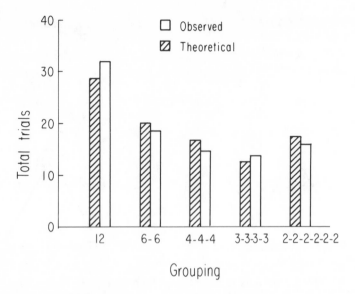

FIGURE 2.4. Predicted and observed trials to learn 12-letter sequences grouped in different ways during presentation in a test of the control-element model. The predicted values reflect the numbers of excitatory and inhibitory associations that must be learned to form the memory representation for each type of grouping.

such learning, and I do not know of any appreciable progress that has been made on the problem during the past 10 years or so.

One might well wonder why there has not been more substantial progress toward a real theory of list learning, considering that Ebbinghaus got the job off to a good start 100 years ago. Evidently the answer has to do in part with an unfortunate tendency among psychologists to label a problem that proves difficult as narrow or simplistic and look for greener fields. Thus, as we follow a sequence of developments in association theory upward through the levels in Fig. 2.2, the next historical development beyond Ebbinghaus's work on direct and remote associations was the introduction of conceptions of parallel associations and hierarchical organization, instigated by the research on free recall and memory for categorized lists that came into popularity in the 1950s. That line of investigation has given rise to current models that are capable of interpreting at least some aspects of free recall, for example, list length and "part–list cueing" effects (Anderson, 1972; Raaijmakers & Shiffrin, 1981).

Working with these models requires some technical background, however, and consequently they would not stand well in a popularity contest. Currently, research on any form of memory for lists is greatly outweighed by the volume of work on memory representations for words and their meanings, and, within the associationist tradition, the type of semantic memory model shown at the top of

Fig. 2.2. The semantic network continues a trend toward hierarchical organization but adds the idea of labeled associations, those in the figure being of two types, one (S) denoting relations of set inclusion between the connected items and the other type (P) denoting a property relationship (Collins & Quillian, 1972; Quillian, 1967).

THE STATUS OF ASSOCIATION THEORY

The variety of theoretical developments now going on under the increasingly broad mantle of association raises the question of what they have in common. What is association theory? I know of no definitive statement that commands general agreement, but nonetheless one can distill a modal conception from the literature. I shall start with what I will term the classical theory, which held sway from the time of Ebbinghaus until first seriously challenged by the cognitive theories of the 1970s. An association is a hypothetical connection between the representations of two items (stimuli and responses, events, concepts) in memory. These connections vary in strength as a function of frequency and recency of activation, but qualitatively they are all of a kind and all obey the same laws. In particular, to enable the growth of complex memory structures from simple components, they must obey some law or laws of combination. The forms of the laws of combination are not universally agreed on, but most often they are taken to be based on independence. The influence of multiple associations on a given element in memory is the result of independent combination of inputs over associative paths.

What has given this theory its long-term viability? Perhaps most important are the convenience and utility of having a common format for analyzing phenomena of learning and memory and a simple and widely understood vocabulary for expressing theoretical ideas. Further, in contrast to other vocabularies that have been proposed (such as the brain fields of Gestalt psychology), interpretations in terms of associations are readily mapped onto graphical depictions or formalized in mathematical or (currently) computer models.

Association concepts are continually subject to critiques and challenges. What are their weaknesses or limitations? The claim that the concept of association is circular, or simply a blank check for writing untestable theories, was refuted by Ebbinghaus. This claim is still sometimes put forward, revealing, in my view, an ignorance of the history of association theory. A claim that must be taken more seriously is that the concepts of association are inadequate to express ideas about organization in memory (Johnson, 1978), as witness the failure of association theory to provide satisfactory derivations of the concepts of chunking or featural encoding. I am not convinced that this claim is justified, but must concede that the task has not been accomplished. Actually, there seem to have been few serious attempts, and some of the occasional efforts to be found in the literature show surprising promise (for example, the work of Adams, 1979 and 1981, on the formation of functionally significant letter groups in reading).

A complaint that has become widespread with the flourishing of semantic memory models is that memory for meaningful relationships requires the assumption of qualitatively distinct varieties of labeled associations, such as those illustrated at the top level in Fig. 2.2. Two answers come to mind. One that is irrefutable but also unsatisfactory is the vague hope that ultimately it will be possible to reduce the labeled associations to combinations of simple ones. More radical, and also more interesting, is the thought that we might consider overhauling the concept of association from the ground up. Ideas along this line appear in some of the other contributions to this volume. I suggest one form such an overhaul might take by means of an example.

Suppose that in a paired-associate or probability-learning experiment an individual observes the occurrence of events A and B in succession, and in a later test situation, when presented with A, exhibits an expectation that B will follow. The interpretation of this behavior in terms of classical association theory is that events A and B had become associated in the individual's memory. But why should this association be the basis for expecting B to follow A, rather than A's following or accompanying B? The memory representation must contain some information in addition to a connection between the two representations. One possible route toward an interpretation is to put aside the concept of a single type of connection and assume that a memory trace for the perceived relationship of succession on a temporal attribute *is* the association between the events in memory (see Glenberg, this volume). The proposal would be that, in effect, all associations are labeled in terms of the relation of the associated events on an attribute that was attended to at the time of learning.

However, assigning labels to associations does little more than give us a way to elaborate graphical depictions of associative nets. When events that have occurred in some relation become associated in memory, where in the memory system does information about the type of relation reside and what form does it take? In a computer model, a natural solution is to represent memory for each of the associated events by a list of features or attribute values, together with a pointer to the address of the other representation. The pointer would correspond to the notion of an association and the information carried by a label would be included in the feature lists. A way of implementing a similar solution in terms of concepts of human memory may be found in a combination of the concepts of trace and associaion.

The concept of a memory trace may be as old as that of association, but it has lagged with regard to theoretical development. Historically, the concept of association derives primarily from experiments on learning of lists of discrete items, the concept of a memory trace from observations on memory for stimulus patterns or complex experiences. Perhaps because the train of research that Ebbinghaus set in motion was mainly of the former character, theoretical development was, for a long period, largely confined to the associative tradition. The trace concept appeared mainly in interpretations of recognition, and then simply as a carrier of a property such as assurance (Hollingworth, 1913) or familiarity, which serves as a basis for recognition judgments.

A perturbation of this tradition that occurred in the late 1960s finally began to shift the status of the trace or engram from a vague label to a genuine theoretical construct. I refer to the rise of interest in encoding as a basis of memory organization in short-term recall, stemming from findings on confusion errors (Conrad, 1964) and "release from proactive inhibition" (Wickens, 1970). The idea that memory traces might generally be encoded in terms of features or attribute values was first given formal development by Bower (1967, 1972) in his conception of multicomponent traces. Adding to this notion those of stimulus sampling yielded a model that brought order to a considerable range of phenomena of recognition and retention, and an offshoot became important in the models of semantic memory that began to appear shortly thereafter (Smith, Shoben, & Rips, 1974).

This elaboration of the trace concept gave rise to a curious situation in memory theory. On the one hand, we had the flourishing of network models in which abstract elements, or nodes, were connected by associations, labeled or unlabeled. On the other hand, there were multicomponent trace models. There was essentially no relation between the two conceptions. Network models were applied to interpret recall, language processing, and the organization of knowledge, whereas trace models were largely confined to explanations of recognition and similarity judgments.

A suggestion as to how the two kinds of models might fit together came, not directly from memory research, but indirectly from concurrent research on speech perception and letter and word recognition. In the information-processing framework that became fairly standard in the 1970s, it was held that input from speech or printed text activates feature detectors, which in turn, via associative pathways, activate memory representations for letters or phonological units and finally words (Estes, 1975; LaBerge & Samuels, 1974; Massaro, 1975). These representations presumably take the form of multicomponent traces, but at the same time they serve as the nodes in an associative network. They are not inert nodes, however, but interactive filters, which allow activation to proceed along associative pathways only when specific combinations of conditions are satisfied (Estes, 1975, 1976; Foss & Harwood, 1975). Thus, in the example of events A and B occurring in succession, later reinstatement of A may lead to recall of B only if both the attributes of A and of the context in which it occurred are activated in the trace representing its earlier occurrence. The activation of B will carry information about the earlier temporal succession by virtue of the components of its trace that represent the temporal attribute.

Finally, the formerly common criticism that association theory is limited to accounting for rote, or verbatim, memory is met (up to a point) by the current models in which the units associated are concepts or propositions (Anderson,

1976, 1983; Anderson & Bower, 1973; Rumelhart, Lindsay, & Norman, 1972). My qualification has to do with the large conceptual gap between classical association theory and models in which the elements associated are as complex as concepts or propositions. In the spirit of association theory, we should be expected to show how the representation of a proposition or concept in memory can itself be expressed in terms of simpler notions. This task has thus far been bypassed by the propositional theorists, and not yet undertaken seriously by those closer to the classical tradition. At present, the applicability of the concepts of association to these "high-level" models rests on the premise that ways can be found to represent concepts and propositions as multicomponent traces, or vectors, and the assumption (not without some support) that whatever the detailed character of the units associated, the dynamic properties of association will carry over from one theoretical level to another (Anderson, 1981; Estes, 1976).

RETENTION AND FORGETTING

From its inception, research on memory seems to have been motivated to an important degree by two somewhat contradictory aspects of memory in ordinary life. One is that a majority of the events we experience and the greater part of material we perceive either are never stored in memory or are lost rapidly and for the most part irretrievably. The other aspect is that some memories that are thought to have been lost recover unexpectedly. This paradoxical state of affairs was well recognized by Ebbinghaus (1885/1913):

> All sorts of ideas, if left to themselves, are gradually forgotten. This fact is generally known. Groups or a series of ideas which at first we could easily recollect or which recurred frequently of their own accord and in lively colors, gradually return more rarely and in paler colors, and can be reproduced by voluntary effort only with difficulty and in part. After a longer period even this fails, except, to be sure, in rare instances. Names, faces, bits of knowledge and experience that had seemed lost for years suddenly appear before the mind . . . and it is hard to see whence they came and how they managed to keep hidden so well in the meantime. (p. 62)

Ebbinghaus went on to note that psychologists of his period interpreted these everyday facts from several disparate points of view. One group put most importance on the revival of some memories even after long periods. They hypothesized that the memory traces or images laid down by perceptual experiences continue to exist in the memory system at their original "intensity," but eventually lose out in competition for retrieval with newer traces that, in some sense, overlay the older ones. This view was attributed to Aristotle and said by Ebbinghaus still to be authoritative.

The second and third groups mentioned by Ebbinghaus are not easy to distinguish and I am inclined to lump their views together. Their common assumption was that memory traces or associations do not remain permanently in the system at their original strength but rather are subject to some process of erosion or weakening. As time passes following a learning experience, the associations among the ideas or memory traces involved progressively weaken with the result that constituent elements become more loosely connected and may reunite in new combinations. Another manifestation is that components of the original memory trace may simply be lost so that what is available on a test for retention after a long interval may be not a weakened version of the original memory trace but simply an incomplete or a fragmentary one.

The development of the theory of retention and forgetting over the past 100 years (summarized in Table 2.1) may be seen as flowing from the two principal motifs sketched by Ebbinghaus. The interpretation of forgetting in terms of competition between newer and older memory traces (or responses associated at different times to the same cue) has, with a good deal of embellishment and substantial experimental support, continued to the present as an important component of an interpretation of forgetting. McGeoch (1932) argued that the competition among memory traces having elements in common, or between responses to stimuli that have elements in common, was so well substantiated as a

TABLE 2.1
Important Concepts in the Theoretical Interpretation of Forgetting

Concept	Associated Investigators
Decay	Broadbent (1958)
	Ebbinghaus (1885/1913)
	Thorndike (1931)
Competition	McGeoch (1932)
Unlearning	Melton and Irwin (1940)
Context shift and fluctuation	Bower (1972)
	Estes (1955, 1971)
	Martin (1972)
	Robinson (1932)
Search and retrieval	Anderson (1976)
	Feigenbaum (1963)
	Shiffrin (1970)
Perturbation of attribute values	Estes (1972)
	Michon (1967)

cause of forgetting that it was unnecessary to assume any process of inevitable decay of memories.

An unsatisfactory aspect of the competition concept is that it is not obvious why multiple associations need compete with mutually deleterious effects. Why should I not learn, without interference, to associate with a certain person the name Miss Brown on one occasion, the label "the kindergarten teacher" on another occasion, and the name Mrs. Anderson on a still later one? One proposed answer, which was incorporated into an influential theory of memory interference by Melton and Irwin (1940), is that the association learned later causes unlearning of associations learned earlier to the same cue. A great deal of experimentation aimed at detecting and assessing unlearning in paired-association and list-learning situations has produced fairly convincing evidence that such a process occurs, but, I would say, little reason to believe that it constitutes a major component of forgetting. Much the same could be said about the notion of competition, although it has continued to occur more conspicuously in modern theories under such appellations as "cue overload" (Watkins, 1979) and the "fan effect" (Anderson, 1976, 1981). In the information-processing tradition, the metaphor is changed, and phenomena that have been taken to signify competition or unlearning are subsumed under the idea that the retrievability of a given learned item from memory is strongly influenced by later learning, which may increase the number of similar items or the number of paths in an associative network that needs to be searched on a later test occasion in order to locate the given item. Prolongation of a memory search necessarily increases retrieval time, and it may also increase the probability of failure because there is always a hazard that a search will be interrupted by some chance distraction.

Also important is another concept that was emphasized by McGeoch (1932) and that underwent considerable theoretical development by later investigators, namely the idea that context shift plays an important role in memory. The basic notion is that during any learning experience the memory trace or associations formed include elements of the background context in which the learning occurs. Changes in this context between the original learning experience and a later test for retention are detrimental to both recognition and recall. This idea was elevated to the status of a "law of context" by Robinson (1932) in his history of association theory and is basic to some recent quantitative models of retention loss over time (Bower, 1972; Estes, 1955, 1971). These models are based on the observation that some fluctuation of background context between any two learning or testing experiences is virtually inevitable, and it is reasonable to view any context as depending on or including numerous elements or aspects whose availability may fluctuate randomly over the course of time. As a consequence, the availability or retrievability of an earlier formed memory trace or association will likewise fluctuate over a period of time and the quantitative properties of this variation appear to fit quite well many of the observed properties of forgetting functions (Bower, 1972; Estes, 1959).

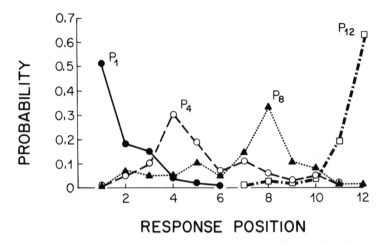

RESPONSE POSITION

FIGURE 2.5.   Observed certainty gradients for items presented in positions P_i of a 12-consonant list. Each point represents the proportion of cases in which subjects recalled an item presented at position P_i in the indicated response position. Data from Lee and Estes (1977).

The final type of mechanism listed in Table 2.1 represents the line of theoretical development I have been engaged in for the past dozen years or so, aimed at interpreting the loss of inner structure of memory traces, cited by Ebbinghaus as one of the principal alternatives to the notion of competition. The basic mechanism in my theory is much the same as one proposed by Michon (1967) in a model of memory for short intervals in a theory of motor performance. In my case, the idea originated in the observation that in short-term memory situations even items that continue to be remembered accurately may drift out of their correct order in recall. My hypothesis was that the temporal position of an item within the time frame of a trial is encoded at the time of its occurrence, and that over a subsequent period of time, the encoded representation loses precision in a systematic way so that the representation of the item in memory comes to be describable by an "uncertainty distribution." Fig. 2.5, taken from a study of recall of 12-item sequences, shows the empirical distributions of remembered positions of items presented in positions 2, 5, 8, or 11 of the 12-item list. Fig. 2.6 shows that the predicted distributions computed from what has come to be dubbed the "perturbation model" (Cunningham, Healy, & Williams, 1984; Estes, 1972, 1980; Lee & Estes, 1977) capture the salient properties of the empirical functions.

In more recent work I have been investigating the idea that encodings of items on other dimensions have similar properties and undergo perturbation processes similar to those that hold for the temporal dimension. As one example, Fig. 2.7 illustrates a recent experiment from my laboratory on memory for the heights of

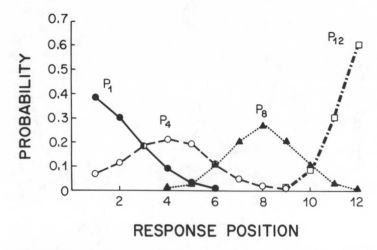

RESPONSE POSITION

FIGURE 2.6   Gradients predicted by the perturbation model for the data of Fig. 2.5.

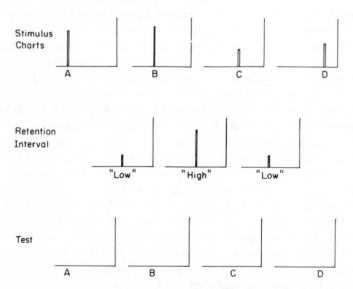

FIGURE 2.7   Design of an experiment on memory for bar heights. The top row shows typical displays presented briefly for study, the middle row displays presented for categorization during the retention interval, and the bottom row the test displays on which subjects attempted to reproduce the bars from memory.

bars in bar diagrams. The top row shows a series of single-bar diagrams shown in rapid sequence to subjects in the course of a single trial of an experiment. The second row shows high and low bars that were presented and that had to be categorized by the subject during a retention interval to preclude rehearsal. The bottom row shows a series of frames with labels presented to the subjects on a subsequent retention test.

Extending the model for temporal memory to this case, I assumed that the heights of the bars would be encoded in memory when they were perceived but that these encoded representations would become fuzzy over the course of the filled retention interval in the same way that memories of temporal position become fuzzy. As can be seen in Fig. 2.8, this supposition seems well borne out. The upper panel shows empirical distributions of remembered bar heights at an

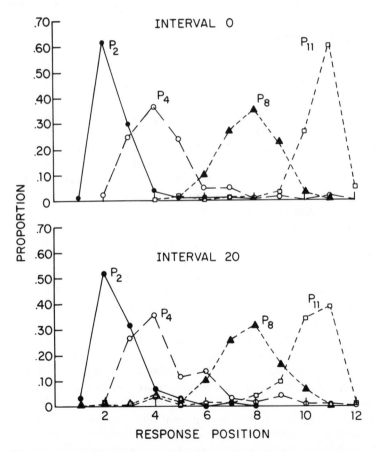

FIGURE 2.8. Observed uncertainty gradients for the experiment on; bar memory, analogous in form to Fig. 2.5 except that the horizontal axis represents bar height rather than temporal position.

initial retention test for bars whose actual heights at presentation were 2, 4, 8, or 11 and the lower panel shows the corresponding distributions of remembered heights for the same bars after a retention interval of 20 time units. We see that just as in the case of temporal memories, the variances of the distributions of remembered heights increased systematically with time, more rapidly for interior values than for end values on the given dimension.

Because the perturbation process is probabilistic, the result is that, on the average, memory for an attribute becomes progressively imprecise with time. Nonetheless, in some instances memory may be accurate even after very long retention intervals. On the supposition that similar encoding and perturbation processes occur with respect to all of the attributes on which events or items are encoded in memory, we may have the basis for an interpretation of both of the conspicuous aspects of memory mentioned by Ebbinghaus—that on the whole, memories become less precise with time but some may be fully recovered even after very long intervals.

THE SITUATION IN MEMORY THEORY

With respect to the overall picture of memory theory, the most striking change since the time of Ebbinghaus is not the (inevitable) increase in volume and diversity of work, but rather the emergence of distinct levels of theorizing. At a miminum, we must recognize a "molar" level of information-processing theories, a more "molecular" level of network and distributed memory theories, and a third level that constitutes a mixture.

A few contemporary investigators associated with each of these levels of theorizing are listed in Table 2.2. The model of Atkinson and Shiffrin (1968) is the prototype of an information-processing model of memory. It remains influential, if not fashionable, after a longer period than many models in this area. Others, ranging along a continuum from cognitive psychology to artificial intelligence, are associated with Simon and his associates (Anzai & Simon, 1979; Gilmartin, Newell, & Simon, 1976), Kolodner (1983), and Rumelhart, Lindsay, and Norman (1972). In these models, concepts are defined at a level of analysis closer to that of artificial intelligence than to traditional theories of learning and memory. The basic substance of memory is information and the basic processes are storage and retrieval. Memory representations of learning experiences take the form of units of information entered in memory stores or arrays. The flow of information and the operations that transform and utilize it are interpreted in terms that are applicable to any symbol-manipulating system—transmission channels, data structures, operations of search, comparison, and evaluation.

In contrast, distributed memory and related network models are formulated in terms of relations among a small number of abstract entities—nodes and paths or the equivalent—with no direct correspondence between the workings of the

TABLE 2.2
Conceptual Levels of Contemporary Memory Models and Theorists
Associated with Models at Each Level

Level	Theorists
Information processing	Atkinson and Shiffrin (1968)
	Kolodner (1983)
	Newell and Simon (1972)
	Rumelhart, Lindsay, and Norman
	(1972)
Mixtures	J. R. Anderson (1983)
	Collins and Loftus (1975)
	Ratcliff (1978)
Associative networks and distributed	J. A. Anderson (1973)
memories	McClelland and Rumelhart (1981)
	Murdock (1982)
	Raaijmakers and Shiffrin (1981)

model and information-processing units or operations. In this category, the models of Anderson (1973), Knapp and Anderson (1984), and Murdock (1982) are based on distributed memories, and those of McClelland and Rumelhart (1981) and Raaijmakers and Shiffrin (1981) are based on networks of localized informational elements.

A collection of models including those of Anderson (1983), Collins and Loftus (1975), and Ratcliff (1978, 1981) is not as clearly classifiable. The information stored in and retrieved from memory is characterized here in terms of units at the level of concepts and propositions, with relations among them often represented by conducting pathways. The representations are in some instances subject to information-processing operations but in others to an abstract process of activation that spreads along pathways between units. It remains to be seen whether these (apparently) hybrid models will prove stable or will move toward the higher or lower level.

Why should multiple levels of theory be needed? Information-processing concepts have the advantage of being similar to those generally used to characterize the information-processing problems people face in their ordinary environments and the intellectual functions and activities involved in attempts at solution. Thus, this level provides the most comfortable and intuitively natural concepts for the analysis of practical situations and the design of intelligent systems. The more molecular level generally admits more powerful mathematical methods of analysis and is commonly thought to be closer to effective rapprochement with neural science. For the latter reason, and because the relatively abstract concepts are generalizable across broad empirical domains, the molecular level may provide a kind of explanatory power not available at the information-processing level alone (Estes, 1979). The appearance and persistence of multiple levels of memory theory is perhaps a natural development, in view of the experience of other sciences (Illustrated, for example, by the long coexistence of models at the levels of mechanical interactions, thermodynamics, and statistical laws in the theory of gases, or those of genes and DNA structures in genetics).

My assessment of the current situation is that those who long for a return to informal, qualitative methods and simple theories expressible in the intuitive language of everyday life are doomed to feel disappointment. One of the principal products of the century of work conducted since Ebbinghaus is the now firmly rooted appreciation of the difficulty of the problems of memory and, in general, cognitive science, and of the commensurate power of the theoretical methods needed to attack them effectively. The challenges to research and theory in our area seem adequate for the most venturesome, and the potential payoffs seem high in terms of possible long-term contributions to solving human problems. However, the cost of staying in the game is commitment to lifelong learning of new methods and pursuit of interactions with other similarly fast-growing disciplines that may from time to time yield valuable inputs to ours.

WHERE IS THE ACTION?

A ubiquitous and often polemical issue throughout the history of the scientific study of memory is whether theories are better based on the results of laboratory experiments employing artificial materials, or on the results of less formal observation of phenomena of memory in everyday life settings. Ebbinghaus is deservedly credited with major responsibility for the dominance of methodologies based on the laboratory and the artificial over the past century, although his stand was neither very dogmatic nor excessively sanguine. He states (1885/1913):

> It is because of the indefinite and little specialized character of our knowledge that the theories concerning the processes of memory, reproduction, and association have been up to the present time of so little value for a proper comprehension of those processes. For example, to express our ideas concerning their physical basis we use different metaphors—stored up ideas; engrained images, well-beaten paths. There is only one thing certain about these figures of speech and that is that they are not suitable.
>
> Of course the existence of all these deficiencies has its perfectly sufficient basis in the extraordinary difficulty and complexity of the matter. It remains to be proved whether, in spite of the clearest insight into the inadequacy of our knowledge, we shall ever make any actual progress. (p. 5–6)

Ebbinghaus felt that the remoteness of his laboratory situation from the phenomena of everyday life was inevitable in the tradition of natural science, and he worried that it might not be sufficiently simplified to yield reproducible and interpretable results.

This stance on method has been shared by many of the investigators responsible for a century's research, spanning dimensions far beyond any that Ebbinghaus could possibly have foreseen. Still, every so often we hear the criticism that the laboratory method, as it has evolved, is missing the "big questions," and the suggestion that we need to turn to fresh observation of memory in everyday life for inspiration (Neisser, 1982).

Should the increasing technicality of research questions be taken as a warning that the laboratory approach is showing hardening of the arteries? In fact, it seems to have been characteristic of every science for research to evolve from an early stage in which the questions at issue derive from everyday life to a later one in which the questions addressed are generated by previous research and theoretical developments. In early natural science, research often took the form of direct attacks on such problems as why some bodies fall to the earth while others float in the air, why heavenly bodies follow regular paths, why fresh water freezes faster than saltwater. But at present, even popular journals such as *Scientific American* show investigators at work on questions remote from ordinary life—the creation and annihilation of quarks, spins of nuclear particles, black holes in distant space.

On a modest scale, we see a similar progression in the psychology of memory. Some research questions (by no means fully resolved) are readily comprehensible by the layman: Why are some experiences quickly forgotten while others leave durable memories? How can effects of amnesia be sharply localized in time? How can some people perform prodigious mnemonic feats? However, most research is directed to problems that seem more esoteric—the possibility of indirect associations, the capacity of short-term memory, the relation between levels of encoding and retention. Some bemoan this drift away from homely concerns, but on it goes; and perhaps necessarily so if the field is to progress toward theoretical maturity. I think our first-order concern should be not to mirror the surface structure of everyday life but to continue moving toward deeper understanding of memory by flexible and adaptive use of the machine Ebbinghaus set in motion—the experimental method driven by theoretical ideas.

ACKNOWLEDGMENTS

Work reported in this chapter was supported by grants BNS 79–21028 and BNS 80–26656 from the National Science Foundation. Laura Beck assisted with the experiment on bar memory.

3 Memory Before Ebbinghaus

Douglas J. Herrmann
Hamilton College

Roger Chaffin
Trenton State College

In 1885 Hermann Ebbinghaus showed the world how the scientific method could be applied to the elusive phenomena of memory. Because of Ebbinghaus' contribution, considerable progress has been made in investigating a wide variety of memory phenomena. Nevertheless, this progress has entailed a sacrifice, the nature of which few are aware. Memory researchers have come to ignore the scholarship on memory that preceded Ebbinghaus. To read a current text on memory, one might suppose that Ebbinghaus was the first person to give serious thought to memory phenomena. For example, current popular and scholarly texts on memory usually cite no more than two or three memory scholars before 1885, and these citations are made just in passing.

Ebbinghaus was not the first to ponder the mysteries of memory. Thinkers have been concerned with memory since the earliest times. We argue that it is a mistake for modern researchers to ignore the memory scholarship before Ebbinghaus, and that the field should take advantage of this scholarship (see Boring, 1950; Crutchfield & Krech, 1963; Watson, 1960).

There are two reasons that modern memory researchers do not read and study memory scholarship before Ebbinghaus. First, Ebbinghaus's experimental method involved a paradigm shift (Kuhn, 1962) from the method of natural observation used by pre-Ebbinghaus scholars. A second reason has to do with the attitudes of modern psychology about what sources constitute the literature that a psychologist should know and cite. Typically, current citation practice requires that a researcher cite relevant work that has been published only within the past 20 or so years; citation of work older than 20 years is optional.

This chapter will show that the current conception of the literature in human memory needs redefinition to include the scholarship that preceded, as well as followed, Ebbinghaus. We illustrate the relevance of pre-Ebbinghaus scholarship to post-Ebbinghaus researchers, first, by briefly reviewing the work on memory before Ebbinghaus. Second, we indicate three specific ways that knowledge of pre-Ebbinghaus scholarship may benefit modern researchers.

A BRIEF HISTORY OF MEMORY BEFORE EBBINGHAUS

Few scholars studied memory until the Renaissance. This is shown by the exponential function in Fig. 3.1. This figure presents a count of the memory scholars cited in Young's (1961) bibliography of memory. (This count did not include scholars who produced special-purpose publications such as posters, cards, and pamphlets.) The figure shows only the quantitative development of interest in memory; appreciation of the qualitative aspects of this development requires examination of the works themselves.

Several brief histories have described memory scholarship before Ebbinghaus (Beare, 1906; Burnham, 1888; Edgell, 1924; Marshall & Fryer, 1978; Mitchell, 1911; Murray, 1976; Yates, 1966). We present below an historical review that

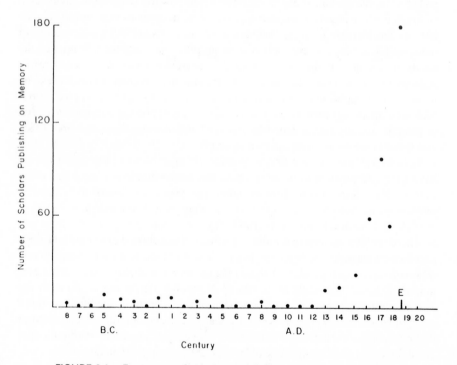

FIGURE 3.1.   Frequency of scholars publishing on memory as a function of the century in which the scholars lived.

pays special attention to the *approaches* taken to the study of memory by pre-Ebbinghaus scholars. Our review focuses on the work of 24 scholars whose writings have importance to the development of thought about memory. Table 3.1 lists these scholars as well as the title of each scholar's works on memory; sources for these works are listed by the scholar's name in the reference section. Reprints of these writings may be found in *Memory in historical perspective* (Herrmann & Chaffin, 1987).

In our view, there were four approaches to memory scholarship before Ebbinghaus. The *pragmatic* approach sought ways to improve a person's ability to learn and remember. The *empirical* approach documented the existence and nature of memory phenomena. Scholars taking a *theoretical* approach explained the mechanisms of memory. The *pretheoretical* approach characterized memory in an intuitive and informal manner. The right-hand column of Table 3.1 indicates the approach, or approaches, taken by each scholar.

The earliest extant writing on memory is Hesiod's account of Greek mythology. There are good reasons for believing that writings on memory existed before Hesiod but apparently none has survived (Yates, 1966). Hesiod's account indicates that the Greeks regarded psychology highly in conceiving of it as the goddess Psyche (shown in Fig. 3.2a). Their regard for memory was high also, as reflected by their giving responsibility for memory not to Psyche but to another goddess, Mnemosyne, created to handle just this responsibility. Mnemosyne, shown in Fig. 3.2b, was one of Zeus' wives and was the mother of the Muses, the spiritual promoters of the arts. Later, in the 5th century B.C., an anonymous author wrote an incomprehensible riddle entitled *Mnemosyne,* apparently to express the view of memory as an enigma.

The first practical writing on how to improve memory was a fragment written in the 5th century B.C. called the *Dialexis,* this fragment advised that attentiveness and rehearsal aided learning (Yates, 1966). In the same century, Heraclitus also made practical observations; for example, he noted that ''the eyes are more exact witnesses than the ears.'' Aristophanes pointed out the role of motivation in memory when he observed that memory is of two sorts: ''If I'm owed anything, I'm mindful, very. But it I owe, (Oh, dear!) forgetful, very''.

Plato and Aristotle were the first theoreticians of memory. Furthermore, Plato produced the first models of memory. The wax tablet model represented memory traces as impressions in wax; the aviary model represented each memory as a bird of a different species; and the scribe model represented in memory a person's experience according to the whims of the scribe. Aristotle, shown i Fig. 3.2c teaching the young Alexander the Great, set forth the basic ''laws'' of associationism, advanced fundamental analyses of memory retrieval, and also pointed out various memory phenomena, e.g. the decline of memory with age.

Interest in the pragmatic aspects of memory grew in the Roman period. Cicero, shown in Fig. 3.2d, as well as the anonymous author of *Ad herennium* (long erroneously attributed to Cicero; Yates 1966) championed the use of the

TABLE 3.1
The Literature before Ebbinghaus

Classical Writing	Approach
8th Century B.C.	
Hesiod	"T"
Theogony	
5th Century B.C.	
Anonymous	P
Dialexis	
Anonymous	"T"
Mnemosyne	
Heraclitus	P
Fragments	
4th Century B.C.	
Aristophanes	"T"
Clouds	
Plato	E,T
Meno, Phaedo; Greater Hippas; Republic; Phaedrus; Theaetatus; Philebus; Timaeus	
Aristotle	E,T
Analytica Priora; Analytica Posteriora; Topica; De Anima; The Parva Naturalia; De Memoria et Reminiscentia, De Somnus, De Somno et Virgilia; Historia Animalium; De Motu Animalium; Physiognomonica; Metaphysica; Magna Moralia; Ethica Eudemia; De Virtubus et Vitius; Rhetorica	
1st Century B.C.	
Cicero	P
De Oratore; Tusculan Disputations	
Anonymous	P
Ad Herrenium, often attributed to Cicero	
1st Century, A.D.	
Pliny	E,"T"
Natural History	
Quintillian	E,T,P
Institutio	
3rd Century	
Plotinus	E,T,P
The Enneods	
5th Century	
Augustine	T
Confessions; The Trinity; The Image in Outward Man; Later Works	

TABLE 3.1   (*Continued*)

Classical Writing	Approach
5th Century Martianus Capella *The Marriage of Philology and Mercury*	E,"T",P
13th Century Thomas Aquinas *Suma Theologiae; Commentary on the Metaphysics of Aristotle*	T
14th Century Da Vinci *The Literary Works of*	P
16th Century Michel Eyguen De Montaigne *Essays*	E
17th Century Francis Bacon *Of The Advancement of Learning; Novum Organum, De* *Augmentis Scientorum* John Locke *An Essay Concerning Human Understanding*	T T
18th Century David Hume *Theory of Knowledge* Immanuel Kant *Critique of Pure Reason* Thomas Reid *The Essays on the Intellectual Powers of Man* Samuel Rogers *The Pleasures of Memory* and *The Pains of Memory,* an addendum by Robert Merry	T T T E,T
19th Century Thomas Brown *Lectures on the Philosophy of the Human Mind*	E,T

Note: P = Practical   E = Empirical
        T = Theoretical   "T" = Pretheoretical

"method of loci" in memorization. Quintillian also taught Cicero's methods but with a note of skepticism not found in Cicero. In particular, Quintillian feared that the method of loci would slow remembering because the loci and the to-be-remembered information imposed a "double task" on memory.

Augustine, shown in Fig. 3.2e, was the third major theoretician of memory. He wrote about a wide variety of issues, especially about the different kinds of memory. Like Plato, Augustine advanced metaphorical models of memory such as likening acquisition to the digestive processes of the stomach, and remembering to the exploration of caverns. Additionally, Augustine discussed the relationship between memory and emotions, noting that the knowledge of the emotion held during an experience "clung to my memory so that I can call it to mind." Also in the 5th century B.C., Martianus Cappella wrote a mythology that, like the Greek one described by Hesiod, represented memory and its relationship to the other psychological faculties. Cappella characterized memory as a god whose role was to make Psyche behave in a more realistic manner.

During the Dark Ages, work on memory (and all other topics) decreased. Fig. 3.1 shows that substantive writings on memory from the 5th century B.C. into the medieval period were very rare (or have since been lost; Yates, 1966, and Young, 1961). In the 13th century, Aquinas brought Aristotle's views on memory into prominence again. However, Aquinas' theoretical interests were unusual for Aquinas's time. In the Renaissance to follow, the focus was primarily on the practical use of the visual arts for the improvement of memory (Yates, 1966).

In the 16th and 17th centuries, interest in the arts of memory had run its course and the number of works declined. This is reflected in the frequency count in Fig. 3.1, which shows a marked deviation from the overall growth function in the 17th century. During this century, the approach to memory scholarship shifted from the practical to the theoretical, a shift that led to a new spurt in memory scholarship. Scholars such as Francis Bacon, John Locke, David Hume, and Immanuel Kant (shown in Figs. 3.2f–i), as well as Thomas Reid, Thomas Brown, and many others gave a great deal of thought to memory. Theoretical interest in memory was so great in this period that even poets (Samuel Rogers and Robert Merry) wrote poems to express their theories of how memory registers, and is influenced by, emotion.

Then, in 1885, Ebbinghaus published his monograph and the world of memory shifted its axis (see Hoffman, Bramberg, & Klein's chapter in this volume).

BENEFITS TO MODERN RESEARCHERS OF A
KNOWLEDGE OF MEMORY BEFORE EBBINGHAUS

A general knowledge of the history of a discipline is valuable to a scholar because it enlarges his or her understanding of how progress is made in the discipline. In the field of memory, understanding may be enhanced in three

FIGURE 3.2.   (a) *Psyche* by Sergio Franchesi, 1832 (at the Fitzwilliam Museum, Cambridge, England), (b) *Mnemosye* by Dante Gabriel Rossetti ca. 1879 (see Surtees, 1971), (c) *Aristotle Teaching Alexander the Great* by J. L. G. Ferrii (see Ruoff, 1910), (d) *Marcus Tullius Cicero* (see Ruoff, 1910), (e) *St. Augustine* by Fra Filippo Lippi (see Ruoff, 1910), (f) *Francis Bacon* (see Ruoff, 1910), (g) *John Locke* (see Ruoff, 1910), (h) *David Hume* (see Ruoff, 1910), (i) *Immanuel Kant* (see Ruoff, 1910).

392. *Mnemosyne* (Cat. no. 261)

FIGURE 3.2b

ARISTOTLE TEACHING ALEXANDER THE GREAT
From the painting by J. L. G. Ferris

FIGURE 3.2c

Marcus Tullius Cicero

Bettmann Archive

FIGURE 3.2d

ST. AUGUSTINE
From the painting of Fra Filippo Lippi

FIGURE 3.2e

FRANCIS BACON
From a painting

FIGURE 3.2f

JOHN LOCKE
From a painting

FIGURE 3.2g

David Hume   Bettmann Archive

FIGURE 3.2h

IMMANUEL KANT
From a painting

FIGURE 3.2i

ways. First, a general knowledge of pre-Ebbinghaus scholarship may give a researcher a better appreciation of the current *zeitgeist* in memory, its origins, its rivals, and its potential for change. Second, this scholarship may offer a researcher insights into memory phenomena of investigative interest. Third, knowledge of this scholarship will help a researcher to avoid duplicating past discoveries and to investigate questions about memory that are truly new. Below we provide concrete examples of these benefits.

Awareness of the Zeitgest

REASON - METHODOLOGY   SPIRIT of THE TIME

It is difficult for researchers to be aware of the extent to which their work is directed by the *zeitgeist*. Greater awareness of its nature would allow researchers to make better-informed judgment about the direction of their research. One way that a researcher may understand the *zeitgeist* better is through the study of the historical development of his or her research area.

To demonstrate that a knowledge of pre-Ebbinghaus scholarship may have such an effect, it will be useful to review, briefly, the approaches to memory of the scholars listed in Table 3.1. For example, prior to Ebbinghaus, the theoretical approach flourished in the 4th century B.C. in the work of Plato and Aristotle; it emerged again the 5th century A.D. with Augustine's writing, in the 13th century with Aquinas, and in the 18th century with many scholars. Similarly, the empirical approach was taken by scholars in the 4th century B.C. (Aristotle; Plato), in the period from the 1st through the 5th century A.D. (e.g., Cicero), and at the end of the 18th century. The practical approach emerged first in the 5th century B.C. in the anonymous work entitled *Dialexis* and in the writings of Heraclitus; this approach was taken again by several scholars from the 1st through the 5th century A.D., and by many disciples of the arts of memory around the Renaissance (Yates, 1966). The presence of the same approach by one or more scholars from the same or next centuries may be regarded as a *zeitgeist* in the broad sense of this term. Dominance of different approaches in adjacent time periods represent a shift in the *zeitgeist*. As inspection of the table shows, approaches to memory shifted several times from the 8th century B.C. to the period of Ebbinghaus.

A knowledge of the approaches to memory before Ebbinghaus is valuable to a modern researcher because these approaches are still with us. Armed with this knowledge, a researcher will recognize changes in the *zeitgeist* more easily. It may also help the researcher to decide about how to react to these changes. Familiarity with earlier changes should make a researcher less gullible when confronted with the inflated promises of zealous advocates of the latest approach.

Consider the recent enthusiasm over everyday memory. Discussion concerning this "new" movement has been at times quite heated in the last several years. Some people have gone so far as to claim that the laboratory can never be of use to memory research; others have asserted that everyday memory research will never yield interpretable data. Many researchers on both sides of this debate have treated the everyday memory movement as new, i.e., as historically unique. But this is not the case; the everyday memory movement is a resurgence of the practical approach to memory. Bahrick (1985) recently pointed out that the shift from a theoretical/empirical focus to a practical one has occurred twice in this century; and we have shown here that this kind of shift has occurred several times in earlier centuries. We believe that debates about the *zeitgest,* such as the one about everyday memory, might be more temperate and would be more productive if those involved were mindful of the reoccurrence of approaches to memory throughout history.

We must point out that the empirical, practical, theoretical, and pretheoretical themes are not the only identifiable themes in pre-Ebbinghaus scholarship. For example, a researcher may choose to study the approaches taken by pre-Ebbinghaus scholars to his or her current research (e.g., short- versus long-term memory, the role of imagery in learning).

Insights

The writings on memory before Ebbinghaus offer a researcher insights about memory. They do so because of the nontechnical manner in which the observations and theoretical views were presented by the pre-Ebbinghaus scholars. We believe that these writings invariably trigger valuable insights. Because researchers focus on different facets of memory, it is not possible to demonstrate this point in a way that might be helpful to all researchers. Instead, we demonstrate the value of pre-Ebbinghaus scholarship for one issue that arose in our own research into everyday memory.

In the past several years, interest has been growing in the use of external memory aids (thanks largely to the work of John Harris, 1980). One question that was raised at conferences on everyday memory dealt with the potentially reactive aspect of everyday memory aids. It was proposed that memory aids may lessen a person's memory ability by leading the person to rely more on the memory aid and less on memory itself. We recall the nods of enlightenment when this point about reactivity was raised. Comments were made for and against this ''new'' idea, i.e., that an aid might actually have deleterious effects.

However, the notion that an aid may lessen ability is not new at all. Plato, as well as some of his followers, held strong reservations about the widespread teaching of writing because writing (a memory aid) would allow a person to avoid relying on memory and, hence, lessen memory ability. Quintillian similarly objected to Cicero's internal memory aids because their use might lessen a person's understanding of the memorized material. Now suppose that the researchers at those early conferences on everyday memory had read the scholarship before Ebbinghaus pertaining to memory aids; they would have already developed an understanding of the reactivity issue. This insight would surely have facilitated and elevated the discussions about memory aids.

The issue of memory aid reactivity is one small point in the universe of questions about memory. But the resolution of many small points facilitates the development of sound theories.

Historical information that fosters insight into a research problem may be found for some problems in one of the several histories of memory. However, this information is not available for many other research problems in these histories. General histories do not, and cannot be expected to, address the issues that concern each and every researcher. In order to discover the historical background of most research problems, a reading of pre-Ebbinghaus sources is necessary.

Original Contributions to Knowledge About Memory

Knowledge of pre-Ebbinghaus scholarship also prepares a researcher to recognize questions about memory that are truly new. It might be argued that the pre-Ebbinghaus work on memory could not provide the germ for modern research because this work relied only on natural observation and reason. Because the experiment is a far more powerful tool than natural observation and reason, so the argument runs, the pre-Ebbinghaus work should not be trusted by modern researchers. Although the power of the experimental method cannot be denied, a reading of the pre-Ebbinghaus literature demonstrates that natural observation and intuition successfully identified, without experiments, many of the main phenomena of memory. Because many modern investigations of memory are concerned with the same topics that concerned the pre-Ebbinghaus scholars, the early scholarship has a contribution to make to the understanding of the basic phenomena and mechanisms of memory.

Researchers who are ignorant of history may pursue intractable ideas or may rediscover phenomena and theoretical constructs. Rediscoveries are undesirable, not just because they represent a waste of time, or because of the injustice done to the work of past scholars, but because rediscoveries do not advance knowledge when more informed research might have done so (Boring, 1950; Crutchfield & Krech, 1963; Watson, 1960).

In the present state of ignorance about pre-Ebbinghaus scholarship, a rediscovery may sometimes be desirable. If a phenomenon has been lost to a scientific community, it is desirable for a scientist to rediscover it and to educate the scientific community about the forgotten work. Nevertheless, this rediscovery also entails a duplication of effort that might have been avoided had past work not been forgotten.

Rediscovery is not a rare event in memory research (or in other areas of psychology, e.g., Cole & Rudnicky, 1983). To illustrate the point, imagine what most memory psychologists would say when asked to name the major phenomena of memory and the people who discovered them. For example, what would most memory psychologists say if asked who first discovered: ab-

stract/concrete memory codes, attributes of encoding, levels of processing, retrieval failures, and the semantic–episodic distinction? The typical answer would
likely cite 20th century psychologists; however, all of the above phenomena
were addressed in some fashion by pre-Ebbinghaus scholars. Before discussing
these instances, we must offer a caveat about the credit and responsibility for the
rediscoveries. Numerous studies could have been selected to illustrate rediscovery (including some of our own work!). The instances examined here were
selected over others only because of their prominence in the modern research
literature. In addition, scholars who make a rediscovery deserve credit for the
work involved because without the rediscovery the phenomena and related constructs might remain unknown. These scholars also cannot be held at fault for the
waste of effort that a rediscovery represents because rediscoveries are made
necessary by the prevailing conventions of scholarship in the field of human
memory. "Blame" for the rediscovery lies with the field rather than with individuals making rediscoveries because the field has followed a tacit standard of
scholarship that does not require the citation of work before Ebbinghaus (or, for
that matter, of work more than 20 years old).

Some instances in which pre-Ebbinghaus ideas have been rediscovered by
post-Ebbinghaus scholars are presented in Table 3.2. These instances involve
memory constructs and attendant phenomena that are commonly held to be the
discoveries of our age. The modern scholars who have investigated and written
about each construct are listed in the center column of the table. The scholars
before Ebbinghaus who wote about these constructs are listed in the right hand
column. Some of the modern scholars in the table pointed out in their seminal

TABLE 3.2
Rediscoveries by Post-Ebbinghaus Scholars of Constructs
Discovered by Pre-Ebbinghaus Scholars

Construct	Post-Ebbinghaus Scholars	Pre-Ebbinghaus Scholars
Abstract/concrete mem-ory types	Paivio (1969)	Cicero, Augustine, Aquinas[1]
Attributes of memory	Bower (1967) Underwood (1969) Wickens (1970)	Brown (Aristotle, Reid and others)
Levels of processing	Craik and Lockhart (1972)	F. Bacon[1,2]
Retrieval failure	Shiffrin (1970) Tulving (1983)	Aristotle, Quintillian, F. Bacon, J. Mill
Semantic-episodic mem-ory types	Tulving (1972)	Aristotle, Augustine, Aquinas, Brown, Abercrombie, and Bain[3]

Note: [1]see also Marshall and Fryer (1978)
        [2]see also Murray (1976)
        [3]see also Herrmann (1982)

works the connection between their research and the ideas of one or more pre-Ebbinghaus scholars: Paivio (1969) has indicated in considerable detail the pre-Ebbinghaus sources that are important to dual coding theory; Shiffrin (1970) quoted William James's (1890) distillation of James Mill's views on retrieval. It is beyond the scope of this chapter to ascertain how much the modern constructs in Table 3.2 reproduce the ideas of scholars before Ebbinghaus. The important point is that the germ of the modern construct was available to the field of post-Ebbinghaus researchers, if modern researchers had consulted the pre-Ebbinghaus literature.

One wonders how research involving the constructs in the table would have developed had post-Ebbinghaus scholars been aware of the pre-Ebbinghaus literature. Had the field of human memory been aware of pre-Ebbinghaus scholarship, debate about these constructs would have been more focused to begin with, the research would have moved more quickly from demonstration experiments to functional experiments, and the present level of knowledge about these constructs would be higher today. In their brief history of memory research, Marshall and Fryer (1978) lamented that modern memory theories appeared not to have advanced much over the theories of early scholars. Tulving (1983) recently expressed a similar view. But how can a discipline expect to rise above past scholarly achievements if it ignores them?

CONCLUSION

Ebbinghaus's monograph eclipsed all that preceded it. We believe that Ebbinghaus would have disapproved of this eclipse. For example, Ebbinghaus cited Aristotle, Bain, Herbart, and others in his seminal monograph. We have discussed three reasons why work on memory before Ebbinghaus should be regarded as part of the literature that researchers should know and cite. Knowledge of this literature may make a researcher more sensitive to changes in the *zeitgeist*, may foster insights about research issues, and may direct attention to little-explored research questions. We conclude that it has been a mistake that the scholarship before Ebbinghaus has come to be so thoroughly ignored by post-Ebbinghaus researchers.

If it is accepted that pre-Ebbinghaus scholarship deserves to be part of a researcher's standard literature, certain practices in our discipline will require change. First, students of memory at the graduate and undergraduate levels should be taught something of memory before Ebbinghaus. Second, publication standards should be revised so that authors are required to clearly show how their research makes a contribution beyond what was known previously, including the knowledge about memory developed before Ebbinghaus. It may seem that this proposal would result in cluttering the literature with an excessive number of citations. However, the literature would not become cluttered because only a few of the pre-Ebbinghaus sources are relevant to most research topics (see Table 3.2) and citation of this scholarship would become unnecessary once research on a topic had moved clearly beyond the ideas of pre-Ebbinghaus scholars. Implementation of these two proposals would require effort. We believe that this effort would be amply repaid in the improvement of post-Ebbinghaus scholarship.

ACKNOWLEDGMENTS

We thank Richard C. Atkinson and David J. Murray for advice on our historical research. We also thank Bob Hoffman, Tom Verhave, and especially Dick Somer, for valuable advice on the writing of this chapter.

4 Some Historical Observations on Ebbinghaus

Robert R. Hoffman
Adelphi University

Michael Bamberg
Clark University

Wolfgang Bringmann
University of South Alabama

Richard Klein
Adelphi University

> *If by any chance a way to a deeper penetration of this matter should present itself, surely, considering the significance of memory for all mental phenomena, it should be our wish to enter that path at once. For at the very worst we should prefer to see resignation arise from the failure of earnest investigations rather than from persistent, helpless astonishment in the face of their difficulties.*
> —Ebbinghaus, 1885/1964

Hermann Ebbinghaus' books, research, and ideas had an effect on early psychology that was as great as the impact of any of its "founding fathers." It is now 100 years since the publication of Ebbinghaus' classic work, *On Memory* (Über das Gedächtnis) (1885). This work is regarded as a major accomplishment in the application of experimental methods to psychological questions. It has had a profound influence on experimental psychology, and yet very little is generally known about Ebbinghaus and his work. Little is written about him in English or in German, there is no biography, and Ebbinghaus left few autobiographical notes, especially notes that referred to the important period he spent traveling in England and France.[1]

---

[1] A biography, and a motion picture about the life and work of Ebbinghaus are being prepared by Wolfgang Bringmann, Department of Psychology, University of South Alabama, Mobile, AL 36688, and Gisela Schuster–Tyroller, Institut für Geschichte der Neueren Psychologie, Passau University, 8390 Passau, West Germany.

Prior to Ebbinghaus' work there was some research on learning (Stigler, 1978; see also Hermann & Chaffin, this volume). However, Ebbinghaus is generally credited with founding the experimental psychology of the "higher mental processes." Once his research became known, the field "took off" in a flurry of activity involving studies on the learning of various types of materials in various tasks (e.g., Glaze, 1928; Müller & Schumann, 1894; Pressey, 1926; see the chapter by Newman, this volume).

A goal of this chapter is to help set the stage for the chapters to follow that focus on modern research and theories. In this chapter we discuss Ebbinghaus' life, the research on memory, and his work after the publication of his memory research. Along the way we will be presenting information that should be new to most American psychologists and historians. We conclude by raising some questions about Ebbinghaus that we feel will be of interest to psychologists and that merit further historical investigation. Before getting into our discussion of Ebbinghaus' life, we begin with a rather tantalizing appetizer.

THE MYTH OF NONSENSE SYLLABLES

Ebbinghaus' memory experiments were a very ambitious project and required great effort. For example, one study involved memorizing 420 lists of 16 syllables each by repeating each list many times. Some of the lists were studied for nearly three-quarters of an hour and the experiment involved a total of about 14,000 repetitions. . . and this was just one of the experiments!

Ebbinghaus' efforts were of heroic proportions, and myths befit heroes. One such myth involves the concept of the "nonsense syllable." The phrase nonsense syllable appears four times in Hilgard's three-page introduction to the popular Dover Press edition (1964) and has always been a salient feature of discussions of Ebbinghaus' work by American psychologists (e.g., Woodworth, 1938). In his review of Ebbinghaus' work in *Science*, James (1885) called the stimuli "meaningless syllables" and was quite correct in employing this literal translation of *"sinnlose Silben"* although Ebbinghaus provided no examples of his materials in either of his two early works (1880, 1885). The phrase *"sinnlose Silben"* appears twice in the monograph (1885), and is translated in the English edition as the term "nonsense syllable" (1913/1964). The phrase appears first on page 30 (1885) as a subheading for the methodology chapter, and appears only once again, on page 35. It is also used in the memory chapter in Ebbinghaus's general psychology text, *Grundzüge der Psychologie* (1897).

Ebbinghaus actually referred to his stimuli with a number of phrases, such as *"völlig sinnloses Material"* ("completely meaningless material"), *"alle überhaupt möglichen Silben"* ("all possible syllables"), and especially *"sinnlose Silbenreihen"* ("nonsense syllable series"). In the context of his methods and methodology, he seemed to prefer to refer to entire rows or lists or lines of unfamiliar sequences and not just to individual syllables that were devoid of meaning. More often than not, he referred to the stimuli as *"Vorstellungsreihen"* or "presentation series."

Ebbinghaus never put much stock in the idea that his stimuli were truly "nonsense syllables." The critical passage in Ebbinghaus (1885/1913) is often overlooked:

> The nonsense material [series of syllables] just described offers many advantages in part because of this very lack of meaning. First of all, it is relatively simple and relatively homogeneous. In the case of . . . poetry or prose, the content is now narrative in style, now descriptive, or now reflective . . . its metaphors are sometimes beautiful, sometimes harsh . . . There is thus brought into play a multiplicity of influences which change without regularity and are therefore disturbing. Such are associations which dart here and there, different degrees of interest, lines of verse recalled because of their striking quality or their beauty, and the like. All this is avoided with our syllables. Among many thousand combinations there occur scarcely a few dozen that have a meaning and among these there are again only a few whose meaning was realised while they were being memorised. . . . However, the simplicity and homogeneity of the material must not be overestimated. . . . These series exhibit . . . almost incomprehensible variations as to the ease or difficulty with which they are learned . . . the differences between sense and nonsense material were not nearly so great as one would be inclined a priori to imagine. (p. 23)

What was important to Ebbinghaus was the systematic generation of homogeneous learning materials and systematic control of the experimental task. What was critical about the syllables was not their lack of meaning, because they actually varied in their meaningfulness, but that in the list-learning task there would be no previous semantic associations among the items. The materials for his studies were rows or lines or nonsense syllable series (*"sinnlose Silbenreihen"*) and not individual "nonsense syllables," as has been traditionally assumed. It was was not the syllables that were nonsense, but the lists. Only in this sense does Ebbinghaus refer to the task as involving an "impression of nonsense" (p. 21) in that one had to learn an unconnected list of syllables.

Ebbinghaus did not regard the association process as a passive thing. Nor was he especially fond of the British "mental chemistry" metaphors. Of greater importance to him were meaning, imagery, and individual differences in cognitive styles. Indeed, the term he preferred for his lists, *Vorstellungsreihen*, could just as well be translated as "image series," and in the original manuscript (1880/1971, Sec. 2) Ebbinghaus begins with a discussion of how the strength and vividness of memory pictures should be related to the effort taken in learning them. He gives the example of an actor who, after considerable experience, can read material that is to be learned and tell how much practice would be needed in order to obtain strong, vivid memory images (Sec. 3).

Ebbinghaus was also concerned with the use of what are today called "mediators." Although he professed that he had no knowledge of mnemonic techniques and did not use mnemonics in his experiments, he found it impossible not to use a mediator: Each list of syllables was read in a poetic meter and the rhythm was used to group and remember the lists.

It would be safe to say that the popular idea about "nonsense syllables" is something of a myth. Given that relatively little is known about Ebbinghaus and that he left little in the way of autobiographical notes, one might expect there to be a number of open questions about various aspects of his life and work.

EBBINGHAUS' LIFE

Ebbinghaus was born near the stroke of midnight on January 23, 1850 in the rapidly developing industrial town of Barmen, in the Rhine Province of the Kingdom of Prussia, near Bonn and Köln in what is now West Germany. His father was a paper and textile merchant and the family was rather wealthy. In his student days at the universities of Bonn, Halle, and Berlin he studied classical languages, history, and philosophy. After serving during the Franco–Prussian War of 1870–1871 he completed his doctoral dissertation, *Über die Hartmannsche Philosophie des Unbewussten* ("On Hartmann's philosophy of the unconscious") in 1873. Karl Marbe (1909) reported that colleagues had told him that Ebbinghaus' performance at the final oral exam was outstanding.

Ebbinghaus spent the next few years in travels to France and England, engaging in independent studies and teaching at two small schools in southern England (Bringmann & Bringmann, 1985). It was about this time that he read Fechner's (1860) *Elemente der Psychophysik* and became inspired to initiate studies of the "higher mental processes."

Returning to Berlin in 1878, Ebbinghaus began his formal experiments on memory in his home. The first series of studies, conducted in 1879 and 1880, were written up as his *Habilitationschrift* (Ebbinghaus, 1880/1971), a paper in support of his application for approval as a lecturer on the philosophical faculty of Berlin University. He was approved as an unsalaried lecturer (*Privatdozent*) in the fall of 1880. He offered his first course on sensory psychology that winter, paid only by student fees (Bringmann & King, 1985).

It is clear that he was not satisfied that the first series of studies (1879/80) presented a complete picture. He continued to conduct studies, many of which were never formally reported, though he alludes to them in his 1885 monograph. There are important differences between the 1879/80 and 1883/84 sets of studies. For example, the experiments conducted in 1879/80 involved a learning criterion of two perfect recitations, but the studies of the second period (1883/84) involved a criterion of one perfect recitation. Perhaps he realized that the earlier studies demanded more effort than the effects required. The work was definitely tedious and boring, and caused a good many headaches (1885/1964, p. 55). The monograph *Über das Gedächtnis* was published in 1885. Within a year he was promoted to *Ausserordentlicher* (''Irregular'') professor, a nontenure track position, but salaried. He remained at Berlin for the next 8 years.

Almost immediately following its publication, other psychologists picked up the idea of research on verbal memory. Müller and Schumann (1894) did Ebbinghaus one better by controlling for the use of poetic meter (by using a pneumograph to measure breathing pauses). They also eliminated all the words from the syllable lists, and invented the memory drum so that not all of the stimuli in a list could be seen at once. With these modifications, Müller tested his notion of ''retroactive inhibition.'' Once Ebbinghaus' work became known in the U.S., research followed that examined the effects of the meaningfulness of the syllables (Glaze, 1928; Hull, 1933). The American educational psychologist Pressey (1926) conducted studies of students' retention of material from an introductory psychology course.

Ebbinghaus' monograph received mixed reviews when it was published. James (1885) praised the work and devoted a substantial portion of his short review pointing out Ebbinghaus' ''heroic efforts'' and his ''high critical acumen.'' From James' review we see a picture of an exacting, thorough scientist, working in the tradition of Weber and Fechner, devoting a major portion of his life to his science and coming up with some interesting discoveries. To James, ''this particular series of experiments [was] the entering wedge of a new method of incalculable reach'' (p. 199).

Although Titchener shared Ebbinghaus' concern about contamination of stimuli with meaning (the ''stimulus error''), he was not so enamored of Ebbinghaus' research, believing that the use of nonsense syllables took the focus away from conscious contents. Yet, Titchener clearly respected Ebbinghaus' accomplishments: ''It is not too much to say that the recourse to nonsense syllables, as a means to the study of association, marks the most considerable advance in this chapter of psychology since the time of Aristotle'' (1928, p. 125).

New psychology journals were beginning to spring up everywhere and Germany needed a general journal, since the only one being published regularly was the *Philosophische Studien*, which consisted of reports from Wundt's Leipzig laboratory. Along with Arthur König, Ewald Hering, Carl Stumpf, Hermann Helmholtz, and others, Ebbinghaus established (and edited for 22 years) the *Zeitschrift für Psychologie und Physiologie der Sinnesorgane* (Journal for the Psychology and Physiology of the Sense Organs), which was a major journal then and is flourishing today as the *Zeitschrift für Psychologie*.

In the fall of 1893 Carl Stumpf (1848–1936) was called to Berlin University as professor of philosophy and director of the ''Seminar for Psychology,'' with the full support of the senior faculty of the College of Arts and Sciences. Ebbinghaus in turn accepted a call to a full professorship at Breslau University in the Prussian province of Silesia, not far from the Polish border. Although historians have speculated why Stumpf, rather than Ebbinghaus, was appointed to the prestigious chair at Berlin University, little factual information is available. One should remember, however, that Ebbinghaus had published relatively few research reports and that major German universities frowned on so-called "inside" promotions.

Ebbinghaus' important text, *Grundzüge der Psychologie* (Principles of psychology), appeared in 1897 and went through a number of subsequent revisions and expansions. For many years, Ebbinghaus' text was the most popular and widely-used general psychology text, as was his later (1908) and briefer *Abriss der Psychologie* (Outline of psychology). In fact, the demand for his texts was so great that the *Grundzüge* appeared in its final form (the fourth edition) under the editorship of Durr, who completed the second volume of the work after Ebbinghaus' death. Titchener (1910) asserted that the *Grundzüge* would ultimately be more important to experimental psychology than either Wundt's or Brentano's general psychology texts. The *Grundzüge* was highly regarded, even by those who were critical of Ebbinghaus' memory research, and even by those whose own research was criticized by Ebbinghaus (Uhlein, 1985).

Ebbinghaus was known as an eloquent lecturer and excellent teacher, a man with vision and a tolerance for views that differed from his own, and a man with a good sense of humor. Indeed, Boring called him "the James of Germany, if there can be another James anywhere!" (1929, p. 384). Ebbinghaus' papers at the meetings of the *Psychologische Gesellschaft* reportedly attracted large audiences.

Ebbinghaus' Later Memory Research

Though he was busy teaching courses in psychology, philosophy, and aesthetics, and busy writing textbooks, Ebbinghaus did not drop the idea of conducting research. Indeed, he set up modest psychology laboratories wherever he taught, despite the Prussian government's hesitation in supporting experimental psychology (Robinson, 1985). Some of Ebbinghaus' later memory research is described in the *Grundzüge*. There, Ebbinghaus reviewed some of his psychophysical experiments (e.g., 1887, 1890) in which he had applied Weber's Law to brightness and color contrast, and he presented a theory of color vision. He also reviewed some new memory research he had conducted.

The school board of Breslau had commissioned Ebbinghaus, among others, to generate mental tests that could be used to determine the best distribution of study hours for schoolchildren. At the time, schoolchildren were engaged in a single session from 8 a.m. until 1 p.m. and their irritability and fatigue as the day went on were apparent to their teachers (Hothersall, 1984, p. 141). An attempt had been made to measure mental fatigue, using a two-point discrimination psychophysical method, but Ebbinghaus did not feel that this test was well suited to the purpose, and the Breslau board agreed. Ebbinghaus devised a task that was related to the kinds of things the schoolchildren did. He invented the completion method (which he called the "method of combinations") to see how well children could perceive relationships, combine information, and arrive at correct conclusions. In the task, students would have to fill in the missing letters in sentences such as "WH-- WILLY --- TWO ----- OLD, HE ----- -- - RED FARM-----." This type of task is still used in modern intelligence and aptitude tests. Along with digit memory and a rapid calculation task, the results showed a clear effect of age and individual differences. However, only the results from the method of combinations showed a fit with the children's grades.

Binet was working on testing at the time, and knew of Ebbinghaus' work through a report (in French) that Ebbinghaus had prepared. Binet was both encouraged and influenced by Ebbinghaus' studies of schoolchildren (Peterson, 1925, p. 111), and the original Binet–Simon scale included Ebbinghaus' method of relearning of lists (of words) as well as the sentence-completion task. Ebbinghaus' work on intelligence testing was thus some of the very first research on this topic. According to Woodworth (1909), the completion method was probably a better test of intelligence than any other method available at the time.

Other research on learning and memory that Ebbinghaus summarized in the *Gründzuge* is of importance to experimental psychology. For example, the classic Ebbinghaus "forgetting curve" (which he called the "curve of oblivis-cence") does not appear in *Über das Gedächtnis,* but was actually first reported in the second edition of the first volume of the *Grundzüge* (1905, p. 680), and was popularized in England and the U.S. by McDougall (1923, p. 295) and Woodworth (1938, p. 31, 53). The research reported in the *Grundzüge* also includes the first discussion of primacy and recency effects. Using the "prompting method," he learned 48 lists of 10 words each and counted the number of promptings needed for the recall of each item. He found that fewer promptings were needed for items that fell near the beginnings and endings of the lists. He explained this result as being an effect of the distribution of attention.

Ebbinghaus' Impact

With regard to the impact of his memory research, Ebbinghaus provided experimental psychology with just the model it apparently needed and wanted. Ebbinghaus became a model of the "hard-nosed" experimentalist, whose writings about experimental methods were thorough and whose writings about theoretical speculations and hypothetical mentalistic mechanisms were brief and cautious. He provided experimental psychology with a model for the use of statistics. He provided a model for "effort." By that we mean that his work had an impact in proportion to the effort it represented: Dozens of experiments, replications, and control experiments, each involving multiple trials and hour after hour of data collection and careful record keeping. There could be no doubt that the results were robust and the relations between dependent and independent variables were "tight." He provided a model for the use of "experimental logic." This included the testing of alternative hypotheses by setting up experimental situations where rival hypotheses would make different predictions, and also a sensitivity to what are today called "experimenter bias effects" (especially important to Ebbinghaus because he was his own subject). Finally, he provided experimental psychology with a model for preparing a research report: the now-traditional ordering of introduction, methods, results, and discussion sections.

Apart from his memory research, Ebbinghaus' efforts had another effect on psychology: He helped separate psychology from philosophy (Boring, 1950, p. 392). Even one of the four "theses" (or hypotheses) that Ebbinghaus defended publicly as part of his final oral Ph.D. examination stated that psychology should not be a part of philosophy (Ebbinghaus, 1873). *On memory* was subtitled "An investigation in experimental psychology," and the title page contained the statement: "From the most ancient subject we shall produce the newest science." In the *Abriss* he opened with the often-quoted line, "Psychology has a long past but a short history." In the brief historical sketch that begins the *Abriss,* Ebbinghaus says:

> When Weber in 1829 [1834] had the seemingly petty curiosity to want to know at what distances apart two touches on the skin could be just perceived as two, and later, with what accuracy he could distinguish between two weights laid on the hand . . . his curiosity resulted in more real progress in psychology than all the combined distinctions, definitions and classifications of the time from Aristotle to Hobbs (inclusive). (p. 17)

Thus, Ebbinghaus was a champion of the view that psychology should be emancipated from philosophy. He believed that the higher mental processes could be studied experimentally with a precision that rivaled the physical sciences and with mental testing methods that did not rely exclusively on introspection.

Ebbinghaus died unexpectedly of pneumonia in 1909. He had not published much research—only a dozen or so research reports—and he had few important pupils. He apparently had no desire to have "disciples" (Jaensch, 1909). Nevertheless, his importance to experimental psychology was foremost in the thoughts of psychologists around the world. Indeed, Knight Dunlap (1927) gave Ebbinghaus the credit for launching psychology on the path toward behaviorism, that is, for orienting psychology toward the experimentalist and functionalist attitudes. Psychology had lost one of its most careful and systematic researchers, and one of its most original, insightful, critical, and admired thinkers. At the famous 1909 psychology conference marking the 20th anniversary of Clark University (to which Ebbinghaus had been invited), Titchener began with a eulogy:

> As I approach the topic of this lecture, what is uppermost in my mind is a sense of irreparable loss. When the cable brought the bad news, last February, that Eb-

binghaus was dead . . . the feeling that took precedence even of personal sorrow was the wonder of what experimental psychology would do without him (1910, p. 405)

Having briefly discussed the life of Ebbinghaus, we now turn to an overview of his classic research *On memory*.

ÜBER DAS GEDÄCHTNIS

The monograph *On memory* has three basic components or aspects: the experiments themselves, a discussion of statistical analyses of data, and some theorizing.

The use of statistical averages and standard errors as a measure of variability had been established by Fechner and others. Ebbinghaus' discussion of the basic statistical methods was so clear and exacting, however, that many psychologists had their students read Ebbinghaus just for the discussion of statistics. Each data point that entered into his analyses was an average of the learning times (or average number of repetitions needed to reach a learning criterion) over a large number of lists. The averages were used to compute a distribution of means, and results were then described in terms of standard errors: the percentage of cases falling under a given area of the distribution.

Although the theoretical discussions do not take up much space, one must be impressed by the clarity and sophistication of Ebbinghaus' thought (1885/1964) especially his awareness of the use of metaphors and analogies:

> To express our ideas concerning [the physical basis of memory] we use different metaphors—stored up ideas, engraved images, well-beaten paths. There is only one thing certain about these figures of speech and that is that they are not suitable. (p. 5)

Later in the monograph he says:

> Who could, with even tolerable exactness, describe in its gradual course the supposed overlaying or sinking or crumbling of ideas? Who can say anything satisfactory about the inhibitions caused by series of ideas of different extent, or about the disintegration that a firm complex of any kind suffers by the use of its components in new connections? Everybody has his private "explanation" of these processes, but the actual conditions which are to be explained are, after all, equally unknown to all of us. (p. 64)

And later still:

> If use is made of the language of psychology, then, as in the case of all unconscious processes, expression can be only figurative and inexact. (p. 122)

He is quite explicit in saying that his research on memory was based on analogies. One was psychophysical, a comparison of the strength of memory impressions to the "intensity of a representation in consciousness." He also relied on Herbart's (1834) metaphor that ideas can be "bound" and "forced" together and can become "dim" over time (Ebbinghaus, 1885/1964, p. 90–94). His sense of humor shows in his poetic discussion of the metaphorical hypotheses of associationism where he describes the "associative threads which are spun" between the items in a list (1885/1964, p. 94, 123).

He drew analogies to physics in comparing his relearning functions with the processes of certain chemical reactions: An initial sharp rise is followed by a slow approach to an asymptote (1880/1971, Sec. 16). He speculated that since the same lawful regularity was involved, the function he obtained may say something about the underlying neurochemical processes that occur after a neuron is stimulated.

Much of Ebbinghaus' writing in *On memory* is highly reminiscent of James Mill's (1829) analysis of the strength and vividness of associations. Perhaps this is what led many historians of psychology to place Ebbinghaus' work squarely in the tradition of the British associationists. However, the theorizing in *On memory* was actually a modest discussion of the ideas of Herbart and Lotze. Following Herbart, Ebbinghaus sought "mathematical rules for mental events," especially for the vividness or strength of memories. He also discussed hypotheses from Bain and Delboeuf about the physiological basis of memory. There are no other salient references.

Although Ebbinghaus discussed the hypotheses of the associationists (in the *Grundzüge* he discussed them at length), he preferred to refer to memory in terms of the "strength and vividness of imagination" (which was commonly mistranslated as "strength of associations"). One could safely conclude that Ebbinghaus' work could just as well be included in the tradition of the Herbartians as it could in the tradition of the British associationists, with which it is usually linked.

The Experiments

In terms of the experiments, the monograph consists of some 19 studies of the learning of lists of syllables, conducted in the years 1879–80 and 1883–84. The experiments touch on at least ten separate topics. (In the original manuscript, he alludes to some observations on the effect of the amount of sleep on retention, but no data are provided and this topic is not discussed in the monograph.)

He first prepared a pool of 2300 syllables, but these were not consonant–vowel–consonant trigrams, as is reported in most history of psychology texts. Ebbinghaus included a number of phonetic elements that relate to the German language (diphthongs and consonant clusters). The stimuli were syllables, but quite a few were words or were at least very word-like. Here are some examples: *heim, beis, ship, dush, noir, noch, dach, wash, born, for, zuch, dauch, shok, hal, dauf, fich, theif, haum, shish,* and *rur.*[2] In discussing the materials, Ebbinghaus referred to their simplicity or homogeneity and to the ease with which they could be systematically varied, but not to their "meaninglessness." In the list of examples above, the first 10 are all meanginful in one or another of the languages Ebbinghaus knew.

He also went to great lengths to control other experimental conditions. He reported that he had led a ritualistic and almost monastic life during the experiments. He kept careful records of the times of day during which he engaged in the learning tasks, and found, for example, that it was easier to learn lists at 10–11 a.m. than at 6–8 p.m. Thus, he could calculate a percentage correction for effort for a list that had been originally learned in the morning and subjected to a memory test in the evening.

In the discussion that follows we refer to the experiments in the order in which they are first mentioned in the monograph (see Table 4.1 for page references).

Experiments 1 and 2 are demonstrations of the viability of the basic method. After systematically generating syllables, Ebbinghaus composed lists of various lengths. Pacing himself with either a metronome or a watch, and reading the lists aloud with a poetic meter (three or four syllables per "foot" with an accent on the first syllable in each foot), he proceeded to memorize the lists of syllables. He relied on memory when possible, and refreshed his memory, when needed, by a glance at the list. Using a set of buttons on a string, he was able to keep track of the number of repetitions he needed in order to learn a list to the point that he could give one perfect recitation of it (for the 1879/80 set of experiments the criterion was two perfect recitations).

The first two experiments had the goal of showing that the variability of the average learning times over a large number of lists was within limits that would be scientifically acceptable. He emphasized that the standard errors he obtained compared very favorably with the precision of measurement in the physical and biological sciences (e.g., Helmholtz's measurement of the speed of neural conduction; Joule's measurements of the mechanical equivalent of heat). In fact, his "probable errors" of about 7% were more precise than the physical measurements and very close to those for the biological measurements.

Experiments 3–7 explored a phenomenon that Ebbinghaus called the "oscillation of attention." Early on, it became evident to Ebbinghaus that the work was tedious and boring, and that many headaches lay ahead. Rather than causing a cumulative fatigue, however, performance tended to oscillate, with relatively poor performance on a list followed by good performance on the next, and so on. This observation led directly to an insightful discussion of what are today called "floor effects" in verbal learning tasks: the tendency for performance to be more

---

[2]These examples are from archival sources and were made publicly available in a poster announcing the meeting at Passau University (See Footnote 3).

variable on trials where it falls above the mean (that is, performance is somehow limited to fall above a certain level).

In Experiments 8 and 9, Ebbinghaus observed that the time needed for learning to criterion increased sharply as the list length increased. For instance, a list of length 36 took 50 times the number of repetitions as a list of length 7. The orderliness of the data allowed him to give a precise description of the functional relation, and this was extremely pleasing to Ebbinghaus.

Experiments 10 and 11 were on the "method of savings." He speculated that learning can lead to "deeper" memory traces for material that is practiced beyond the point of one perfect recitation. To test this, he studied lists for different amounts of time and tested himself a day later by seeing how much study was needed to bring the lists back to memory. Though sometimes not accompanied by conscious recognition of a list, he found that relearning only took about one-third the number of repetitions as the original learning had, and this was pretty much independent of list length.

Experiments 12, 13, and 14 focused on "obliviscence," that is, on what is forgotten rather than on what is remembered. Using the savings method, Ebbinghaus showed that savings decrease systematically with the delay in testing. For a 1-hour delay, relearning took about 50% of the original effort, for an 8-hour delay, relearning took about 75% of the original effort. The amount retained divided by the amount forgotten varied as the inverse of the extent of the delay. Ebbinghaus was obviously very pleased that such precise relations could be obtained, since he had as a major goal the generation of true laws of higher mental processes, laws that would compare in precision with those in other sciences.

Experiment 15 looked at the effects of repeated relearning. As the number of repetitions increases, the lists should be engraved more and more deeply and indelibly in some mental substratum (1885/1964, p. 53). Over 6 days of repeated learning trials, the number of repetitions that was needed to reach criterion dropped, but the drop depended on list length. There was a 33% savings for 12-syllable lists, but a 58% savings for 36-syllable lists. In other words, that which was learned with greater difficulty was better retained.

Almost incidental to his discussion of the main result of Experiment 15 is a paragraph in which Ebbinghaus (1885/1964) mentions rather casually that distributing the repetitions over days had a greater effect than massing the repetitions in one day: "With any considerable number of repetitions a suitable distribution of them over a space of time is decidedly more advantageous than the massing of them at a single time" (p. 89). Could he have imagined that his systematic demonstration of the difference between distributed and massed practice would find itself mentioned in psychology texts for decades to come?

Experiments 16, 17, and 18 tested the notion of "strength" of associations. Are associations only between contiguous items or do they bind items that are separated? Over time, associations may dim or become inhibited, and thus the effects of contiguous items on each other may appear stronger. According to Herbart's (1834) theorizing on the laws of association, the strength of association between two ideas should be a function of the number of ideas that intervene between them. Furthermore, "secret threads are spun which bind together the series" (Ebbinghaus, 1885/1964, p. 123). To test these notions, Ebbinghaus learned many sets of lists, with the order of the syllables varied across the repetitions of a given list. If associations are formed between all the items, and not just between contiguous items, one should expect to find some savings on the relearning of the reordered lists, and this is exactly what Ebbinghaus found. The greater the extent of the reordering of a list, the less was the savings, but even for the greatest amounts of reordering, there was a reliable savings in terms of the time it took to reach criterion (on the order of 12 out of 420 seconds). For Experiment 18, tests were done on the relearning of lists in the reversed order. The tests yielded a savings of about 12% of the effort it took in the original learning, suggesting that associations may have some reversed connections.

Included in the discussion of these experiments is an insightful consideration of the possible effect of experimenter bias and "warpings of the truth" (1885/1964, p. 29). Ebbinghaus was concerned that a biasing factor might lead him to get the very results he wanted. When doing a series of the relearning experiments with reordered lists, he could not avoid being curious about which list it was that was being relearned, that is, to determine which type of reordering was involved. It was easy to notice the lists that involved little reordering, and harder to notice the lists that involved more reordering. Thus, there was a variation in attention over the types of reorderings, giving an inflated estimate of the savings for the lists that did not involve much reordering. Yet, there was still an effect of associative strength in Experiment 18, in which he kept all the lists and results hidden from view until the experiment was completed.

Almost incidental to his discussion of the results of Experiments 16, 17, and 18 is a rather remarkable passage, one which antedates modern discussions of the short-term memory span:

> I wish to add a few words concerning the . . . derivation of the association of successive ideas from the unitary consciousness of a unitary soul. . . . the number of syllables which I can repeat without error after a single reading is about seven. One can, with a certain justification, look upon this number as a measure of the ideas of this sort which I can grasp in a single unitary conscious act. (p. 109)

Jacobs (1887) picked up on this notion and it is his studies of the "memory span" that were cited by Cattell (1890) and subsequent American researchers.

Experiment 19 is a study of the effect of the number of repetitions on the strength of associations. In initial learning, he repeated lists either 16 or 64 times. On relearning, he studied reordered lists and found a savings of about 100 seconds for the lists that had initially been repeated 16 times, and a savings of

161 seconds for the lists that had been studied 64 times. The strength of remote associations did not increase proportionately to the number of repetitions, as was the case for associations between immediately successive items (Experiments 10 and 11). The effect of repetitions repetitions decreased more quickly for remote than for immediate associations.

Although it is rather obvious that this program of 19 experiments involved a great deal of work, we were surprised to find that no one has tried to figure out exactly how much work was involved. Our attempt to do so was made difficult by the fact that different portions of the results from the various experiments are reported in more than one place in the monograph. Furthermore, the results for some experiments are reported in terms of the average savings in time per list and for other experiments in terms of the average savings of repetitions. To make matters worse, for some of the experiments Ebbinghaus reports the time taken to read each syllable and one must compute the time taken to learn the lists by multiplying the number of repetitions by the time taken per syllable.

Despite these difficulties, we were able to compile the experiments, as is shown in Table 4.1. The totals for syllables do not include repetitions of the lists. Total time for Experiment 1 seems disproportionately small because this study involved a relatively small number (6–18) of repetitions. Conversely, total times for experiments 10 and 15 seem disproportionately large because these experiments involved as many as 64 repetitions. The time for experiment 15 takes into account that part of the results presented earlier in the monograph. Totals for lists and syllables for Experiment 15 are included in Experiment 8. Experiments 3, 5, 6, 9, and 12 were conducted in 1879/80 and some of the results from them were reported in the original manuscript (1880/1971) as well as in the monograph (1885/1964).

As Table 4.1 shows, the research did involve a great deal of work. Can you imagine sitting in front of a metronome or pocket watch and chunking in 84,600 syllables in 6600 lists, taking more than 830 hours! Although the number of list repetitions involved for each experiment is not presented in Table 4.1 since it cannot be computed for some of the studies on the basis of Ebbinghaus's report, for Experiment 2 alone, Ebbinghaus engaged in 189,501 repetitions of lists. A great deal of work indeed!

Although it is traditional to praise Ebbinghaus for the amount of effort it took him to conduct his research, in retrospect the effort may not seem all that great. A number of the studies reported in the other chapters in this volume represent such effort, as do many studies on verbal learning and memory that are reported in modern journals. This does not detract from his achievement, in our view. He was breaking new ground and his research required an effort comparable to modern research that has followed in his footsteps.

Looking across all his research with lists of syllables, there are a number of important findings:

TABLE 4.1
A Compilation of Ebbinghaus' Experiments on the Learning of Lists
of Syllables

Study	Page	Number of Syllables per List	Total Number of Lists	Total Number of Syllables	Approximate Time per Experiment
1	31	16	168	2688	3.8 hours
2	31	12,16,24,36	350	5796	22.9
3	35,42	13	736	9568	28.4
4	36,43	16	504	8064	29.4
5	39,40	13	234	3042	12.0
6	39,40	13	304	3952	11.7
7	40	13	160	2080	4.9
8	43,46	12,16,24,36	350	5796	31.7
9	49	10,13,16,19	1056	13380	34.4
10	54–58	16	420	6720	245.2
11	60	12	96	1152	14.4
12	65–79	13	1304	16952	84.1
13	79	10	90	900	2.3
14	80	12	63	756	2.6
15	82	12,24,36			226.7
16	95–101	16	330	1056	37.5
17	102–106	16	180	576	20.6
18	110–114	16	168	1344	9.3
19	114–123	16	96	768	10.7
		Totals	6,609	84,590	832.6 hours

Note: The studies are numbered in order of mention in the monograph. (Page numbers refer to the 1964 Dover edition.)

(a) Demonstration of the viability of the method of savings or "ease of relearning" as a means of measuring retention.

(b) Demonstration of the effects of fatigue and time of day on retention.

(c) Measurement of the effect of list length on the number of repetitions it takes to learn material to a given criterion.

(d) Measurement of the "decay of memory" as a function of the delay between acquisition and memory test (with delays spanning hours, days, weeks, and even years).

(e) Demonstration of the effect of "distributed" versus "massed" practice.

(f) Demonstration of primacy and recency effects in serial recall.

(g) Demonstration of the existence of "remote" associations.

(h) Measurement of the short-term memory span.

To say that this list includes some important findings would be to understate things considerably. The list certainly includes all the basic phenomena that are the focus of the other chapters in this volume.

The Don Juan Experiment

One topic is conspicuous by its absence from the previous list: The effect of meaningfulness of the material on the ease of relearning. Ebbinghaus demonstrated that also, and this brings us to a discussion of what we call his Experiment 20, although the results of this study are alluded to throughout the monograph (1885/1964, pp. 43–44, 50–51, 82–83). In this study, Ebbinghaus memorized some stanzas from Byron's *Don Juan* (in English) in order to directly address the question of the role of meaningfulness in the associative process. Over a period of 4 days he conducted seven separate tests, each test involving the learning of six stanzas. Each test took about 20 minutes and involved about eight repetitions of each stanza. Given that each stanza consisted of about 80 syllables, he could compute that meaningfulness resulted in a big advantage: about one-tenth the effort in terms of the number of repetitions needed to allow one perfect recitation.

More important to Ebbinghaus, however, was the fact that the findings with the poetry confirmed the findings for the syllables: General laws were in operation, such as the principle of the oscillation of attention.

SOME QUESTIONS ABOUT EBBINGHAUS

Our discussion of the results of the studies with stanzas from Byron leads us directly back to the idea that there are many interesting historical questions about Ebbinghaus and his work. The most interesting question is the most difficult one to answer: What led Ebbinghaus to the idea of doing experiments on memory? This question has two aspects to it: Where did he get the idea for the syllables and where did he get the idea for his tasks? Our answers, though tentative, rely on evidence about the sources of inspiration for Ebbinghaus: the work of Fechner, and Ebbinghaus' knowledge of poetry. As we will show, the *Don Juan* experiment was probably more critical than most historians have supposed.

The Influence of Fechner

Following Jaensch (1909) and Shakow (1930), it has been believed that Ebbinghaus was introduced to the work of Fechner by a secondhand copy of the *Elemente*, which Ebbinghaus discovered during his travels to Paris. Actually, Ebbinghaus bought Fechner's classic two-volume work between April and December 1875 in London (Bringmann & Bringmann, 1985). Ebbinghaus was no doubt inspired by reading Fechner because he dedicated his *Grundzüge* to him ("I owe everything to you") and even sent a signed copy of his monograph to Fechner once it was published (Fechner was 84). This copy has recently been discovered in the archives of the American Psychological Association. (It is not known how the book reached the United States and the A.P.A. [Benjamin, 1985]). Ebbinghaus and Fechner never met. Fechner had died by the time Ebbinghaus wrote Wundt to inquire about him (Robinson, 1985).

Ebbinghaus' original manuscript (1880/1971) begins with a discussion of psychophysical methods and the search for relations between the intensity of stimulation and the vividness of the resulting impression. The influence of Fechnerian psychophysics is clear in Ebbinghaus' intellectual search for a task that would be appropriate for the study of memory.

However, there is still something of a mystery here. If Fechner had been so influential, why did Ebbinghaus not cite him, either in the original manuscript or in the finished monograph? He quoted very few authors in the manuscript (1880/1971) and the monograph (1885/1964). He was clearly heavily influenced by Herbart (1834), who had proposed the search for lawful relations for mental events, but who had not followed through with actual observations on the vividness of memory images. Ebbinghaus began both the original manuscript and the monograph with statements to the effect that he wanted to extend Herbart's notion of "strength of imagination" to real measurements of the vividness of memory images. Fechner is mentioned nowhere.

Beyond the influence of Fechner's and Herbart's work, we are somewhat in the dark as to the factors or events that led Ebbinghaus to conduct his memory experiments. Some speculation is possible, however, and this is where the *Don Juan* experiment comes in.

The Influence of Poetry

Ebbinghaus definitely did not begin his memory studies with the lists of syllables. In the original manuscript he mentions that he had first thought of learning a series of tones (that would require two experimenters) and also lists of numbers. In fact, the first actual experiments he conducted were on lists of numbers, and not with himself as subject, but with a 14-year-old child (1880/1971, Sec. 14). Although this is speculation on our part, this child was probably one of the students he was teaching in England. This preliminary study showed that the task of learning multiple lists was very tedious, and he apparently had some qualms about subjecting people other than himself to its rigors, although he may also have conducted research with one of his students in France (Shakow, 1930) and he definitely conducted some unreported studies using his son Julius as a subject (Bahrick, 1985).

Left unsatisfied with tones and numbers, he turned to poetry. Although the description of the results of the *Don Juan* experiment in the 1885 monograph mentions that the formal studies were conducted in 1884, he definitely conducted some experiments on his memory for *Don Juan* in the 1879–80 period. He also alludes to preliminary experiments that *preceded* the studies of 1879/80. This means that he may have conducted pilot studies of his memory for poetry while he was in England and France.

In the original manuscript (Sec. 5) he mentions that it was very important to him to study poetry and prose. However, he also says that his preliminary trials with poetry showed that the material was learned too quickly. He found no need for multiple repetitions (meaning that he could not get enough data about trials and time to criterion in order to generate statistically reliable laws) and he was also concerned that the material could not be systematically and quantitatively varied (lists of numbers did not afford enough variety either).

Both in the original manuscript and in the monograph, Ebbinghaus refers repeatedly to the *Don Juan* experiments, no doubt in part because the idea of learning a poem is an experience that would be familiar to his readers. Yet, references to the Don Juan example occur exactly at points where Ebbinghaus is describing the basic logic of his methods. It is also important to remember that Ebbinghaus learned his lists of syllables by using a poetic meter to chunk them.

One final fact to be considered is that Ebbinghaus continued to conduct studies of his memory for poems long after the publication of his 1885 book. In the *Grundzüge* (Volume 1) he reported that he tested his memory for stanzas that had been learned 5 and 17 years earlier, yielding a savings of about 20%.

All these facts taken together suggest to us that Ebbinghaus may have first hit upon the idea of the method of savings by testing his memory for Byron's poetry. He may have learned some stanzas when he studied English in England. At a later date, probably while in England but almost certainly within a short time thereafter, and while pondering the idea of experiments on higher mental processes, he may have attempted to recall the poetry he may have learned as early as his mid-20s, and then asked himself how much additional studying he would have to do to recall the stanzas without error. Perhaps it then occurred to him that the effort involved in relearning might be used as a sensitive measure of the processes of association.

Our reasoning about the importance of poetry is also supported by the possibility that he may have hit on the idea of his syllables from reading the popular nonsense poetry and children's literature of the day. Shakow (1930) speculated that Ebbinghaus had read Lewis Carroll's *Through the Looking Glass* (1872) while he was in England.

No Apologies, Please

Today we see criticisms of the Ebbinghaus tradition and the questioning of the generality of his findings (e.g., Erdelyi & Kleinbard, 1978). Surely Ebbinghaus would have been disappointed with us had we not modified and refined his results on the basis of further experimentation. Modern treatments of Ebbinghaus seem sometimes to be apologizing for Ebbinghaus, for example, by saying that he was so systematic that he invented nonsense syllables in order to eliminate all meaning (see the chapter on learning in just about any introductory psychology text). In point of fact, Ebbinghaus' research on the learning of stanzas of poetry was much more extensive, and more important to him, than most historical treatments suppose.

Human learning is extremely complex, and one should not at all be distressed that experimental psychology is still struggling to explain the phenomena that Ebbinghaus demonstrated. As he recognized, it will take a great deal of complex research on a large array of methods and materials in order for psychology to generate a corpus of lawful regularities in learning.

Some Other Questions

Offhand, we can think of a number of interesting questions, but alas, we can only list them because no facts are currently available: Why did he turn from his studies of philosophy and history to the study of psychology? How much psychology had he read before he conceived the idea of the memory experiments? Had he read Wundt's *Physiological psychology* (1873)? Had he read any of the works of the British associationists? Precisely when did he read Fechner's *Elemente der Psychophysik*? Was he aware of other work on memory that was being conducted (cf. Stigler, 1978)? What was going on in his personal life that may have influenced his work? We know that he was married, and that his archives include letters to his fiancé. Certainly much can be learned about Ebbinghaus' scientific life through investigations of information about the personal side of his life. We know that he came from a wealthy family. What role did the desire for an academic position play in his life? How did he view his own work and career?

Certainly the centennial celebrations of Ebbinghaus in the United States (the present volume) and also in Europe[3] will encourage historical investigations through which we will learn more about the man and his work.

ACKNOWLEDGMENTS

The authors would like to thank Henry Roediger, Rob Wozniak, and David Gorfein for their comments on an earlier version of this chapter. We would also like to thank the office of the executive director of the American Psychological Association for lending us the signed copy of Ebbinghaus' monograph so that it could be displayed at the conference.

---

[3]*Internationales Hermann Ebbinghaus Symposion,* held at the Institut für Geschichte der Neueren Psychologie, Passau University, 8390 Passau, West Germany, May 30 through June 2, 1985.

5 Ebbinghaus' *On Memory*: Some Effects on Early American Research

Slater E. Newman
North Carolina State University

Among my early tasks while preparing this chapter was to read *On Memory* (1885) again, identifying Ebbinghaus' many contributions—such as the nonsense syllable, the method of savings, the use of the serial task, the method of derived lists, and his mathematical treatment of the data—plus the several problems he had worked on such as the length–difficulty relationship, the effects of repetition, the shape of the forgetting curve, the comparison of poetry and nonsense-syllable learning, and the occurrence of remote and backward associations.

This chapter is a review of American research during the period 1885–1905 with a focus on the impact of Ebbinghaus' work. It is organized chronologically and is divided into four periods with a summary of American research on memory during each of those periods. The emphasis is on experimental research using normal human subjects and published in four American periodicals, the *American Journal of Psychology, Psychological Bulletin, Psychological Review* and *Psychological Review Monograph Supplements.*

1885–1890

The first period is from 1885–1890. There are four items that I comment on: (a) a review of Ebbinghaus' book by William James that appeared in *Science* in 1885, (b) another review, also in 1885, by Joseph Jacobs that appeared in the British journal, *Mind,* (c) the founding in 1887 of the *American Journal of Psychology,* and (d) the appearance in that journal in 1889 of a summary of Ebbinghaus' work.

Ebbinghaus' *On Memory* was reviewed in *Science* by William James just after it had been published. James was especially impressed by two "incidental results" (p. 199), by the rapid early drop in memory and by the results from studies using derived lists. He was not much impressed with most of the remaining results, which, in respect to the laws of memory ". . . we are sorry to say add nothing to our gross experience of the matter" (p. 299). James was also, however, favorably impressed by Ebbinghaus' "heroism in the pursuit of true averages, his high critical acumen, his modest tone, and his polished style . . . [suggesting that] . . . we have a newcomer in psychology, from whom the best may be expected" (p. 199).

The review by Jacobs, also in 1885, was somewhat longer than James' and was also predominantly favorable. In this review, Jacobs summarized some of the main aspects of Ebbinghaus' method as well as some of the major findings from his experiments, concluding that the book was remarkable more for its method than for its results, most of which ". . . scarcely seem to need two years of strenuous and exhausting labor to establish" (p. 458). However, Jacobs proposed that these experiments ". . . deserve, and will repay, the attention of earnest students of psychology . . . [since they] . . . may claim to be the first on any considerable scale in which quantitative relations have been obtained for psychical facts, apart either from physiological concomitants or physical reference" (p. 454). Jacobs continued:

May we hope to see the day, when school registers will record that such and such a lad possesses 36 British Association units of memory power or when we shall be able to calculate how long a mind of 17 'macaulays' will take to learn Book ii of *Paradise Lost* . . . Meanwhile, let us not part from him without a word of recognition for the astonishing patience, painstaking diligence, and scientific caution and accuracy shown in his work . . . (to be regarded), with wonder and admiration. (p. 459)

A third major event relating to American research during this period was the founding in 1887 by G. Stanley Hall of the *American Journal of Psychology*. The first issue of this journal was published in November 1887 and, as is the case today, it was published quarterly. The main objective of this journal was, according to its editor, ". . . to record the progress of scientific psychology for which no organ now exists in English" (Hall, 1887, p. 4). The journal contained three sections: original contributions of a scientific character, digests and reviews of important psychological literature and scientific books, and a section called notes, news, brief mentions, etc. The articles that I have reviewed for this chapter come from the first section.

A four-part article entitled, "Memory, historically and experimentally considered," by W. H. Burnham, appeared in the four issues of Volume 2 (published between November 1888 and August 1889). Most of this treatise (all but

28 of the 187 pages) summarized the views about memory from the earliest mythology up to 1885. But in the final section Burnham presented Ebbinghaus' work in some detail, describing the procedures used and the results from what he termed "the most important attempt to apply the methods of experimental psychology to the study of memory" (p. 581). Burnham suggested also, however, that a simpler method of studying memory than the learning of nonsense-syllables is ". . . to test the power of recognizing a sense-impression when repeated," (p. 604). He pointed out that the results from some of Wolfe's (1886) experiments in that vein with short retention intervals were consonant with those of Ebbinghaus (obtained with longer intervals). Burnham then described some of the psychophysical studies of Wolfe and provided brief summaries of a number of other studies on a variety of memory-related topics, such as the memory span, the association of ideas and the "latent memories" observed in the study of hypnotic tests of memory. He concluded with the listing of a number of questions still to be answered, such as the extent of cerebral localization, the relative accuracy of memory among the different senses, and the genesis of memory in children. These papers by Burnham were the only papers on memory in this journal during this first period ending in 1890.

1891–1895

A major event during this next period, was the beginning of another new journal, the *Psychological Review*. According to Wozniak (1984), a number of younger psychologists, led by James Mark Baldwin and James McKeen Cattell, had become disappointed with Hall's editorial policies for the *American Journal of Psychology*. They thus proposed that either the editorial board of the *American Journal of Psychology* be broadened or that Hall sell the publication. When he did neither, they set up the *Psychological Review* in 1894. Each of the six issues of the first volume of the *Review* contained the following sections: articles, discussions, psychological literature (which included a three-page summary by James R. Angell of the two 1893 papers by Müller and Schumann), a list of new books, and notes. In addition, the final issue of this first volume contained the first annual appearance of the *Psychological Index*, described as "A Bibliography of the Literature of Psychology and Cognate Subjects for 1894" (Warren & Farrand, 1895, p. i) which was the precursor of *Psychological Abstracts*. The first issue of this index listed 1312 titles, including 32 on "memory and association," of which more than one-third were American. In 1895 the *Psychological Review Monograph Supplements* began publication, with a single monograph during that year.

What I have done for this 5-year period and for the 2 that follow is to examine each of the empirical (and mainly experimental) papers on memory, noting especially references to Ebbinghaus' *On Memory*, and to the methods and results therein, and attempting also to describe the nature of American research on memory during each of these three periods. I expected to find that, at the beginning of this period, a large proportion of the papers would make reference to Ebbinghaus, and that his methods would be in wide use. Over the course of these three periods totaling 15 years, I expected also to find that there would be an increase in the amount of research on memory, in the proportion of papers that reference Ebbinghaus' work, and in the use of his methods. These expectations were not fully confirmed.

During this first 5-year period there were 13 papers on memory (Baldwin & Shaw, 1895; Bergstrom, 1893, 1894a, 1894b; Bigham, 1894; Bolton, 1892; Calkins, 1894; Daniels, 1895; Howe, 1894; Kirkpatrick, 1894; Leuba, 1893; Münsterberg & Bigham, 1894; Warren & Shaw, 1895). Of these, six appeared in the *Psychological Review,* and seven in the *American Journal of Psychology.* Of those in the *Psychological Review,* three were from the Harvard laboratory (Bigham, 1894; Calkins, 1894; Münsterberg & Bigham, 1894) and were reported by Hugo Münsterberg, and two of the papers (Baldwin & Shaw, 1895; Warren & Shaw, 1895) were from the Princeton laboratory and were reported by H. C. Warren. These papers were progress reports of work under way or recently completed, and they usually contained few references. Another such paper from the Cornell laboratory (Howe, 1894) was reported in the *American Journal of Psychology* by Titchener.[1] In addition, it contained four papers from Clark University, three of which were by Bergstrom (1893, 1894a, 1894b), plus the paper by Bolton (1892).

Direct reference to Ebbinghaus' *On Memory* appeared in three of these 13 papers. In one of them, Bergstrom mentioned that he had learned the nonsense syllables ". . . by the method used by Ebbinghaus" (1894a, p. 248). In this same paper, Bergstrom noted that his results for an increase in interference in the learning of consecutive lists were similar to those of Ebbinghaus (p. 269). He mentioned also Ebbinghaus' observation of a "rhythmic oscillation" in some experiments (p. 269), and his report that learning lists took longer in the early evening than in the morning (p. 267). In another paper Bergstrom refers to ". . . repetitions like those employed by Ebbinghaus with the nonsense syllables . . ." (1893, p. 366).

The paper by Münsterberg and Bigham (1894) begins this way:

> The experimental study of memory, important both for psychology and ped-agogics, is as yet only begun. The only experiments we have are those of Eb-binghaus, which cover simply the question of the influence of repetition and of the time-interval, made with but one material (syllables), and with only one subject. (p. 34)

---

[1]Similar "progress reports" from the two subsequent 5-year periods are those of Calkins (1896a, 1898), Gordon (1903), Heywood and Vortriede (1905), W. G. Smith (1896), and Whitehead (1896).

They then go on to point out, however, that neither the work of Ebbinghaus, nor that of Müller and Schumann (1893, which was strongly influenced by Ebbinghaus' work) are directly related to their own investigation, ". . . the purpose of which was to determine the action of disparate senses in recollection, especially to discover whether the different senses act at the same time independently, or help, or hinder each other" (p. 34).

Other evidence of Ebbinghaus' influence during this period is the use of nonsense syllables in several studies (Bergstrom, 1894a; Bigham, 1894; Howe, 1894) or reference to them (Bergstrom, 1893, 1894a, 1894b; Daniels, 1895; Münsterberg & Bigham, 1894) the use of the serial recall task (Bergstrom, 1894a) and references to the work of Müller and Schumann (Bergstrom, 1893, 1894b; Münsterberg & Bigham, 1894).

I was surprised at the variety of methods used in the studies of this period. There were, of course, some studies (Bergstrom, 1894a; Bigham, 1894) that used the serial task in the way that Ebbinghaus had done. In others, the serial task appeared as the memory-span task (Bolton, 1892), or as the method of serial reconstruction (Bigham, 1894; Münsterberg & Bigham, 1894) in which on the test the subject physically arranged the items of the series in the order that they had been presented during the study trial. However, both Calkins (1894) and Howe (1894) used a paired-associate task; Kirkpatrick (1894) used single-trial free recall, while recognition was tested in the studies by Baldwin and Shaw (1895) and also by Kirkpatrick (1894). Add to this the use by Bergstrom (1893, 1894a, 1894b) of a card-sorting task to study transfer and retroactive interference, and it is evident that a number of the tasks that were to become standard in the laboratory study of learning and memory had appeared by 1895.

There was variety, too, in the topics studied. Baldwin and Shaw (1895), for example, sought to determine the course of memory for size; Bergstrom (1893) to determine whether old habits interfere with new ones; Bigham (1894), to study ". . . the influence of the time interval between learning and recollecting with regard to its length and its filling" (p. 453); and Calkins (1894), to learn about the ". . . relative significance of frequency, vividness, recency and earliness as conditions of association" (p. 476).

Let me mention briefly some other characteristics of these papers. In most of the experiments, subjects were given a single trial and were then tested immediately. For some, however, the independent variable was the length of the retention interval, the range being from 2 to 30 seconds in one study (Bigham, 1894), and from immediately to 3 days in another (Kirkpatrick, 1894). Most experiments used 10 or fewer subjects (in two there was only a single subject—the experimenter in one, and his wife in the other), but in other studies the number of subjects ranged from 35 (Calkins, 1894) to more than 1500 (Bolton, 1892). In one of the papers, Warren and Shaw (1895) argued that ". . . single experiments on a number of subjects . . . [are under certain circumstances preferable to] . . . a series of experiments on a single individual" (p. 243).

In addition to nonsense syllables, colors (Bigham, 1894; Calkins, 1894; Münsterberg & Bigham, 1894), forms (Baldwin & Shaw, 1895; Bigham, 1894; Warren & Shaw, 1895), objects (Kirkpatrick, 1894), numbers (Bigham, 1894; Bolton, 1892; Calkins, 1894; Daniels, 1895; Münsterberg & Bigham, 1894), brightnesses (Leuba, 1893), and French (Howe, 1894), German (Howe, 1894) and English words (Bergstrom, 1893, 1894a, 1894b; Bigham, 1894; Howe, 1894; Kirkpatrick, 1894) comprised the materials in one or more experiments.

Other aspects of interest were the presentation of serial-position curves (Bigham, 1894; Bolton, 1892), the classification of errors into various types (Bigham, 1894; Bolton, 1892; Kirkpatrick, 1894), some evidence for the buildup of proactive interference (Bergstrom, 1894a), and the use by Bigham (1894) of a 2 × 2 design which permitted the study of selective interference involving the visual and the auditory modalities.

1896–1900

The next period is from 1896–1900. During this period there were 19 memory papers that appeared in the two journals and the *Psychological Monographs*. Of these 19 papers, 3 were questionnaire studies (Bolton, 1896a; Colegrove, 1899; Franz & Houston, 1896), 3 tested memory mainly for psychometric purposes (Moore, 1896; Quantz, 1897; Sharp, 1899), 1 compared blacks and whites on the recall of four-line verses written by Eugene Field (Stetson, 1897) 1 reported an attempt by the author to train her own visual memory (Talbot, 1897), and 1 by Calkins (1896b) reported the same findings that she had reported in a previously published paper (Calkins, 1896a). In the 10 remaining articles (Angell, 1900; Angell & Harwood, 1899; Bentley, 1899; Calkins, 1896a, 1898; Dearborn, 1899; Hawkins, 1897; T. Smith, 1896; W. Smith, 1896; Whitehead, 1896), there is reference to Ebbinghaus and to Müller and Schumann in 4 (Angell & Harwood, 1899; Bentley, 1899; W. Smith, 1896; Whitehead, 1896) and to Ebbinghaus alone in another (T. Smith, 1896).

The paper by Whitehead (1896), comparing serial recall of visually and auditorily presented nonsense syllables, contains the most references to Ebbinghaus. Whitehead discussed several methodological concerns with what he called the "Ebbinghaus–Müller–Schumann method of procedure" (p. 258) that he said ". . . was essentially . . . now familiar to everyone by the work of the authors already cited" (p. 259). His methodological concerns included the fast rate of presentation, the use of rhythmic presentation, the heterogeneity of the nonsense syllables as well as the difficulty in equating them, particularly across presentation modalities, and the use of the number of repetitions as a dependent variable. Whitehead reported, nevertheless, that he had replicated Ebbinghaus' finding of an inverse relationship between the number of repetitions in the original learning of a list and its relearning.

Among other references to Ebbinghaus were those of Angell and Harwood (1899), who wondered whether the memory processes involved in Ebbinghaus' experiments are ". . . similar to those involved in discriminating between pairs of stimuli" (p. 70) and of T. L. Smith (1896), asserting that "The first psychologist to attempt a definite memory problem was Hermann Ebbinghaus, who undertook and carried out in person a series of experiments little short of heroic" (p. 455). Other references during this period included those of W. G. Smith (1896) stating that as for the effects of repetition, ". . . hitherto there has been no attempt experimentally to study this factor beyond the experiments of Ebbinghaus . . ." (p. 21) and of Madison Bentley (1899) who noted that results similar to those for retention of nonsense syllables, and of tones have been obtained for retention of letters, time intervals, visual length, visual size, digits, extent and direction of movement, lifted weights, tactual space perceptions, colors and brightnesses, noises, letters and words, and odors (p. 12).

Also evident was the use of serial recall (Hawkins, 1897; T. Smith, 1896; W. Smith, 1896; Whitehead, 1896) of nonsense syllables (Calkins, 1896a; T. Smith, 1896; W. Smith, 1896; Whitehead, 1896) and of relearning (Whitehead, 1896). There were additional references to nonsense syllables by Angell and Harwood (1899) and by Bentley (1899). Again, too, there was a variety both in the method and in the problems studied. In addition to serial recall, free recall (Calkins, 1898; Hawkins, 1897), paired-associate (Calkins, 1896a) and recognition tasks (Angell, 1900; Angell & Harwood, 1899; Bentley, 1899; Dearborn, 1899) were employed in one or more of these experiments. There was a wide range of retention intervals, and most experiments used fewer than 10 subjects. In addition to nonsense syllables, materials included colors (Calkins, 1896a), numbers (Calkins, 1896a; Hawkins, 1897), words (Calkins, 1898; Hawkins, 1897), tones (Angell, 1900; Angell & Harwood, 1899), brightnesses (Bentley, 1899), inkblots (Dearborn, 1899), and letters of the alphabet (T. Smith, 1896).

Again, serial-position curves were presented in some papers (Calkins, 1898; W. Smith, 1896) as were the results for various types of errors (Calkins, 1898; T. Smith, 1896; W. Smith, 1896). Of particular interest were: (a) the request by Dearborn (1899) that his subjects indicate the certainty of their responses through the quickness of their key presses and the amount of pressure they exerted, (b) the manipulation in a single experiment (Angell, 1900) of four independent variables, and (c) the proposal by Whitehead (1896) that ". . . the rate which permitted the most rapid and satisfactory memorizing was essentially that of the pulse" (p. 260). Again there was a variety of problems such as the question of whether an item (in this case, an inkblot) could be recognized if its position were changed (Dearborn, 1899), and the question of the effect of articulation during learning on recall (T. Smith, 1896). There were also attempts to replicate the findings of Wolfe (Angell & Harwood, 1899) and of Kirkpatrick (Calkins, 1898).

One other memory-related event of consequence during this period was the appearance in 1898 in the *Psychological Review* of a paper by Kennedy entitled

"On the experimental investigation of memory." Kennedy's purpose was ". . . to give a critical survey of experimental research on memory" (p. 477). In this paper, Kennedy distinguished between the two major methods for studying memory, the reproduction method (which was that used by Ebbinghaus) and the two forms of the recognition method. Next he described the material that had been used in those studies and then summarized the research characterized as the "two great memory problems" (p. 45), "Discovering the relation of the character of the reception of the object into consciousness to the accuracy of recollection, [and] ascertaining the relation of the transformation of the memory image to the same" (p. 486). His bibliography lists 86 entries, approximately one-third of which each were in American, in French, and in German journals. In Kennedy's paper, reference was made to Ebbinghaus' methods, to his materials, to some of his findings, and to his formula for relating the results for recall to the length of the retention interval. Ebbinghaus' name was the most mentioned and Wolfe's was next.

1901–1905

The final period is from 1901 to 1905. During this period a new journal, the *Psychological Bulletin,* began publication and first published in 1904. Its first volume also contained reports of experimentation as well as general reviews, a summary of psychological literature, and discussion and correspondence. This period also saw the publication of 16 *Psychological Monographs.*

For this period there were 12 papers on memory (Bair, 1903; Gordon, 1903; Henderson, 1903; Heywood & Vortriede, 1905; Peterson, 1903; Potwin, 1901; Seashore & Kent, 1905; Swift, 1905; Whipple, 1901, 1902, 1903; Wissler, 1901). Of these, 1 paper (Wissler, 1901) was mainly psychometric whereas in another, Potwin (1901), through use of questionnaires, attempted to get information about her subjects' earliest memories. In those remaining there was mention of Ebbinghaus' work by Bair (1903), Gordon (1903), and Henderson (1903) and of Müller and Schumann by Bair (1903) and Peterson (1903). Nonsense syllables were used by Gordon (1903), and by Heywood and Vortriede (1903) whereas Peterson (1903) used nonsense words of varying lengths. Reference was made to nonsense syllables by Bair (1903), Gordon (1903), Henderson (1903), Peterson (1903) and Seashore and Kent (1905). The serial recall task was used by Gordon (1903) who also tested for retention through relearning, and by Seashore and Kent (1905).

Again, in addition to serial recall there were several other tasks, paired-associate (Peterson, 1903), free-recall (Peterson, 1903), motor skills (Bair, 1903; Swift, 1905), recognition judgments (Whipple, 1901, 1902, 1903) and the recall of paragraph material (Henderson, 1903). In that study, Henderson, in considering the modifications that occurred in his subjects' recall of these paragraphs wondered, in a manner anticipating Bartlett (1932), whether the ''. . . modifications are sometimes made in order to make the ideas consistent with the experience or preconceptions of the individual'' (p. 68).

Other interesting aspects of the research during this period involved the use of a paired-associate task in which odors were paired with pictures, or with colors, the odors then being used later as retrieval cues (Heywood & Vortriede, 1905); and the bidirectional testing by Peterson (1903) of various types of item pairs. Again there was variety, too, in the length of the retention intervals, in the number of subjects (fewer than 10 in most studies) and in the materials; tones (Whipple, 1901, 1902, 1903) pictures, (Heywood & Vortriede, 1905) words (Peterson, 1903), movements (Peterson, 1903; Swift, 1905), tone sequences (Seashore & Kent, 1905), chords (Whipple, 1903) and melodies (Whipple, 1903), as well as the nonsense syllables, and nonsense words, odors and paragraphs previously referred to. Other items of interest were Gordon's (1903) reference to Külpe's (1895) speculation about the possibility of a von Restorff-like effect, (i.e., ''The more a content differs from its surroundings, the easier will be unification and recall'' (p. 269)), the use of odors as distractors in a study of the memory image by Whipple (1901), and the more-than-20 pages of introspections that he reported in that paper.

CONCLUDING STATEMENTS

This completes the brief survey of early American research on memory. We find that there was a sharp increase in the amount of that research during the second period (1891–1895), as compared with the first period (1885–1890), but that, as indicated in Table 5.1, there was no systematic change in amount of research during the next two 5-year periods. Table 5.1 shows also that during the last three periods, (from 1891–1905) a majority of the papers did not make reference to Ebbinghaus (or to Müller and Schumann) nor did the majority of the studies make use of any of the three individual aspects of method considered here. The number of direct references to his book or to those individual methods did not increase over these three 5-year periods. When, however, we combine the direct and derived references with the use of one or more of those aspects of method (or reference to them) we find that 21 of the 33 papers we have considered have, in at least one of these ways, taken account of Ebbinghaus' *On Memory*.

This attempt to assess the influence of Ebbinghaus' *On Memory* is not free of imperfections. There are several: some subjectivity in selecting the articles to be considered; the weighting of each article in the same way; the possibility that other aspects of method (e.g., the attempt to avoid mnemonics, the use of poetry, the method of derived lists) may also have had their effects; the possible influence of others (aside from Müller and Schumann) on whom Ebbinghaus had an influence; and the existence of other research by American psychologists in

TABLE 5.1

Frequency of Selected Measures Relating to Influence
of Ebbinghaus' *On Memory*[a]

Period	Memory Papers	Papers Selected	References to Ebbinghaus	References to Müller and Schumann	Use of Nonsense Syllables	Reference to Nonsense Materials	Serial Task	Relearning	All
1891–1895	13	13	3	3	3	5	5	0	8
1896–1900	19	10	5	4	4	2	4	1	7
1901–1905	12	10	3	2	2	5	2	1	6
Total	44	33	11	9	9	12	11	2	21

[a]See text for fuller explanation of these measures.

journals or books, American or otherwise, which we did not examine. We have not considered the number of memory articles (or pages) in relation to the total number of articles (or pages) published in these journals during this period either.

There are, of course, other and more general aspects of Ebbinghaus' work that may have had their effects: his objectivity (and the concomitant de-emphasis of introspection), the carefulness of his experimentation, his quantitative emphasis both analytical and theoretical, and his overall demonstration that it was possible to carry out with excellence a program of research on the learning and memory of complex material. These we have not attempted to assess here. Nor have we attempted to speculate about the direction that research on memory would have taken had Ebbinghaus' *On Memory* not been published. Of some possible relevance here, however, is that not long after Ebbinghaus' book appeared there was an increase in variety both in the tasks and in the materials that were used in research on memory.

Preparing this chapter has been for me both instructive and pleasurable. I hope, too, that this chapter has been helpful in enhancing the reader's knowledge about the state of early American research on memory, and how that research may to some extent have been influenced by Ebbinghaus' *On Memory*.

ACKNOWLEDGMENTS

I am grateful to Ben Underwood for his introduction to the domain of Ebbinghaus. I also thank Randy Craig for comments about earlier drafts of this chapter, Pat Newman for her strong support during its preparation, and the Small Grants and Research Fund of the School of Education at North Carolina State University for the provision of financial support for some of the tasks incidental to its completion. Finally, I appreciate the help from the following sources, none of which are specifically cited in the text: Boring (1929), Cofer (1979), Heidbreder (1933), Hilgard (1964), Ladd and Woodworth (1911), McGeoch (1942), Murray (1976), Osier and Wozniak (1984), Postman (1968), Shakow (1930), Titchener (1910), Watson (1974), and Woodworth (1909, 1938).

6 The Winds of Doctrine: Ebbinghaus and His Reputation in America

Thom Verhave
Queens College, City University of New York

Willem van Hoorn
University of Amsterdam, The Netherlands

A dramatic shift in the reputation of Ebbinghaus in America occurred during the 1960s. Acclaimed since his death in 1909, he has been disparaged since the 1960s. What happened? The answers to this question tell us something that is a bit worrisome concerning the level of historical scholarship in experimental psychology. Indeed, to us, the situation is rather scandalous.

This chapter is organized into an introductory section and four major sections, each of which focuses on what we regard as a "scandal." The first involves misinterpretations of Ebbinghaus' memory research. The second involves misrepresentations of Ebbinghaus during the "verbal behavior" or "psycholinguistic" revolution. The third section involves psychologists' ignorance of Ebbinghaus' major work, the *Grundzüge der Psychologie*. The fourth scandal involves psychologists' general lack of historical scholarship. The goal of this chapter is not just to point out inaccuracies in historical accounts, but to point beyond those inaccuracies to their fundamental causes in the dynamics of psychology's history and the practices and attitudes of psychologists.

THE FALL FROM GRACE

In American psychology of the early 1900s, Ebbinghaus' work was held in very high regard. Titchener (1909) was effusive in his praise: "It is not too much to say that the recourse to nonsense syllables, as the means to the study of (conscious) association, marks the most considerable advance in this chapter of psychology, since the time of Aristotle" (pp. 380–381). Wrote R. M. Yerkes in 1911: "It is now impossible for me to perceive Professor Ebbinghaus' *Grund-*

züge der Psychologie without having old sensations (sense images), familiar affections, and old ideas appear as part of the experience'' (pp. 169). These are fond memories of his student days with Münsterberg at Harvard or perhaps even a personal meeting with Ebbinghaus during a trip to Germany in 1902 (Yerkes, 1930).

As with many others since the late 1800s, William James found most of Ebbinghaus' quantitative data to be uninspiring. Not so the results of the derived list experiments. James thought the results said something very important about the relations of consciousness and memory. The interest of James (1890) was piqued since he recognized that the results of these experiments

> add one more fact to the set of facts which prove that association is subtler than consciousness, and that a nerve-process may, without producing consciousness, be effective in the same way in which consciousness would have seemed to be effective if it had been there. (Vol. I, p. 678)

In an important footnote, James related his interpretation of the derived list data to the work of Binet on hysterical subjects with anesthetic hands. A lengthy description of these "curious observations" can be found in the same volume under the title *Unconsciousness in Hysterics* (pp. 202–213). James refers here to a series of articles by Alfred Binet published in English in 1889. In the 1905 edition of *On Double Consciousness*, Binet's (1905) conclusion from the work with hysterics was

> that the limits of introspection are not those of consciousness; and that where we have not consciousness, there is not necessarily unconsciousness. Such are the very important and curious facts that to me seem destined to reconstruct the theory of the unconscious. (p. 43)

James, Freud, and Binet were all in agreement (Taylor, 1984). In 1908, G. Stanley Hall invited Ebbinghaus as well as Freud to attend the now-famous Clark University conference in 1909.

According to Gardner Murphy (1929/1949): "The subjection of both learning and forgetting to quantitative treatment . . . was probably the greatest triumph of original genius in experimental psychology since Weber" (pp. 189, 179).

Hilgard (1951) pointed out the wide applicability of the methods Ebbinghaus had invented:

> The pattern of the nonsense-syllable experiment can be followed with other verbal materials, such as adjectives or related discourse. With appropriate changes the methods may be used for the study of memory for objects or pictures or tasks. The study of testimony, as originated by Münsterberg (1908), is one such variation. (p. 525)

Fame is as fickle as fate and fortune. After World War II, a new generation of American psychologists was vying for attention after the demise of prewar theoretical systems and the deaths of Clark Hull in 1952 and Edwin Tolman in 1959 (Estes et al., 1954).

Postman, in 1968, found it necessary to defend Ebbinghaus and the "verbal learning" tradition of which Postman is a representative. That tradition, with which the name of Ebbinghaus had become associated in the U.S., was then under attack from the newly emerging "subculture of memory" as well as the new psycholinguistics, both offshoots of the new cognitivism (Postman, 1968a,b).

> We have hundreds and thousands of little facts, we can make quantitative instead of qualitative statements, we can talk about all kinds of fine details in experimental data and characteristic underlying processes, but the broad picture we have of human memory does not differ from that in 1870.

So wrote Tulving and Madigan in their *Annual Review of Psychology* article in 1970. The work of Ebbinghaus was, by implication, dismissed as trivial and irrelevant (cf. Neisser, 1982).

When did the currently prevailing negative picture of Ebbinghaus begin? Not with William James (1890), Robert Woodworth (1938), or E. G. Boring (1957). It all started with the "psycholinguistic revolution" or cognitive "paradigm shift." Both were built on the quicksand of historical ignorance. The evidence for these charges? One need only examine a number of the papers presented at the Kentucky Symposium of 1966 and published by T. R. Dixon and D. L. Horton in 1968. The editors correctly sensed that a revolution was in the making (1968). The rest, however, is shoddy history.

THE FIRST SCANDAL

Ebbinghaus could not have defended himself had he been present at the Kentucky conference. Even his very success was held against him. R. K. Young (1968) gave three reasons "why his conception of serial learning, in an area in which no theory seems to last very long without considerable modification, should have stood for nearly three quarters of a century without serious attack." So much for Bartlett! In any event, Young's (1968) first reason was that Ebbinghaus'

> results were in agreement with what might be expected from a common sense point of view. . . . Second, results such as the serial position curve, found by later workers, were easily assimilated into his system. Finally, the third reason for the extended success of the Ebbinghaus viewpoint is that his methods were exact, his

procedures clear, and his data overwhelming. Upon reading *Uber das Gedächtnis,* even in translation, it is easy to understand why his work remained seriously unchallenged for so long. Subsequent research workers sought, perhaps, to supplement his work, but little effort was made to examine his system and the procedures he used. (p. 122)

Are we to believe then that psychology would have been better off had Ebbinghaus used less exact methods, hidden his clear procedures behind turgid prose, and published only half of his overwhelming data? That way psychology would have made more rapid progress; it would not have fallen under his spell.

The "older" generation of experimentalists present at the Kentucky conference, Cofer, Osgood, and Postman represented the "establishment." They felt "that their positions were distorted and caricatured. Opponents felt that the establishment was being evasive and blind" (Jenkins, 1968, p. 538). Cofer (1982) is still wondering what happened in Kentucky in 1966. The general social context, the Vietnam War, and more specifically, the general antiestablishment attitude of that overheated decade among so many college students and younger faculty members, seems to be a good topic to look into for further enlightenment; more so than the tedious literature on "paradigm shifts," a concept that is misused by modern psychologists in their never-ending ideological squabbles.

If the participants at the Kentucky conference had read Chapter 3 in Ebbinghaus' *On Memory* (1885/1913), they would have discovered that

the differences between sense and nonsense material were not nearly so great as one would be inclined a priori to imagine. At least I found in the case of learning by heart a few cantos from Byron's *Don Juan* no greater range of distribution of the separate numerical measures than in the case of a series of nonsense syllables in the learning of which an approximately equal time had been spent. In the former case the innumerable disturbing influences mentioned above seem to have compensated each other in producing similar effect; whereas in the latter case the predisposition, due to the influence of the mother tongue, for certain combinations of letters and syllables must be a very heterogeneous one. (pp. 23–33)

Because few have read the *Grundzüge,* few, with the exception of Gardner Murphy (1929/1949), have been aware of the fact that

Twenty-two years later he relearned many of the stanzas (of *Don Juan*), having in the meantime completely forgotten them so far as his introspective memory or capacity for recall was concerned. Comparing these with the new stanzas memorized, he found an appreciable difference in learning time. The saving method revealed some retention over the twenty-two year period. (pp. 194–195/p. 179)

Murphy tells only half the story. When Ebbinghaus had originally planned these long-term retention studies, he had intentionally memorized a number of selected stanzas four times on each of four successive days. These he relearned by heart again 17 years after they were first memorized. The degree of savings he obtained when compared with the amount of time required to memorize stanzas never learned before, was nearly 20%. The savings score for the material that he had previously memorized only once and relearned 22 years later was only 7%. Here is the classic single-subject design, planned and faithfully executed over a period of 22 years (Ebbinghaus, Vol. 1, 1919, edition, p. 722).

Perhaps if there is to be a second edition of Professor Neisser's *Memory Observed: Remembering in Natural Contexts* (1982), he might consider adding Ebbinghaus as a modest footnote to the bibliography of D. C. Rubin's study on "very long-term memory for prose and verse" (Rubin, 1977; partially reprinted in Neisser, 1982). From Bartlett (1932) through Neisser (1982), it seems that only Gardner Murphy (1929, 1949) has been aware of Ebbinghaus's studies of long-term retention of prosodic material.

The "Sins" of the Revolution

The "post-revolutionary" crop of our experimental colleagues apparently believes that Ebbinghaus was another one of those dreadfully dull German professors. A dedicated, even heroic scientist perhaps, but dull and boring; most certainly misguided, if not possibly dim-witted. As Aristotle had his tedious syllogisms, so Ebbinghaus had a nonsense syllable for every occasion. He used rote learning, where meaningful and insightful learning should have been studied instead (Asch, 1968). Although fluent in German, French and English, Ebbinghaus "stripped away" meaningful associations and thus bypassed "the learner's pre-established habits of thought."

Better and smarter psychologists "soon discovered that some nonsense syllables are more nonsensical than others" (Miller & Buckhout, 1973, pp. 239–240). Because subjects in human memorization experiments "do, and sometimes must, utilize old information in acquiring new associations . . . the program of memory research advocated by Ebbinghaus could not succeed. . . ." (Hoffman & Senter, 1978). We are asked to believe that Ebbinghaus was unaware of organizational factors such as those involved with the mnemonic methods.

Miller and Buckhout (1973) showed Ebbinghaus up:

> The author once constructed a list of paired nonsense syllables deliberately made exceedingly difficult. . . . After thirty-nine presentations on a memory drum, most people could correctly anticipate only three or four. . . . One day a young man learned every single item in a matter of six presentations, only then revealing that he was a native of Latvia where what is linguistically nonsensical to Americans makes perfect sense to Latvians. (p. 241)

Posner seems to believe that Bartlett's *Thinking* (1958) and Bruner, Goodnow, and Austin's *A Study of Thinking* (1956) "helped to free many researchers from the belief that the higher mental processes were not amenable to experimental investigation" (1979, p. 372). Ebbinghaus had, mistakenly it would appear, thought he had done exactly that in 1880.

Scandalous. Incomplete information about Ebbinghaus' actual research and research interests, combined with misinterpretation. A second scandal was in the works as well—the misrepresentation of Ebbinghaus as an "associationist."

THE SECOND SCANDAL

In their paper at the Kentucky conference, Bever, Fodor, and Garrett provided formal proof that the entire associationist enterprise had been misguided in believing it could ever explain the higher mental processes ". . . certain human abilities lie beyond the upper bound on any set of learning principles that could reasonably be called associative" (1968, p. 582). Ebbinghaus, as the arch-associationist, had thus kept psychologists from the more exciting analysis of deep structure, grammatically correct sentences, and prose. Ebbinghaus stood condemned by way of guilt by association with S–R psychologists, connectionists, behaviorists, atheoretical functionalists and other such "empiricist" nitwits (Anderson & Bower, 1974; Deese, 1968; Weimer, 1973).

By traveling to foggy England, Ebbinghaus had been infected by that philosophical disease called "British Associationism" (Deese, 1968; cf. Cofer, 1968, p. 523). Ebbinghaus, Thorndike, and Pavlov, it seems, were all cut of the same associationist cloth. Mere use of the suspect word "association" is taken as evidence nowadays of complicity in leading generations of psychologists astray. According to Lachman, Lachman, and Butterfield (1979): "Ebbinghaus and Pavlov both induced associations in laboratory experiments, and they are responsible for the fact that for 60 years psychological research focused so heavily on laboratory-induced associations" (p. 44). Hilgard and Bower (1974) in the fourth edition of *Theories of Learning* state that:

> Associationism led to the experimental investigation of learning. The first experiments on human memory . . . by Ebbinghaus (1885), explicitly set out to test certain proposals within associationist doctrine; the first experimental monograph on animal learning, by . . . Thorndike (1898), was titled *Animal Intelligence: An experimental study of the associative processes in animals*. Developments within the American "schools of psychology" over the next 60 years have done little to alter that associationistic approach. . . . It is thus fair to say that empiricism and associationism laid down the mold (the rut?) into which contemporary learning theory has flowed and jelled, perhaps even solidified. (1975, pp. 6–7)

The odd notion that Ebbinghaus was a (British) associationist seems to have originated with Boring (1929/1957): "For the principles of method, he relied on Fechner. The problem of memory he got from British associationists, a very natural acquisition for a young philosopher spending time in study in England" (p. 378/p. 387).

The anecdote that Ebbinghaus acquired a copy of Fechner's *Elemente der Psychophysik* (1860) "at a second-hand bookshop in Paris" (Boring, 1929, p. 379; 1957, p. 387), stems, according to Traxel (1985), from Jaensch (1909). Both erroneous stories are retold by Murphy (1929, 1949). After Ebbinghaus had obtained his Ph.D. with the dissertation *Concerning Hartmann's Philosophy of the Unconscious* (1873), he "spent the following years in Berlin, England, and France. He supported himself by teaching or tutoring and received an assignment as a French tutor at the Imperial Court in Berlin with the aid of his friend, the historian, Hans Delbruck" (Traxel, 1985, p. 38).

Ebbinghaus bought his copy of Fechner's *Elements* in London, not Paris (Traxel, 1985). How could Boring possibly write that Ebbinghaus got the problem of memory from the British associationsist? Why not from the French sensationalists or Ribot and Richet, since he traveled in France also? That suggestion is equally silly, of course; the "problem" of memory is millennia old. As a German classical scholar as well as a tutor of French, Ebbinghaus did not have to read further than Herbart and von Hartmann (or observe his own pupils) in order to run into the problems of memory!

Ebbinghaus and Herbart

As far as the topic of memory was concerned, the contemporary views held by Herbart "and his adherents," such as T. Waitz in his *Lehrbuch der Psychologie als Naturwissenschaft* (1849), were the most important ones to Ebbinghaus. The question of whether Ebbinghaus was an associationist, or a Herbartian, is a complex one. The answer depends on what is meant by "associationism," a subject about which few authors are very clear (see Brett, 1930; Eisler, 1904; James, 1890; Robinson, 1932; Rozeboom, 1965; or Woodworth, 1938, as examples of better-informed sources).

Because Herbart's psychology was so important in Germany throughout the 19th century, one may ask if his use of "association" was descriptive or theoretical. That question need not be settled here. Herbart's "was a peculiar type of associationism," as Wolman puts it (1968a, p. 37) and Ebbinghaus was most certainly not a pure Herbartian as Young (1968) makes him out to be.

Like Herbart, Kant, and Wundt, Ebbinghaus also used the concept of "apperception," which has a complex history in German philosophy and psychology (Eisler, 1904; Lange, 1894). It is largely unfamiliar to the current crop of experimental cognitivists. Ebbinghaus certainly was not a British, but a German philosopher who was familiar with Leibnitz, Christian Wolff, and Kant (Brett, 1930; Verhave, 1967). His views, in many ways, seem closer to William James, who in the *Grundzüge* is so frequently referred to. We must leave it at that; the relationship to Herbart, James, and anyone else for that matter, needs careful analysis.

Association Versus Retrieval Versus Reproduction

Deese (1968) asserted that "the classical view of the associative process is determined, I think it is fairly obvious to see, by the most evident and superficial property of the flow of ideas, their temporal succession" (p. 97). We are led to believe that Ebbinghaus was a reductionist, who boiled the riches of human memory down to nothing but drill and retention, a mere "acquisition mechanism" (Hilgard & Bower, 1975, p. 7). Ebbinghaus was a dogmatist, whose verdicts had retarded the study of free recall (Tulving, 1968, p. 4). Ebbinghaus "failed to discriminate among the process of encoding information, the memory structure that encoded that information, and the process of retrieving information from that memory structure" (Anderson & Bower, 1974, p. 125).

Anyone who contemplates Herbart's concepts and the experiments of Ebbinghaus will realize that the latter could not possibly have been a "contiguity theorist." The belief that all associationists, including the "German experimentalists," were contiguity theorists (Deese, 1968) is uninformed.

So is the notion that "associationists" assume that "association and retrieval are the same thing" (Schacter, 1982). A reading of the chapters on "Association" and "Memory" in the *Principles of Psychology* by William James (1890) will disabuse one of that belief. Associationists, according to Schacter (1982), make the problem of retrieval processes uninteresting: "They simply assumed that association and retrieval are the same thing. . . Thus Ebbinghaus used the terms association and reproduction interchangeably" (p. 168).

Was Ebbinghaus unaware of the distinction between "association and retrieval," as Schacter concluded on the basis of one sentence in the English translation of the *Abriss* (1908)? We need only quote that sentence in context. The "crucial" sentence (in the Max Mayer translation) reads as follows: "We refer to this ability of expansion by the term memory, to the actual process of expansion by reproduction or association" (2908, p. 93). What did Ebbinghaus intend the term expansion to refer to?

In the *Grundzüge*, Ebbinghaus' general discussion of memory (*Allgemeines über das Gedächtnis*), is preceded by a long chapter dealing with the problem of attention (*die Aufmerksamkeit*), a problem which he regarded "a real embarrassment to psychology" (1919, Vol. I, p. 652). For Ebbinghaus, as for James (1890), attention refers to the limited or reduced content of the conscious mind at any moment. Attention is selective, as in Broadbent's "filter model" (1957) which otherwise uses a very different vocabulary. Whereas attention "limits" or "shrinks" the moment to moment content of consciousness, memory (*Gedächtnis*) "expands" and "enriches" it again. Here, memory refers to this "general activity of the mind" (*Die algemeine Fähigkeit der Seele zu dieser Leistung bezeichnet man als Gedächtnis*), (1919, Vol. I, p. 679).

Common language, Ebbinghaus points out, does not have a general term to refer to "the general facts of the reoccurrence of earlier experiences" (*Die Tatsache selbst des Widerhervortretens früherer Erlebnisse*, p. 679). Common German only has a special word "for a predominant instance or practical interest" (*für einen praktisch vorwiegend interessierenden Fall*). That word is "Erinnerung." Because there is nothing to be gained by the use of such an arbitrarily restricted word, "scientific terminology has introduced the (generic) term "reproduction" (*Reproduktion*), "which quite generally refers to the return to consciousness of experience once been" (*der ganz allgemein den Vorgang der Vorstellungswiederkehr früher dagewesener Erlebnisse bezeichnet*, p. 679). Reproduction is a descriptive term and the German technical psychological equivalent of Tulving's and Schacter's "retrieval." The distinction between *Gedächtnis* and *Reproduktion* is a special case of the Aristotelian potential versus actual distinction, or in terms of the analogy used by Ebbinghaus, between energy and work.

Did Ebbinghaus equate retrieval and association? To paraphrase Ebbinghaus, scientific usage has still another term , "association," which attempts to attribute the occurrence of a particular memory to a suspected cause. The reproduction of mental images which previously were experienced together in awareness, can readily be explained by the assumption that such images became closely joined and knotted together, so that any one of them will always elicit the others. Such a connection between thoughts is referred to by the word association. The meaning of the word, however, is frequently also carried over to what the term reproduction refers to, i.e., not just the suspected inner cause (*den vermuteten inneren Grund*) of reproduction, but reproduction (retrieval) itself, the actual occurrence of particular mental contents according to the intimately tied-up knots of those thoughts. "Disregarding this widespread extended usage," writes Ebbinghaus, "the word (association), will in this work, as much as possible, be used in its original (descriptive) meaning only" (pp. 679–680).

Our discussion of the second scandal—the misrepresentation of Ebbinghaus as an "associationist"—involved considerable reference to his major work, the *Grundzüge der Psychologie*. Modern psychologists' lack of awareness of this work constitutes a third scandal.

THE THIRD SCANDAL

Ebbinghaus wrote three major works during his lifetime: A dissertation (1873) about von Hartmann's (1872) philosophy of the unconscious; another paper

(*Habilitationsschrift*), dealing with his memory experiments (1880) and currently known as the *Uhrmanusscript* of the well-known monograph *On Memory*, published in 1885. Finally, he wrote a systematic textbook, the *Grundzüge der Psychologie* (1897), and an abridgement of the latter, the *Abriss der Psychologie* (1908). Of these works, the 1885 monograph in its English translation of 1913 is the best known, and the first sentence of the *Abriss*—"Psychology has a long past, yet its real history is short"—is perhaps the most widely quoted in the American literature. The dissertation about von Hartmann's philosophy is the least-known work, and deserves careful study in its own right. It indicates an early interest in a fashionable 19th-century topic (Ellenberger, 1970), a topic that crops up in his later experimental work.

The *Grundzüge* was cited and reviewed early in this century, but the reputation of Ebbinghaus in the American literature after about 1920 rested mainly on the translation of the 1885 monograph rather than the *Grundzüge* or any of Ebbinghaus' articles published in scientific journals. The impact of some of these articles was not insignificant, however, and they were cited by some American psychologists during the first decade of this century. A theory of color vision was published in 1893. Two articles were published in French in 1897. These articles influenced Binet (1905) and had an impact on the development of intelligence tests (see Boring, 1957, pp. 390 and 432; and Hoffman et al., this volume).

One cannot get an adequate picture of Ebbinghaus as psychologist unless one goes beyond his *Über das Gedächtnis* to the *Grundzüge der Psychologie*, a textbook that according to Titchener ". . . might prove as important to experimental psychology as Wundt's *Physiologische Psychologie* (1872–1874) or Brentano's *Psychologie vom empirisckhen Standpunkte* (1874)" (Titchener, 1910, p. 405). Whereas *On Memory* is a brief and circumscribed research monograph, the *Grundzüge* is a systematic statement that reviews the entire field of psychology as it then existed.

The man who singlehandedly turned the study of learning, memory and the "reproduction" of mental images (*Seelische Gebilde*) or representations (*Vorstellungen*) into a systematic and experimentally informed natural-science enterprise, had a lucid and sober intellect of the first order. It is unfortunate that except for its greatly abridged textbook version, translated by Max Meyer in 1908, there is no English translation of this superb overview of the entire domain of psychology at the turn of this century by one of its great pioneer experimentalists. The table of contents and indexes of its two hefty volumes give an indication of its scope and the scholarship of its author. Few had so generous and wide-ranging a vision of his field as Ebbinghaus. It is rather scandalous that the English translation of *Über das Gedächtnis* (1913), is, unfortunately, still the best known of his publications in the U.S. The fact that his reputation came to rest on his memory research rather than the *Grundzüge* was to have major repercussions.

How did it come about that "few modern psychologists know that (Ebbinghaus) published two textbooks during the final years of his life" (Ühlein, 1985)? We can restate that question: How did the *Grundzüge* get buried? The simple answer is that it was never translated and thus became inaccessible, but there is more to it than that.

Psychologists, Americans and Europeans alike, are still suffering the consequences of World War I. The weight of power, (industrial, technological, financial, and scientific) shifted across the Atlantic. American students no longer went to Germany to get their education in the sciences or, like Robert Yerkes, went on a brief European tour to visit its research laboratories after obtaining their doctoral degree. The direct personal contact between successive generations of scientists so crucial to the maintenance of mutual respect and understanding was irreparably damaged. The direct contact between German mentors and American graduate students, as well as the collegial exchanges of views between German and American investigators, had been disrupted by the war. After World War I had ended and especially after Hitler came to power, American psychologists were going their own "isolationist" ways; they have continued to do so until this day (Rosenzweig, 1984). Thus, the *Grundzüge* came to be a forgotten work, and knowledge of Ebbinghaus a blur of misinformation.

In Germany from 1933 to 1945, all liberal voices were stifled; only a few lucky German psychologists, such as Köhler, Wertheimer, Lewin, and Werner made it to the United States. In Europe, an entire generation of young men had lost their lives in the muddy trenches of Flanders. That and the economic disaster that hit the Weimar Republic during the 1920s delayed the rebuilding of German universities and scientific institutions. The period between the wars, dominated by the Nazis, was hardly conducive to the restoration of the necessary direct person-to-person dialogue between German and American psychologists. This ensured that the diverse voices and factions that constituted German psychology at the time of the *Grundzüge* would not get a fair hearing (Ash, 1982; Brett, 1930). The disruption in the transmission of the diverse traditions of psychology that existed before 1914 to postwar generations was never undone.

There is a theme that cuts across the three scandals we have described—the general lack of historical scholarship in psychology. This constitutes the fourth, and final, scandal we shall discuss.

THE FOURTH SCANDAL

As historians of psychology, we protest the way Ebbinghaus is mauled in the current literature of psychology, particularly in the U.S. To be blunt, the contemporary image of Ebbinghaus that is imparted to students, graduate and undergraduate alike, is a farce. Aside from Brett (1921) and Murphy (1929), the honorable exceptions, even scholars who should have consulted the *Grundzüge*, did not (e.g., Boring, 1929, 1957; Murray, 1976; Schacter, 1982).

Once the papers presented at the Ebbinghaus centennial celebrations in Germany have been published and assimilated by historians of psychology, it may be possible to improve on our historical accounts. A critical re-evaluation of Ebbinghaus' work is long overdue but will take more than a few commemorative papers. We will have to restudy all of his works and compare them with those of his contemporaries. That will be a long and time-consuming task, to be undertaken by a few dedicated scholars.

The problem here goes far beyond the inexcusable treatment accorded Ebbinghaus. The history of associationism, memory, learning, perception, and cognition are all treated in an unscholarly fashion. Wrote George Sarton (1930), the Belgian historian of science and founding editor of *Isis*: "Nowhere does the immaturity of our studies appear more clearly than here: scholars who would feel dishonored by the commission of scientific errors which they could have easily avoided, indulge in historical statements with the utmost levity (pp. 147–148).

How many psychologists in the U.S. or Canada know anything about the writings of Ludwig Klages (1872–1956), Ganzheit psychologists such as Felix Krueger (1874–1948) and Albert Wellek (1904–1972), or Eduard Spranger (1881–1911) and Willy Hellpach (1877–1955), who extended Wundt's *Völkerpsychologie*? On the basis of similar ignorance, Ebbinghaus was turned into the mere "father of verbal learning."

Oversimplified "historical" accounts can be found in journal articles and these are further reinforced in "history and systems of psychology" books by authors with little historical or philosophical sophistication. Most of them are unable to read German or French and, apparently, are unwilling, unable, or too lazy to read much of the relevant secondary literature in such journals as the *Journal of the History of the Behavioral Sciences*, the *History of Psychology Newsletter*, *Isis*, or the *Journal of the History of Ideas*. To the extent that psychologists do not meet even the lowest standards of historical and scholarly accuracy, they do a disservice to the field (Young, 1966).

If one examines the lists of references in the chapters of books edited by Hearst (1979) and Kimble and Schlesinger (1985), one cannot but fail to notice that editors and authors alike seem unaware of the fact that a professional literature on the history of psychology has come into existence since Robert Watson published *The History of Psychology: A Neglected Area* (1960). Only Littman's article (1979) shows historical sophistication and refers to a few articles by historians of psychology. Concerning the rest, American psychology seems to have lost sight of the considerable impact of various European influences (for documentation see Ash, 1982; Rieber & Salzinger, 1977; Rieber, 1980; or Woodward & Ash, 1982). For those who proudly consider themselves hard-nosed experimentalists, the possible relevance of any social context to the development of psychology is a thought that has yet to dawn (for documentation see

Ash, 1982; Buss, 1979; Danziger, 1979; 1985; Ellenberger, 1970; Fellman & Fellman, 1981; Littman, 1979; Sarason, 1981; Scull, 1981; Van Hoorn & Verhave, 1977; Verhave & Van Hoorn, 1984).

A factor that contributed to this state of affairs was the elimination of foreign language requirements for the Ph.D. degree in psychology, and the general unfamiliarity with the German language in the U.S. Other factors are (a) the relaxation of academic standards in colleges and universities beginning in the 1960s, (b) the consequences of the ever-increasing specialization in all fields, including psychology, and history of psychology, and (c) the pleasures of settling "old scores" between the in- and out-groups of successive generations of psychologists. As the new cognitivism swept in, "good guys" became "bad guys," even though they had been dead for more than half a century.

"Can history be revised?" asked E. G. Boring in the preface to the second edition of his *A History of Experimental Psychology*. He answered in the affirmative: "As time goes on, there come to be second thoughts about the interpretation of it. There are also new discoveries" (1957, p. xiii). "Strange as it may seem," he wrote in the preface to the first edition, "the present changes the past; and as the focus and range of psychology shift in the present, new parts of the past enter into its history and other parts drop out." (1929, p. vii and 1957, p. ix). Contemporary psychologists have been busy thus revising their history in the light of the various new cognitivisms. There is a difference, however, between inaccuracies stemming from a lack of familiarity with primary and secondary historical literature, and what passes for "history" in much that is written in today's books and journals (e.g., Muller & Van de Kemp, 1985; Samuelson, 1985; Sokal, 1985).

What is to be Done?

How can we put an end to the embarrassing state of historical scholarship among psychologists? By giving support to full-time historians, an endangered subspecies of the profession. Sokal (1985) has suggested that the time-tested journal peer-review process include historians. We fully endorse that modest proposal. Psychology may have, as Ebbinghaus stated, a long past and short history because psychologists have short memories. Each new palace revolution wipes the collective memory clean (cf. Jacoby, 1975). The active involvement of knowledgeable historians could help stop the abuse we have described in this chapter.

Psychologists have been the losers. Whatever ruts we have gotten into—structuralism, functionalism, behaviorism, neobehaviorism and cognitivism—have been of our own making. Creative minds are rare; open minds are rarer still. Psychology needs all it can get. We need to rethink our history, not on the basis of rumors, but on the solid basis of methodologically sound research by professional historians. We need to train a new generation of psychologists with the breadth of vision and the historical depth of Ebbinghaus, trained to respect colleagues who listen to the sounds of different drummers. Psychology, like the House of the Lord, has many mansions. We need more teachers like William James, Hermann Ebbinghaus, and Robert Woodworth. We need to get rid of the divisive "isms" and partisan pseudohistory that pervade the current literature from introductory textbooks to journal articles. A lack of hubris, a quiet modesty, an open-minded inquisitive attitude, a willingness to give any informed opinion in psychology a fair hearing, are all attitudes that characterized Ebbinghaus. May that be his legacy to us yet, belatedly . . . after a hundred years.

III CONTEXT AND MEMORY

7 The Law of Frequency

Norman J. Slamecka
University of Toronto

> *General knowledge concerning these laws is as old as psychology itself,*
> *but on the other hand a more precise formulation of them has remained—*
> *characteristically enough—a matter of dispute up to the very present*

—Ebbinghaus, 1885/1964

INTRODUCTION

This conference celebrates the centennial anniversary of the publication of Hermann Ebbinghaus' profoundly influential and seminal monograph, *Über das Gedächtnis,* in 1885. That landmark achievement was nothing less than the first programmatic experimental investigation into the psychology of learning and it took place within the domain of human learning, and specifically within the arena of rote verbal memorization. Among other things, it constituted the formal and systematic introduction of the philosophical tradition of associationism into the experimental analysis of the so-called higher mental processes, and brought them down to earth. From its classical beginnings with Aristotle to its subsequent intellectual extension and elaboration at the hands of the English and Scottish philosophers (Anderson & Bower, 1973; Boring, 1950), associationism paid substantial scientific dividends through the work of Ebbinghaus, and like a well-managed enterprise, has never failed to declare a dividend since, through good times and bad.

The conference that provided the genesis for this book afforded an appropriate occasion to pause and see where the past has led us. It gives a rare opportunity to take a serious look at an old idea to see how well it has held up in the crucible of subsequent experimental tests. This chapter is one attempt to do just that. The organizational scheme of my remarks is as follows. I begin by offering some personal opinions about Ebbinghaus' metatheoretical orientation, followed by comments on his treatment of the laws of association, and then point the discussion toward the law of frequency. After certain preliminary considerations about repetition have been aired, the main part of the chapter consists of a review of contemporary published experiments whose designs can tell us something about the degree of robustness of this principle of repetition. Finally, I present two new experiments for consideration and then draw an overall conclusion about the tenability of the law of frequency.

EBBINGHAUS

The underlying conceptual and descriptive framework that made up the warp and woof of Ebbinghaus' pioneering research was, above all, in the spirit of associationism wherein learning is to be understood as the weaving of metaphorical "invisible threads" (in Ebbinghaus' felicitous phrase) that connect ideas to each other, and serve to determine their arousability and their order of appearance upon the stage of consciousness. Superficially at least, this was a mentalistic or a subjectively oriented associationism in that it purported to account for the selectivity and succession of privately experienced mental events. It antedated by many years the deliberately objective S–R associationism that committed itself to the functional analysis of the relations between overt stimulating conditions and publicly observable responses. However, Ebbinghaus' own treatments of his findings never really entailed any intrinsically mentalistic explanatory mechanisms. He indulged in little more than some relatively neutral suggestions about indirect associative connections. No elaborate edifice of multistage mental manipulations was ever constructed, nor was any tortuous flow chart ever offered for depicting information being teased into submission.

In decided contrast to his scrupulously minimalist armamentarium, our contemporary cornucopia of cognitive conceptualizations has struck more than one observer as verging on speculative abandon. Underwood (1972, p. 1) once made a point of this, and his original list of supposed mental mechanisms has recently been amusingly amplified into a *reductio ad absurdum* by Tulving (1983) to include such invented inner processes as

accepting, activating, adding, analyzing, anticipating, arousing, attenuating, categorizing, choosing, communicating, comparing, comprehending, computing, consolidating, copying, deciding, desiring, discriminating, distracting, eliciting, estimating, examining, extinguishing, filtering, going, generating, inhibiting, interfering, interpreting, locating, looking, marking, matching, mismatching, operating, pigeonholing, placing, reaching, recovering, rehearsing, rejecting, replacing, requesting, retrieving, scanning, searching, selecting, sending, sorting, supplementing, suppressing, switching, tagging, transferring, transforming, understanding, and using. (p. 141)

This is not to say that one or more of the previous might not serve as handy metaphorical props to shore up someone's otherwise frail purchase upon certain selected phenomena, but it is to say that Ebbinghaus' disciplined approach had no need for such overkill in order to handle the problems that he examined. Indeed, Ebbinghaus' brand of mentalism was so restrained and so parsimonious as to lie barely a just-noticeable-difference away from a straightforward empirical treatment. I have by now become persuaded that underneath the conventional lip service that Ebbinghaus paid in the form of occasional mentalistic terminology (which may have been more a matter of the expository style of the day rather than a reflection of deep commitment) there beat the heart of a first-class functionalist. He systematically explored verbal acquisition and retention as a function of a host of basic independent variables. He presented his findings as lawful relations relatively unadorned and unencumbered by gratuitous theoretical entities, and thereby laid a solid empirical foundation for the field.

Laws of Association

The philosophy of associationism has proffered a miscellaneous collection of laws or principles of thought and memory (summarized in Robinson, 1932). Although neither their exact composition nor their relative importance were ever fixed by common agreement, the laws of contiguity, similarity, contrast, vividness, recency, and frequency were prominent members of the group. They served the purpose of identifying, in a mostly broad and general sense, the major conditions that determine association formation and/or associative strength. These principles are understandably rather vague because the contributing philosophers did not attempt to carry out experiments that would have given such principles a sharper definition. Nor, with one or two possible exceptions, can Ebbinghaus be said to have actually tested aspects of any of the hoary laws of association. The one clear exception may be the law of contiguity, which was examined almost incidentally as a by-product of his derived-lists experiments on remote associations, and whose outcomes led him to repudiate the then-prevailing mentalistic formulation of that principle (Ebbinghaus, 1885/1964, pp. 109–110; Slamecka, 1985).

With regard to the laws of similarity, and of contrast, and even of vividness, he effectively ignored them in the sense that none of his experiments incorporated the systematic variation of materials along any of those dimensions. His occasional use of poetry materials did not constitute a systematic exploration of those laws. Ebbinghaus did not seek to validate the law of recency so much as to exhibit or illustrate it, with the most elaborate illustration being his famous curve of forgetting. His analytical interest in that regard was focused on developing a mathematical description, or model, of the function that related retention to the recency of acquisition (Ebbinghaus, 1885/1964, pp. 77–78).

Finally we come to the law of frequency, also known by such names as the law of repetition, the law of practice, the law of exercise, and the law of use. Because it is sufficient for the present review, I will entertain a theoretically neutral version of the law, which would simply say that memory performance is an increasing function of the number of presentations of the to-be-remembered material. It can be fairly asserted that although Ebbinghaus did not attempt to investigate the comparative importance of this principle by pitting it against other conditions that were thought to affect learning, he certainly did utilize it. He relied exclusively on list repetition as the formal instrument for acquiring his series of nonsense syllables, and for mediating his relearning-based measurements of memory. As he put it, ". . . learning was carried on solely by the influence of the mere repetitions upon the natural memory" (Ebbinghaus, 1885/1964, pp. 25).

Since that time, all subsequent experimenters' dependence on some form of repeated exposure to the materials as the operational route to performance increments has continued unabated. Indeed, how could it be otherwise? Has anyone ever produced a curve of learning to mastery which was based upon only a single exposure followed by nothing but test trials? It would seem to be in the very nature of things that repeated presentation of a supraspan list is necessary in order to accomplish its memorization. When regarded from this most general viewpoint, the law of frequency approaches the bland and unremarkable status of a self-evident truth. However, given its ubiquity of application from the very beginnings of our field, perhaps it deserves another and closer look, one that may suggest some interesting properties after all.

The following discussion will not concern theoretical accounts of how frequency manages to work its beneficial effects; whether by incremental strengthening of items or of their connections to context, by encouraging encoding elaboration or encoding distinctiveness, by permitting improved list organization or chunking, by laying down multiple copies of traces, by affording another opportunity for all-or-none item learning, or whatnot. Rather, in emulation of Ebbinghaus' preference for remaining close to the level of descriptive analysis, I focus my efforts on a relatively limited empirical question about the law of frequency. But before formulating that question, I first address a preliminary and basic conceptual problem, one whose answer will help to delimit the scope of the question. The problem is, how are we to conceive of a repetition in a learning situation?

What Is Repeated?

At the most rigorous level one can flatly deny any realistic possibility of a strict and literal law of frequency by pointing out that nothing is ever able to be repeated exactly. However carefully and fastidiously the experimenter may proceed, however painstaking his arrangements, uncontrollable variations in count-less details of the physical circumstances that surround a succession of list presentations are unavoidable. Even more intractable, since it is intrinsically beyond the scope of any technical control, is the fact that the experimental subject is always one trial older and wiser at the start of the next presentation. A second trial is inevitably a different subjective episode from the first one, since it is superimposed upon the experiential residue that lingers from the first. The learner, himself, has undergone a change of inner state. As trials mount there is a growing sense of familiarity with the materials, there is a clearer perception of the list structure, a more decisive encoding of elements, a heightened (or lessened) confidence about strategy, and so forth.

This progressive shaping of the learner's cognitive condition is the experien-tial or subjective manifestation of the acquisition process, the inner accompani-ment to the objective gains in performance that define the curve of learning. Indeed, as long as learning is taking place, there cannot and should not be any exact duplication of experience from one trial to the next.

None of this is any news, for we know from our introductory philosophy course that the ancient thinker Heraclitus couched similar sentiments in terms of the impossibility of stepping into the same river more than once. In the case of verbal learning, the constantly flowing river of experience guarantees no exact reliving of anything.

Granting, therefore, that precise repetition of inner experience is both beyond the realm of experimental artifice and fundamentally incompatible with the very idea of learning as such, we must reject it as a plausible dimension along which to explore the law of frequency. By elimination, this draws us back to the alternative of the repetition of objective conditions. Although weaker, its feasi-bility makes it the more promising avenue for assessing the empirical force of the law. It must be conceded that countless minutiae of the external learning situa-tion (the experimenter's intonation and gestures, errant shadows, visual angles, extraneous noises) are never perfectly stable over time. Yet, they probably tend to vary only moderately around some mean value under well-controlled condi-tions (this problem of constancy of conditions was introduced by Ebbinghaus in the second chapter of his monograph).

Such relatively minor and random perturbations reflect a closer approximation to the ideal of exact repeatability than do the deliberately cumulative and system-atic alterations of the subject's cognitive state that occur across trials. According-ly, we are led to conclude that the law of frequency is intelligible only with reference to the admittedly imperfect repetition of objective circumstances, and we shall deal with it at that level.

The Question

The question to be examined in this review now reduces to the following:

In verbal list-learning tasks involving repeated presentation of familiar target items, to what extent is the overall rate of gain in their recallability independent of manipulations of the objective encoding or contextual environment? That is, how necessary is it to keep the encoding or contextual conditions constant in order to obtain the full benefits of repeating the same nominal collection of items? At one extreme, it is possible that even a slight change of any kind in the input conditions could preclude normal list-wide performance growth. At the other extreme, the slope of the learning curve would remain steadfastly invariant across even the most radical alterations of input circumstances. In the former case, the law of frequency would be too fragile or too narrow in scope to be accorded much weight, while in the latter instance it would be both pervasive and important. In short, how robust is the law of frequency?

The question at issue refers only to memorization tasks, that is, tasks in which intentional learning instructions are given. The reason for this is that mere repetition of a list may not always be sufficient to mediate acquisition gains in the absence of whatever processes are set into motion when memorization is explicitly required. There is no reason to insist that frequency cannot have a predisposing condition for its operational efficacy, and specific instructions to learn the target items can readily be accepted as constituting such a requirement. Although there is evidence that even incidentally learned items can enjoy the usual recall increments associated with repetition (for instance, Mechanic, 1962, 1964), there is also evidence in the contrary direction. McGeoch (1942) relates:

> the incident described by Radossawljevitch (1907) of the subject who, because of his imperfect German, failed to comprehend the instructions. . . . The subject read aloud a series of eight syllables time after time, but at the forty-sixth repetition he had not yet signaled that he had mastered the list. . . . Radossawljevitch stopped the apparatus and asked if he could recite the series. "What! Am I to learn the syllables by heart?" was the reply. He could not recite them. . . . (p. 275)

The best contemporary example of such a situation is from Tulving (1966), where subjects were asked simply to read aloud a list of 22 high-frequency nouns for 6 trials, in a different order on each trial. These subjects were then given the identical 22 words to learn for 12 free-recall trials. Their acquisition curve was indistinguishable from that of control subjects whose irrelevant prior reading task consisted of male names. Mean correct recalls over the 12 trials were 15.71 versus 15.91. This zero-transfer outcome persuades us to focus our deliberations on intentional learning situations, where the processing appropriate to learning can be assumed to be under way.

Our question also refers only to cases where the nominal identity, or what can be called the surface form, of every repeated item is maintained across presentations. This simply means that the visual appearance and/or the sound of each repeated input chunk remains the same across trials. Apart from this, all other changes, such as those which might induce variations in encoding through alteration of context or through whatever other means, are fair game for experimental manipulations. This restriction is not particularly severe because the overwhelming majority of reported frequency manipulations have conserved the surface features of the repeated items.

When surface features are deliberately changed to destroy the integrity of input chunks from one trial to the next, cumulative learning can be brought to a dead stop. The most instructive worst-case illustration of this was reported by Bower and Winzenz (1969), using a variation of the Hebb (1961) paradigm. Within a block of auditorily presented nine-digit strings, some strings had the identical digit sequence, whereas the remaining strings were unique. For the recurrent strings, one type kept the digit subgroupings intact across presentations, such as (17) (683) (945) (2). The other type varied the subgroupings or chunks at each presentation by a change in pronunciation that regrouped the same digit sequence into new chunks as (176) (8) (394) (52), or (1) (768) (39) (452). Immediate serial recall steadily improved across the four trials only in the constant-chunk condition. The varied-chunk treatment revealed no gains at all.

Although it has not been attempted, the word-string counterpart of such a treatment would present, for example, "brushfire, flypaper, weight. . ." on one trial and "brush, firefly, paperweight. . ." on the next. I have no doubt that, with such inconsistency, the learning curve would also be flat because there would be no repetitions across trials of either the letter groups or the semantic chunks. Attempts to maintain the continuity of semantic features while letting surface features vary, by employing synonyms and translations (Kolers & Gonzalez, 1980) or other words from the same category (Mathews & Tulving, 1973), cannot guarantee exact repeatability of meaning, as compared with exact repetition of surface units.

Because the focus of this inquiry is on the cumulative growth of list-wide learning, a distinction must be made between the kind of repetition that permits such growth and the kind that does not. The distinction rests on whether repetition has its origin in the environment, or in the subject. Only in the former case can the curve of learning proceed to mastery, because all items, both learned and unlearned, are presented on every trial. In the latter case, the subject is limited to representing to himself only those items that are already learned and retrievable, but this provides no means for the learning of additional ones.

This self-dependent form of repetition is the process of rehearsal, and its benefits are expressed in the improved retainability of accessible items. Some list-wide growth of performance has been observed as a consequence only of opportunities to retrieve, but these gains are small in magnitude and can probably be understood in terms of extended retrieval time (Postman, Fraser, & Burns, 1968; Richardson & Gropper, 1964; Roediger & Thorpe, 1978). These rehearsal or test effects are legitimate topics of interest in their own right, but they represent a different path from the one I choose to take in this review.

DIRECT CHALLENGES TO THE LAW OF FREQUENCY

I now present three kinds of observations whose initial impact was to challenge outright the basic validity of the law of frequency. Two of these involved learning under conditions where nonrepeated items were systematically substituted into the list from one trial to the next. The deceptively simple paradigm developed by Rock and his associates (Rock, 1957; Rock & Heimer, 1959) was the earliest of these. The control group acquired a list of letter-number paired-associates list to mastery by the conventional method of repeating all items across trials. The experimental group experienced drastic changes in the composition of its list, achieved by dropping out any item that the subject had not recalled on the prior trial, and substituting for it a randomly chosen new pair from a large pool of pairs. This prevented the reappearance of any previously unlearned material. Initial reports were that there was no difference between the groups in the number of trials taken to one errorless performance of the list, thereby denying the importance of repetition.

However, subsequent investigations by others showed that there were two aspects to this demonstration that made it less than persuasive. First, the null finding was not readily replicable. Both Postman (1962), and Underwood, Rehula, and Keppel (1962), carried out many experiments of this type, and obtained an overall learning advantage for the control condition. In their Experiments 2–5, the latter researchers even used the same paired letter-number materials that Rock had employed, and still found a superiority for the standard repetition group.

Second, it was established that this paradigm harbored an item-selection artifact that would favor the dropout condition (Postman, 1962; Underwood, Rehula, & Keppel, 1962; Williams, 1961). The control group had to stay with the items originally given, whereas the dropout group could, in effect, eliminate its difficult pairs and have easier ones, on average, substituted for them. This was shown by the fact that the terminal list acquired by dropout subjects tended to be easier than that of the controls, when given to other subjects to learn. It was a tradeoff between the disadvantage of no repetition and the advantage of item selection that determined the dropout learning curve. Sometimes the net effect was even, and sometimes it was detrimental, but at no time did this paradigm really constitute a denial of the efficacy of frequency.

The second type of observation that challenged the law of frequency came from an experiment conducted by Murdock and Babick (1961). A list of 25 words was presented once, and followed by a recall test. Then a second list was presented that contained all different items, save for one critical word that was re-presented in each successive list until it was eventually recalled. Every subject had 80 such lists. The key finding was that the likelihood of critical item recall was independent of the number of lists in which it had appeared. Its prior repetition as a member of other lists did not raise its probability of recall, ergo, frequency was irrelevant.

The subjects in this situation were not really dealing with a cumulative multi-trial memorization task. Rather, they experienced a lengthy series of separate lists and always had to restrict their output to the contents of the most recent one, trying to avoid giving intrusions from prior ones. In short, they were faced with a mammoth list-discrimination problem. The circumstances lent themselves admirably to the establishment of a high criterion for responding, such that the subjects effectively nullified what might otherwise have been the beneficial and detectable consequences of repetition. It was the unique noncritical words that distinguished a current list from its predecessor whereas the critical one did not. If the critical item came to mind, it was a very good candidate for rejection on the ground of relative uncertainty of its proper list membership.

The forgoing scenario, however plausible it may be, is completely speculative because, unfortunately, no one has yet published a follow-up of this procedure aimed at delineating its effect on the subject's response criterion. Unless and until this is done, the relevance of these findings to the law of frequency must remain, at best, inconclusive.

The third type of observation that challenges the law of frequency stems from the part-to-whole transfer paradigm originated by Tulving (1966). He reported that the rate of multitrial free-recall learning of a list of unrelated nouns was actually retarded by the prior acquisition of a shorter list consisting of a random half of those same items. This was by comparison with a control group whose prior list contained no words in common with the transfer list. Thus, the phenomenon of negative part-to-whole transfer seriously questioned the validity of the law of frequency. According to that latter principle, initial acquisition of a part list could only facilitate the subsequent learning of the whole list.

The developments that followed this initial paper paralleled those that drastically transformed our understanding of the Rock paradigm. With respect to generality of replication, although the negative transfer effect could be readily duplicated with lists of unrelated nouns, this being the class of materials first used, quite the opposite effect was obtained when slightly different materials were employed. Slamecka, Moore, and Carey (1972, Experiment 1) presented categorized part lists under conditions designed to bias the subjects' encodings either toward optimality or nonoptimality with respect to the categorized transfer list. It turned out that regardless of this encoding compatibility manipulation, both part list groups exhibited very substantial and equivalent amounts of positive transfer, as compared with two control conditions.

A second example comes from Hicks and Young (1972). In two experiments, these researchers employed lists of adjectives instead of the usual noun materials. Both of their sets of data revealed a clear-cut superiority for the part list group in executing the transfer task. These outcomes are completely in keeping with the law of frequency, and they stand in sharp contrast to the originally reported effects. The reasons for this empirically clouded situation are not known.

The specter of artifactuality has also raised its head within this paradigm. Slamecka, Moore, and Carey (1972, Experiment 2) hypothesized that the part list condition normally induces a more stringent criterion for response emission because the subject is more uncertain of the list membership of transfer list items than he would be in the control condition. They found that, with low-criterion instructions that encouraged more response output for both groups, the part list group in fact showed positive transfer. This suggests that the advantage of repetition was masked in Tulving's (1966) study by the presence of differential performance criteria under the usual instructions. The same reasoning may apply to the whole-to-part version of this paradigm as well (Tulving & Osler, 1967).

Gorfein and Viviani (1978) conducted the last major examination of part-to-whole transfer with categorized materials (word lists). Along with new categories, one group's final list had half the instances of old categories carried over from the first list. Uncertainty as to which old instances had carried over might induce a generally conservative high-criterion attitude for the entire transfer task. Indeed, the authors' Table 5, Condition 7, shows negative transfer for both old and new categories. In referring to this literature for other purposes, Neisser (1982, p. 7) said: "Tulving's finding seemed to undermine one of the commonplace principles, but it was an empty threat. The flaws in the experiment were soon revealed . . . and the status quo restored."

In my estimation, none of the preceding three direct challenges to the law of frequency has sustained itself in the long run. Accordingly, I now feel free to go on and examine other experiments, no matter what their originally stated intent, from the point of view of what they may tell us concerning the empirical viability of the principle of repetition. This sampling of the literature will confine itself to what we may call the contemporary period, spanning the last 25 years of research.

THE EFFECTS OF CONTEXTUAL VARIABILITY

Input Ordering

There is a group of experiments that have investigated free-recall learning as a function of variation in the input ordering of unrelated words across trials. Typically they compare the effect, on the learning curve, of a fixed-order sequence versus a haphazardly ordered sequence of the items on each study trial. Broadly viewed, this is a manipulation of the local stimulus context within which each item is studied. A word will have either the same neighbors all the time, or its immediate item surround will change randomly from one presentation to the next, giving it no stable intraserial context. From a more specific associative view, the varied order condition should effectively preclude the formation and strengthening of adjacent connections that are based on temporal contiguity, thereby removing one possible source of performance gains. Just how much difference will this make to the rate of acquisition?

The earliest of these free-recall studies was conducted by Waugh, in 1961. Her subjects learned lists of 48 words by the study-test method for six trials. She found virtually identical learning curves for the varied and the constant order conditions. Because performances topped out at about 40%, there was no question of ceiling effects. On each trial the between-group differences were unreliable and, in absolute terms, minuscule. This decidedly striking null finding doubtless served to galvanize other researchers into making similar attempts of their own, as follows.

Jung and Skeebo (1967) tested children on lists of 12 and 24 monosyllabic nouns, for six study-test trials. The findings were mixed, in that there was an interaction between list length and input sequence. The shorter list was not influenced by item order whereas the longer list showed better learning with a fixed order. This later advantage averaged out to barely 2 words per trial. Lachman and Laughery (1968) reported two experiments that investigated the role of test trials in multitrial free recall, which also included comparisons of fixed versus variable input sequences. Lists of 30 words were used. The first experiment revealed reliably better performance for the fixed order. As estimated from the authors' Fig. 4 (group A), this superiority over the varied condition amounted to less than 2 words when averaged across the eight test trials. The second experiment also used lists of 30 words, and showed a similar pattern. There was an interaction between trials and word order, such that the fixed sequence mediated higher performances as of the third trial. Its overall superiority was 1.37 words per trial, across all seven trials, according to the authors' Table 1 (group A).

A further comparison can briefly be mentioned from part of a larger study conducted by Mandler and Dean (1969). Two successive lists of 16 common nouns were acquired over 17 study-test trials. For both stages of practice, the fixed order inputs were reported to be superior to varied orders. The actual extents of these differences can not be estimated from the authors' Fig. 1, but it does appear that conditions finished out at virtually the same performance levels.

Additional information about order effects comes from an experiment on practice in multitrial free recall by Postman, Burns, and Hasher (1970). It included random versus fixed presentation order manipulations, and the latter were each subdivided according to instructions, these being either the standard ones or ones that encouraged organization. Each subject learned two successive 20-word lists for six study-test trials. Results showed that for either stage of practice and for either type of instructional condition, the constant input ordering permitted better performance. The absolute magnitude of this advantage, calculated across instructions, lists, and trials, was only 1.03 words.

In a multitrial free recall experiment by Maki and Hasher (1975, Experiment 1), a list of 47 unrelated words was presented as a succession of arbitrary groupings of words. Subjects were encouraged to use these groups as a basis for organization. In one condition a critical item in each group remained fixed within that group across trials, whereas in another condition it was moved randomly to a different group on each repetition. The learning curves for the 12 critical items showed no differences as a function of same versus varied context.

Single-Trial Studies

There is also another smaller group of studies that represent a variant of the preceding designs. These studies involved only one presentation trial, with repetition of items being within the list so that no learning curves as such were obtainable. Nonetheless, the effects of various local contextual manipulations upon the single, subsequent free-recall performance trial could be assessed.

Wallace (1969) used a list composed of 16 unrelated words, of which 12 appeared three times. For one condition, these 12 were arranged into six pairs, such that the same word of a pair directly followed the other one on the three occasions. For the other condition, the 12 words each appeared in three different sequential pairs. In spite of the less-stable local context obtaining across repetitions for the latter group, its free recall was not reliably inferior (in fact, it was absolutely higher) relative to that of the constant-context group. Part of a larger report on the effects of massed-versus-distributed repetitions by Shaughnesy, Zimmerman, and Underwood (1974) is also relevant in this regard. They displayed a long list of words in a paired-associates format, such that the response members given two or three presentations were either accompanied by the same stimulus member or by a new word each time. As measured by the free recall of responses, the cumulative benefits of repetition were unaffected by this contextual manipulation.

In yet another study of the distribution effect, Maskarinec and Thompson (1976, Experiment 1) presented lists of 40 words once, for free recall. Every subject had four lists. Four critical items each occurred three times in a list. In one condition they were always embedded in the same local context of 2 preceding and 1 following word. In another condition they were surrounded by different items at each occurrence. There was no reliable influence of contextual stability upon the recall of these repeated words, although the usual performance inferiority accruing to a massed practice condition was obtained.

Evaluation

Overall, what do these experiments tell us about the robustness of the law of frequency in the face of contextual variation, whether manipulated by list-wide randomization across trials or by more limited subgroup changes across intralist repetitions? Does alteration of the surround act to preclude learning, or even to retard it severely? In my judgment the answer would seem to be no. The influence of contextual change in multitrial designs ranges from absolutely nil to relatively modest, and its influence in single-trial repetition designs is even less impressive. On that score therefore, the law of frequency holds up remarkably well.

As is well known, within-list designs can yield substantially different recall levels, depending on whether the reappearances of an item take place in immediate succession, or are distributed throughout the list (Crowder, 1976). Doesn't this fact alone impugn the validity of the principle of repetition? As originally described previously, no, because massed practice does not eliminate performance gains. A more interesting question would be whether distribution has only additive effects or whether it interacts with the number of repetitions. That is, does the magnitude of the performance gain from, say, two to three presentations depend on whether they were massed or spaced? If this difference is independent of massing versus spacing, then the latter is just another variable that can influence performance, but it has nothing to do with determining the amount of benefit conferred through repetition per se. As will be seen, formulating this question is far easier than answering it.

I have looked for experiments that fulfilled the requirement of including more than just one level of actual repetition, and have found the best source to be a report by Underwood (1969). It permits five comparisons of free recall under massed-versus-distributed study, at repetition frequencies of 2, 3, and 4. For Experiment 1, the interaction between massed-versus-spaced repetition and presentation frequency was significant. However, for Experiment 2 it was not. For Experiment 3 the analysis was not reported, but judging from the author's Fig. 2, the first-list slopes did diverge slightly whereas the second-list slopes were decidedly parallel. For Experiment 5 the interaction was significant. Obviously, one cannot draw a clear conclusion in the face of such mixed outcomes.

There is yet another problem, no matter how univocal the data of any such experiments. At even the lowest repetition frequency of 2, the massed and spaced conditions are already at different levels of recall, since this defines the distribution phenomenon. With more repetitions, the group curves move upward, describing either a diverging or a parallel course. This means that they fall into the class of uninterpretable interactions, given the usual assumption of only a monotonic relation to an underlying scale (see Loftus, 1978, Fig. 3). This fact alone muddies the interpretative waters to such an extent that the whole question must at this time be relegated to the limbo of inconclusivity, and therefore removed from current consideration as a way of assessing the law of frequency.

The preceding remarks also generally apply to what is called the lag effect where, under conditions where *all* repetitions are distributed, there is sometimes found a direct relation between amount recalled and the number of items intervening between distributed repetitions (lag). I am also hesitant to place much weight upon the findings of lag effect studies for another reason, namely, that the lag effect does not appear to be a very reliable phenomenon.

I was first apprised of this through a conversation with Bennet Murdock, who commented that his research has never turned up a persuasive lag effect, in spite of numerous opportunities for its emergence. The most telling public evidence in that regard is a recent paper by Toppino and Gracen (1985). Those authors doggedly carried out a total of nine well-conducted lag experiments, and failed to obtain the effect. They note that the ". . . lag effect in free recall does not invariably occur and apparently is limited by boundary conditions that have not yet been determined'' (p. 191). Consequently, it seems inadvisable to use this apparently fragile and undependable phenomenon as a standard against which to evaluate the much more dependable phenomenon of the repetition effect.

ENCODING VARIABILITY

Having reviewed the findings typical of studies that used unrelated items, I move on to a somewhat different class of experiments. These attempt, by one means or another, to manipulate more directly the range of encoding that a subject will impose on studied items. One way of doing this is to present each target word in conjunction with some deliberately contrived sense-biasing context, in what amounts practically to a paired-associates format. A variant of this is the employment of homographs or homophones in order to achieve the same end. The focus of interest is on the extent to which the benefits of repetition are influenced by induced encoding changes in targets whose surface features remain constant, but whose semantic features have presumably undergone some alteration.

An interesting series of three experiments by Postman and Knecht (1983) represents the best-conducted work on encoding variation without the employment of homographic material. In Experiment 1, a list of 48 sentences was presented for three study trials and then tested by free or by cued recall. The subject noun of each sentence was the target. In the constant condition, the sentence remained the same across all trials, whereas in the varied condition a different sentence frame was used for each presentation as, *"The hospital built a parking garage," "The hospital employed many local people," "The hospital covered several city blocks."* The free recalls were virtually identical for the two groups. Similarly, when recall was cued by all three sentence frames together, there was still no significant difference between the groups.

Experiment 2 had the same input treatments as above, tested by free and cued recall at two retention intervals. Free-recall levels were again the same for both encoding conditions, at both intervals. For cued recall, the constant condition had its single frame and the varied condition had its set of three frames. Performance for the constant group was superior at both intervals, reflecting the greater strength of the cue-target associations for the sentences that had been repeated during study, over those that had not.

Postman and Knecht's Experiment 3 was a methodologically improved version of certain studies by Bevan and Dukes (1967), and Bevan, Dukes, and Avant (1966). A list of 48 adjective-noun phrases was given three study trials followed by a free-recall test of the noun targets. The constant condition kept the same modifier across trials, such as *"hard hat,"* whereas the varied condition altered it as *"hard hat, straw hat, top hat."* There were standard-versus-imagery instructions, and two retention intervals. Results showed no free-recall differences under the standard instructions, at either interval. Under imagery instructions, the constant group showed a slight but significant advantage. As estimated from the authors' Fig. 3, this latter amounted to only about one word. The general impression gained from this group of observations is that encoding variability did relatively little or nothing to reduce the benefits of repetition for target recallability.

Experiments Using Homographs

A number of experiments used the alternative procedure of biasing the encodings of homographic (and/or homophonic) targets. Such materials readily lend themselves to more extreme manipulations of semantic feature encoding than do ordinary words, while still keeping the surface features constant.

Bobrow (1970) gave his subjects a list of 60 sentences whose subject and object nouns were both homographs. These noun pairs were then repeated on a second sentence-study trial. Recall for each object noun was tested by cueing with the subject noun. The two conditions of present interest are The Similar Meaning Condition, where the second sentence preserved the semantic encodings, and The Different Meaning Condition, where the second sentence occurrence biased subjects toward a totally unrelated encoding of both cue and target. An initial sentence, such as *"The hi-powered drill entered the masonry blocks,"* had a Similar version, as *"The electrical drill pierced the stone blocks,"* and a Different version, as *"The fire drill cleared the city's blocks."* Cued recall was higher for the Similar Meaning condition, with Different Meaning being no better than for once-presented items. A second experiment produced comparable results. This outcome is inconsistent with a strict frequency expectation, since repetition gains were not obtained for The Different Meaning condition, in spite of constancy of the surface features of cue-target pairs.

A related experiment by Thios (1972) used Bobrow's materials and also obtained better cued recall of Similar over Different encodings. Unaccountably, this time even the Different condition yielded better performance than the once-presented items.

In an investigation of distribution effects, Gartman and Johnson (1972) gave one study and one free-recall trial on a long list of words. It contained certain homographs that occurred twice, under two conditions. The Similar words were immediately preceded by an item that imparted a consistent bias, such as *"leg, foot,"* and *"arm, foot."* Different words were preceded by an inconsistently biasing item, such as *"leg, foot,"* and *"inch, foot."* These biasing items were part of the to-be-recalled list. The first experiment found free recall of homographs to be totally unaffected by this treatment, it being about 55% correct for both groups. However, subsequent experiments introduced two preceding biasing items at each occurrence, and now found that Different items were considerably better recalled than Similar ones, with both higher than once presented items. These are somewhat mixed results, and the superiority of different over similar not only denies an invariance of frequency benefits, but is also unexplainedly in contradiction to the pattern reported by Bobrow (1970) and by Thios (1972).

In another study of distribution effects, Johnston, Coots, and Flickinger (1972) employed single-trial free recall. Four homograph targets appeared twice in a list, each either accompanied by the same semantic biasing word on the two occasions, or by two words that biased separate meanings, such as *"sports-FAN," "electric-FAN."* Their recalls for the two experimental conditions did not differ, and were superior to those of nonrepeated control items.

Wood (1972, Experiment 4) presented a list of 55 words to be learned for six study-test trials. Eleven of the words were homographs. In the Constant condition these critical items were embedded in the same categorical unit across trials, while for the Varied condition they alternated between semantically unrelated units, as *"priest, cardinal, minister"* and *"robin, cardinal, sparrow."* The free-recall acquisition performances under these treatments were statistically indistinguishable. Maki and Hasher (1975, Experiment 2) had subjects learn a list of 20 homographs by the study-test method, taking free recall to an 80% performance criterion. Long-term retention was also assessed through another free-recall test 1 week later. For the groups of present interest, every study trial displayed a target in the company of another word that biased a particular meaning of the homograph. In the Stable condition, this was the same word on every trial. In the Unstable condition, each of two words that biased unrelated meanings were employed on alternate trials. Results showed no difference in either speed of learning to criterion, or in long-term retention.

A study by Slamecka and Barlow (1979) employed long lists of paired associates in three within-list experiments wherein each response item was a homograph, and the stimulus biased one of its meanings. The test was immediate cued recall, using all of the stimulus cues that had been seen. In addition to once-occurring-targets, there were two types of repeated targets widely distributed in the list. For Same Meaning Targets, the repetition involved a stimulus that called for the same semantic encoding, as *"shortstop-pitcher, catcher-pitcher,"* while Different Meaning Targets called for disparate encodings, as *"shortstop-pitcher, jug-pitcher."* Tests designed to assess memory for the meaning of the targets indicated that these biasing manipulations were effective. Nonetheless, the cued recall levels were virtually indistinguishable.

It was concluded that these equal repetition increments were mediated solely by the constancy of target surface features, and that preservation of semantic features played no role in determining the gains at all. A follow-up of this work was later carried out by Dicaire (1983), with a new set of materials and some improvements in details of design. The original pattern of findings was replicated in all respects.

Experiments Using Homophones

Finally, I consider two relevant studies which, although they do not quite meet my stated inclusion criterion of strict preservation of surface features, are more interesting and informative because of that very fact. Instead of displaying homographs and attempting to bias their semantic encodings by accompanying cues, these experiments employed homophones, i.e., words that differ in meaning and spelling, but sound exactly alike such as *"sail"* and *"sale."* With visual presentation, these materials are semantically unambiguous since their spelling automatically specifies a particular meaning. Unlike homophonic homographs, however, all of whose surface features are identical, homophones differ in their visual appearance. Their employment therefore involves only a partial conservation of surface features across repetitions. This poses an even more severe test of the question at issue because not only will semantic features be varied, but visual features will also vary along with them. Use of such stimuli allows one to ask: To what extent can preservation of only the acoustic features still mediate the cumulative benefits of repetition?

In the first of two transfer experiments, Laurence (1970) had subjects learn a list of 10 paired associates to an overlearning criterion of two errorless trials by the method of written anticipation. The pairs were unrelated words, with the response member being a homophone. The common transfer list for the Experimental group had the same stimuli and the corresponding homophones for responses, as *"table-raise, table rays."* A control group had new pairs, such as *"block-eyes, table-rays.* There was almost perfect positive transfer for the Experimental group. On the first anticipation trial, its performance was about 95% correct, and was essentially perfect thereafter. In spite of the change in visual and semantic features, the benefits of prior learning were conserved.

Laurence's second experiment involved free-recall learning of two successive 30-word lists, each with 10 visual study and written test trials. The common transfer list was composed entirely of homophones. The Experimental group had a first list of homophones and a transfer list of their counterparts, such as *"raise, rays."* The Controls had a first list of nonhomophones that were unrelated to the second list. Although the control performance was inferior at the start of transfer learning, it surpassed the Experimentals in the second half of the trials.

Why was there not consistent positive transfer? In answer to this, one can speculate that because first-list trials took learning to only a 60% level, in contrast to the overlearning in her first experiment, such learning was inadequate for discriminating first- from second-list spelling requirements of acoustically identical words after only a limited degree of first-list learning. The Control group did not have this disadvantage, since acoustic units were not carried across lists. Laurence's Table 3 lends some credence to this possibility by showing that second-list acoustic confusion errors were more than three times as likely for the

Experimentals than for the Controls. Were this unnecessary complication eliminated by taking the first lists to mastery or beyond (as in her Experiment 1), then considerable positive transfer may again have been revealed.

Two experiments by Nelson and Davis (1972) are also appropriate here. They involved a transfer design, but with serial learning. The first one used written serial anticipation of items displayed on a memory drum. A common transfer list of 10 homophones was learned for six trials. The controls had an initial list of 10 unrelated nonhomophones and the Experimentals had 10 homophones of the second-list items, occupying corresponding serial positions. Although significant positive transfer was observed on the first two trials, it was not reliable thereafter. However, the results of a second experiment were appreciably more decisive. Here, the method of serial recall was used in a study-test procedure. Again, both groups learned a common homophonic transfer list, and first-list treatments were the same as before. Results showed highly significant positive transfer overall, with half of the 32 Experimental subjects giving a perfect performance on the very first trial, in contrast to only one Control subject. Thus, even when the interlist surface features of items are only partly conserved and their semantic features are totally unrelated, the benefits of prior list repetitions can still transfer to a considerable extent.

EVALUATION OF CONTEXTUAL AND ENCODING VARIABILITY STUDIES

This concludes my sampling of studies that looked at the consequences of contextual and of encoding variability. I do not claim to have made an exhaustive compilation of all reports bearing on this question, if that would even be possible, but I tried to include the most informative and best designed contributions, and feel that this coverage is a fair representation of such work in general. What do these experiments tell us about the robustness of the law of frequency?

On the one hand, by a modest criterion that would ask only whether repetition is rendered ineffective whenever a contextual or encoding change occurs, the law of frequency is upheld. Repetitions do act, inexorably, to raise the level of performance in the face of these other manipulations. On the other hand, by the highest criterion, which would demand an absolute invariance of repetition gains in spite of any and all contextual or encoding changes, there is at least partial confirmation. The majority of the relevant experiments revealed either no perturbation of repetition benefits or else relatively little in that regard. Only a very few showed a more substantial influence, some in favor of constancy and others in favor of variability. As Young and Bellezza (1982) recently put it, ". . . conditions seem to exist under which either encoding variability or encoding constancy may enhance memory performance" (p. 556). Still, the actuarial norm seems to be that of no noteworthy difference between such conditions, or no power over and above that of frequency.

Actually, there is a dearth of the kind of data that one would most like to see on this issue. Most experiments simply compare one versus two presentations, and that is not really enough. What is needed is more levels of repetition as such, with the data reported trial by trial as in a learning curve. Then, one can see whether repetitions (starting at two presentations) mediate different slopes of acquisition. In spite of the additional vexations of the scaling problem, at least the empirical substrate would be at hand. But, taking what there is in the spirit of one who sees the glass as half full, encoding variability does not seem to force us to repeal the law of frequency.

TWO NEW EXPERIMENTS: THE "SHIFT" DESIGN

This final section is devoted to a presentation of two new experiments, new in the sense of not having been reported before, although they were carried out some years ago. Both of them satisfy our inclusion criteria of dealing with intentional recall and of maintaining the constancy of target surface features. They contribute further information about the degree to which repetition gains are independent from changes in task requirements and from changes in encoding requirements, respectively. The work was carried out at the University of Toronto with the able collaboration of Lori McElroy.

Method

Because the two experiments are both alike in their basic conception and design, they can be described simultaneously for the most part. They are what we call "shift" designs in that sometime during a multitrial learning task, some salient aspect of the situation was abruptly and unannouncedly shifted to a contrasting version for the remainder of the trials. The question of interest is whether the imposition of the change midway through acquisition would disturb the normal course of the learning curve.

The design was a $2 \times 2 \times 2 \times 5$ factorial, all factors within subjects. The first factor was the type of Task, with Generate-versus-Read as levels. This variable was aimed at producing what is called the generation effect (Slamecka & Graf, 1978), wherein a word generated by a subject on the basis of constraining stimuli is better recalled than is the same word when it is simply read. The second factor was the type of Rule, with Opposite-versus-Rhyme as the two levels. This variable refers to the constraining rule that expresses the relationship between the stimulus item and the target word. It is characteristically found that target recall under the opposite rule is better than under the Rhyme rule (Slamecka & Graf, 1978). The third factor was the type of Condition, with Shift-versus-Nonshift as levels, and it was the critical manipulation. In Experiment 1 some items were shifted from Generate-to-Read and others from Read-to-Generate, after learning was already under way. In Experiment 2 some items were shifted from Opposite-to-Rhyme, and others from Rhyme-to-Opposite. These were the task and encoding changes whose effects upon repetition gains were to be assessed. The fourth factor was Trials, and it consisted of five study-test sequences on the list.

The learning materials were a list of 48 paired words, 24 exemplifying an Opposite, and 24 a Rhyme relation. The particular rule in force was always known to the subject. For the Read task, both displayed words ("hot-cold") had to be spoken aloud. For the Generate task, the stimulus and the first letter of the prescribed response were displayed (hot-c), and both the stimulus and the generated target word were to be spoken aloud. An important property of these materials was that every target item was capable of being encoded in terms of both Opposite and Rhyme rules. Examples are *"lose-win, sin-win,"* and *"hot-cold, fold-cold."* This property, later independently utilized by Gardiner and Arthurs (1982), permitted the Rule shift of Experiment 2 to be imposed without changing the surface features of the responses.

Items were blocked by Rule, blocks being counterbalanced across subjects, and a signal indicated the rule in effect at the start of each block. Within each Rule block, the items were blocked by Task, with 12 Generate and 12 Read items, the order of blocks being counterbalanced. Each target was equally often represented, across subjects, at both levels of Task, Rule, and Condition. Item order was varied across Trials.

Thirty-two undergraduate psychology students at the University of Toronto served as subjects in each of the two experiments. After appropriate instructions, five study-test trials were given. The presentation rate was 4 seconds, and each study trial was followed by 30 seconds of counting-backward distractor activity. The first two trials constituted the preshift phase. Then, starting with the third study trial, half of the items were shifted to the other Condition level while the rest remained as before. No statement was made to the subject about this manipulation. For Experiment 1 the shift was with reference to Task, wherein 12 items changed from Read to Generate, and another 12 changed from Generate to Read. For Experiment 2 the shift was with reference to Rule, wherein 12 items changed from Opposite to Rhyme encoding, and another 12 changed from Rhyme to Opposite. The tests were written free recall of all targets, with 4 minutes allowed.

Results

Results of the first experiment are seen in Fig. 7.1. The satisfaction of two preconditions necessary for going on with the analysis is apparent in the preshift phase. First, a main effect of Trials established that learning was taking place. Second, a main effect of Task established the presence of the generation effect. The critical analysis focuses upon the postshift phase, where the progress of the

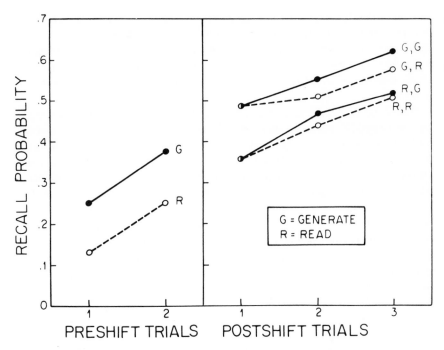

FIGURE 7.1.   Experiment 1 learning curves showing recall as a function of a shift versus no shift in the Task (Generate or Read).

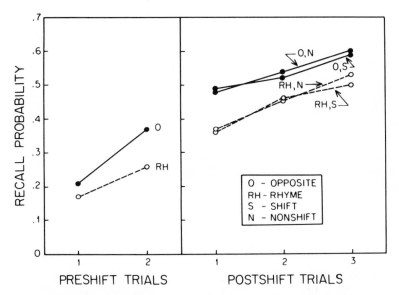

FIGURE 7.2.   Experiment 1 data replotted in terms of the encoding Rule (Opposite or Rhyme).

four subgroups is seen on the last three trials. There was a main effect of Trials, showing continued learning. There was no main effect of Condition (*F*-ratio < 1.00), which means that the recall of shifted items was no different from that of nonshifted ones. There were no interactions present, further reinforcing the tenor of this pattern. Of the 11 possible interactions, not a single one was statistically significant.

Figure 7.2 shows the same data replotted, with Rule as the parameter. In the preshift phase the expected superiority of Opposite over Rhyme is seen, and was verified statistically by a main effect. For the postshift phase, an obtained main effect of Rule meant that the recall of opposites continued to be better than that of Rhymes. As the aforementioned lack of interactions suggests, shifting from one task to another, did not impair repetition gains across trials for either.

Next, I consider the results of Experiment 2, as displayed in Fig. 7.3. The meeting of two preconditions necessary for pursuing subsequent analyses is evident in the preshift phase. First, a main effect of Trials showed that learning was under way. Second, a main effect of Rules revealed the usual levels-of-processing advantage of a semantic Opposite encoding over a phonemic Rhyme encoding.

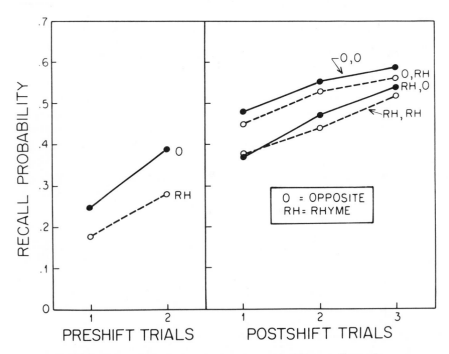

FIGURE 7.3. Experiment 2 learning curves showing recall as a function of a shift versus no shift in the encoding Rule (Opposite or Rhyme).

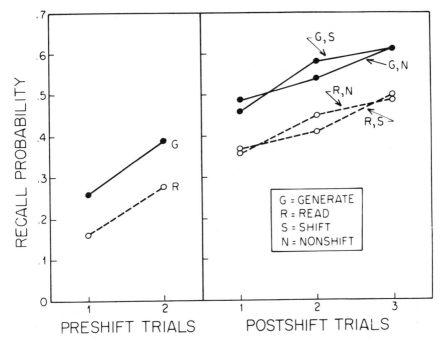

FIGURE 7.4.   Experiment 2 data replotted in terms of the Task (Generate or Read).

The fates of the four subgroups formed in the postshift phase are as follows. There was a main effect of Rule, such that the originally Opposite items were still superior to those that were originally Rhyme. Thee was also a main effect of Trials, indicating progress in learning. There was no main effect of Condition (F-ratio < 1.00), which indicates that performance on the part of shifted words was no different from that of nonshifted words. Evaluation of all the interaction terms served to underscore the straightforward nature of the results by the fact that none of the 11 was statistically significant.

Fig. 7.4 presents the same data, replotted in terms of the Task parameter. The preshift phase exhibits the usual generation advantage, one that is statistically reliable. In the postshift phase there was a main effect of Task, indicating that performance under the Generate task maintained its superiority throughout. The complete absence of interactions justifies the conclusion that a shift from one Rule to the other did not affect the magnitude of repetition increments observed across trials for either Task.

Both experiments are strikingly similar in all details of their outcomes, and are univocal in the conclusion that they suggest. This latter adds up to the message that, in spite of some relatively drastic alterations in what the subject was supposed to do or how each word was to be encoded, the curve of learning was invariant with respect to these manipulations. The cumulative gains produced by way of repetition of surface features were notable for their constancy.

CONCLUDING STATEMENT

I began this inquiry by asking just how robust the law of frequency has actually turned out to be in practice (pun intended). One hundred years of research on verbal learning have yielded a goodly sampling of relevant comparisons by which to judge the associationistic philosophers' conviction that a principle of repetition is a fundamental and necessary notion. My survey of representative experiments from the contemporary period, together with the two additional ones reported herein, has reinforced my conviction that such a principle does indeed merit continued recognition as a valid empirical generalization.

We have seen that it is not easy to divert the learning curve away from its characteristic course, and when upon occasion that can be made to happen, the perturbation is usually of relatively modest magnitude. Even these latter instances are not a disproof of a principle of repetition, any more than observations of objects moving upward constitute a rejection of the law of gravitational attraction. Demonstrable countervailing as well as supplementing influences can be identified in psychology, as well as in physics. In the last comprehensive treatment of the laws of association, Robinson (1932) observed:

> The curve of learning gives the relationship between strength of associative connection and frequency of repetition. . . . But frequency is only one of the variables with which strength of association is correlated. The factors of time-interval, assimilation, intensity, and set are also important determiners. . . . (p. 99)

Since that time, psychologists have considerably extended the list of effective variables, but the impression that I receive from my review is that these other variables tend to play out their roles superimposed against a larger background, which reduces them almost to local eddies that are swept along in the irresistible tide of repetition increments. They may retard or enhance cumulative performance benefits to a degree, but they can ultimately neither reverse nor nullify the monotonic growth of the curve of learning. Practice does make perfect. My concluding statement is that, on balance, the law of frequency is robust enough to be elevated to the capitalized scientific stature of The Law of Frequency.

ACKNOWLEDGMENTS

Preparation of this chapter was supported by Grant A7663 from the National Sciences and Engineering Research Council of Canada. The author gratefully acknowledges the assistance of Lori McElroy.

8 Comments on Chapter 7 by Slamecka

Murray Glanzer
New York University

Professor Slamecka has presented a general theoretical argument and some data. I summarize the argument and indicate another way of looking at some of the data that are used to support the argument. I also indicate a way to make the argument stronger or more general.

The array of data he has presented is not univocal in support of his argument (see Underwood, 1969), as he does note. It is possible to bring in additional data that would weaken the argument further: data that show interactions of various experimental conditions with repetition (Marks & Miller, 1964; Miller 1958). I focus here, however, on the argument and the data presented by Professor Slamecka.

Professor Slamecka's argument is that the effect of frequency or repetition on intentional learning: (a) is continuous, (b) cannot be eliminated unless surface features are changed, and (c) is not variable. Where it seems variable, that variability is due to another additive factor. To argue for the first assertion, he reviews the one-trial learning controversy; for the second he reviews cases such as part–whole transfer; for the third he presents, among other items, data from experiments on shift of encoding.

The assertion about continuity is one that might have pleased Ebbinghaus. Indeed Ebbinghaus (1885) states:

> These relations can be described figuratively by speaking of the series as being more or less deeply engraved in some mental substratum. To carry out this figure: as the number of repetitions increases, the series are engraved more and more deeply and indelibly. . . . (pp. 52–53)

Ebbinghaus does, however, clearly identify the image as a metaphor.

I am not sure that it is necessary to subscribe to the first assertion, that the effects of repetition are continuous, that every repetition has an effect on every item in a group of items. I only note the following: The assertion about continuity was argued through in the literature on expeiments by Rock, Estes, and Bower. The outcome of that work was that although some simple cases of verbal learning can be handled with one-element or one-stage (that is, noncontinuity) theories, others require either a continuous theory or a multiple-stage/multiple-element theory. No clear decision was arrived at. The history of this controversy is presented in Hilgard and Bower (1975).

The second assertion is a special case of the third. The third is the one I address in detail. The third assertion, that the effect of repetition is not variable, is the strongest assertion. It is accompanied by an argument that when there seems to be a factor that varies the effect of repetition, it is an additive factor— one that just raises performance at every level of performance.

As Professor Slamecka says, "A more interesting question would be whether distribution has only additive effects or whether it interacts with the number of repetitions." Professor Slamecka then analyzes some curves of Underwood (1969), showing the relation between the number of repetitions and performance under different distribution conditions. He checks to see whether distribution and repetition interact. The same examination is carried out on the effects of encoding variability. Again he examines whether encoding interacts with repetitions, or whether, as he argues, it simply adds onto repetition.

It may help to consider the argument fully if we look at a full sequence of repetition effects, and some learning curves. It should be noted that Professor Slamecka recommends such an examination.

Fig. 8.1 shows data from a study by Cieutat, Stockwell, and Noble (1958) (The curves have been selected for their clarity, not for their particular relevance to the arguments about specific variables.) The curves have the following characteristics: (a) They differ in the rate at which they approach symptote, and (b) They seem to be going to the same asymptote.

It is clear that the repetitions interact with the four meaningfulness conditions labeled H-H, L-H, H-L, L-L in the figure. It is also clear that we could select out segments of the data that would not give a statistically significant interaction effect, for example, trials 6 through 12 in conditions HH and LH, or trials 9 throughout 12 in condition HL and LL. Curves such as those shown are usually seen as generated by a learning process with different constants.

Fig. 8.2 shows two theoretically generated curves, one with a learning constant of .20, the other with .10. The equation is also given. The equation, parenthetically, is neutral with respect to the continuity issue. It describes both continuous and noncontinuous learning (The top curve, by chance, turns out to fit the H–L curve in the preceding figure fairly well.)

Note again that the overall solid curves show an interaction of conditions with

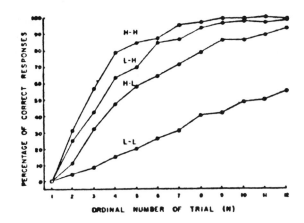

FIGURE 8.1.   Acquisition curves for lists of 10 paired associates in four different conditions as a function of practice (N). The four conditions were obtained from combinations of low (L) and high (H) meaningfulness (m) of cue and response items. (From Cieutat, Stockwell, & Noble, 1958, reproduced with permission.)

repetitions (trials), but there are sections in which such an interaction would not be clear, for example, trials 12 to 18.

If we now look at the Underwood data on massing versus distribution of repetitions, as shown in Fig. 8.3, we see a pattern like the bottom part of the curves in Fig. 8.2. We see pairs of curves with different learning constants.

Let us consider the cases mentioned concerning the switch in encoding with the curves and constants of Fig. 8.2 in mind. If encoding is switched for a set of material during a sequence of trials, the learning constants would change and the learning curves change course. In Fig. 8.2 the dotted line marked with the label "switch" is the curve that results when the subject switches from poor encoding (rate constant $C = 0.10$) to good encoding (rate constant $C = 0.20$) on trial 11. It moves from the bottom curve and toward the top curve. A similar but opposed movement would occur if the subject moved from good encoding to poor encoding.

Professor Slamecka's data for the several Generate and Read conditions in the Experiment 1 are what you would expect with a shift of the rate parameters. The curves for unswitched conditions continue; the curves for the switched conditions start to migrate toward the other curve's track. Examination of his Figs. 8.1 and 8.3 shows that they fit this description. There is no evidence for additivity alone or evidence against interaction.

In summary, there is no doubt that repetition has strong effects on performance. The effect cannot, however, be divorced from other conditions, such as encoding conditions. Attempts to set up that divorce on the basis of absence of

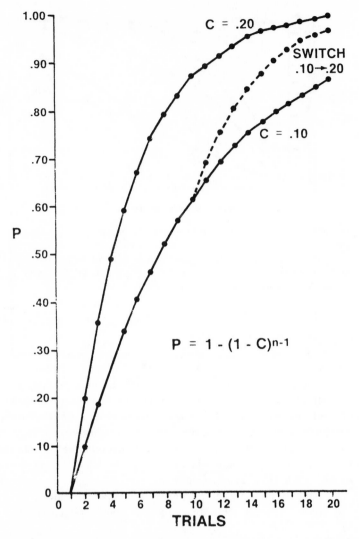

FIGURE 8.2.   Curves generated by the equation $P = 1 - (1-C)^{n-1}$ with two different values for C.

interactions are not likely to work. Any conventional picture of learning curves gives interactions if a sufficient and appropriate amount of data is examined.

This may not be satisfying if one is underlining the raw power of repetitions. I therefore offer Professor Slamecka something instead. In his original formulation, the assertion about the effect of repetition was restricted to intentional learning. I suggest that the effect does not have to be restricted to intentional learning. If we change from recall measures to recognition measures, then the

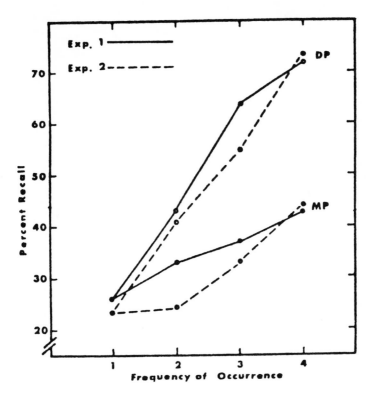

FIGURE 8.3.   Recall as a function of frequency and massed-versus-distributed presentation (MP–DP) for two experiments (from Underwood, 1969, reproduced with permission).

restriction can be dropped. The controversy about the role of maintenance rehearsal that started with the depth-of-processing proposal showed that number of rehearsals (i.e., repetitions) had no or little effect on recall when the subject did not intend to learn. The same repetitions in the same condition had a clear effect on recognition (Woodward, Bjork, & Jongeward, 1973). It is in recognition that the power of simple repetition shows most clearly.

9

The Dual Meanings of Context: Implications for Research, Theory, and Applications

Delos D. Wickens
Colorado State University

INTRODUCTION

During recent years, the term "context" has occurred more and more often in the technical literature of psychology, the concept being used with increasing frequency to account for many behavioral phenomena. If one looks up the word "context" in some standard dictionary, one finds that it has two basically different meanings. Webster's *Third International Dictionary* lists the following: (a) the interrelated conditions in which something exists, and (b) the part or parts of a written or spoken passage preceding or following a word or group of words and so intimately associated with them as to throw light on their meaning.

The first of these definitions, which describes what I shall call "context alpha," simply refers to the environmental surrounds in which some event exists or occurs, and it contains no implication that the context or the environment influences that event or is related to it in any significant way. The second definition, which describes what I shall call "context beta," states essentially that the context is needed to clarify the meaning of a particular word or group of words, or some action; otherwise the event, verbal or other, is ambiguous. Psychological research on context has used both of these meanings somewhat loosely and indiscriminately and because the underlying mechanisms involved in determining the behavioral outcome differ, depending on which meaning of context is being investigated, it would seem to behoove a science to make a clear conceptual distinction between the experimental operations and basic psychological processes appropriate to each meaning.

To do so we must begin by making a clear linguistic discrimination between the two meanings of the term. This does seem to be occurring with the term "environmental context" being used for what I have called context alpha. Baddeley (1982) has suggested the terms "independent" and "interactive" for what I've called context alpha and beta, respectively. (I prefer that the neutral terms alpha and beta be used because they carry no excess meanings.) Thus the level of performance on a task may show a fairly strong dependence on the environment or context in the instance of context alpha as research to be described later will show. I think we might be better off by using neutral terms which separate the objective nature of the task rather than ones which might imply some performance characteristic which could lead to confusion.

A preview of my plans for this chapter seems to be in order. Its major focus will be on context alpha, but because it and context beta may on occasions be conjointly operative, there is need to discuss context beta, however briefly. In both instances I mention the animal literature on the topic when I feel that it contributes to the understanding of context at the human level.

The Ebbinghaus Conference and the Topic of Context

It is this writer's impression that it may come as a surprise to some that the topic of context would appear on a program honoring Ebbinghaus. The heavy modern emphasis on the role of context and memory seems to have appeared on the scene circa 1980 with little apparent appreciation of earlier research or interest in the concept.

Actually one finds a considerable degree of appreciation of the importance of context among the Chicago functionalists in the 1920s and 1930s. Carr, for example, has a section called Environmental Conditions in his introductory text (p. 250ff.) and the examples he cites are very much the same as might appear in a modern textbook on learning and memory. One of these is worthy of quoting. "Subjects who memorized material in a certain room and in the presence of a given experimenter make poorer records when tested for recall by another person in a different room than they do when tested under the conditions that are obtained when the material was memorized" (p. 251).

It was the Chicago group and its students who maintained, almost singlehandedly, the Ebbinghaus tradition in both methodology and subject matter until the burgeoning of interest in human learning and memory occurred in this country in the mid to late 1950s.

So, with this aside on the appropriateness of the topic of context on a conference honoring Ebbinghaus, I turn now to a consideration of context beta.

CONTEXT BETA

Context beta refers to the situation in which one stimulus event combines with another stimulus event to define the correct response or meaning of the event. Each stimulus or stimulus attribute by itself is ambiguous and the concurrence of the two classes of environmental events is a necessary condition for indicating the correct or appropriate response.

Although conjunctive concept formation is a clear instance of context beta, it does not, at least as yet, seem to have been incorporated into the discussion of context. Perhaps this is due to the fact that concept formation has a long history, has been recognized as a cognitive activity for an equally long period of time, and hence has an independent status of its own.

The research on context beta with humans seems to have been less directed toward understanding the phenomenon itself than toward using it as a tool for investigating some other topic. One line of this research has addressed itself to the structure of semantic memory, namely whether words are stored as composites of their attributes (Atkinson & Shiffrin, 1968; Collins & Quillian, 1969) or as unique wholes. Another extensive usage of context beta is to explain the basis for the superiority of spaced as opposed to massed presentations of verbal material.

A study by Light and Carter–Sobell (1970) approached the nature of the store question by presenting homographs whose particular meanings were determined by the sentences in which they occurred. These targeted words were later included in a recognition test. The independent variable introduced was either holding constant or varying the words' meaning in successive presentations by use of contextual manipulations. In one instance the two presentations might be: *"They sat on the bank and fished all afternoon"* and *"He skillfully guided the canoe to the bank."* In the varied meaning condition, the second sentence might read: *"She cashed the check at the bank."* Subsequent research has varied context by using single prefixing words (Bobrow, 1970; Davis, Lockhart, & Thompson, 1972; Slamecka & Barlow, 1979; Thios, 1972). Generally, the experiments demonstrate a positive effect of the change context; it is superior to a single presentation of the word but inferior to a dual presentation in the same context. The results across experiments vary in the magnitude of the effect, just as will be reported in the case of context alpha.

The facilitating effect of spacing the repetition of words in a list to be learned rather than using a contiguous presentation is a robust phenomenon as measured either by recognition or recall (Melton, 1970). Of the various explanations of it, a somewhat favored and promising one stems from the concept of variable encoding (Martin, 1968). This hypothesis holds that the preceding word or words, although unrelated to the word in question, supply a context that influences the encoding of that word. If a word is presented and then immediately repeated, it is encoded in the same manner each time because the context is unchanged. However, if other words intervene between the two presentations, the context differs in the separate presentation, and, it is assumed, so does the nature of the encoding of the critical word. Memory performance is enhanced because the word has two retrieval routes to it rather than only one. The variable encoding interpretation of the spacing effect can be tested by using homographs and controlling their encoding through the introduction of biasing words immediately preceding the target word's presentation. If "BANK" is the target word, its two occurrences may result in the same semantic outcome if on its first occurrence it is preceded by "*river*," and by "*canal*" on the second. However, if it is preceded by "*mortgage*" on its representation, two semantic events, each quite different from the other, will have been encoded.

A number of experiments have used this type of procedure (Bobrow, 1970; Davis, Lockhart, & Thompson, 1973; Gartman & Johnson, 1972; Johnston, Coots, & Flickinger, 1972; Thios, 1972), and they met with modest success in supporting the variable encoding interpretation of the massed-spaced phenomenon.

In contrast to the studies with humans, much of the animal research on the topic has been directed toward the investigation of context beta itself, even though the studies are not specifically identified with the word context. Basically the research has been concerned with the situation in which the meaning of some specific stimulus differs as a function of the occurrence of another stimulus or environmental arrangement. As a general rule, the paradigms are of the two-choice discrimination variety with the nature of the response to the cue stimulus being determined by the conjunction of it with another stimulus. Typically, each of the stimuli have only two values, their psychological significance being determined by the conjunctive relationship between the values of each. If, as in the Lashley study (Lashley, 1938), one is working with the form of triangles and circles, and employing vertical and horizontal stripes to produce the ground, no single physical value is a sign for the appropriate way of responding; a conjunction is required. Thus an isolated physical stimulus—one point on its dimension—will acquire both excitatory and inhibitory characteristics.

The major paradigms in animal behavior that fall into the context beta classification differ in various features from each other. They also tend to go by different names: conditional discrimination (Lashley, 1938); matching and delayed matching to sample (Honig & Wasserman, 1981); oddity discrimination (Spaet & Harlow, 1943); the ambiguous cue problem (Richards, 1981); and "switching" (Asratian, 1972). All of these special paradigms share a common feature, namely, that there is no specific form, hue, or other aspect that is always reinforced or never reinforced, their significance depending on their conjunction with some other equally ambiguous physical attribute. Typically such tasks are more difficult to master than is a simple discrimination (Honig & Wasserman, 1981), and the capacity to perform them adequately is closely related to chronological age (Harlow & Mears, 1979). They require the learner to react exclusively to the *gestalten* and not to the individual components.

CONTEXT ALPHA

Context alpha refers to a situation in which the context, or environmental surround, is essentially irrelevant to the central task, whose demands and characteristics remain the same regardless of the context. Thus, the basic aims and content of a lecture remain unchanged, regardless of the classroom in which it is delivered; if one must learn a list of French–English vocabulary words, the pairing of the words remains the same wherever the student studies it; the required motor pattern for successfully shooting a foul shot remains the same on the home or on an away court.

Despite the identity of the objective task demands, in the examples given above, the individual may remember the lecture or the vocabulary list less well in a different situation and the basketball player may shoot fouls less accurately on an away but neutral court.

In his classic paper, "Forgetting and the law of disuse" (1932), McGeoch, a Chicago Ph.D., has referred to context alpha as follows: "the learner is forming associations, not only intrinsic to the material being learned, but also between the parts of this material and the manifold features of the context or environment in which the learning is taking place" (p. 365).

There is a usage of the term "context" that seems of little value and that smacks of the old-wine-in-a-new-bottle gambit, but yet is one that is occasionally applied to paired-associate learning. In it, "context" becomes a substitute for the older term "stimulus," or the more modern term "cue," with which the response term is paired. In such a usage, context becomes a highly specific term, appropriate only to a specific response in contrast to its use as a variable effecting performance on the list as a whole. The specific use not only seems to add nothing to the understanding of paired associate learning but actually dilutes the strength of the "context" term and weakens the value of the concept in general. Similarly, it would not be appropriate to term the CS as the context for making the conditioned response, but it would be appropriate to refer to the general environment as a context that facilitates the occurrence of the CR when the CS is administered.

The usage of the term cited in the preceding paragraph should be differentiated from the case where the other items on a list are said to serve as the context for a particular item or items. An example of the influence of context in this situation can be illustrated by the comparison of transfer effects obtained by the use of the mixed versus unmixed list design in paired associate learning (Twedt & Underwood, 1959). The Osgood (1946) transfer surface predicts that, when stimuli of the two lists are the same and the response terms of the second list become increasingly unlike those of the first list until they are opposed in meaning, the transfer declines with decreasing similarity, becoming negative if the responses are opposed. Empirical tests of the theory have used synonyms or antonyms of the first-list responses to represent the highly similar and opposed conditions, with the inclusion of a condition where the response terms were quite different in the successive lists. When the experiment is conducted in an unmixed list design, with a separate group for each condition, both the synonym and antonym groups show positive transfer, with antonyms producing slightly higher positive transfer than the synonyms. If, however, a mixed list procedure is used, wherein the second list for each subject is composed of an equal proportion of pairs of each of the three types—synonyms, antonyms, and unrelated—the antonym condition produces slight negative transfer effects (Wickens & Cermak, 1967). Clearly, the composition of the list forms a context which interacts with the magnitude and direction of the particular interference paradigm being considered. In the unmixed list design, all pairs consistently point toward a particular class of response required—always an antonym, a synonym, or an unrelated word; in the mixed list, the totality of other responses favors no consistent relational nature of the various responses.

To summarize, in the instance of context alpha, various aspects of the environment present at the time of learning have some likelihood of becoming associated with the learned response and may, at some later time, influence the probability of occurrence of that response. The term "some likelihood" is used because, as research to be reviewed will show, the magnitude or the context effect is variable.

Logically, context alpha, intrinsically unrelated to the central task as it is, is not a necessary condition for the occurrence of the response, as demonstrated by the fact that the response may be given to the appropriate stimulus in an environment quite different from that in which the learning took place (Liddell, 1946). A shock-induced leg withdrawal response in a sheep was conditioned in the laboratory to the CS of scratching the animal's rib cage. Later, when the sheep was safely grazing in the meadow outside, a CR was given to the same CS. Quite clearly the laboratory environment and the affixed electrodes were not necessary for the making of the CR. Nor on the other hand should context serve as a sufficient condition for a given behavior; if so, the intertrial responding in a shuttle box would completely obfuscate measurement of a conditioned avoidance response to the conditioned stimulus.

Adjustive behavior is ordinarily guided by specific phasic stimulus changes, and it would be unadaptive if context alone became a sufficient condition for the emission of a particular response which is inappropriate at that moment. In free recall, any of the responses in the list are correct, but in the paired-associate situation, they are correct only if they are given to a particular stimulus or cue word. How context can facilitate performance in both free recall and paired-associate recall, as it does. is a topic to be addressed quite fully later. Before doing so, it seems necessary to describe the basic methodological designs of context research as well as a sample of the outcomes of a number of experiments.

THE MAGNITUDE AND THE DIRECTION OF THE
CONTEXT ALPHA EFFECT

In this section a few of the many context alpha experiments will be reported in order to demonstrate the wide variation in the effectiveness of the manipulation. This is being done not for the purpose of denigrating the concept as an important determinant of behavior, but rather to indicate the need for research identifying the cause or basis for the variation. Some of the research to be cited uses humans as the subjects and some lower animals; some are primarily concerned with memory and others are more in the nature of transfer studies.

The basic design of the experiments on context consists of the following sequence: first, the presentation of a learning task to a group of subjects in a specific environment or context; then a division of the original into two groups; and, finally, the presentation of a test to the group that stays in the same stage-one environment and also to the group which has been shifted to a different environment. There are, of course, numerous variations and counterbalancing in such experiments, but basically the difference in performance between those who *Stay* and those who *Change* is the critical context measurement, and hereafter Stay and Change will be used to identify the groups in the terms of this type of procedure.

In addition, the experimenters' purposes may have one of two orientations. One of these is concerned with the topic of *Transfer* of what has been learned in one environment to performance in a different environment. The other will be termed the *Interference* design, which always requires the acquisition of material in at least two tasks (or lists) where the retention of one or other of the two tasks is reduced because of having learned the other task—the proactive or retroactive inhibition situation. The context manipulation is to have both lists learned in the same environment and the recall of the target list is made in that environment. Performance on the target list is compared with another group, which acquires one list in one environment and the second list in a different environment, with recall for the target list occurring in the environment where it was learned. Sometimes, but not always, a group which learns only a single list is also included as a control.

It should be noted that in the Transfer design, the Stay group is expected to perform better than the Change group, whereas just the opposite is true for the interference design. Thus, context serves as a prompter hiding in the wings. Unfortunately, it may give the wrong as well as the right prompt for the play on stage, depending on which playbook the prompter holds. In the former cases performance is inhibited; in the latter it is facilitated.

CONTEXT ALPHA IN THE INTERFERENCE DESIGN

In the Bilodeau and Schlosberg study (1951), which seems to be the first research to investigate the role of context alpha in relation to specifically introduced interference, the subjects learned two paired-associate lists in either the same or different environments. The environments were either a normal classroom or a small closet, these being counterbalanced. Since this was a retroactive paradigm, recall was tested in the room where the first list learning took place. The recall performance of the Change group was above that of the Stay group, showing a superiority of about 110%. Both groups were, however, inferior to a control group that learned only a single list, thus indicating that context alone does not completely eliminate the interference effect. A later study by Greenspoon and Ranyard (1957) replicated this finding, obtaining about the same advantage for the Change group.

Context effects were investigated in the proactive inhibition situation by Dallett and Wilcox (1968), who manipulated the interference by the successive learning of noun lists across days, with the recall of the previous day's list being given before learning the current day's list. The context variable produced a superiority of 75% for the Change group, for whom the context shift was made after the first day, but it dropped to only 30% when the change was made after three prior lists. This decrement in the effectiveness of context alpha with increased experience in the environment will be discussed later.

Wickens, Tuber, and Wickens (1983) used a classical conditioning paradigm with cats in an experiment closely modeled after proactive paired associate work with humans and obtained a superiority for the Change group of 450%. The proactive condition was the random pre-exposure to the potential CS and UCS and the magnitude of the context change varied as a function of the degree of similarity between the stimuli used in the first and second learning.

These few experiments indicate the wide effectiveness of context alpha from 30 up to 450% in its capacity to dampen, but not to eliminate, the induced interference effects. The range is far too great to be disregarded in any statement about the role of context alpha in behavior.

CONTEXT ALPHA IN THE TRANSFER DESIGN

A similar range of results is found for context alpha in experiments of the transfer variety. In these studies, the research is not specifically directed toward the topic of memory, although memory is involved since the transfer test always occurs some period of time after first task learning.

A prototypical study, one with obvious ecological validity, is an experiment by Abernathy (1940). During the regular course in introductory psychology, special lectures were given on such topics as sensory functions or principles of learning, for which carefully standardized tests had been developed. Later, the examinations were administered in the same room with the same proctor, or in a different but standard classroom with the chairs rotated 180 degrees from normal and with a different proctor. The change in context produced a decrement of only 4%, a result that was not significant. (Parenthetically, results such as these should be most encouraging to a dedicated teacher who hopes that the knowledge imparted in the classroom carries over to the extra-classroom environment.) Smith (1979) had college students learn a list of words in a pleasantly furnished laboratory and recall them a day later either in the same or in a soundproofed chamber located in a larger room that contained a considerable amount of computer equipment. His Stay group performed about 50% better than did the Change group.

The animal literature on context alpha also shows variation in context's effectiveness. Bouton and Bolles (1979) established a conditioned emotional response (CER) in one chamber and then extinguished it in a very different chamber. When the animals were returned to the original chamber, their CERs did not differ from those of a group that had never undergone extinction. In short, the effect of the context change was complete. Gordon et al., (1981), working with rats and the CER, found an approximate 300% advantage for the Change over the Stay Groups. A study by Siegel, Hinson, Frank and McCully (1982) has demonstrated a context alpha effect in drug addiction. In phase 1, rats were given increasingly larger, but nonlethal, doses of heroin in a particular environment over a number of days, thus producing increased tolerance for the drug. In phase 2, they were injected with a near-lethal dosage, either in the same or a different environment. Both the Stay and Change groups showed a mortality rate which was considerably less than for a control group which had received injections of dextrose while the other groups had been receiving their tolerance development doses. This result is clear evidence of physiological adaptation to heroin, suggesting an addiction. The mortality rate for the control animals was more than 95%; the rate for the Change group was about 60%, while that for the Stay animals was slightly more than 30%. When converted to our measure of context measure effectiveness, the value is about 100%. Thomas and McKelvie (1982), using the key peck response of pigeons, found a difference between the two groups—stay and change—of about 45%.

In summary, the transfer effect has ranged from being infinitely large, as in the Bouton and Bolles work, to little if any in the Abernathy (1940) study. The wide range in the effectiveness of context alpha presents a challenge to the experimental psychologist and to his general reputation as a scientist—for little respect will accrue to a discipline whose only answer to a research question will be "Sometimes no, sometimes a little, sometimes a lot, and sometimes completely." It seems to me that we are now at the stage wherein there is a clear recognition that context variation can play a role in the determination of behavior, and we should direct our theory and research toward predicting the magnitude of the effect in any given situation.

A hypothetical example of this need could be found in the development of a trainer for one or another purpose where the question arises as to how closely the context must approach that of the actual life situation. It may be possible, but very costly, to increase the similarity of the trainer to the real world situation, but if the gain in transfer is minuscule it may not be worth the cost. Costs can be estimated by the engineers; the psychologists should be able to estimate the benefit. The following section will contain speculations as to why the variance in the context alpha effect is so large.

THE BASIS FOR VARIATION IN CONTEXT ALPHA
EFFECTIVENESS

It seems obvious that for context alpha to be effective at all, the subjects must perceive, at some minimal level, the context change, and furthermore, it would seem that the more salient the change the greater the magnitude of the differential in performance between the Stay and Change groups. Given those assumptions one would expect to find a considerable context change resulting from learning under water and recalling on land or vice versa. Godden and Baddeley (1975) conducted such an experiment with members of a scuba-diving club, and they found the Stay condition to be about 50% better than the Change condition. This magnitude is very similar to that in the previously mentioned research by Smith (1979), yet there would seem to be a much greater difference in the saliency of the shift in the Godden and Baddeley experiment than in the one by Smith. In the Dallett and Wilcox study (1968), flashing lights were used in one of their two environments, producing a disco-like effect which was so potent that some of the subjects complained of nausea and requested to withdraw from the experiment. Yet, in spite of the high saliency of the manipulation, the magnitude of the context alpha effect did not differ much from that in the Bilodeau and Schlosberg (1951) research with its less-flamboyant environmental modification. Although some perception of the environmental differences certainly underlies the context alpha effect, there must be other psychological processes involved that are more closely related to the variance in effectiveness than are mere environmental differences.

In the experiments mentioned in the previous section, it may have been noted that research with lower animals typically shows a greater context alpha effect than does research done with humans. Before concluding that there is a basic phylogenetic factor accounting for this difference, one should consider a possible environmental confounding, namely the amount of experience these different organisms have had in different environments and in the various activities experienced in these environments prior to the experiment itself. The typical rat subject in experiments on conditional emotional responses (CER), remains in a small cage in the animal housing quarters until the time that the experimenter considers it to be of appropriate age to serve as a subject in the experiment. It then is taken to the laboratory in its own cage or a similarly structured holding cage and placed into the experimental chamber, the construction of which differs in many respects from the home environment. Therein it might learn to lick a tube to obtain water or press a bar for either food or water. If the training is to be on-line, the static features of the box are unchanged while the tone-shock pairings occur. If off-line, the bar may be withdrawn and the pellet or water dispenser obscured while the conditioning training occurs. The context manipulation may be achieved bv extinguishing the CER in a different as opposed to the reward-delivering chamber, and later tested for the persistence of the extinction experience in the training box. Obviously the procedures differ but they do not depart greatly from this general schema.

What is important for the present argument is the fact that the typical rat subject has experienced only a very small number of different environments and has not engaged in many different activities in its entire life. If an unusual event, such as a shock, is received for the first time in the rat's life and only in one of the few environments it has ever experienced, that environment becomes quite relevant to the shock's occurrence. Perhaps as a result, theories derived from this type of animal research attribute great weight to context.

A situation of this sort should be contrasted to the lifetime of classroom experience of college students, as in the Abernathy (1940) research. From an early age they have been in various classrooms, and they have engaged in many different formal learnings as well as other activities in these rooms; they have been bored, amused, intellectually stimulated, to mention but a few, and, importantly, they have been tested for their knowledge of many different materials. Thus, despite differences among particular rooms, the rooms become, as a class (no pun intended), a place where many kinds of learning are acquired and tested. Out of this experience, in which many different materials are learned—some neutral to each other, some consonant, and some even conflicting—students also learn that the classroom per se is not a dependable cue for some specific response or specific set of responses. This is not meant to imply that a conscious decision concerning the irrelevance of the static environment is made by the individual; the difference is produced simply as a consequence of the many disparate experiences and the true irrelevance of the classroom to the central task.

A recent experiment by Smith (1982) adds support to the conjecture offered above. In his Experiment 3, one group experienced three different free-recall lists in the same room and recalled either in that same room or in a different room. Another major group was presented the three lists each in a different room, and they recalled them either in one of the three presentation rooms or in a different room. There was no significant effect of same or different room for this group, its Stay condition being only 5% superior to the Change condition. However, for the single-room condition, there was about a 50% superiority for the Change group. Its performance was superior to that of the three-room group in the Stay condition, but was inferior by about the same magnitude in the Change condition.

The conclusion that can be drawn from the foregoing discussion is that the disparity in the magnitude of the context alpha effect between humans and lower animals may very well arise from the experiential background of the subjects prior to the experiment rather than to phylogenetic differences. None of this discussion is meant to imply that research with lower animals has no relevance to the human condition. On the contrary, animal subjects afford the experimenter the opportunity to investigate the topic more systematically than can be done with human subjects because the animal researcher has a greater ability to control the amount and variety of the animals' experience before conducting the critical context experiment, and to relate these to the magnitude of the context alpha effect.

The conclusion that can be drawn from this survey of studies on context in humans and animals and the wide variation in magnitude is that an important determinant of the magnitude is the degree and kinds of experience the subject has had in the class of environment used in the experimental manipulation. If the prior experience in variants of the environment is multiple, then a context shift may have only a minimal effect but will have a large effect if the prior experience has been limited. To turn to a practical problem that might confront a human factors psychologist advising on the design of some new training device, the degree of verisimilitude of the trainer to the eventual environment may be of less importance if the population to be trained has had a great deal of experience on tasks of the sort, as opposed to a population with a lesser degree of experience.

THE BASIS OF THE CONTEXT ALPHA EFFECT

It seems appropriate at this point to return to McGeoch's descriptive statement concerning context alpha, namely that associations are formed not only among the materials to be learned but also with manifold features of the environment in which the learning takes place. Given that such associations are formed, the question arises as to how the static environment can influence a response which ordinarily is appropriately given only in relationship to a particular phasic stimulus. In simple conditioning, for example, the experimenter typically will have presented the CS–UCS pair at irregular intervals to avoid establishing a rhythm of responding which coincides with the CS onset, and the execution of the response in the absence of the prior onset of the CS is not considered a conditioned response. How, then, can an environment which is static in nature facilitate correct responding? It will serve to do so if it lowers the threshold of the response (Balaz, Capra, Hartl, & Miller, 1980) making it more available when the appropriate cue, in this case the CS, occurs. By doing so the probability of responding is increased. Such an interpretation as this is consonant with the view stated earlier that, in the proper state of affairs, context is neither a necessary or sufficient condition for making the response. By the proper state of affairs I mean that experimenters require that the probability of responding be greater during a short period of time following CS onset than during some equal window of time when the CS has not occurred. The suppression ratio was devised to measure this differential.

In the classical conditioning situation, one can assume that the context simply adds its activating strength to that which has been acquired by the conditioned stimulus itself, which triggers the conditioned response. However, work by Liddell (1946) described earlier demonstrates the CS alone can produce the CR in a quite different context from that in which it was learned. Obviously this means that the CS can acquire sufficient strength to become independent of the context in which it was formed.

When one turns to more complex learnings, such as unrelated noun lists or the even more restrictive paired associate learning, one must account for the fact that context can influence performance on a number of independent responses that often are unrelated to each other. If it is a paired-associate experiment, the usual requirement is that the response must be given to a particular stimulus. Because the environment—the context—is static, it seems most unlikely that each response becomes associated with a different feature of the environment. Also, if the presentation of the items is paced, as usually is the case, the subject has little time or inclination to gaze about and encode different aspects of the environment with particular responses, so as to use these aspects as retrieval cues later. However, if the context serves to activate the list as a whole, making the entire set of responses of which the list is composed more aailable, then context will enhance performance, provided, of course, that only a single list was acquired in that context.

There are several lines of research supporting the view that the retrieval process operates on the level of list as a whole rather than item by item. In a study on recognition memory by Wickens, Moody, and Dow (1981), which involved an extension of the Sternberg (1969) paradigm, it was found that retrieval time was the same for a two- and four-item memory set, implying that set was retrieved as a unit, not item by item. A considerable amount of research using paired-associate lists has been conducted by Postman and students, which supports the view that interference occurs primarily at the level of the list or set of responses (Postman, Stark, & Fraser, 1968). The previously mentioned Wickens et al. (1981) experiment also found evidence for interference operating at the set rather than item level.

An interesting source of support for the response set interpretation of the context effect is found in Experiment 1 of the previously mentioned Smith (1982) article. In this experiment the subjects were presented four lists, either all in the same room; two lists in one room and two in a different room; or, for the third group, each list in a different room. This was followed by a free-recall test. Not only did the number of items recalled differ between the groups, favoring the multiple groups, but especially significant for the response set interpretation is the finding that the clustering score (Bousfield, 1953) increased monotonically with the number of rooms used in the learning situation. The clustering score was based on the adjacency of recalled items from the same list. Because clustering is evidence for organization, this finding is very much in accord with the view that context produces its effect by operating at the list level.

In summary, it is suggested that context alpha has its effect by means of increasing the availability of the response or set of responses experienced in that environment. In the case where only a single response is learned, as is ordinarily true of classical conditioning, this interpretation need no further elaboration. However, when, multiple responses are involved, as in free recall and especially in paired-associate learning, mechanisms which increase the availability of the group of responses must be included. This is the concept that context operates to increase the availability of the set of responses in the list. In the free recall situation, the increase in response availability of the list as a whole is sufficient to account for the facilitation of context; in a paired-associate situation, one may assume that if responses are more available they are more likely to be given when the appropriate stimulus term occurs. In the transfer design, the list activation facilitates the performance for the Stay group, but in the interference design it inhibits performance for the Stay group because it activates both lists.

Response Availability Theory and Recognition Memory

The response availability interpretation is predictive of the findings that context alpha is ineffective in recognition memory (Baddely, 1982; Cuccar, Egstrom, Weltman, & Willis, 1975; Davis, Lockhart, & Thompson, 1972; Godden Baddely, 1975; Smith, 1983). In testing for recognition memory, the experimenters supply the responses to the subject, and thereby deprive the context of the role that it normally makes, namely of making the responses more available. Since responses are completely available in the recognition situation, performance in the stay condition has little or no advantage over the change condition.

THE INTERACTION OF CONTEXTS ALPHA AND BETA

Although this article has emphasized the operational and psychological differences between context alpha and context beta, it is not meant to imply that the two may not simultaneously operate in the same situation. A case in point is the research on mood as context (Bower, 1981). In this experiment, a happy or sad mood was generated in the subjects, followed by the presentation of a word list, which was later recalled whether in the original or opposite mood. Retention was superior if the mood was the same in learning and recall. These results could be attributed to a combination of context alpha and context beta. Many words are ambiguous, with their current meanings being determined by the mood of the moment. Hence a context beta effect could influence the original encoding of the word. At the same time the mood itself could serve as an environmental state as in context alpha. A change in each context type would operate in the same direction, namely, to inhibit recall. The differentiation that I have made between the two types of context does not imply that they may not operate in the same situation. Very simply the view is that, with respect to their underlying psychological mechanisms, they are very different processes. Indeed it is unlikely that, were it not for prior and well-established usage in the lay vocabulary, we would have adopted the same term "context" to refer to these two psychologically disparate processes.

The state dependent effect has not been included as an example of context, although it is quite likely that it should be. If, for example, "uppers" and "downers" were the drugs used, their effects could function in the same fashion as suggested for the mood manipulation that we have described. Motivational or drive states have been shown to function as context beta by both Hull (1943) and Leeper (1935) when they demonstrated that rats could learn to turn in one or another direction at the choice point of a T-maze, depending on whether they had been deprived of food or water. One might say that the meaning of the stimulus of the choice point is changed as a function of the drive condition. Hull handled these data by endowing his drive stimulus with a cognitive as well as an energizing function. An example of context alpha can be found in the research of Wickens, Hall, and Reid (1949) which used a retroactive inhibition paradigm modeled after the Bilodeau and Schlosberg (1951) study, but used rats in a single unit T-maze and hunger and thirst drives as the context alpha manipulation in a habit reversal paradigm. It found the *change* group to be superior to the *stay* group in relearning the first habit. I have not specifically included these types of manipulations under context simply because the term is already heavily laden, and because the state dependent manipulation is not completely consistent in its outcome (Eich, 1980). It is most desirable, however, to recognize the basic relationship between context and these types of operation.

CONCLUSIONS AND SUGGESTED RESEARCH

In this final section, I wish to emphasize the personal belief that the concept of context is an important and necessary one for the full accounting of behavior. Unfortunately the term, by historical precedence, has two quite different meanings related only in that both meanings make reference to the surrounds in which an event occurs. For the weaker meaning of the term, which I have designated context alpha, there is no inherent relationship between the surrounds and the specific activity that is being learned. In the instance of its strong meaning—termed context beta—the context is needed to define the meaning of at least some of the task's components.

Although in context alpha the relationship between the environment and the task is an adventitious one, associations are often formed between it and aspects of the environment, such that performance on this activity may differ when executed in the same environment or in a different one. Research with both humans and animals has shown a considerable range in the effect of context alpha. This is to be expected of a variable which logically is not a necessary condition for performing the task.

It must be apparent that both of the major conclusions concerning context alpha drawn in this chapter are amenable to evaluation by research. A few suggestions of what the author considers to be feasible approaches will be mentioned.

The Range in the Effectiveness of Context Alpha

One problem in obtaining a true measure of the power of context deals with nonsignificant findings. Unless such findings become an integral part of an evaluative program, they are not likely to appear in the professional journals. If, however, they are a part of an expressed systematic effort to find the variable or variables associated with the degree of the context effect, rather than an isolated attempt to work with one or another manipulation, a negative finding becomes meaningful. It was suggested earlier that work with animals lends itself quite readily to systematic research varying the degree of prior experience in various classes of environments on the magnitude of the context manipulation. In the human field, particularly in the human factors area, more precise knowledge of the effect of context fidelity is required for the psychologist to be of maximal usefulness as a consultant. Obviously a similar programmatic orientation is desirable in context research with humans. This is not to suggest that a single, large program is the only answer, but that individuals keep in mind this broader purpose of context research as they plan and interpret their research.

Response Availability as the Basis for the Context Alpha Effect

Advanced methods for the investigation of this topic are already available. This is to be found in the paradigms invented for the analytical study of transfer and interference during the late 1950s and the 1960s. It includes not only such paradigms as the A–B, A–D; A–B, C–D, and A–B, A–Br, but various choices of measuring performance, such as free recall, modified free recall (mfr), and modified modified free recall (mmfr). These paradigms evolved as means of analyzing performance in both transfer and memory. Because of the proven analytical power of the paradigm, they promise to be equally effective when applied to the study of the role played by context in the transfer and memory situations. It must be apparent that my interpretation of the context effect would predict that the major impact of the context manipulation would be found on the response side.

A RESEARCH UPDATE

Subsequent to the conference and submitting this chapter to the editorial process, several studies have appeared that are very relevant to the chapter. A few recent studies relate to positions I have taken on the question of the robustness of the context alpha effect.

One is a report by Saufley, Otaka, and Bavaresco (1985) on the influence of context change on examination performance by California college students at Berkley. Conceptually, the research was the same as in the Abernathy (1940) study, but is more extensive in nature. The report contains seven experiments comparing Stay versus Change groups. In no instance did the two types of groups differ significantly and there was no clear trend for one type of group to surpass the other in mean score. The article represents an excellent example of adapting laboratory methodology to the real-world environment.

Another extremely relevant article is one by Fernandez and Glenberg (1985). It is a report of eight experiments dealing with various manipulations which might be assumed to relate to the degree of impact the context manipulation would have. In none of the first seven experiments was a significant effect obtained. The eighth experiment was a slight modification of one performed by Smith (1979), which had reported significant effects of the context manipulation. The modification consisted of more than doubling the N per group, using only auditory presentation, and omitting one group Smith had used but which was not required for the purposes of the basic replication. Because Smith had conducted his research in the same laboratory (University of Wisconsin at Madison), the authors were able to use one room that Smith used; the other rooms were highly similar to his and in the same building. Their results did not replicate those obtained by Smith.

These experiments support my conclusion that there is indeed a wide variation in effect of context alpha. They imply furthermore that we should address in our research and theory the reason or reasons for the variation.

A final experiment to be cited is one by Eich (1985). It relates to my interpretation of how context operates in the situation where the response is correct only if given to a particular stimulus, as in the paired-associate situation. It was suggested that, in the usual paced situation, the subject may not have time to relate a particular pair to some object in the environment. The Eich experiment addressed this problem by presenting word pairs to subjects using two different instructions, one of which was simply to create an image of the word and the other to create an interactive image which included some object present in the room. Recall was tested under either a Stay or Change condition. The presentation was self-paced and the time required for the subjects to complete the list was recorded.

The results show that the Stay and Change groups differed in their recall performance 2 days later in the expected direction only for those subjects given the "interactive image" directions. However, the two groups also differed in the mean study time per pair, with those given the interactive directions spending 20.7 seconds per pair and the isolated image group 17.8 seconds per pair. This study time difference was significant, and the author points out that the performance difference could arise from the fact that the interactive group spent more time studying the items than did the Isolated image group. Once again, the robustness of the context effect is questioned by this research.

These three carefully conducted sets of studies support the opinion that the magnitude of the context effect does vary considerably. We need to address our research to the problem of identifying the factors responsible for this variation.

10 Explaining Context Effects on Short-Term Memory

David S. Gorfein
Adelphi University,
Garden City, New York

A quarter of a century ago John Brown (1958) and Lloyd and Margaret Peterson (1959) reported the creation of a new memory technique that allowed the investigation of memory for a subspan amount of material over the course of a relatively brief retention interval. The variations of their procedure have become known as the short-term memory task (STM), the distractor task, or the Brown–Peterson paradigm. It is the aim of this chapter to demonstrate that two distinct types of context, "environmental" and "semantic," have powerful effects on performance in this task, and to offer a theoretical interpretation of the operation of these contextual factors. To accomplish this aim, we will begin by describing the procedure and reviewing three major classes of findings with respect to the procedures. We will go on to introduce the term "context" in its several meanings, review the literature with respect to contextual manipulations in STM, and finally, offer our theoretical view.

In the Brown–Peterson procedure, a trial consists of the cycle of events described in Table 10.1. Typically a "ready signal" is followed by the presentation of a to-be-remembered item (usually a word or consonant triad). Next is a verbal distractor task (such as shadowing numbers), a signaled recall period, and, in many studies, an intertrial interval prior to the repetition of the trial cycle to create a block of trials. In the 15 years subsequent to the initial experimental reports of Brown (1958) and of Peterson and Peterson (1959), approximately 1000 studies were published employing the distractor task. Some of the range of experimental manipulations is described in Table 10.1.

TABLE 10.1
An Outline of the Distractor Task and its Manipulation

Task Event	Range of Manipulation	Experimental Purpose
1. Ready signal	1. Typically 1–2 sec but ranges up to duration of retention interval. Typically word "ready" or a symbol.	1. Warning signal
	2. Subject to context manipulation (Falkenberg, 1972; Gorfein & Spata, in preparation).	2. As context for encoding
2. To-be-remembered item.	CCCs, single words, word triads; Classes of materials (Wickens, 1972).	1. Study of "semantic release"
3. Distractor task	1. Verbal activities, including mental arithmetic, Stroop.	1. Rehearsal prevention
	2. Typical duration retention.	2. Study of interval duration
	3. As context for retrieval	3. Study effect of similarity to ready signal
4. Recall signal	1. Symbol such as question marks to signal time to recall (3–10 sec duration).	1. Occasion for recall
	2. Recognition alternatives, Gorfein and Jacobson (1972, 1973), Bennett (1975)	2. To assess effects of competition
5. Intertrial interval	0–300 sec (Loess & Waugh, 1967; Kincaid & Wickens, 1970). Context may be manipulated (Gorfein & Schulze, 1975).	Typically as a rest period between trials (or to study temporal release)
6. Repetition of above cycle		

STM: THE MAJOR FINDINGS

A number of very interesting and well-established findings emerged from this surge of work and have been widely cited in the textbooks of the field. I briefly review the three major classes of findings: the existence of proactive interference in the Brown–Peterson paradigm, the occurrence of "semantic release," and the occurrence of "temporal release."

The first finding of the distractor task is the demonstration of the existence of proactive inhibition or proactive interference (called PI hereafter to maintain an atheoretical position). What is meant by PI is illustrated by Fig. 10.1.

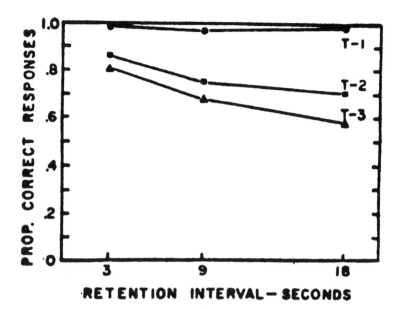

FIGURE 10.1.   Effect of retention interval as a function of trial in experiment (reproduced with permission from the Journal of Verbal Learning and Verbal Behavior, Keppel & Underwood, 1962).

The data for this figure were generated in an experiment by Keppel and Underwood (1962) in which different groups of participants were assigned to different orderings of three retention intervals (3, 9, and 18 sec) for three trials in a distractor task. The usual precautions of balancing intervals and materials were observed. What we see is that there is a decline in performance over trials and that there is a trial-by-retention interval interaction, whereby on Trial 1, interval has no statistically significant effect, but by Trial 3 we see a substantial decline in memory performance as retention interval increases. By PI we mean this systematic decline in performance across trials and across retention intervals.

Wickens, Born, and Allen in 1963 showed dramatic improvement in performance resulted from the manipulation of the type of to-be-remembered material. If after several trials of one class of to-be-remembered items the class was altered, performance improved. This study and a number of others resulted in the general class of item manipulations known as *PI Release* studies (Wickens, 1970). In these "semantic release" experiments, triads of related words are presented for a number of trials, then a shift is made in the type of triad presented, such as in the taxonomic category from which the words are drawn. Performance is compared with a control condition where the type of to-be-remembered item is not altered. The improvement obtained is measured as the difference in the Trial 4 scores between the experimental (shift condition) and the control (no shift condition).

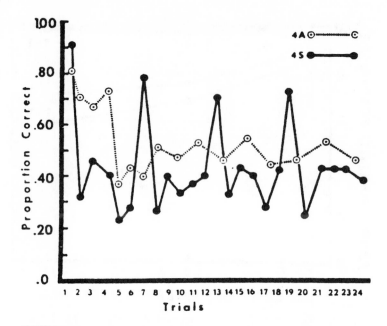

FIGURE 10.2.   Performance as a function of category shifts in (A) Alternating and (S) Successive blocks of categories (reproduced with permission from the Journal of Verbal Learning and Verbal Behavior, Loess, 1968).

Wickens (1970) notes that we can define two highly related measures on these data. What we will call *Absolute Release* is defined by the numerical difference on the performance measure between the experimental and control conditions at the point of the shift trial. The other measure expresses this result as a percentage of the recovery from the decrement observed in the control condition from the first trial to the point of the shift trial. This measure is called *Relative Release.*

It should be noted that once the category is shifted there is a subsequent decline in performance across trials of the new material, and release can again occur if an additional shift trial is introduced. Fig. 10.2, from a study by Loess (1968) illustrates this.

When release from PI is obtained under conditions in which material is manipulated to maximize judged semantic dissimilarity of adjacent trial blocks, the same type of trial by retention interval interaction such as that observed by Keppel and Underwood (1962) occurs. Fig. 10.3 shows that interaction obtained in a study reported by Gorfein and Viviani (1980). Performance on the first trial after a category shift is the same with a retention interval of 6 or 15 sec. The two retention intervals do have different effects on trials 2–4 subsequent to the shift.

The final class of findings to be reviewed are on "temporal release"; the findings with respect to the manipulation of the intertrial intervals. Two distinct

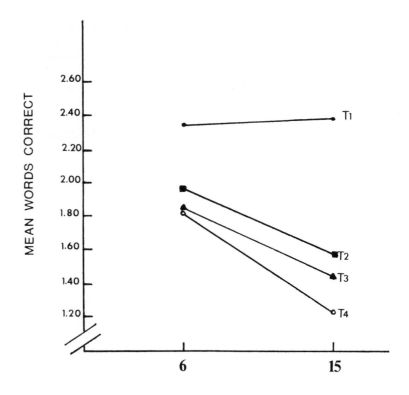

RETENTION INTERVAL - SECONDS

FIGURE 10.3.   Effect of retention interval as a function of trial in categorized block in a semantic release experiment (Gorfein & Viviani, 1980).

variations of this manipulation exist. In one of these, the duration of each intertrial interval in a block of trials is held constant, but the length of the intertrial interval is varied between trial blocks. In this case we find that the longer the within-block, intertrial interval, the less steep is the decline in performance; the less "PI buildup," occurs in that block. Fig. 10.4 from a paper by Loess and Waugh (1967) illustrates that long intertrial intervals serve to retard performance decrements across trials.

In the other form of intertrial interval manipulation, the intertrial interval is kept constant and relatively short for several trials, and after performance has declined to its asymptotic level a long intertrial interval is introduced. Fig. 10.5 drawn from Kincaid and Wickens (1970) illustrates that performance on the postinterval trial improves as a function of the length of the intertrial interval. Gorfein (1974) employed a recognition measure of STM, and showed (1974) that

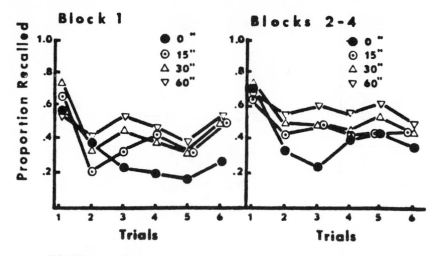

FIGURE 10.4. Performance as a function of within-block intertrial interval (reproduced with permission from the Journal of Verbal Learning and Verbal Behavior, Loess & Waugh, 1967).

the amount of absolute release obtained over a long intertrial interval following two trials was approximately twice as great as the release obtained when an intertrial interval of the same length followed four trials. In short, PI release is an inverse function of the amount of PI present.

Finally, note that the effects observed are quite robust across experimental manipulations. Thus PI and its semantic and temporal release have been demonstrated both in recall studies (as cited previously) and in recognition (Gorfein & Jacobson, 1972; Gorfein, 1974) and using both accuracy and latency measures (Gorfein & Jacobson, 1973; Murdock, 1961).

DEFINITIONS OF CONTEXT

"Context" is used to stand for at least two distinct classes of concepts in the short-term memory literature, one of which I refer to as "environmental" context and the other which I call "semantic" context (See Wickens' chapter in this volume.)

The first of these, *environmental* context, refers to the stimulus environment at the time the to-be-remembered-item is presented for study and to the environment in which memory is examined. Environmental context includes the physical setting, the psychological state of the participant, and the characteristics of the experimental trial other than the characteristics of the to-be-remembered

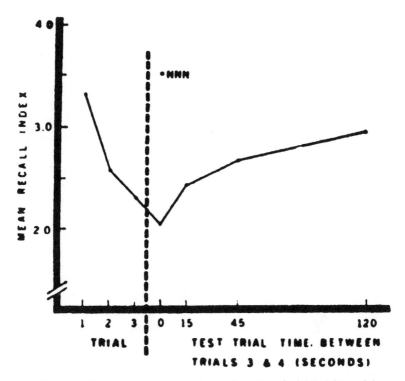

FIGURE 10.5.   Trial 3 performance as a function of trial 2–3 intertrial interval (reproduced with permission from the Journal of Experimental Psychology, Kincaid & Wickens, 1970).

materials. Melton (1963) pointed out that, historically, "context" in memory research has been used to refer to the dependence of retrieval on the reinstatement at retrieval of the stimulus situation present at the time of encoding. Some changes in stimuli are directly manipulated experimentally, as in studies of stimulus generalization in conditioning. In memory studies some of the altered stimulus conditions or altered psychological "set" of the subject are a consequence of our inability to completely control the total situation and maintain constant conditions from encoding to retrieval. This inability to experimentally maintain context may be considered in relation to stimulus fluctuations in stimulus sampling theory as outlined by Estes (1950). It will be shown that both of these factors (experimentally altered stimulus situations and stimulus fluctuation) enter into the performance in the Brown–Peterson task.

The second use of the word context, which I label *semantic* context, refers to the semantic setting of the to-be-remembered materials, i.e., the to-be-remembered word in relation to other words in the experiment.

THE LITERATURE WITH RESPECT TO
ENVIRONMENTAL CONTEXT

The literature with respect to environmental context can be classified into two types, studies that use context as a hypothetical construct or explanatory variable, and studies that have deliberately manipulated the environmental context. I reserve my discussion of environmental context as a hypothetical construct for the section on theory, and describe here some of the few studies that have actively manipulated environmental context.

The research of Falkenberg (1972) would come closest to testing the question of how much retrieval is dependent on the reinstatement of the same context at retrieval as was present at encoding. In a simple variation on the original Peterson and Peterson study, Falkenberg (Experiment 1) employed the identical counting backwards task before the study of the to-be-remembered item that was employed during the retention interval. Falkenberg compared this effect with that of a replication of the Peterson and Peterson (1959) procedure and found superior performance for his experimental condition. The procedure chosen had the unfortunate confound of manipulating the intertrial interval at the same time as context was manipulated. In Falkenberg's procedure the retention interval and the task prior to presentation of the to-be-remembered item were of the same duration. When the retention interval was to be 12 sec of the distractor task, the item was also preceded by 12 sec of that task, whereas in the Peterson procedure the ready signal was a constant 2 sec. In Falkenberg's experiment 4, the confound was controlled in one condition and tested in another. The context effect was shown to exist above and beyond the possible confound of intertrial interval variation.

A few studies investigating release from PI addressed themselves to the stimulus environment of the to-be-remembered item. Both Turvey and Egan (1969), who manipulated location and size of area of the slide on which the to-be-remembered item was presented, and Reutener (1972), who manipulated the slide background of the to-be-remembered item, obtained small PI release effects with these manipulations.

A recent study in my laboratory by Andrea Spata, (Gorfein & Spata, in preparation), will serve to illustrate more completely the effects of contextual stimuli, as defined by the activity required of the subject. Two tasks were employed, number shadowing and Stroop color naming. In a manner similar to that of Falkenberg, we employed these tasks as both the ready signal and the retention interval activity, although we did not try to keep any specific numbers or colors associated with the to-be-remembered item, nor did we covary the duration of the retention interval and the ready signal. Four combinations of activity were employed: the factorial combination of Stroop and number shadowing as the "ready" signal and as the intertrial interval activity. The condition where the ready signal and retention interval activity are of the same type (i.e.,

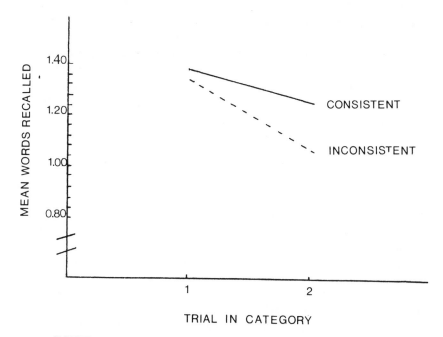

FIGURE 10.6.   Recall as a function of trial in block and consistency of context (Gorfein & Spata, in preparation).

both number shadowing or both Stroop, are called the consistent context condition). The other two combinations are the inconsistent context condition. The materials employed in this study were pairs of words drawn from taxonomic categories with the pairs arranged in categorized blocks of two trials each. After every two trials a semantic shift (new category) occurred. Within the experiment across the two trials of a block, all 16 combinations of ready signal and retention interval activity were employed twice, for a total of 32 blocks.

Fig. 10.6 shows the effect of the consistency manipulation. We see that performance with the consistent context is superior to that with the inconsistent context. The advantage of the consistent context is far greater on the second trials of the categorized blocks. The effect of consistency is clearly not independent of semantic release.

Gorfein and Schulze (1975) reasoned that one possible explanation of the effectiveness of long intertrial intervals in producing PI release (temporal release) was that the long interval allowed the opportunity for contextual fluctuation. Thus, if context changes sufficiently, then the item following a long interval could be coded uniquely with respect to items that preceded the interval. By varying the similarity of the intertrial interval activity to the normal trial activity, we demonstrated support for that hypothesis, because performance on the trial following the intertrial interval was significantly greater when the intertrial interval activity was dissimilar to the normal retention interval activity.

In summary, the manipulation of environmental context can be demonstrated to have a significant effect on performance. Consistency of context within a trial (Falkenberg, 1972; Gorfein & Spata, in preparation) improves performance. When context is altered in the intertrial interval, this facilitates performance on a subsequent trial (Gorfein & Schulze, 1975).

THE LITERATURE WITH RESPECT TO SEMANTIC CONTEXT

The major findings on semantic context have been the phenomena associated with semantic shifts and the consequent semantic release. Manipulations of materials that have produced substantial release include shifts in taxonomic category, dimensions on the semantic differential, and sense impression (cf. Wickens, 1972 for a substantive review).

Underwood (1972) raised the question of whether the observed PI release can tell us how individuals encode words in isolation. The suggestion was that in the typical "semantic" release experiment, the experimental manipulation requires that the subject process a number of examples of a category prior to the category shift, and perhaps this influences the encoding. Bennett and Bennett (1974) explicitly tested this idea in an experiment that used the relatively subtle categories of sense impressions, specifically words that elicited the sense impression "white" or "round." The experimental manipulation was a between-groups design in which the category shift occurred after 1, 2, 3, or 4 trials of the first category. A control condition compared performance on the word triads after 1 or 4 trials on consonant trigrams. Fig. 10.7 shows the results of this study.

Amount of release is the performance in the shift category compared with the most extreme case of the PI buildup function, i.e., performance on the fourth trial of the groups who received four trials prior to release. Clearly in the sense-impression domain, release is, as Underwood suggests, dependent on the amount of experience with the preshift materials. The control condition indicates that when the classes of materials are more salient (CCCs versus word triads), experience is not a factor. A similar conclusion can be drawn from Loess (1968), as shown in Fig. 10.2. In the condition 4A where a new triad from differing taxonomic categories is alternated on the first four trials, we see little PI buildup, indicating relatively complete semantic release from trial to trial.

A study from my laboratory (Gorfein & Viviani, 1981) sheds some light on semantic context effects. The study assessed the effects of semantic context on the encoding and recognition of a subclass of homographs that we call heterophones, those homographs that are nonhomophonic in their multiple meanings. The materials included the words "bass," "close," "dove," "minute," "re-

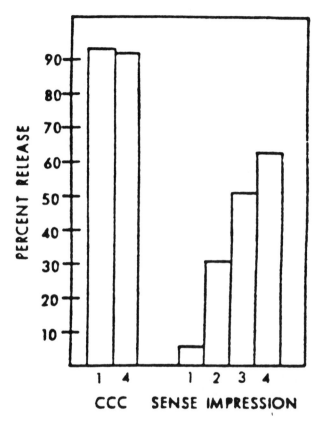

FIGURE 10.7. PI release following a category shift as a function of trial of shift and preshift material (reproduced with permission from the *Journal of Verbal Learning and Verbal Behavior,* Bennett & Bennett, 1974).

fuse,'' ''sow,'' ''tear,'' and ''wound,'' all of which have two distinct meanings and whose distinct meanings are signaled in conversation by distinct pronunciations. A recognition-latency version of the distractor task was employed (Gorfein & Jacobson, 1973). In one condition of the experiment, each of the heterophones was employed as a to-be-remembered item on trial 3 of a five-item block. On Trials 1 or 2 of the block, the to-be-remembered item was related to the secondary meaning of the heterophone as determined by association norms (Gorfein, Viviani, & Leddo, 1982). For example, the heterophone ''minute'' was preceded by trials on which the to-be-remembered item was ''small'' and ''tiny.'' The trial following the heterophone had as its to-be-remembered item a word that was related to the primary meaning of the heterophone (e.g., the word ''hour'' was a to-be-remembered item on the trial following ''minute''). One other experimental manipulation was involved—the length of the intertrial interval

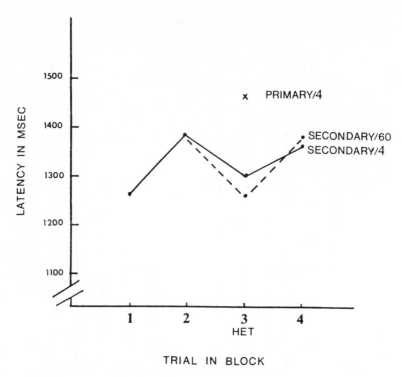

FIGURE 10.8a.   Decision latency as a function of trial in block and intertrial interval (Gorfein & Viviani, 1981).

between Trial 2 and the heterophone trial was either short (4 sec) or long (60 sec).

   Participants were required to pronounce each to-be-remembered item aloud at encoding. Therefore, we can examine the proportion of the time each heterophone was pronounced in a given direction. In the experiment after the short, 4 sec, intertrial interval, 50.9% of the heterophones were pronounced in the direction of the secondary meaning whereas at the longer intertrial interval of 60 sec, only 36.5% of the items were pronounced in accord with the secondary meaning. This compares with an expected value of 21.6% based on the homograph association norms.

   Recognition performance can be examined in two ways. We analyzed latency with respect to correct decisions and the number of errors made. With respect to response latency and accuracy, we see, in Fig. 10.8, that whereas PI builds up from Trials 1 to 2, the heterophone item has slightly fewer errors and is recognized slightly faster than the Trial 2 item even in the short intertrial interval condition. The point marked "X" in each figure represents the performance on the same heterophone in a condition where the Trial 1 and Trial 2 to-be-remembered items are related to the heterophone's primary meaning. Nevertheless,

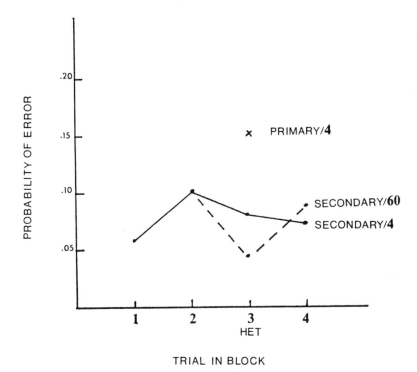

FIGURE 10.8b. Error as a function of trial in block and intertrial interval (Gorfein & Viviani, 1981).

there is PI present as we see when we compare the long intertrial interval condition with the 4-sec condition. The occurrence of temporal release in both latency and errors confirms the existence of PI. One last thing to be noted is the performance on the Trial 4 item, which was a word that was related to the primary meaning of the homograph. We see between Trials 3 and 4 an interesting crossover interaction, whereby on Trial 3, performance is better in the long intertrial interval condition, whereas on Trial 4, this performance is worse.

In summary, the literature on semantic context effects includes a substantial body of studies that show "semantic release." In the case of nonsalient categories of materials, considerable experience with the category is needed before shifts have an effect. Materials on early trials tend to prime subsequent items presented for memory.

A THEORETICAL INTERPRETATION OF CONTEXT EFFECTS

There is a range of provocative findings with respect to short-term memory, some data on the manipulation of environmental context, and a substantial literature with respect to semantic context manipulation. I now undertake a brief review of the existing theories of short-term memory to see how they account for the data described and then I present a theory that, I believe, can explain the phenomena associated with the distractor task. My task is simplified by the work of Bennett (1975), who demonstrated that any theory of performance in the distractor task had to be one of "trace selection," as contrasted to a pure "trace decay" theory (see Bennett, 1975, for the details of this argument). As a consequence of Bennett's analysis we are left with a few models of "trace selection" including the classical interference theory as applied to STM by Keppel and Underwood (1962), Bennett's model (1975), and our theory (Gorfein & Viviani, 1981).

According to interference theory, PI results from an extinction of an association and its spontaneous recovery over a retention interval. The classical interference theory requires an A–B, A–C situation to produce the unlearning and consequent spontaneous recovery. Context has been implicated by Bennett (1975) as the stimulus for paired associates. Specifically, he suggests that a good description of the Keppel and Underwood application of interference theory to the Brown–Peterson experiment can be obtained by considering each trial in the Brown-Peterson experiment as analogous to a single paired associate. The response member of the paired associate is the current to-be-remembered item and the stimulus member is the current experimental context. To the degree that the response is associated with a relatively invariant context, each trial represents the learning of what might be called X–A, X–B, or X–C associates where the X represents the invariant environmental stimulus, and A, B, and C represent the to-be-remembered items on successive trials. By this interpretation we have the conditions sufficient to produce extinction and spontaneous recovery.

In a slightly different way, Bennett's own theory (1975) makes use of environmental context as a hypothetical construct. In his research, Bennett (1975) employed a forced-choice recognition modification of the distractor task in which one element of a current to-be-remembered item was paired with an element of a prior to-be-remembered item which served as a foil. One variable that was manipulated was the source of the foil (i.e., how far back in terms of trials the foil was chosen), a variable called foil lag. The data in Fig. 10.9 show that the likelihood of an error in recognition was a monotonic decreasing function of foil lag.

In developing his theoretic explanation of the foil lag function, Bennett made use of a component of Melton's analysis of context, the part which refers to our inability to control the stimulus situation completely and the consequent stimulus fluctuation. Employing a model not unlike stimulus sampling theory, Bennett suggested that the subject encodes the trace of the to-be-remembered item with a sample of the context at the time of presentation, and at retrieval searches memory for an item that best fits the context at the time of retrieval. A random-walk model of contextual fluctuation can account for much of the foil lag function, according to this analysis.

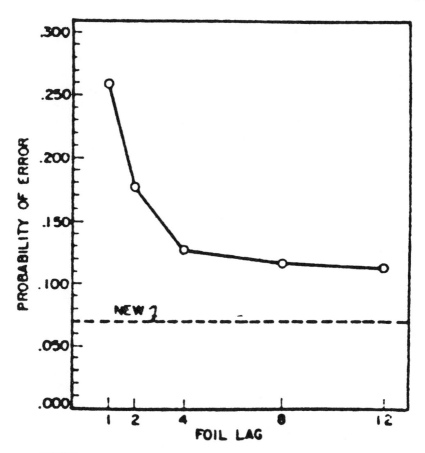

FIGURE 10.9.   Errors in forced-choice recognition as a function of the source lag of the distractor alternative (reproduced with permission from the Journal of Verbal Learning and Verbal Behavior, Bennett, 1975).

With respect to the role of context manipulations in the Brown–Peterson task, both the classical position and Bennett's model have the promise of helping us interpret the literature on "environmental" context. With respect to "semantic" release, the classical theory, developed before the demonstrations of semantic release, must be extended to account for semantic release findings, possibly in the direction of a list-differentiation principle. Bennett mentions several possible mechanisms for semantic release, involving a "criterion set" established at encoding that could serve either as a selective filter at retrieval, or to guide memory search, or as both a filter and a guide. Experiment 1 of Gorfein and Jacobson (1973) renders the selective filter role of the "criterion set" unlikely because semantic release was shown to occur in latency of recall of single words. A selective filter would act after a search process and thus we might expect to obtain improvements in accuracy of performance but not necessarily in speed of performance. Thus, neither theory offers a compelling explanation of semantic release.

I would like to sketch a theory of performance in the distractor task (Gorfein & Viviani, 1981), which I believe accounts for the data that has been discussed and has generality to a range of memory tasks. The theory proposes a mechanism for "spreading activation" (Collins & Loftus, 1975) and for the interaction of environmental and semantic context.

The theory focuses on the encoding of the to-be-remembered item. The seven basic principles of the theory are these:

1. Words are represented by an ordered set of attributes.

2. The processing of a word activates a number (N) of attributes, the number is limited by: (a) task constraints—the number necessary to meet the requirements of the task; and (b) the time available, if it is less than the time needed to meet the task demand.

3. In isolation, the first N attributes of a word are activated.

4. Set Principle: Processing a word in the context of active attributes will result in the use of those attributes to the extent that the word possesses attributes in common to those that are active. An illustration of how the principle might operate follows:

Given an item "Y" with attributes in hierarchical order of processing ABCDEFGH and an item "Z" with an order of processing IJKLABCD, and a task that requires the activation of four attributes, it follows that:

(a) If "Y" is processed in isolation, then attributes A, B, C, and D are likely to be activated. If "Z" is then presented for processing, these common attributes, if active, will be utilized.

(b) If "Z" occurs in isolation, attributes I, J, K, and L, unique to Z, will be activated, and no change would result in "Y's" processing hierarchy if "Y" were presented subsequent to "Z."

5. Attributes are activated an amount (S) that is determined by the time available and the task's requirements. Use of a matching attribute results in an increment in activation, while a nonmatch decrements the activity of an active attribute.

6. Activation of an attribute is accompanied by the permanent marking of the attribute with a sampled number of elements of the current environmental context from a universe of potential contextual elements. *Context* is used in a manner equivalent to the "stimulus sample" in stimulus sampling theory as proposed by Estes (1950).

7. Activation decays over time as a function of initial strength. The probability that an attribute remains active over a period of K sec is an exponentially

decreasing function of the length of the period and an increasing function of initial strength. Therefore, the probability that an attribute active at time T is still active K sec later can be defined mathematically as equal to $e^{-K/S}$.

The heart of the theoretical view is the *set principle*. Although a number of models offer "context effects" as a hypothetical construct in explaining memory in different tasks (both semantic and episodic), the set principle offers a mechanism for the operation of "semantic" context. We chose to use "set" rather than "priming" for two principle reasons. First and foremost, I see the postulated mechanism as a process that is continuous and consistent with other conceptions of set, i.e., not unlike *Einstellung* (Luchins, 1942) or "functional fixity (Duncker, 1945)." These, in my view, are the result of cognitive processing in the presence of ongoing active elements that influence that processing. I see "set" as an automatic effect of encoding a word in the presence of an active semantic context. Second, I feel that "priming" connotes a facilitation effect. I believe that "set" is neutral and that the same process that enhances lexical decisions is the process that increases competition or "trace confusability" in the distractor task.

According to the present view, the Brown–Peterson task is a hybrid of an immediate memory task and a task acting primarily on long-term or secondary memory. Wickens and his colleagues (Wickens, Moody, & Dow, 1981) have presented the case for a secondary memory component for the distractor task. In my view, the activation helps support the immediate memory of items. In fact, there is suggestive evidence (Gorfein & Viviani, 1980) that duration of activation is a "control" process. Thus under Principle 5, the participant activates semantic attributes for the duration necessary to optimize task performance.

The application of the theory to the heterophone experiment can readily be described. In that experiment, when there was a short intertrial interval, the items that were related to the secondary context had a stronger influence on the encoding of the heterophone, causing it to be encoded in a manner similar to the prior words and thereby creating difficulty in retrieving that item. Because in that condition the item tended to be "set" in the direction of the "secondary" meaning of the heterophone, it failed to compete with the Trial 4 item which was related to the primary meaning of the heterophone, producing PI release for that item. In the long intertrial interval condition, the activation of Trial 1 and 2 secondary items had a fair probability of decaying over the long intertrial interval. Therefore the heterophone had a higher probability of being encoded in its primary meaning, producing release on that item (lack of competition with prior items) and competition with the Trial 4 item.

The theory thus explains temporal release with two principles: First, the length of the interval results in a decay of activation of attributes from previous items. This reduces set in the encoding of the current (post-intertrial interval) to-be-remembered item. Therefore, there is less similarity to the encoding to the

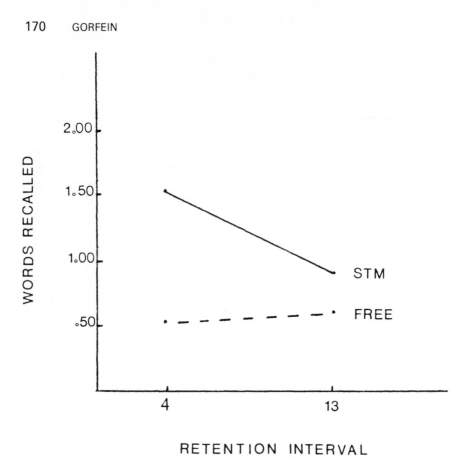

FIGURE 10.10.   Immediate and free recall of items originally presented in short-term memory as a function of original retention interval
(Gorfein & Spata, in preparation).

previous item and less competition. The second is that long intertrial intervals are
an opportunity for environmental context fluctuations that result in encoding and
retrieval contexts that are more unique to the current to-be-remembered item.

The theory is compatible with the other data cited. With respect to retention
intervals, we would expect performance to decline both with the decay of activation and the fluctuation in context. As shown in Figs. 10.1 and 10.4, on either
the first trial of an experiment (Keppel & Underwood, 1961) or on the first trial
following a semantic shift (Gorfein & Viviani, 1980), we obtain a flat curve as a
function of the duration of retention interval. The theory allows memory search
on the basis of either residual semantic activation or contextual information
retrieval. On the first trial of a material, even a minimum of residual activation
would act as a guide to memory and would allow immediate and accurate
performance due to the absence of similarly coded competitors.

The Bennett and Bennett (1974) finding (the need for experience with a preshift category to obtain semantic release on a category shift) is explainable with the set principle. An attribute that is high in an item's hierarchy will be activated and will tend to (select that attribute) set in the meaning of other words. With a nonsalient attribute, the probability of the attribute being activated will depend on one or more of the words having that attribute high enough in the hierarchy to be activated. The greater the number of words processed, the greater the likelihood that one of them will have the attribute high enough to be activated initially. In general, with salient attributes such as taxonomic category, this will not be a problem, since all or almost all of the words will have the taxonomic class as a high-level attribute.

In our theoretical view, environmental context is extremely important because retrieval (in the absence of activation) depends on the amount of contextual coding in order to guide the memory process. The longer retention period at 13 sec would allow more contextual fluctuation prior to retrieval, resulting in more environmental context information being attached to the retrieved item at 13 sec than at 4 sec. Thus, we might expect that the superiority of items recalled at short retention intervals observed in Brown–Peterson procedures would not have an advantage in a free recall of those items.

In the study by Gorfein and Spata cited previously, one of the variables manipulated was retention interval. Fig. 10.10 compares the performance at 4 and at 13 sec in the STM task with that in a subsequent free-recall task in which the participants were asked to recall all the words from a prior block of 16 trials. The advantage of the short retention interval for performance in the Brown–Peterson task does not carry over to long-term retrieval even when we consider retrieval as an additional opportunity to rehearse (approximately 1½ items are rehearsed at 4 sec for every one item rehearsed at 13).

BEYOND THE BROWN–PETERSON TASK

The *set principle* can be understood as basic to the functioning of semantic memory. As such it predicts (postdicts) the occurrence of unidirectionality in lexical priming experiments. Priming depends on the activated attributes of the first (prime) item being part of the attribute hierarchy of the to-be-primed item. In the illustration cited under Principle 4 of the theory we see an example of a situation where word "Y" primes word "Z" but "Z" does not serve as a prime for "Y." We are currently involved in a program of research to make the hypothetical point concrete, i.e., to use items in a known attribute hierarchy in the lexical task.

The theory has generality to the long-term memory literature, because the set principle provides a mechanism for "encoding specificity [Tulving & Thomson, 1973]." We believe that the set principle can be applied to any cognitive processing. To the degree that the organism's activity has elements (attributes) in common with the materials being processed, they will be selected for use in that process. Attributes that are selected may facilitate performance in priming studies, as in lexical decision experiments, or may inhibit performance by increasing item similarity and producing PI in STM studies. We are moving ahead in investigating the generality of our principle.

11 Temporal Context and Recency

Arthur M. Glenberg
University of Wisconsin, Madison

Since Ebbinghaus's time, theories of memory have had to prove their mettle by accounting for recency effects in recall. The recency effect is the dramatic improvement in recall for items near the end of a series of to-be-remembered (TBR) elements. It is found in a variety of situations including free recall, serial recall (as in Ebbinghaus's research), and recall from generic memory (see Crowder, 1976, for a review). The recency effect takes on added significance when it is considered from a different perspective: The effect is also a forgetting curve; information presented nearest in time to the recall test is remembered best, information presented farther removed from the test is, generally, recalled less. Thus understanding recency effects may hold one of the keys to an understanding of remembering and forgetting in general.

In this chapter I review evidence consistent with a temporal distinctiveness account of recency effects that are found in free recall. This account goes a long way toward explaining recency effects found when certain constraints are met. I begin with and focus on a description of the long-term recency effect because data from that domain prompted development of the distinctiveness account.

LONG-TERM RECENCY AND THE RATIO RULE

At one time it seemed clear that the recency effect in free recall was produced by retrieving the last few items in a series from some form of limited capacity short-term rehearsal buffer (e.g., Atkinson & Shiffrin, 1968). Although the details differed from theory to theory, the "modal" model did a credible job of accounting for the recency effect, negative recency effect (Craik, 1970), effects of

173

interpolated activity on the size of recency effects (Glanzer & Cunitz, 1966), as well as other related phenomena.

Trouble for the short-term buffer account of recency began to appear in the early 1970s. For example, Baddeley and Hitch (1974, 1977) reported that the recency effect could be found even when short-term store was engaged in maintaining a sizeable amount of information. The introduction of a distractor paradigm by Whitten and Bjork (1972; Bjork & Whitten, 1974) produced further trouble for the modal account. In an attempt to eliminate serial position effects, Whitten and Bjork interpolated a series of mathematics distractor problems into the interpresentation interval (IPI) before each TBR item and into a long retention interval (RI) following the last TBR item. Contrary to predictions from the modal model, both recency and primacy effects were found. Apparently, interpolating distractor activity into the IPIs insulated the recency effect from the consequences of a distractor-filled RI, even when the length of the RI was beyond the usual extent of a short-term buffer. Bjork and Whitten (1974) went on to demonstrate that this long-term recency effect is much reduced (or nonexistent) when memory is assessed by a recognition procedure rather than a recall procedure (later replicated by Glenberg & Kraus, 1981), thus strengthening the case for a retrieval interpretation of the effect as discussed in the next section. By comparing across a number of experiments and procedures, Bjork and Whitten adduced a ratio rule: Recency effects are positively correlated with the ratio of the IPI to the RI. In standard free recall, when both the IPI and the RI are short (e.g., less than a second), recency is robust. When the IPI is short (e.g., less than a second) relative to the RI (e.g., 15 sec, see Glanzer & Cunitz, 1966) recency is reduced. In the distractor paradigm, the IPI may be substantial (e.g., 4–30 sec), and so a recency effect is found even with a long RI.

The ratio rule was demonstrated quantitatively by Glenberg, Bradley, Kraus, and Renzaglia (1983). As a measure of the size of the recency effect, they used the slope of the least-squares regression line relating proportion recalled to serial position over the last three serial positions. (This slope is equal to half the difference between recall of the last and third to last TBR items.) This measure captures the notion of recency as a dramatic improvement in recall, and, to the extent that ceiling and floor effects are avoided, it does not depend on the absolute level of recall. Glenberg et al. (1983) reanalyzed data from an earlier publication (Glenberg, Bradley, Stevenson, Kraus, Tkachuk, Gretz, Fish, & Turpin, 1980) that reported data from the distractor paradigm using IPIs of 4, 12, and 36 sec, and RIs of 12, 36, and 72 sec. As suggested by the ratio rule, the size of recency increased with the ratio of the IPI and the RI. Specifically, 86% of the variability among the mean size of recency scores was accounted for by the linear relationship between the size of the recency effect and the logarithm of the ratio of the IPI to the RI. Glenberg et al. (1983) went on to modify the paradigm so that it could be used to examine recency effects for IPIs of 5 min, 20 min, 1 day, and 7 days and RIs of 40 min, 1 day, and 14 days. For these data, the linear relationship between the mean size of recency and the logarithm of the ratio of the IPI to the RI accounted for 91% of the variability in the recency scores. Thus, the ratio rule applies to recency effects found after a few days as well as after a few seconds. Apparently a basic memory process is being tapped.

TEMPORAL DISTINCTIVENESS THEORY

Bjork and Whitten (1974) and Crowder (1976) proposed an account of the ratio rule in terms of an analogy to vision: When sighting along a series of telephone poles (e.g., down a railroad track), those poles nearer to the observer (more recent) appear more distinct than those farther away. Furthermore, the relatively nondistinct poles can be made more distinctive by increasing their separation (IPI). The temporal distinctiveness theory presented here and in Glenberg and Swanson (1986) translates this analogy into a memory model. The distinctiveness account is related to some of my work describing the use of context in retrieval (e.g., Glenberg et al., 1983), and it takes into consideration arguments advanced by Gardiner (1983), as well as data presented in Glenberg and Swanson (and in this chapter) illustrating the specific temporal nature of the effects.

In overview, the theory proposes that subjects attempt retrieval by forming multiple, temporally defined search sets. Each search set includes items presented during a particular temporal interval. Success in the recall task depends on the distribution of items within the search sets: When an item is alone in a search set, it is temporally distinctive and recalled well. Thus the theory describes how temporal information, that is, temporal context, plays a role in generating the recency effect.

Temporal distinctiveness theory is not a complete model of memory; it does not address questions regarding the structure of memory, nor does it take into account all that we have learned regarding memory processes, such as rehearsal, organization, or levels of processing. It deals only with retrieval from memory under the following relatively impoverished conditions. First, the memorizer has not engaged in mnemonic activities that would organize or interassociate TBR information. I am not claiming that these activities are unimportant, only that temporal distinctiveness theory is not designed to account for the effects of these mnemonic activities. Second, the retrieval environment is devoid of cues presented by the experimenter (e.g., associates or category names). Also, many self-generated cues that a subject might otherwise use (e.g., themes of self-generated stories) are obviated by this condition. What is left is a situation in which a subject experiences a sequence of TBR items, each presented and processed during a specific temporal interval. The theory addresses how subjects use temporal information in recall.

The first assumption of distinctiveness theory is that the trace of a TBR item includes a component representing the time of presentation of that item. Importantly, the component does not specify the time of presentation exactly, instead, it is assumed that a distribution of possible presentation times are more or less

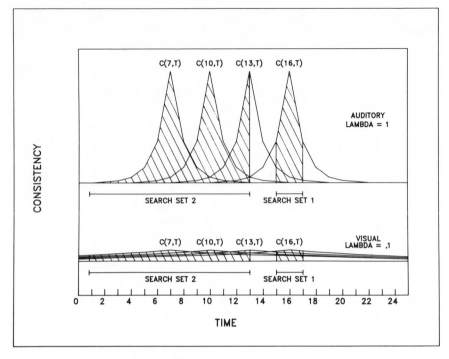

FIGURE 11.1.   Each curve represents the consistency ($c(t_i, t)$ on the ordinate) of the representation of time of presentation for an item encoded at time t_i with other times (t). The curves near the top of the figure represent fine-grained encoding of time of presentation, those near the bottom represent coarse-grained encoding of time of presentation. Also illustrated are the temporal boundaries (widths) of search sets centered on the presentation times for Items one (left) and four (right). The degree to which each item is included in a search set corresponds to the shading of the consistency functions. *Note.* From "A temporal distinctiveness theory of recency and modality effects" by A. M. Glenberg and N. G. Swanson, 1986, *Journal of Experimental Psychology: Learning, Memory, and Cognition,* 12, p. 5. Copyright 1986 by the American Psychological Association. Reprinted by permission.

consistent with the encoded time of presentation. A series of consistency functions is illustrated in Fig. 11.1.

The value of $c(t_i, t)$ is the consistency of a time t with the component encoding time of presentation of an item presented at time t_i. The actual time of presentation is always the most consistent with the encoded component, and times further removed from the actual time decrease in consistency. Until we learn more about what produces consistency functions, their exact form is unspecified by the general theory. For computational ease, double exponential functions are used in fitting the specific mathematical model discussed here. The model has a free parameter, lambda, indexing the rate of decay of the exponential, or the spread of the consistency function. Specifically:

$$c(t_i, t) = \lambda \exp(-\lambda \mid t_i - t \mid). \tag{1}$$

The parameter can be thought of as an index of the grain of temporal encoding. A small lambda (see bottom of Fig. 11.1) corresponds to a large grain, or equivalently, a wide consistency function. A large lambda (see top of Fig. 11.1) indicates a fine-grained encoding of time of presentation so that only a narrow band of times are consistent with the encoded time of presentation. As demonstrated later, factors that affect the size of lambda have a large influence on recall.

Given impoverished retrieval conditions, retrieval proceeds by defining multiple search sets in the temporal domain. Two such search sets are illustrated in Fig. 11.1. Three assumptions are made about the operation of the search sets. First, the width of the search set (its temporal extent) increases as the temporal distance between the center of the search set and the recall test increases. This assumption is consistent with results of Bellezza (1982). In the mathematical model, the temporal extent of a search set centered at time t_j, when the recall test is at time t_t, is given by

$$\text{width}_j = w_2 \times \ln(t_t - t_j - w_1). \tag{2}$$

The w_1 parameter allows for the reinstatement of the temporal context w_1 sec preceding the test, so that widening of the search set does not begin until that point. The w_2 parameter is for scaling.

The second assumption is that the probability of retrieving an item from a search set is a function of the number of items included in the search set. Specifically, the membership of an item in a search set is given by the area under the item's consistency function bounded by the search set. Membership in a search set is indicated by shading in Fig. 11.1. Referring to the figure, membership in search set 1 of the item presented at time 16 is greater than the membership in search set 1 of the item presented at time 13. The probability of retrieving a specific item from a search set is the degree of membership of that item in the search set divided by the sum of the memberships in the search set (plus a noise index). This is a cue-overload assumption: The more items included in a search set, the less likely any one of them is retrieved. The noise index, $\text{width}_j \times n$, represents noise included in the search set, (e.g., the subject's thoughts) that decreases the probability that any trace is retrieved.

Finally, the theory includes the assumption that subjects construct multiple search sets. As specified by the previous assumptions, those search sets that are centered near the end of the list are temporally constrained (width_j is small); those centered on earlier times are temporally more extensive. Probability of recall is determined by combining the independent probabilities of retrieval of a given item from all search sets.

Currently, the theory does not specify the number or location of the search sets. Fitting the quantitative model requires two stages. In the first stage a free parameter is assigned to each serial position to index the probability of forming a search set at that location. In the second stage, inspection of the values of these parameters is used to induce a retrieval strategy (which can usually be captured with one free parameter) for a second fit. For the fits illustrated in Figs. 11.3, 11.4, and 11.6 the following retrieval strategy was used. The probability of forming a search set centered on position j, $draw_j$, for a list of length L is

$$(3) \ draw_j = \begin{cases} d + (1 - d)/2 & \text{for } J = 1 \\ 0 & \text{for } 1 < j < L - 2 \\ d & \text{for } J = L - 2 \\ d + (1 - d)/2 & \text{for } J = L - 1 \\ 1 & \text{for } J = L \end{cases}$$

where d is a free parameter (without a clear psychological interpretation) bounded by 0 and 1.

Clearly, the theory is limited. It does not attempt to deal with more complex retrieval situations, such as when both temporal and semantic cues are available. As mentioned previously, it does not deal with factors such as organization, levels of processing, or differential rehearsal. Indeed, the model does not predict the usual primacy effect. This should not be considered a liability, however because the theory is meant only to explicate use of temporal context. Glenberg et al. (1980) demonstrated that the primacy effect (at least in the distractor paradigm) is completely attributable to differential rehearsal of the first few list items. As will be evident in the data presented shortly, when the experimental procedures strongly discourage differential rehearsal, the long-term primacy effect is greatly reduced or eliminated.

The theory explains the recency effect as follows. When subjects attempt to retrieve the most recent TBR items, the search set will be relatively narrow (e.g., search set 1 in the upper portion of Fig. 11.1), and it will include the last TBR item and few others. That is, within the end-of-list search set, the last item is temporally distinct and recalled well. In attempting to retrieve TBR items presented earlier, the search set is wider so that multiple items are included in the search set (e.g., search set 2 in Fig. 11.1). Consequently, none of these items is distinct and none is recalled well.

TESTING DISTINCTIVENESS THEORY

The theory is consistent with data from a number of sources. First, it provides an explanation for the ratio rule that recency effects are positively correlated with the IPI to RI ratio. As the RI increases (reducing the ratio), the end-of-list search set becomes wider (see Equation 2). Because the search set is wider, more TBR items are included and recall drops, thereby reducing the recency effect. Even with a wide end-of-list search set, the recency effect can be reinstated by increasing the IPI (increasing the ratio). Increasing the IPI increases the separation between the consistency functions. With a greater separation, the last item will be temporally distinctive even in a wide end-of-list search set, reinstating the recency effect.

Fig. 11.2 illustrates the quantitative fit of the model to the ratio rule data from

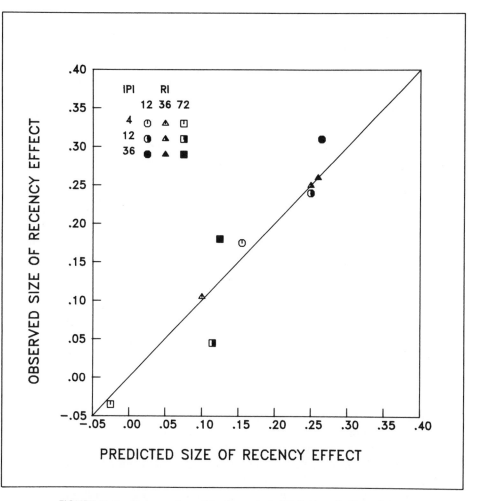

FIGURE 11.2. Data are from Glenberg et al. (1980, Exp. 1). Size of the recency effect is the slope over the last three serial positions. Since RI was a between-subject variable, different parameter estimates were obtained for each level of the RI. Parameter estimates may be obtained from the author.

Glenberg et al. (1980). Each symbol represents a specific combination of IPIs and RIs. The position of the symbol relative to the ordinate indicates the observed size of recency, whereas the abscissa gives the predicted size of recency. The ratio rule is illustrated by the increase in the observed size of recency as the IPI increases (going from open to solid symbols) for any given RI (geometrical shape). Fit of the model is indicated by the extent to which the symbols fall on the diagonal.

The theory also accounts for the level of recall effect found with the distractor paradigm (Glenberg et al. 1980, 1983; the effect can also be seen in Greene & Crowder, 1984). This effect is that at a constant RI, the absolute level of recall of the last TBR item increases with the length of the IPI. The effect is probably closely related to the "release from proactive interference" found with long intertrial times in the Brown–Peterson paradigm (Loess & Waugh, 1967). According to temporal distinctiveness theory, increasing the IPI tends to temporally isolate successive items. As the final TBR item becomes more isolated from its predecessor, it is more likely to be the sole item in the end-of-list search set and recall increases.

An illustration of the level-of-recall effect and the fit of the model comes from Glenberg and Swanson (1986). This experiment (as well as others from my laboratory reported later) used a variant of the distractor procedure designed to eliminate displaced rehearsal of TBR items and yet maintain a reasonable level of recall. The TBR items were pairs of common words presented over a loudspeaker. Subjects were required to respond to each pair by pressing one of two buttons to indicate which of the words referred to the larger object. Pairs were presented for 2.5 sec. The distractor task during both the IPIs and the RI consisted of two components. A three-term addition problem with an answer was presented on a display terminal every 2 sec. The subjects were required to press one of two buttons to indicate whether or not the answer was the correct sum. Subjects' responses were monitored by a computer and difficulty of the problems adjusted to maintain performance at 80% correct. While responding to the addition task, subjects were required to engage in an articulatory suppression task by overtly saying the syllable "bla" 3–4 times a sec.

In Glenberg and Swanson's Experiment 2, each list was followed by a 20-sec RI. One important independent variable was the location of a 20-sec isolating interval. It was inserted before the first TBR item (Condition B1) before the third (B3), or before the last (B5). All other IPIs were 0 sec.

The results are illustrated on the left-hand side of Fig. 11.3. Predictions derived from the mathematical model appear on the right-hand side of the figure. Comparison of the two sides of the figure demonstrates that the model captures the major trends in the data. One important trend is the level of recall of the last TBR item when it is preceded by a 0-sec IPI (Condition B1 and B3) compared with when it is preceded by a 20-sec isolating interval (Condition B5). The observed increase in recall with the longer interval (Condition B5) is the level of

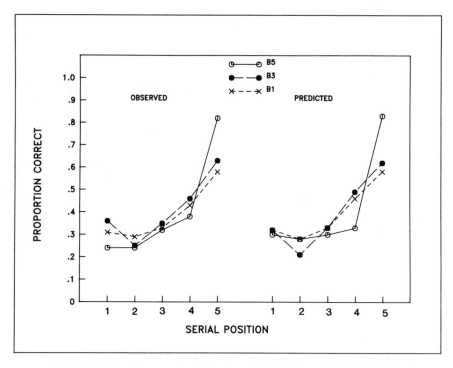

FIGURE 11.3. Data are from Glenberg and Swanson (1986, Exp. 2). Proportion recalled as a function of serial position and location of a 20-sec distractor interval (before the last TBR item, B5; before the third TBR item, B3; before the first TBR item, B1). Parameters for the distinctiveness model are lambda = 0.27, w_1 = 21.99, w_2 = 1.46, n = 0.053, d = 0.24, RMSE = 0.05.

recall effect. Presumably, it reflects greater temporal distinctiveness of the last item in the end-of-list search set.

The foregoing reasoning suggests that a very large IPI can affect recall at earlier serial positions. In their Experiment 3, Glenberg and Swanson compared the effects of a 40-sec IPI and a 4-sec IPI between the first and second TBR items (pairs of auditory words). All other IPIs were 4 sec and the RI was 10 sec. Although the search set used in retrieving the initial item is very wide (see, for example, Fig. 11.1), if the initial item is sufficiently segregated from the second item, the initial item will be temporally distinct and recalled well. (Imagine the consistency function on the far left in the upper part of Fig. 11.1 shifted much farther to the left, thus representing an initial item presented much earlier than the others. A search set centered at the time this item was presented will be consistent with few other items.) The data in Fig. 11.4 confirm this prediction. Note that the initial item in the 40-sec condition has a substantially longer total

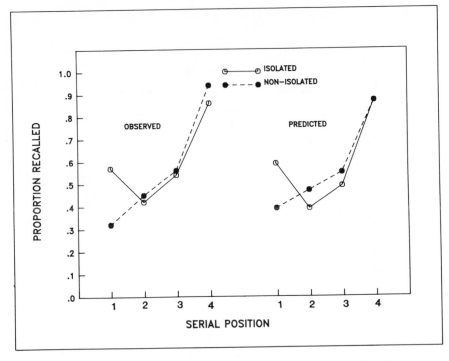

FIGURE 11.4. Data are from Glenberg and Swanson (1986, Exp. 3). The dashed line illustrates recall in the control condition in which all TBR pairs were preceded by a 4-sec interval. The solid line illustrates recall when the first and second pairs were separated by a 40-sec interval. Parameters for the distinctiveness model are lambda = 0.66, w_1 = 12.55, w_2 = 1.39, n = 0.01, d = 0.58, RMSE = 0.05.

retention interval than the initial item in the 4-sec condition. Nonetheless, the temporally isolated item is recalled better. Once again, the predictions illustrated in the right-hand part of the figure capture the major trends in the data.

According to the distinctiveness theory, the recency effect arises when subjects use a temporally based retrieval strategy. Thus changing the retrieval strategy should change the recency effect. This is probably why Bjork and Whitten (1974) and Glenberg and Kraus (1981) failed to find long-term recency effects using a recognition procedure. When given copy cues, subjects need not rely primarily on the temporal context. Greene and Crowder (1984) demonstrated that categorical similarity between TBR items also reduces the long-term recency effect. Categorical similarity may disrupt the use of temporal search sets in at least two ways. First, the similarity may encourage displaced rehearsal which would smear temporal cues. Second, subjects may use the category name as a retrieval cue instead of temporal cues.

SPECIFICITY OF TEMPORAL SEARCH SETS

Baddeley and Hitch (1974, 1977) suggested that recency may arise from the operation of an ordinal retrieval strategy applied to any memory organization (e.g., items in working memory, or items in any grouping in long-term store such as "movies seen recently"). Thus separate recency effects may be observed for each of the organizations. In an earlier paper (Glenberg et al., 1983), I demonstrated that this proposal was incomplete; one must also consider the temporal distribution of TBR items within an organization. Nonetheless, the idea that multiple recency effects can be generated is intriguing and almost surely correct. That is, people would almost certainly generate separate recency effects in recalling, for example, the movies seen recently, the sporting events watched, and the graduate degree committees on which they have served.

Watkins and Peynircioglu (1983) made this point experimentally by demonstrating three recency effects at the same time. Three different types of stimuli (e.g., riddles, sounds, and objects) were mixed in a single list, each stimulus being presented for 10 sec. They observed a recency effect for each type of stimulus in the list, consistent with the view that multiple recency effects can be obtained for different organizations. A critical feature of their procedure may well have been the mixing of the different types of stimuli and the relatively long presentation intervals. These two features ensure a relatively long temporal spacing (IPI) between successive items of the same type. With this temporal spacing, the last few items in any organization are temporally distinct from the initial items in the organization, and a recency effect is predicted by temporal distinctiveness theory.

The Watkins and Peynircioglu results force a modification in the conception of a search set in temporal distinctiveness theory. The demonstration of multiple recency effects implies that search sets may be specific to specific types of items, or organizations, in addition to being specific to temporal intervals represented within those organizations.

Working with this extension, Huang and Glenberg (1986) examined the possibility that temporal search sets are specific to modality of presentation and stimulus familiarity. They used a combination of the distractor paradigm and a "suffix" procedure. Following the last TBR pair and a 10-sec RI, a suffix item was presented. Subjects processed the suffix using the same orienting task as that used to process the TBR items, although subjects were not responsible for remembering the suffix. In fact, the suffix was already printed on the top of the subject's response sheet. In the control condition a buzzer, but no suffix, followed the RI.

Huang and Glenberg reasoned that if a suffix could be excluded from a search set, it would not interfere with recall of items from that search set. Thus, noninterference between two types of items can be used to indicate dimensions to which search sets are sensitive.

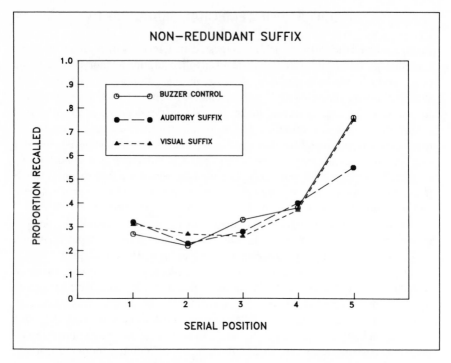

FIGURE 11.5.   Proportion recalled as a function of serial position and suffix condition. *Note.* From "Echoic and retrieval accounts of the long-term modality effect tested using the suffix procedure" by S-T. Huang and A. M. Glenberg, 1986, *American Journal of Psychology*, 99, p. 466. Copyright 1986 by the Board of Trustees of the University of Illinois. Reprinted by permission.

In one experiment the TBR stimuli were pairs of auditory words separated by 4-sec IPIs. The independent variable was suffix presentation modality, auditory, visual, or presentation of the buzzer instead of a suffix. In this experiment the suffix was nonredundant in that it changed from list to list. The data are reproduced in Fig. 11.5. The auditory suffix greatly reduced recall from the end of the list. Presumably, the auditory suffix could not be excluded from the end-of-list search set that was constructed to retrieve auditory TBR items. On the other hand, the visual nonredundant suffix did not affect recall. Thus Huang and Glenberg concluded that search sets can be modality-specific.

An alternative interpretation of the results in Fig. 11.5 is that the auditory suffix interfered with echoic information that would otherwise enhance recall of the last few auditory TBR items. This alternative is ruled out, however, by the results from another of Huang and Glenberg's experiments. In that experiment the same (redundant) suffix was used in each list requiring a suffix. The redundant auditory suffix should disrupt echoic information as well as the nonredundant auditory suffix. In contrast to this prediction, however, compared with the buzzer control condition, the redundant auditory suffix resulted in a nonsignificant 4% decrease in recall in the last serial position. Thus, the disruption illustrated in Fig. 11.5 cannot be accounted for by echoic mechanisms alone.

The contrast between Huang and Glenberg's nonredundant and redundant suffix experiments suggests that search sets are sensitive to an experiential factor, namely, redundancy or well-learnedness. Apparently, the representation of an episodically well-learned stimulus (such as a redundant suffix) can be excluded from a search set consisting of representations otherwise very similar to the excluded representation. This suggestion is in line with Hayes–Roth's (1977) demonstration that overlearned stimuli do not interfere with learning and retrieval of other stimuli.

THE MODALITY EFFECT

Gardiner and Gregg (1979) used a variant of the distractor procedure and manipulated the modality of the TBR items. They found a much more pronounced recency effect for auditory than for visual presentation. This long-term modality effect is quite robust, and it does not seem to be either artifactual or related to well-known mechanisms. For example, Glenberg (1984) demonstrated that the effect is found in the absence of rehearsal of TBR items, and it is not dependent on a specific output order. Also, given that a redundant auditory suffix does not eliminate the auditory recency effect (Huang & Glenberg, 1986), it is unlikely that the long-term modality effect reflects echoic mechanisms.

The temporal distinctiveness account of recency can model the long-term modality effect with the addition of a single assumption: Visual presentation produces less-accurate (larger grain) encoding of time of presentation than does auditory presentation. Thus the consistency functions for visual items (bottom of Fig. 11.1) are flatter and overlap to a greater degree than those for auditory items (top of Fig. 11.1). A consequence of increasing the grain is reduction of recall at the end of the list: Because the consistency functions are so flat, even with a temporally constrained end-of-list search set (such as search set 1 in Fig. 11.1), many visual TBR items will be included in the end-of-list search set. Because retrieval is a function of the number of traces included in the search set, retrieval of visual items from an end-of-list search set will be depressed, compared with retrieval of auditory items.

According to the temporal distinctiveness account, the difference between auditory and visual presentation is generally confined to the end of the list for two reasons. First, middle- and beginning-of-list search sets are wide (e.g., search set 2 in Fig. 11.1). These wide search sets are overloaded (contain many TBR items) regardless of modality, so modality differences are small. Second, visually presented TBR items in the beginning of the list actually have a small advantage over auditory items presented in the beginning of the list. Because the visual consistency functions are flat, visual items presented in the beginning of the list have some probability of being retrieved from end-of-list search sets in addition to beginning-of-list search sets. Indeed, visual presentation occasionally produces superior recall in the primacy portion of the serial position function (see, for example, Gardiner & Gregg, 1979; Glenberg, 1984; and Fig. 11.6 in this chapter).

In principle, the distinctiveness theory can model the long-term modality effect. Is there any evidence, however, that auditory and visual presentation differ in the degree to which time of presentation is encoded? Some such evidence was reported by Metcalfe, Glavanov, and Murdock (1981). In their experiment, auditory and visual stimuli were presented in various spatial locations. Recall was by temporal order of presentation or by spatial location of presentation. Recall by temporal order produced an auditory advantage, whereas recall by spatial location produced a slight visual advantage. One interpretation of these results is that auditory presentation produces a finer grained encoding of time of presentation than does visual presentation, a difference revealed when recall is constrained by temporal order.

Data from Glenberg and Swanson also illustrate the differential sensitivity of auditory and visual presentation to temporal factors. Referring to Fig. 11.3, inserting a 20-sec isolating interval before the item presented in position 5 increased recall of the auditory items 24% (from Condition B1 to Condition B5). In that same experiment, in response to the same manipulation, the corresponding change in recall of visual items was only 6% (from 38% to 44%). A similar difference in sensitivity to temporal factors was found in Glenberg and Swanson's Experiment 3 (see Fig. 11.4). When the first auditory item was separated from the second auditory item by a 40-sec interval, recall of the first auditory item increased by 20%. The corresponding change for visual presentation (not illustrated in Fig. 11.4) was a 4% decrement (from 44% to 40%).

The data in Fig. 11.6 are also instructive on this point. The data are from an unpublished experiment using our standard methodology (pairs of TBR words studied with an orienting task, distractor task of math problems and articulatory suppression). In this experiment, two variables were factorially manipulated, modality of presentation and ratio of the IPI to the RI. For one group of subjects, the IPI was 8 sec and the RI 10 sec, resulting in a fairly large ratio, a large recency effect, and a large modality effect. For the other group, the IPI was 4 sec and the RI was 16 sec, resulting in a smaller ratio, a smaller recency effect, and a smaller modality effect. The data also illustrate the superiority of visual presentation in the beginning of the list. Now focus on just the results for auditory items (filled circles). Note that the last few auditory items are sensitive to the ratio of the IPI to the RI: The greater the ratio, the greater recency effect (slope across the last three serial positions). Now focus on the results for the visual items (crosses). The size

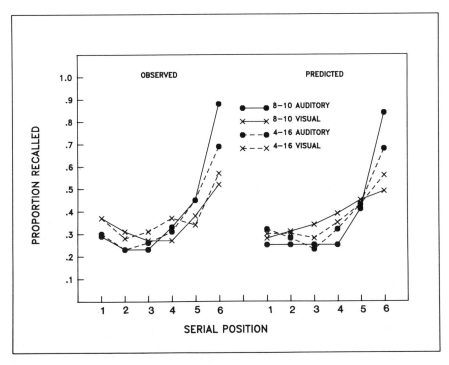

FIGURE 11.6.   Proportion recalled as a function of serial position, presentation modality, and IPI/RI condition. Separate parameter estimates were obtained for the two between-subject IPI/RI conditions.

of the recency effect is hardly changed by the ratio manipulation. In fact, recall of the last visual TBR item actually increased slightly as the ratio decreased. Clearly, visual presentation is not as sensitive to temporal manipulations as is auditory presentation.

Recent work from my laboratory using a different task converges on the supposition that auditory presentation encodes time of presentation more accurately than visual presentation. In this experiment, subjects studied lists of six pairs of TBR items in the distractor paradigm. Each list was followed by a 10-sec RI. For one-third of the lists, memory was tested by free recall; for the majority of the lists memory for order was tested. Each order judgment required the subject to indicate which of two TBR items was the most recent. The two TBR items were either the first two, the middle two, or the last two on the list. The IPI separating the pairs at presentation was 0, 4, or 16 sec.

The data in Table 11.1 show the differences between auditory and visual presentation in accuracy of order judgments. The distinctiveness theory makes three predictions about the order judgments. First, if auditory presentation results in more accurate encoding of time of presentation than visual presentation, then

TABLE 11.1
Difference Between Auditory and Visual Presentation in
Accuracy of Order Judgments

	Location of Tested Pairs			
	Beginning	Middle	End	$\bar{X}$
IPI (sec)				
0	.04	.03	.01	.03
4	.05	.05	.07	.06
16	.15	−.07	.14	.07
$\bar{X}$	.08	.00	.07	

the recency judgments should be more accurate for auditory presentation. Indeed, auditory presentation was more accurate than visual presentation in eight of the nine conditions listed in Table 11.1.

Second, if auditory presentation is more sensitive to temporal manipulations, then the superiority of auditory recency judgments over visual recency judgments should increase with the IPI. This trend can be seen in the last column of Table 11.1.

Finally, we can consider auditory superiority as a function of serial position (beginning, middle, or end of the list). According to the distinctiveness account, time of presentation is encoded more accurately for auditory presentation than for visual presentation at all serial positions. In recall, this difference is not observed at the earlier serial positions because subjects must use wide (and thus overloaded) temporal search sets to retrieve the primacy and middle items. Temporal search sets are probably less important for the recency judgment task because presentation of the TBR items themselves should provide access to the traces without the necessity of forming a temporal search set. Thus in the recency judgment task, differences between auditory and visual presentation should be found at all serial positions, not just the end of the list.

Data from the last row in Table 11.1 are more or less consistent with this prediction. Accuracy of recency judgments is greater following auditory presentation than following visual presentation for both the initial positions and the end positions. Why there was a reversal for the middle items (found only in the 16-sec IPI condition) is unclear.

FUTURE DEVELOPMENT OF THE TEMPORAL DISTINCTIVENESS THEORY

The temporal distinctiveness account of recency provides a coherent account for a number of phenomena associated with recency effects. These phenomena include the ratio rule, the level-of-recall effect, and auditory superiority. Also, as illustrated in the previous section, we are now starting to produce evidence pointing to the specific temporal nature of these phenomena. Nevertheless, temporal distinctiveness theory needs to be developed in several directions, including specification of the basic processes that produce consistency functions, and an account of why search sets increase in temporal extent.

One possible mechanism of temporal coding is that it arises from processing stimuli within a system specialized for speech, such as Crowder's (1983) "grid" model of Precategorical Acoustic Store (PAS). In the grid model a speech stimulus is encoded on a grid formed by the dimensions of time of arrival and source channel. The system extracts features from the acoustic stream and integrates information from other sense modalities (e.g., lip movements) when encoding the stimulus. The system also serves as a rudimentary memory, holding sensory information for a few seconds. Clearly, the memory function of PAS cannot account for the effects reported here; echoic information is too labile to produce the long-term modality differences noted in this chapter. Nonetheless, passage of auditory information through PAS might result in more accurate temporal coding for auditory information than for visual information.

Relating temporal coding to PAS has four complementary benefits. First, it links the distinctiveness account to the standard modality effect and the recent advances Crowder has made reformulating PAS theory (e.g., Crowder, 1983; Greene & Crowder, 1984). Because the grid model provides a mechanism for synthesizing auditory features from multiple sources including vision and proprioception, PAS theory can now account for some of the data regarding lip-read and mouthed stimuli.

Second, this linkage provides a rationale for why memory for auditory items is more sensitive to temporal factors than is memory for visual items. Namely, auditory items are processed by PAS, visual items are not.

Third, the grid model of PAS explicitly requires a representation of time of presentation (or time of arrival). Thus coding of time of presentation can serve both the operation of PAS and temporal distinctiveness theory.

The fourth benefit of linking temporal coding and PAS is to extend the importance of PAS for language processing. As originally conceived, PAS was specialized for speech processing: It facilitated analysis and integration of the acoustic signal encoding words. The integration of words into meaningful propositions was given less consideration. This second sort of integration requires a relatively accurate representation of the sequence of lexical items because grammatical and semantic constraints can extend over many words. Although some accounts of language processing assign the function of maintaining the order of a sequence of words to short-term store (STS), this assignment is rather inelegant. For example, most models of STS propose rather strict limits on the capacity of STS, and yet the extent of grammatical constraints can be quite large. Also, representation of order in STS may require an active rehearsal process, such as Baddeley and Hitch's (1977) "articulatory loop." My own introspections (at least) rarely reveal any sort of repetitive cycling of words while listening to speech.

Temporal distinctiveness theory may solve both of these problems. According to the theory, the representation of time of presentation is included in each trace rather than in a specific memory store. Thus there is no absolute limit as to how far back ordinal grammatical constraints can operate successfully, just a gradual decrease in effectiveness as search sets are widened. Second, maintenance of order does not require an active process. Instead, the burden is placed on retrieval or utilization of order information. That the burden should be on utilization makes sense: As successive words are being processed the extent of the constraints the words engender cannot be known perfectly, thus it makes little sense to expend great effort on actively maintaining order.

Thus, there are theoretical benefits to be gained by linking temporal coding and PAS. Nonetheless, to date there is little empirical evidence consistent with this speculation.

12

The Context of Remembering: Comments on the Chapters by Glenberg, Gorfein, and Wickens

Robert G. Crowder
Yale University

Robert L. Greene
Case Western Reserve University

We begin these remarks by discussing the general status of the concept of context in the study of human learning and memory following the lead of Professor Wickens. First a quotation from Underwood (1977) on temporal codes in memory:

> No single concept is so widely used in theories of memory functioning as the concept of context . . . . never in the history of choice of theoretical mechanisms has one been chosen that has so little support in direct evidence. (p. 43)

Wickens' paper emphasizes that the gap has been closed somewhat in the intervening years, particularly in experiments on the "stay and change" manipulation in both humans and animals. But does the application of the concept in human learning and memory match its sources of empirical support? We think not.

OUR THEORETICAL USE OF CONTEXT

Memory theory cannot do without some representation of the passing of time. McGeoch (1942), having trashed one such representation in his attack on decay theory, embraced another by announcing contextual change (altered stimulus conditions) as one of his three principles of forgetting. We are speaking here of context-alpha to use Wickens' useful distinction; context-beta is only a distant relative of the mechanism that McGeoch had in mind. After McGeoch's time, an unbroken chain can then be traced through influential formal statements that had "contextual drift" (Bower's term) across time as a central working part (Anderson & Bower, 1973; Bower, 1972; Estes, 1955; Glenberg, 1979; Raaijkmakers & Shiffrin, 1981). Contextual drift carries heavy explanatory burdens in at least the following five research areas:

(1) *Lag effects.* The relation between context-alpha and context-beta in research and theory on lag effects has been especially confused: Many of the early experiments were designed like Madigan's (1969) study using homographs to manipulate context-beta. However, theories of contextual drift (context-alpha), such as Estes' (1955), have seemed necessary, if not sufficient, to handle the full range of results in lag experiments, particularly the interaction of presentation lag with testing lag (see Glenberg & Lehmann, 1980).

(2) *Memory for duration.* Block (e.g., 1982) argued that the duration of an episode is represented in memory proportionally to the amount of contextual change there has been during the episode. Although this is an intuitively comfortable notion, and one that is related to a widely believed mechanism (Ornstein, 1969), Block's experiments on contextual change and remembered duration have not been unanimous in supporting it directly.

(3) *Amnesia.* Wickelgren's (1979) theory of amnesia—based on vertical and horizontal associations—includes the assumption that amnesia patients are unable to associate events with context. This fits the clinical observation of "source amnesia" almost perfectly. However, recent evidence (Graf, Squire, & Mandler, 1984) suggests that the explicit-implicit distinction is more fruitful than the item-context distinction in understanding amnesia. For example, Winocur and Kinsbourne (1978) found that amnesia patients were sensitive to a room shift insofar as there was less retroactive inhibition when interfering materials were learned in different contexts than when they were learned in the same context.

(4) *Recency.* The discovery of long-term recency having robbed us of our tried-and-true explanation of recency as a *primary memory* phenomenon (see Glenberg's paper, this volume), many workers turned to time and its surrogate, context, as explanatory principles. Glenberg, in the conference which preceded this book, has been most explicit in such theories. We think the argument rests mainly on faith. No effort has been made to isolate and manipulate particular cues from the context that might guide retrieval in such a way as to produce recency. The temporal parameters themselves—relative spacing—do have an effect and perhaps for this reason Glenberg is increasingly speaking of abstract temporal cues for retrieval.

(5) *Memory for serial position.* The occurrence of events in time is perfectly correlated with their serial order in the overwhelming majority of memory experiments. (Later we present an experimental alternative to this.) Therefore what passes for "temporal coding" in memory should really be associated with ordinal measurement rather than with interval measurement. That we can recall the order of things by their associations to environmental context is a plausible hypothesis (Hintzman, Block, & Somers, 1973; Underwood, 1977); however, again the evidence is conflicting (Block, 1982) and scanty.

WHERE THE EVIDENCE IS

Let us first acknowledge our respect for the concept of context-beta. The interpretation of an event depends on the context prevailing at the time; this is the proper setting, we think, for Tulving's experiments on encoding specificity (Tulving, 1983). Even delicate shades of meaning may be differently encoded, depending on the momentary external and internal context. The use of homographs is a sledgehammer approach to encoding specificity, perhaps a caricature of what happens with ordinary materials. The two meanings of the homograph BEAR are best considered as two separate words (Morton, 1969), just as separate as the heterographic homophones BARE and BEAR or of the heterophonic homographs LEAD and LEAD. It is only an accident of our literacy and of our orthographic history that these pairs tempt us to consider them as one word. Homography and polysemy are linguistically intriguing but they are only distantly related to context alpha, which, we have been arguing, is a critical working principle on the psychology of memory and learning. Gorfein (this volume) has shown, however, one way of relating the two types of context.

Wickens' review makes clear that much of the evidential support for environmental context comes from studies of room shifting (Smith, 1982) and related operations such as the underwater-dry-land experiment of Godden and Baddeley (1975). Another literature with considerable hard evidence concerns state-dependent learning based on pharmocological context (Eich, 1980). These literatures establish that context-alpha is a potent modulator on human learning and retrieval from memory. Should we then relax, satisfied that reliance on context as a concept is matched by strong scientific documentation of it in practice?

No. There is a dangerous mismatch between the context of normal contextual drift and the evidence from experiments on room shifting and drug states. Consider again the research areas in which theory depends on the contextual drift mechanism. We know of no experiments where, for example, an increasing lag between repetitions of a word are interrupted by dashing from one room to another, diving underwater, or quickly getting high on drugs! We act as if we had a handle on the passage of time through the mechanism of context-alpha, but it is an illusion. Once before, in an earlier generation, the psychology of memory enlisted a phantom surrogate for the passage of time—in the interference-theory concept of spontaneous recovery in proactive inhibition. Efforts to tap into that process directly were a notorious failure 20 years ago. Somehow we investigators must come up with ideas on how experimentally to tap into the drift of time as experienced in stream of consciousness by college students as they sit watching a verbal list.

Psychologists have been too complacent about coming to terms with the concepts of time and context. They use these notions readily enough but seldom probe deeply into them either in theoretical or experimental terms. Glenberg's research (Glenberg this volume) could not be more welcome, then, in reversing both trends. His theory of temporal distinctiveness is an explicit formulation of the temporal distribution of experiences. The working parts of his model provide a basis for retrieval of temporally-coded items, albeit a default retrieval plan to be used when other bases for retrieval fail. Glenberg's experiments on the "ratio rule" in long-term recency are among the most sophisticated demonstrations of the dependence of remembering on time that have ever been done.

TEMPORAL DISTINCTIVENESS

We concentrate now on one application of the temporal distinctiveness idea in Glenberg's paper: We have written elsewhere about the currently troubled state of theory in the area of modality and suffix effects in immediate memory (Greene & Crowder, 1984). The situation is more vexing still when we try to explain long-term modality effects (Gardiner & Gregg, 1979; Greene, 1985). For example, the Huang and Glenberg (1985) data seem to show that we must appeal to different mechanisms for the immediate modality and for the long-term modality effects. Glenberg offers here (this volume) a promising new idea for unifying these effects under the temporal distinctiveness theory. He assumes that temporal coding is more accurate in auditory than in visual presentation. This refreshing new approach could potentially explain all modality effects, both immediate and long-term (although it would require added stipulations to deal with the effects of lipreading and mouthing just as the PAS theory has (Greene & Crowder, 1984).

Glenberg's hypothesis that "visual presentation is not as sensitive as auditory presentation to temporal manipulations" has the special and rare virtue that it is capable of disproof. We concentrate on this last feature with evidence from a recent unpublished experiment of ours: Our temporal manipulations were imposed on lists of six letters all permutations of the letters A, B, C, D, E, and F. Somewhat like some of Glenberg's experiments, ours included irregular spacing of the six memory letters in time. In fact, no two successive letters were separated by the same amount of time. In each list the five interitem intervals separating the six letters were permutations of the intervals .5, 1.0, 1.5, 2.0, and 2.5 sec. Graphically a typical list can be represented as below

B   D   E A   C   F

Each letter appeared on the CRT for about .5 sec; the screen went blank during the interitem intervals. The special feature of our study was that we did not ask for recall of the letters or for memory of relative serial order. The latter information would be tapped by asking subjects which had been the later item in terms of ordinal position, E or A. This test has been accepted in the past as a measure of temporal memory, for example, in the pilot work Glenberg summarized in his Table 11.1. We think the relative-order question is not a test of memory for time at all, and the serial order information should be distinguished carefully from temporal information. Instead in our study we gave people three letters from the list they had just seen in their correct serial order and asked which of the two interitem intervals had been the larger, as shown by:

E   A   C

1   2

Which interval was longer, 1 or 2?

Because all the interitem intervals were different, the correct answer was always defined. In our experiment all 20 pairwise combinations of the five possible intervals were tested twice for a total of 40 tests. This session was repeated twice for each subject, one time under instructions to read the letters silently and again under instructions to read the items aloud. Half the subjects began with the silent reading tests and the other half with the aloud tests. If "auditory presentation encodes time of presentation more accurately than visual presentation" (Glenberg, this volume) people should have an easier time with these judgments of duration when the items had been read aloud than when they had been read silently. Our data are shown in Fig. 12.1 in the form of a psychophysical function. The abscissa shows how much longer, algebraically, the second interval was than the first. (Negative values on the abscissa represent conditions in which the first of the two intervals was the larger.) The ordinate shows people's tendencies to choose the second interval as the longer one. There are several data points above some abscissa values because there were several conditions resulting in the same (Interval 2—Interval 1) difference, for example the condition with 1.5 and 2.5 sec for the two intervals and another with .5 and 1.5 sec.

Two aspects of Fig. 12.1 are notable. First, performance was rather good overall. Our subjects complained about the difficulty of the task, but, collectively they did rather well. The overall regression of judgments on true differences gave a correlation coefficient of $+0.93$. The main point is that the data from silent and aloud conditions were virtually indistinguishable, in spite of Glenberg's prediction that the slope of the aloud condition should be reliably steeper than that of the silent condition. (The overall difference between modalities was in the "right" direction, but fell far short of conventional statistical significance.)

One might argue that items read silently or aloud from a screen do not approximate true comparisons of pure auditory and pure visual stimulation. Of course this is true. However, the manipulation of silent and overt reading has been known for years (Conrad & Hull, 1968) to produce the classic auditory-visual difference in memory. Therefore, because this is the very difference we are trying to generalize to, the pure comparison argument carries no weight.

We are not so naïve as to think that a single crucial experiment can overturn a good hypothesis. We need more converging experiments to settle the point. Our experiment shows value in testing the putative auditory advantage in temporal coding outside the recall task, and where serial order is not perfectly correlated with temporal duration.

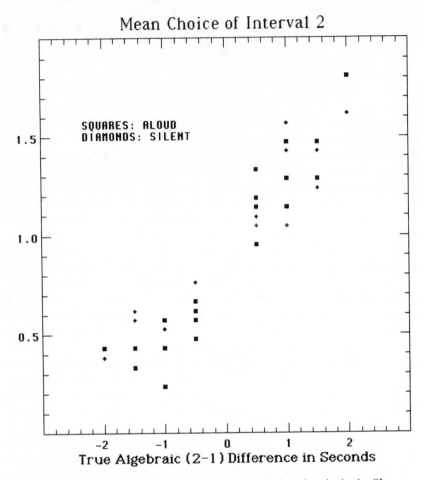

FIGURE 12.1. A psychophysical function relating the algebraic difference between the second and the first of two intervals (separating three items) to the average choice of the second as longer.

THE PUZZLE OF THE BROWN–PETERSON TASK

Like Glenberg, Gorfein (this volume) has taken seriously our responsibility for making explicit assumptions about context and time. Glenberg's assumptions are framed by the memory episodes we all want to model, not sudden plunges underwater, rapid room shifts, or changes in drug state. The Brown–Peterson task is the focus of Gorfein's chapter and of our comments here. If the 100 years since publication of Ebbinghaus' celebrated book seems like a long time, consider that for fully one-quarter of that time we have lived with the Brown–Peterson technique. The findings summarized by Gorfein (this volume) are stable and well known to the extent that they may be considered laws of memory.

Yet, we wish to claim, the Brown–Peterson task is poorly understood. Take the dramatic erosion of performance during less than a minute of counting backwards. The classic data of Peterson and Peterson (1959) and others are actually misleading. Muter (1980) has shown that if people do not expect a test, performance decays to chance in about 2 sec, rather than declining to asymptote in around 20! Muter reasoned that people achieve the better short-term memory we are accustomed to seeing because of something like surreptitious rehearsal. This interpretation is congenial to Gorfein's (this volume) second assumption, about activation and task demands. However, Muter's result is troublesome for those who might have associated the Brown–Peterson decay curve with short-term memory processes. Thus, the traditional trial-to-trial average performance grossly overestimates the capacity of the short-term system.

Paradoxically, the Brown–Peterson technique also underestimates capacity badly: The classic curves are generated by well-practiced subjects, under the influence of proactive inhibition. When a subject first sits down to do the Brown–Peterson assignment, recall is typically perfect, independently of delay. Recall would probably be perfect in Muter's situation, too, if it were possible to arrange the experiment (which it is not). Thus, in this second sense, the classic curves show far too much forgetting.

Why, if this task does not represent forgetting in the short-term system (Muter, 1980) and if it conceals the real (proactive) source of forgetting on a single trial, should we have paid so much attention to it? Probably for reasons its inventors never anticipated: The Brown–Peterson task has commanding ecological relevance, coupled with experimental precision. Our experiences in our external lives are seldom, indeed almost never, registered without a background of previous similar experiences. So the presence of proactive inhibition in remembering them is faithful to life. As a rule, deliberate real-life memorization also contains a conflict between rehearsing (for maintenance and elaboration) what has recently happened versus the new demands that have cropped up since. In the moments after we are introduced to someone at a party we are struggling to perform in a way that will preserve the name in memory, trying at the same time, not to appear dazed or absent in the polite conversation that ensues.

Apart from these commanding ecological credentials, we think the Brown-Peterson method has been useful in uncovering important principles of memory. We shall now conclude with some remarks about what sorts of principles we think these are. Two chief alternatives are apparent to us: Beginning with Brown's (1958) and Broadbent's (1958) proposals for the decay theory, some suggestions have rested on the operation of a seperate short-term forgetting system. The most fully worked-out modern example of this approach is the *perturbation model* of Estes (Estes, 1972; Healy, 1982; Lee & Estes, 1981). It assigns forgetting to processing occurring during the retention interval of a single trial, while the subject is doing the distractor task. Information in short-term storage is carried by ordered timing cycles of constituent elements of the items. With time these cycles are vulnerable to error, and to exchanges of information, which lead to errors.

The second approach to the Brown–Peterson arrangement stresses proactive inhibition. Bennett (1975) and Gorfein (this volume) have advanced specific versions of this approach. One essential assumption is that subjects always face the problem of recalling the most recent memory items—those from the immediate trial. When there is no prior trial, these most recent items are the only ones in storage, and so there is no discrimination problem and no forgetting. On subsequent trials the difficulty of discriminating the most recent trace from earlier ones depends on several factors. If the most recent item has just been presented with little or no retention interval, it is still in the foreground of the temporal context, much like the closest in a line of evenly spaced telephone poles appears if you are standing next to it. Extending the retention interval destroys the special distinctiveness of the most recent item perhaps following the sort of "ratio rule" advanced by Glenberg (this volume) for recency. For example, the clarity of the nearest pole would then depend on the ratio of the distance separating the two last poles and the distance separating the observer from the nearer of them. This accounts qualitatively for why there is no forgetting on the first Brown–Peterson trial and why forgetting increases with retention interval after the first few trials. The data displayed by Gorfein in his Fig. 12.1 (on shifts among stimulus categories and manipulation of the duration of intertrial intervals) are also easily incorporated into this general approach as he and Glenberg have acknowledged at this conference.

If some principle such as Glenberg's ratio rule can accommodate both the within-trial and between-trial forgetting losses, why should we add to it some additional assumption such as perturbation of timing, resulting in an "overexplanation" of the within-trial losses? One reason is that the perturbation model offers elegant interpretations of the detailed nature of the errors that occur in recall and their dependence on the balance of item information, order information, and the spacing of within-trial events (Lee & Estes, 1981). The ratio rule is silent on such matters just as the perturbation model is silent on why there is no forgetting on the first experimental trial.

Perhaps Melton's (1963) concept of "intraunit interference" can help: If the first item in a Brown–Peterson memory experiment were six or seven letters long, rather than three or four, we should perhaps not be surprised to find an erosion of performance as a function of retention interval, even with careful safeguards against a confounding with degree of original learning. Such a loss in the absence of proactive inhibition would vindicate perturbation as a realization of Melton's suggestion. A second reason for enlisting a short-term mechanism, such as decay or perturbation, to go with the more encompassing trace–discrimination–ratio–rule type of approach would be good evidence that asymptotic performance in Brown–Peterson experiments could be dissociated from the approach to asymptote. Crowder (1976) showed that such a dissociation would be possible in principle; however, few investigators have been willing to test the large number of retention intervals necessary to permit inference on this point. In conclusion, we think that this Brown–Peterson task highlights a major puzzle for theory—why it is that forgetting losses seem to require always a combination of both proactive and retroactive inhibition?

ENVOI

If it were not for the occurrence of forgetting, the study of memory would be boring. Indeed, the study of memory would not exist in that circumstance. The most conspicuous feature of forgetting losses has always been their progression with the passage of time. Thus, the recency effect is, as Glenberg (this volume) states, the experimental model for our most important theoretical problem. The work we have reviewed here, on (a) the nature of contextual drift across time, (b) the recency effect itself, and (c) the balance of proactive and retroactive intervals in short-term memory, all signals a return of memory psychology to its very most urgent issues.

ACKNOWLEDGMENTS

The preparation of this chapter and the experimental work included in it were supported by NSF Grant 19662 to R. Crowder. We acknowledge with appreciation the programming assistance of Lucinda DeWitt and the data collection of Laura Fawcett in the experiment reported here.

IV SEMANTIC MEMORY

13 Beyond Associations: Strategic Components in Memory Retrieval

Lynne M. Reder
Carnegie-Mellon University

There are two strong traditions within the contemporary field of memory research, one belonging to Bartlett (1932) and one to Ebbinghaus (original published in 1885; English translation in 1964). The Ebbinghaus tradition is best characterized by its rigor, its precision, and its attempts to uncover invariants in the memory system. His development and use of the "nonsense syllable" reflect his attempts to control for the influence of prior knowledge on list learning. The Bartlett tradition, started a half-century after Ebbinghaus, is quite complementary in its perspective. There is less focus on precise memory "laws," and more concern with how knowledge interacts with learning and memory.

An important component to Ebbinghaus' theory of memory is the formation of associations, direct and remote; learning is essentially the formation of associations. Bartlett's position is that we do not store verbatim memories. Our memories are *reconstructed* on the basis of what we already know. Both theories have had enormous impact on current views of memory, even though their perspectives are largely construed as antithetical.

The position I argue for here is that at times Bartlett's view is correct and at times Ebbinghaus' view is correct. Sometimes memory data seem best explained by Bartlettian principles and sometimes by those described by Ebbinghaus, because people can adopt one of several memory strategies. For example, people can try to retrieve information in a precise search of memory, looking for exact facts studied, or they can try to reconstruct what they have learned in an imprecise way, making use of prior knowledge, as Bartlett suggested. This chapter will illustrate that the same knowledge structure can produce dramatically different results, depending on the processes (or strategies) that are operating on that structure.

The notion that we have multiple strategies to retrieve information from memory has been neglected to a large extent. Only recently has the availability of multiple strategies been a topic of discussion. The contexts under which one strategy is preferred to another has been explored even less. Many theorists who discuss the availability of multiple strategies have assumed that the order of application of strategies is fixed or invariant. The case will be made that not only are there multiple strategies for retrieving the same information, but that the order of selection of strategies is variable. Nonetheless, the factors that contribute to preference for one strategy over another can be understood.

THE ROLE OF ASSOCIATIONS IN MEMORY RETRIEVAL

Numerous scholars have followed Ebbinghaus' tradition and have documented the importance of associations for understanding learning and memory phenomena. One domain within this broad category is that of interference. Much forgetting or difficulty in learning can be thought of in terms of competing responses to the same stimulus association (see Crowder, 1976, for a review). The original paired-associate learning paradigms that demonstrated interference tended to measure performance as probability of recall of nonsense syllables; however, more recently, analogous results using response times have also been found for recognition of sentences (e.g., Anderson, 1974, 1976; Lewis & Anderson, 1976; Thorndyke & Bower, 1974). The paired-associate research showed that the probability of recalling a response to a cue declined if prior or subsequent associations were also learned to that cue or stimulus. The reaction time research showed that the more facts committed to memory about a particular concept, the slower a person is to *recognize* or reject (as not studied) any statement sharing that concept. This result was dubbed the "fan effect" by Anderson because of the assumed underlying propositional representation in which facts are stored as a set of links between concepts, and facts that share the same concepts all "fan out" from the concept node. This finding seemed quite robust. The monotonically increasing RT function with increasing fan was obtained not only for facts about fantasy characters, it was obtained for real facts about famous people (Lewis & Anderson, 1976; Peterson & Potts, 1982). That is, it takes a subject longer to verify that *George Washington chopped down a cherry tree* the more fantasy facts that were also studied about George Washington.

The theoretical explanation for the fan effect is as follows. Information is retrieved by spreading activation from concepts in working memory through the network of associated facts. The time required to retrieve information is a function of the level of activation that the concept nodes receive. Fanning of multiple paths from a concept node dissipates the activation that the node sends down any one path and increases retrieval time.

The fan effect would never have been challenged if everyone subscribed to the Ebbinghaus tradition of using nonsense syllables or at least materials devoid of any inherent interest. Anderson's original materials were sensible statements, but they were random combinations (generated by a computer) of nouns and verbs (screened for sensibility by a human). Smith, Adams, and Schorr (1978) were intrigued by the paradoxical implications of the fan effect, that knowing more was detrimental. They replicated Anderson's findings, but only with statements that were thematically unrelated to one another. Subjects in one condition studied pairs of facts about fictitious individuals, such as: *Marty did not delay the trip* and *Marty broke the bottle*. In another condition, subjects studied these two facts plus a third unrelated fact such as: *Marty painted the old barn*.

Replicating past fan results, subjects were slower in the three-fan condition than in the two-fan condition. In another condition, however, subjects studied a fact that integrated the first two facts into a theme, such as: *Marty christened the ship*.

When the third fact was thematically related to the other two, there was no difference in verification times between the two-fan condition and the three-fan condition.[1] Moeser (1979), too, found that thematicity changed the effects of multiple associations.

The interpretation of the results offered by Smith et al. seemed to follow the Bartlett tradition for the thematically related materials. They adopted the model proposed by Anderson for random pairings, but assumed an entirely different schema-like representation and process for the thematically related or more meaningful materials. Although Smith et al. partly resolved the "paradox of the expert" by showing that knowing more did not interfere when the material to learn was "integrated," several questions remained unanswered. Why would we have completely different knowledge representations and processes depending on whether the material is thematically integrated or not? On the other hand, why were people not *better* at making judgments when they had learned more integrated material than when they had learned less? Thematically related material only made the interference effects smaller. The next section will answer these questions.

Different Strategies for Responding

It is possible to explain the results found by Smith et al. without assuming different knowledge representations in the two conditions. Other work of my own (Reder, 1976, 1979) led me to believe that people may use inferential reasoning to answer a question even when the information is directly stored. The

---

[1]In the Lewis and Anderson study, the fantasy facts about famous characters such as George Washington did not form a consistent theme, i.e., they were random combinations of other predicates.

theory that people often prefer to make plausibility judgments rather than to search for a specific fact helps to explain the "paradox of the expert." The Smith et al. result that the fan effect attenuates with thematically related facts can be explained by assuming that subjects often adopt a plausibility strategy to recognize the facts rather than actually search for a specific fact. That is, subjects decide that "it is *plausible* that I studied this fact if it is thematically consistent with other facts I know I studied." If finding any fact in memory about Marty that is consistent with ship-christening would suffice to "recognize" a specific Marty-ship-christening statement, then, of course, there would be little effect of the number of ship-christening facts associated with Marty. Thus, my analysis of the Smith et al. result is that subjects were using different strategies in the two conditions, not different knowledge representations.

This point of view is supported by the results of Reder and Anderson (1980). We replicated the results of Smith et al. using thematically related materials. However, we only replicated their results when the not-studied test foils were unrelated to the studied theme. A subject might study the following three facts: (1) *The teacher went to the train station.* (2) *The teacher bought a ticket for the 10:00 train.* and (3) *The teacher arrived on time at Grand Central Station.* In the block of trials where the studied statements were tested with unrelated foils, a foil to be rejected (as unstudied) might be: *The teacher called to have a phone installed.*

An unrelated foil like this would allow the subject to judge plausibility or thematic consistency instead of truly making a "recognition" judgment. When the foils were thematically related to the studied theme, such as *The teacher checked the Amtrak schedule.* subjects could not use thematic consistency or plausibility to make accurate recognition judgments. (In all conditions, the to-be-rejected foils were constructed by re-pairing studied predicate and occupation terms. In this way, foils could not be rejected because the subject knew a specific word or phrase was not used during the study.) When the foils precluded use of a plausibility strategy, the fan effect was as large with thematically related material as with unrelated material. Fig. 13.1 shows the different RT functions for recognition judgments depending on the type of foil that was tested with the studied facts.

Very different fan functions were obtained with the same materials in blocks of trials that differed only in terms of the type of not studied foils to reject. Since these different functions were produced by the same subjects, an explanation based on different long-term memory representations for thematically related materials is unlikely. Instead, it seems more reasonable to propose that interference or fan effects obtain in recognition tasks if the materials preclude the use of a plausibility strategy.

The question of why knowing more did not *facilitate* still remained. Other work (Reder, 1982) suggested a possible explanation: Strategy-selection is affected by a number of variables, in addition to the type of foils used. For

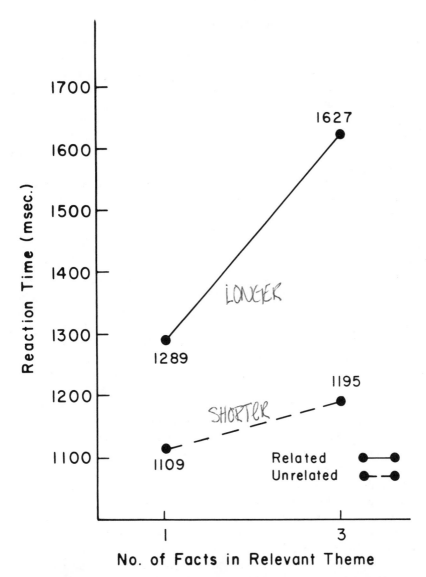

FIGURE 13.1.   Mean RT for correct recognition judgments, plotted as a function of the number of predicates associated with the probed character, and whether the block of trials used thematically related or unrelated folls. The data are averaged over yes and no responses. (Adapted from Reder & Anderson, 1980, Experiment 2, Fig. 4.)

example, the task demands (such as recognition versus plausibility judgments) or the strength of the relevant memory traces can affect which strategy is selected. In many situations there is a *mixture* of strategy use, such that sometimes one strategy is selected and sometimes the other is selected.[2] The flat fan function with thematically related materials might have resulted from a mixture of using the recognition (direct retrieval) strategy some of the time and the plausibility strategy the rest of the time. The fan function when plausibility is precluded shows a positive slope, so perhaps the fan function when plausibility is used exclusively would show a negative slope (yielding a roughly flat function when averaged together).

This speculation, that plausibility judgments would actually be facilitated by knowing more, was tested by Reder and Ross (1983). In this study, too, all subjects learned thematically related sets of information and were tested with those facts in a variety of conditions. As in Reder and Anderson, for some blocks of trials subjects were required to make recognition judgments in the presence of plausible (thematically related) foils, and for other blocks of trials they made recognition judgments in the presence of implausible (thematically inconsistent) foils. In addition, a new condition was used in which subjects were actually told to make thematic consistency judgments rather than recognition judgments. They were to say "yes" to both the studied statements and the plausibly true, namely the thematically related but unstudied statements. They were to say "no" to thematically unrelated statements. Figure 13.2 plots the fan functions for the three types of statements (studied, related, unrelated) used in the thematic relatedness block of trials. (The other blocks of trials replicated the earlier studies.) Here, the fan function for the thematically related not-studied statements showed a sharp, *negative* slope. Those statements could only be accepted by a plausibility-like (or thematic consistency) strategy. So the hypothesis that a plausibility strategy would show facilitation with fan was confirmed.

It is worth noting that the slope for stated probes was also negative, but much less steep than for related, not-studied items. This too can be accounted for by assuming that subjects used a *mixture* of the two strategies, since either one produces a correct response for studied statements. The bias to use plausibility was greater in the blocks where subjects were actually asked to judge thematic relatedness. To the extent that subjects were biased to use the plausibility strategy more often as a first strategy in the block requiring those judgments, the slope for the stated probes should be more negative than in the recognition block. Since only the plausibility strategy produces a correct response for the plausible, not-studied items, the function is much more steeply negative for them. Response times for these statements are also much slower than for the other test items because two strategies must often be tried before a correct response is given. That is, first the direct retrieval strategy is tried, but the statement is not

---

[2]Some of the data supporting these claims will be described later.

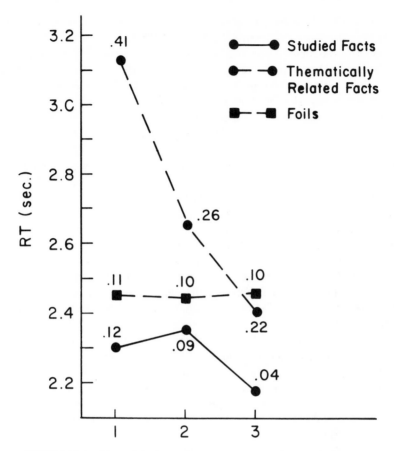

FIGURE 13.2.   Mean RTs (and proportion of errors) as a function of relevant fan and type of probe in the consistency task. (Adapted from Reder & Ross, 1983, Fig. 3a.)

found in memory. If the subject quits with a guess of "no," an error is recorded and the time is not averaged into the mean RT. If the subject elects to go on to make a plausibility judgement, the RTs are necessarily much longer than when only one strategy is used to make a decision. Note the high error rate for these statements as well.

Strategy-Selection is Variable

The account given above implies that strategy-selection for question-answering does not proceed in a fixed order. Previous conceptualizations have assumed that people first attempt to answer a question by searching directly for the statement in memory. Only when it is clear that the fact cannot be found is an inferential strategy evoked (e.g., Lachman & Lachman, 1980, Lehnert, 1977). There are a number of results that support the notion that direct-retrieval is not always the first strategy of choice. For example, data of Reder (1979) indicated that subjects make inferences even when the information is stored in memory. In those studies, subjects were asked to read short stories and make judgments about the plausibility of assertions on the basis of the stories that they read. Some of the statements to be judged had actually been presented in the story as part of the story (randomly determined for each subject). The plausibility of the test sentence with respect to the story affected judgment time even when the item had been explicitly presented. Although there was a clear RT advantage for stated (explicit) probes over not-stated probes, the plausibility of the statements affected stated probes as well. Figure 13.3 plots the data from the stated and not-stated conditions for the highly and moderately plausible probes when tested immediately after reading the relevant story.[3]

One explanation for faster RTs for highly plausible statements assumes that the probability of drawing the inference and then finding it in memory is greater for the highly plausible statements, and that subjects always try to search memory for a specific fact first. The problem with this explanation is that it predicts no plausibility effect for probes that had been stated in the story. A different explanation for both the plausibility effect and the speed advantage for stated probes involves a simple race between the direct retrieval process and the plausibility process, where both processes execute in parallel. By assuming that sometimes one process wins and sometimes the other wins, both effects can be accounted for, the faster times for presented statements and for highly plausible statements.

The simple parallel race model just described can be ruled out, however, if one considers the data of Reder (1982). Those experiments were quite similar to Reder (1979), except that some of the subjects were asked to make recognition judgments instead of plausibility judgments. Judgments were either made right after reading a story, after reading 10 stories, or 2 days after reading all 10 stories. In some conditions, subjects actually were faster at plausibility judgments at longer delays than at shorter delays. This is a result that a simple race model cannot explain. Subjects were faster at a delay in those situations where the direct retrieval strategy could not produce a correct response, namely for not-stated plausible inferences. Figure 13.4 presents the response times and error rates for the two tasks (plausibility and recognition) as a function of delay of test and whether the probes had been stated in the story.

An explanation that can account for this result is to assume that at the shorter delay intervals, subjects are inclined to try the direct retrieval strategy first. That

---

[3]The experiment also included "primed" inferences, and inferences that were verb-based, i.e., they immediately followed from the verb in an assertion. The statements were also tested at various delays. The subset of data graphed here seemed most representative and relevant.

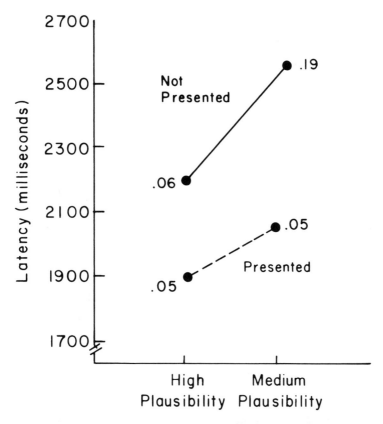

FIGURE 13.3.   Mean RT for correct plausibility judgments (and error rates), plotted as a function of plausibility of the test probe and whether it had been presented in the story. (Adapted from Reder, 1979, Experiment 1, Fig. 1.)

strategy will produce the correct response in many conditions. However, when subjects are asked to make plausibility judgments and fail to find the probe in memory, they must go on to try the plausibility strategy or risk making an error. At longer delay intervals, there is an increased tendency to try the plausibility strategy first. This means that for not-stated plausible inferences, the useless direct-retrieval strategy is avoided, making overall response times faster in that condition.

Other aspects of Reder (1982) also supported the notion that subjects became more inclined with delay to adopt the plausibility strategy first in both the plausibility task and the recognition task. As with Reder (1979), the plausibility of the test questions was also varied. The effect of plausibility, (i.e., the difference in response times between the highly and moderately plausible state-

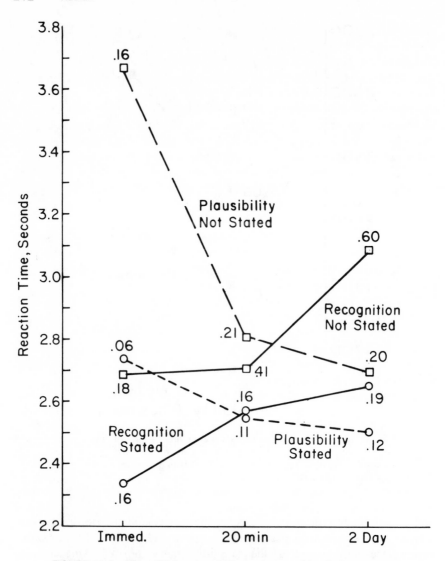

FIGURE 13.4.   Mean RT for plausibility and recognition judgments as a function of whether the probe had been stated in the story, plotted across levels of delay. (Adapted from Reder, 1982, Experiment 1, Fig. 3.)

ments) increased at the longer delay intervals. Also, accuracy declined greatly for not-stated plausibles in the recognition task, especially for the highly plausible statements. Figure 13.4 shows that not-stated items in the recognition task were erroneously accepted 60% of the time. The error rates were 50% for the moderately plausible and 70% for the highly plausible.

Given the theoretical interpretation of Reder (1982), that subjects were more inclined to adopt the plausibility strategy as memory traces faded (i.e., at longer delays), it seemed reasonable to predict that at longer delays the pattern found by Reder and Ross (1983) in the fan paradigm would also show a stronger influence of the plausibility strategy (i.e., more of a negative slope). Reder and Wible (1984) conducted an experiment similar to Reder and Ross, in which the major difference was that subjects were tested 48 hours after learning the material as well as being tested on the day of learning.

As expected, the effect of fan (the number of sentences sharing the same concepts) was strongest in those conditions where only one strategy could produce the correct response. Subjects who were asked to make recognition judgments showed the greatest interference from increased fan for the thematically related, not-studied items. This replicated earlier results. Inconsistent items and stated items could be correctly recognized using the plausibility strategy as well as the direct retrieval strategy, so those RT functions were flatter. On the other hand, those subjects who were asked to make thematic consistency judgments showed the most facilitation from increased fan for the related, not-studied items, since only the plausibility-like strategy would work.

The prediction that subjects would be more inclined to use the plausibility strategy at longer delays was supported by a number of results in Reder and Wible (1984). Figure 13.5 shows the mean facilitation (or speedup) from the first session to second session as a function of task and probe type. For all items, subjects are somewhat faster during the second session, possibly due to practice or due to greater fatigue during the first RT session after learning the materials. It is reasonable to consider the flat line for the stated probes as a baseline of no true facilitation or loss due to strategy shifts, because either strategy works equally well for these items. The most interesting changes in relative speed from the first to the second session are for the related, not-stated items. In the recognition task, where the plausibility strategy would produce the wrong response for these items, there is a relative hindrance due to the strategy shift, i.e., much less speedup than the baseline. In the consistency task, where only the plausibility strategy produces the correct response, there is the greatest speedup. Presumably this occurs because there are far fewer trials where subjects first use the inappropriate direct retrieval strategy prior to the plausibility strategy.

The speedup results just described are inconsistent with a simple, parallel race model for the same reasons that the speedup in Reder (1982) is inconsistent with it. Other aspects of the data also argue for a shift in strategy preference (from direct retrieval to plausibility) with increasing delay. The slopes of the fan

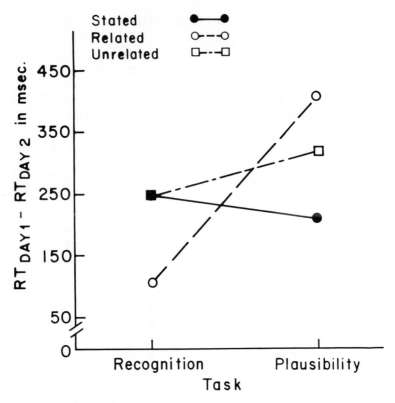

FIGURE 13.5.   Mean facilitation or speed-up from first session to second session, plotted as a function of task and probe type. (Adapted from Reder & Wible, 1984, Fig. 2.)

functions, negative for the consistency task and positive for the recognition task, both become more negative at the 2-day delay. This is because with a greater portion of trials using the plausibility/consistency strategy at a delay, there should be more of a facilitation effect from increased fan.[4]

The accuracy data also showed a shift toward greater use of the plausibility strategy at longer delays. Figure 13.6 displays the accuracy data as a function of relevant fan, task, delay and type of test probe. During the first session, in which the subjects tended to use the direct retrieval strategy for the plausibility task, accuracy was poor for thematically related, not-stated probes, since it produced

---

[4]In the recognition task, the slope changed from a +135 msec. slope to a −65 msec. slope at a delay. In the consistency task, the slope showed less influence of interference initially, starting with a +12 msec. slope and shifting to a greater facilitation than in the recognition task, a −146 msec. slope. These slopes are only computed for the stated and inconsistent probes since only one strategy can be correctly used for the not-stated inconsistent probes.

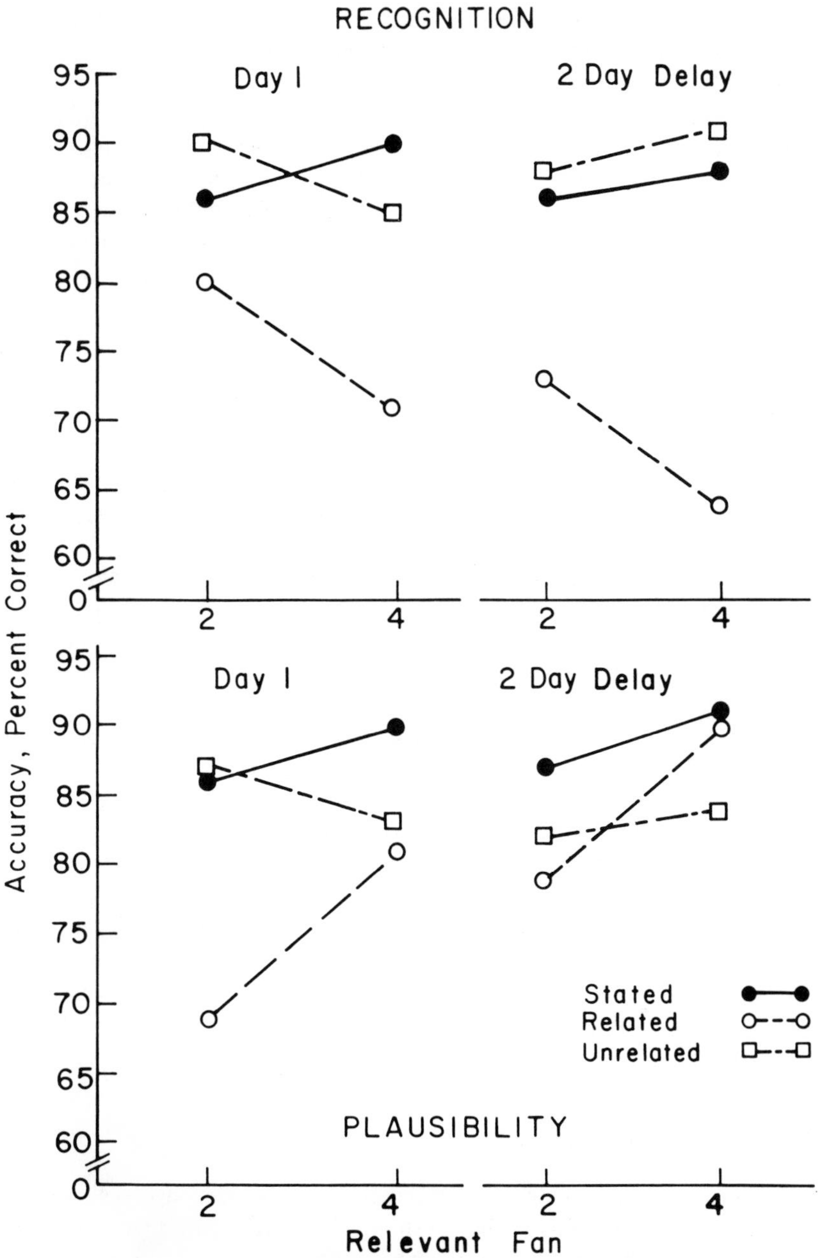

FIGURE 13.6. Mean percentage correct for judgments in the recognition task (top) and consistency task (bottom), plotted as a function of relevant fan for each probe type. The short-delay data are displayed in the left quadrants, and the long-delay test data are plotted on the right. (Adapted from Reder & Wible, 1984, Fig. 3.)

the wrong responses (no's instead of yes's). Accuracy improved 10% for both levels of relevant fan with delay for those statements where both strategies could not work.

The accuracy pattern in the recognition task showed the opposite trend for the related statements for exactly the same reason. These were the only probes that would produce an error when the plausibility strategy was invoked. At the delayed test, there was a greater tendency to use the plausibility strategy and so more errors were made. Furthermore, these probes were 10% worse in accuracy for the high-fan condition, that is, when there was more information consistent with the theme of the not-studied probe.

THE MECHANISMS FOR STRATEGY-SELECTION

Several conclusions seem clear given the results just described. Questions are not always answered by using the same question-answering strategy or process. Which strategy is used to answer a given question varies. The available strategies do not compete for execution by racing against each other to see which one will complete first. A nonfixed order serial model can easily account for the data described. A parallel race model can also account for the data if we assume that the *allocation of processing resources* is unequally distributed for the two strategies. By assuming a shift in the allocation of resources from one strategy to another instead of a shift in which strategy is tried first, the same pattern of speedups, and so forth, can be explained.

Regardless of whether or not one assumes a variable, serial strategy-selection model or a differential allocation of resources in a parallel-race model, it still follows that there must be a preliminary process that determines strategy selection or allocation of resources among strategies. This preliminary process has two sub-components or stages: an initial evaluation of knowledge relevant to the question followed by a decision of which strategy to follow. I propose that the initial evaluation is an automated process while the decision is a conscious, controlled process (e.g., Neely, 1977; Posner & Synder, 1975; Shiffrin & Schneider, 1977).

Initial Evaluation

A number of factors are involved in the initial evaluation. One involves assessing the familiarity of the words in the question. The more familiar the words, the more a person is biased toward using direct retrieval. The initial evaluation also involves assessing how many intersections in memory there are among the words from the question. The more intersections, the more the person is biased toward plausibility.

The idea that we can automatically determine the familiarity of the concepts provided in the question has been proposed elsewhere (e.g., Hasher & Zacks, 1979; Jacoby & Dallas, 1981; Mandler, 1980). The activation level of the terms in memory that were referred to in the probe can be compared with their "resting" activation levels. If they seem higher than expected at the time of questioning, it is assumed that the words were encountered recently.

The proposal that relatedness affects decision times is also not new (e.g., Rips, Shoben & Smith 1973). In my view, the "relatedness" of the concepts in the question is monitored through the interconnections in memory. Relatedness is defined as the degree to which words in a question cause *activation* to intersect in memory. The more intersections that are detected in memory as a result of a query, the more potentially relevant information there is available for question answering.

Familiarity detection and intersection detection are processes that monitor the automatic spread of activation from the concepts in the question. This spread of activation is assumed to be automatic, as are processes that monitor the level of activation and the extent of intersections. The bias to use the direct retrieval strategy "trumps" the plausibility strategy since direct retrieval is a faster and easier strategy than judging plausibility when the queried fact is relatively accessible. This is because when memory search is relatively easy, the plausibility strategy does not have the search-time advantage to counteract its long plausibility computation time.

Strategy Selection

In deciding which strategy to apply, the subject integrates the biases from the initial evaluation along with considerations or factors that are *extrinsic* to the test question. These extrinsic factors include things such as task instructions and probability that a particular strategy will be successful. Some of these variables have already been shown to influence strategy selection, for example, form of the instructions (Gould & Stephenson, 1967; Reder, 1982), ease of discrimination among alternatives (Lorch, 1981; Reder & Ross, 1983; Reder & Wible, 1984), impressions of one's own expertise (Gentner & Collins, 1981), and form of the question (Rips, 1975).

In addition to these variables, it seems reasonable that strategy selection would be affected by recent prior history of success with a strategy, nominal constraints of the task, special knowledge that a strategy will or will not work, and motivation to perform well. The influence of extrinsic factors on strategy selection is partly a function of how strong the bias is from the automatic assessment of "feeling of knowing" from the first stage and how compelling the factors are from this stage. If there is overwhelming evidence that a strategy will not work, or if subjects are heavily penalized for making errors, they may ignore the biasing information from the automatic assessment.

Evidence for the Existence of a Strategy-Selection Stage

I have conducted a number of experiments that are consistent with the idea that there is a preliminary mechanism that allows us to select a particular strategy for question answering (Reder, 1987). Some of these experiments supported the proposal that people can assess their memories before actually doing a careful search of memory. People can estimate that they can answer a question such as, "Who invented the telephone?" significantly faster than they can actually answer it. This faster estimation time is achieved without sacrificing accuracy. That is, those subjects who estimated that they could answer a question typically could answer the question, and they answered as many correctly as those in the answer condition. If accuracy is defined as the ratio of percentage correctly answered to percentage attempted, the estimate group was more accurate (percentage attempted is defined as one minus the probability of saying "can't answer").

Another experiment lent support to the mechanisms hypothesized to influence "feeling of knowing." This experiment primed some of the terms in some of the questions that subjects would later have to estimate or answer. It was expected that having rated the word-frequency of a couple of the terms in a question would give the person an illusory "feeling of knowing." One-third of the questions were primed in this manner. Subjects who were asked to estimate whether or not they thought they could answer a question overestimated their ability to answer difficult questions that had been primed. For subjects who were asked only to give answers, the priming manipulation did not influence the percentage of questions attempted. However, it did affect how long subjects took to decide that they could *not* answer a difficult question: Primed, difficult questions gave an illusory "feeling of knowing," which caused subjects to search much longer before realizing that they did not have the answer. Estimation times, on the other hand, were not affected by priming. If anything, estimation times were faster for those questions that were primed.

Other experiments in Reder (1987) showed that strategy selection was affected by variables extrinsic to the question. One study varied the proportion of the probes to be judged for plausibility that were actually presented as part of the story subjects read. When 80% of the test items had been presented as part of the story, subjects were expected to adopt the direct retrieval strategy. When only 20% were presented as part of the story, subjects were expected to adopt the plausibility strategy. Given that both groups were asked to make plausibility judgments, any difference in response time patterns would be due to sensitivity to the ratio of presented to not-presented statements.

The results quite clearly indicated that subjects were sensitive to the ratio of presented to not-presented test probes. For those subjects who received predominantly presented probes and were therefore biased to use the direct retrieval strategy, there was a large difference in verification RT between presented and not-presented statements, such that the not-presented were much slower. For those who received predominantly not-presented probes and were therefore biased to use the plausibility strategy, there was essentially no difference in verification RT between the presented and not-presented probes. Conversely, there was a large plausibility effect (difference in RT between highly and moderately plausible statements) for subjects biased to use the plausibility strategy, and only a very small effect for subjects biased to use direct retrieval. For the latter group, all of the plausibility effect came from those statements that could not be verified using direct retrieval.

This manipulation of varying the proportion of presented to not-presented statements was done only for the first 6 of the 10 stories in the experiment. Starting with the seventh story, the ratio of presented to not-presented reverted to the standard 50:50. For these last 4 stories, the results showed a return toward a moderate use of each strategy, that is, the bias functions converged. This is also evidence that subjects could adjust their strategies fairly rapidly. It should be pointed out that the bias manipulation and the shift back to neutral was never explicitly mentioned to the subjects.

Another experiment (Reder, 1987) was designed to see whether people can switch strategies at a moment's notice, depending on the advice they receive prior to the question. Again all subjects were asked to make plausibility judgments. However, before each question, they were told whether they would be better off searching for a specific fact in memory or better off trying to actually compute the plausibility of the statement. They were also warned that although the advice would usually be appropriate, it would not always be. When the advice was wrong, they were to still try to answer the question correctly (i.e., to use the other strategy). The advice was correct 80% of the time.

The results clearly indicated that subjects find it quite easy to follow advice and switch strategies from trial to trial. There were clear differences in RT pattern depending on which strategy had been recommended. For example, there was a much bigger RT difference between the moderately and highly plausible presented statements if the advice had been to compute the plausibility of the answer than if the advice had been to search for the fact in memory. Further, when the advised strategy would not produce the correct response, response times were much slower because subjects had to go on and adopt the second strategy as well. Subjects were especially slow for not-presented statements where the (wrong) advice had been to try direct retrieval.[5]

In summary, these experiments lend support to the theory of strategy selection for question answering. We can assess our feeling of knowing, which is sensitive to the recency of exposure to words and the extent of intersection in memory among the concepts referred to in the probe. Further, we integrate our initial

---

[5]It is worth noting that data such as these also argue against a simple parallel race model between the two competing strategies, confirming the view of a strategy-selection process.

evaluation with facts that we can more consciously assess in order to select one strategy to try first (or to which to devote most of our processing capacity).

GENERAL CONCLUSIONS

This volume is in honor of the hundredth anniversary of the publishing of Ebbinghaus' famous treatise on human memory. The message of this contribution is that we should reconsider Ebbinghaus' "laws" from the perspective that memory performance reflects cognitive strategies and that these strategies vary from situation to situation. For example, the same structure of associations can either hurt memory performance or facilitate it, depending on other constraints of the task. It is no wonder then that the conclusions of Ebbinghaus and those of Bartlett seem so contradictory. Each had constructed tasks and tested subjects in situations that encouraged completely different strategies. Ebbinghaus constructed tasks that required veridical, verbatim recall that minimized the usefulness of prior knowledge. Bartlett used tasks that encouraged reconstruction of the information by using prior world knowledge. Both sets of "laws" or principles are useful, so long as we acknowledge that they apply only in contexts that encourage the corresponding memory strategy.

14 Relation Element Theory: A New Account of the Representation and Processing of Semantic Relations

Roger Chaffin
Trenton State College

Douglas J. Herrmann
Hamilton College

Relation knowledge may be viewed in two different ways. First, in a tradition that can be traced from Aristotle through the associationists to present-day network models of memory, associations have been used to explain thought processes. Aristotle used associations to explain the sequence of ideas in recall. For John Locke, associations played the same role and also accounted for the formation of complex from simple ideas and the ability to reason (Rapaport, 1974, pp. 66–85). Current network models of memory continue this tradition (e.g., Anderson, 1976; Norman & Rumelhart, 1975). When used this way, associations function as primitive terms in an explanation. They explain but are not themselves further explained. They are not further decomposed into more primitive entities but are treated as unanalyzable; they are regarded as unitary semantic entities.

Second, relations between concepts can be viewed as themselves a subject for explanation. Hume (1739/1965, pp. 82–86) analyzed the cause–effect relation into the elements of contiguity in space, contiguity in time, succession, and constant conjunction. Other standard semantic relations have been analyzed by Geoffery Leech (1974) and John Lyons (1968, 1977). When viewed this way, standard relations, (e.g., antonymy, part–whole, class inclusion) are not the unanalyzable primitive terms of a psychological explanation but are themselves decomposable into more basic elements. According to the unitary approach, people comprehend relations between concepts by ascertaining whether two words are connected by a labeled associative link. According to the relation element view, people comprehend relations by identifying the elements which make up the relation between two words.

221

The resolution of the discrepancy between the two approaches has important consequences for semantic memory and for other areas of psychology that employ semantic relations to account for mental processes. An improved understanding of the nature of relations may be expected to benefit all those areas of psychology in which relations serve as primitive explanatory constructs.

We review recent studies that have directly compared the two approaches. Two experimental tasks are discussed: a sorting task in which subjects are asked to distinguish similar and different relations, and an analogy task in which subjects select from among several word pairs the one that has the same relation as a target pair. We also describe the various types of relations examined in the research.

RESEARCH ON JUDGMENTS OF RELATION SIMILARITY

There are many different kinds of relations between concepts. Nearly 50 are listed by Apreysan, Mel'cuk, and Zolkovsky (1970). Each relation may be regarded as a different kind of unitary association (e.g., Anderson, 1976; Norman & Rumelhart, 1975). Alternatively, each relation may be regarded as composed of a set of simpler relation elements (e.g., Leech, 1974; Lyons, 1968, 1977).

One phenomenon that lends credibility to the relation element hypothesis is the fact that relations can be grouped in terms of their similarity to each other. Judgments of similarity require the identification of aspects in which things are similar and different (Tversky, 1977). Similarity judgments about relations therefore require that the relations be decomposed into respects in which the relations are similar and different. Numerous taxonomies of associative relations, based on intuition and on associative data, were proposed by early experimental psychologists, such as Wundt, Kraeplin, and Jung (Warren, 1921). We describe a recent study that confirmed some of the main features of these early taxonomies and showed that they also reflect the intuitions of ordinary speakers (Chaffin & Herrmann, 1984).

Our empirical taxonomy of relations was developed by asking subjects to sort examples of relations. Thirty-one relations were identified in the psychological and linguistic literature (Evanechko & Maguire, 1972; Evens, Litowitz, Markovitz, Smith, & Werner, 1983; Leech, 1974; Lyons, 1977; Perfetti, 1967; Riegel & Riegel, 1963; Warren, 1921). This literature suggested that relations fall into five major groups: Contrasts (night–day), Similars (car–auto), Class inclusion (robin–bind), Case relations (farmer–tractor), and Part-whole relations (bike–wheel). Two examples of each relation and the a priori classification of relations into five groups are shown in Table 14.1. The 31 relations selected do not exhaust the variety of relations. Some were excluded so that they could

TABLE 14.1
Examples of 31 Semantic Relations Organized According to an
a priori Classification into 5 Families

I. CONTRASTS

Contrary	old–young, happy–sad
Contradictory	alive–dead, male–female
Reverse	attack–defend, buy–sell
Directional	front–back, left–right
Incompatible	happy–morbid, frank–hypocritical
Asymmetrical contrary	hot–cool, dry–moist
Pseudoantonym	popular–shy, believe–affirm

II. SIMILARS

Synonymity	car–auto, buy–purchase
Dimensional similar	smile–laugh, annoy–torment
Attribute similar	rake–fork, painting–movie
Necessary attribute	tower–high, bachelor–unmarried

III. CLASS INCLUSION

Perceptual	animal–horse, flower–rose
Functional	furniture–chair, tool–hammer
State	disease–polio, emotion–fear
Geographical	state–New Jersey, country–Russia
Activity	game–chess, crime–theft
Action	talk–lecture, cook–fry

IV. CASE RELATIONS

Agent–action	artist–paint, dog–bark
Agent–instrument	farmer–tractor, soldier–gun
Agent–object	baker–bread, sculptor–clay
Action–recipient	sit–chair, hunt–prey
Action–instrument	drink–cup, cut–knife
Invited attribute	food–tasty, hospital–clean

V. PART–WHOLE

Functional object	car–engine, face–nose
Collection	forest–tree, fleet–ship
Group	choir–singer, faculty–professor
Ingredient	table–wood, pizza–cheese
Functional location	kitchen–refrigerator, house–dining room
Place	Germany–Hamburg, Asia–China
Organization	college–admissions, army–supply corps
Measure	mile–yard, pound–ounce

be used in the instructions (coordinates, such as "doctor–lawyer" and reciprocals, such as "judge–defendant"), others because they did not appear in the literature (e.g., referential relations such as "red light–stop," "map–city").

For our research, five word pairs were selected as examples of each relation and typed on cards, five pairs on each card. Forty subjects were then given the task of sorting the 31 cards into piles so that the same or similar relations were put into the same pile and different relations were put into different piles. A 31 × 31 sorting matrix was compiled which summarized the number of times that each pair was sorted with each other pair. A hierarchical clustering analysis of this sorting matrix produced the clustering of relations shown in Fig. 14.1.

Relations joined at a higher proximity level were sorted together by more subjects. Inspection of the figure shows that subjects perceived similarities among relations that were consistent with the a priori classification. There were five main clusters that correspond to the major types of relation identified in earlier taxonomies: Contrasts (big–little), class inclusion (robin–bird), similars (car–auto), case relations (farmer–tractor), and part–whole (foot–toe). We refer to each cluster as a *family* of relations. The five families are organized in terms of their similarity to each other. The major division is between the *family of contrast* relations and the other four families of noncontrast relations. The next major division is between logical and pragmatic relations. The logical relations—class inclusion and similarity—involve overlap in the properties of the two concepts and are thus based on similarity of meaning. The pragmatic relations—case and part–whole relations—do not involve similarity of meaning. Instead, the two concepts are related by a pragmatic association (Klix, 1980). Within each *family*, the specific relations are also organized in terms of similarity. For example, there is a major division of part–whole relations into relations involving discrete parts that are separable from one another and from the whole, (e.g., car–wheel), and relations involving parts which are not readily distinguishable from each other, (e.g., bread–flour and pound–ounce).

The subjects sorted on the basis of the similarity of the *relations*, not on the basis of the similarity of the concepts. For example, car–vehicle and car–wheel were appropriately sorted into the class inclusion and the part–whole relations, respectively. There were only five cases of disagreement with the a priori taxonomy, which was described in Table 14.1. Four of the disagreements were reasonable alternative classifications, (e.g., "invited" attributes (food–tasty) were sorted with the similarity relations instead of with the case relations). The classification appears to be based on the similarity of the concepts rather than the relations in only one case: places (Germany–Hamburg) were sorted with geographical subordinates (country–Russia) and the other class inclusion relations. Even here the subjects' judgments might have been influenced by a distinction that the experimenters overlooked: country–Russia is a class membership rather than a class inclusion relation since Russia is an individual not a class (Miller & Johnson–Laird, 1976, p. 245). Thus this example pair has at least as much in common with the place relation as with the class inclusion relations.

PROXIMITY LEVEL

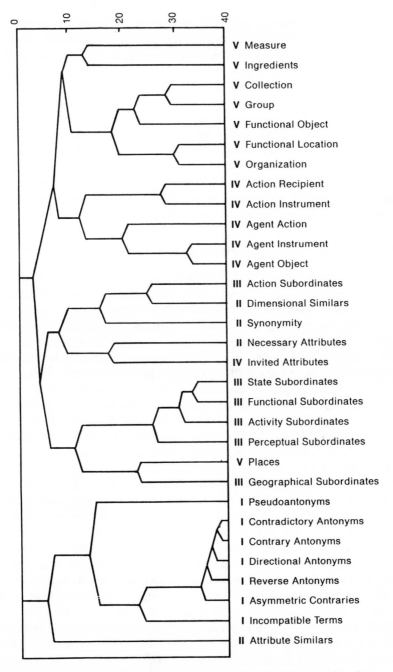

FIGURE 14.1. Hierarchical clustering solution for 31 semantic relations with a priori classification represented by Roman numerals (from Chaffin & Herrmann, 1984).

The subjects were thus able to identify *families* of relations, to perceive differences in the similarity of one family to another, and, within each family, to perceive differences in the similarity of one specific relation to another. The ability of subjects to make similarity judgments about relations requires explanation. The perception of similarities and differences requires the identification of respects in which things are the same and respects in which they are different (Tversky, 1977), as is recognized in the aphorism, "You can't compare apples and oranges." This is true if apples and oranges are compared as unanalyzable wholes. As soon as one decomposes the wholes into aspects in which they are the same (size, shape, nutritional value) and different (texture, taste, color), the comparison can be made. The ability of subjects to compare relations for similarity suggests that they decomposed the relations into elements or aspects in which they are the same and elements or aspects in which they differ.

The Unitary Account of Relation Similarity

What account might the unitary view of relations give of the sorting data? The unitary position is represented at present by network models of memory in which relations between concepts are represented by labeled links (see Johnson–Laird, Herrmann & Chaffin, 1984, for a review). Network models explain similarity judgments about relations as a process of tracing pathways between nodes and matching relation markers. If two markers or series of markers match, the relation is the same; if the markers do not match, the relations are different. Two versions of the unitary position must be considered. The *specific marker* version assumes that each specific relation is represented in memory by a different type of marker. The *family marker* version assumes that only the family to which each relation belongs is represented by a marker. The family marker position is closest to that of current network models which have typically been parsimonious in postulating markers, since these are the primitive terms of the theories. For example, Norman and Rumelhart (1975) use a single "hasa" relation to represent the various types of part–whole relations. There is, however, nothing other than a commitment to parsimony to prevent network models from adopting a specific marker position and using a larger number of more specific markers.

According to the specific marker hypothesis, each of the 31 relations in Fig. 14.1 would be represented by a different marker. This would recognize the variety of relations but not the similarities among them. Because each marker is unitary there would be no basis for judging it as more similar to one marker than any other.

The family marker hypothesis is more successful in accounting for the sorting data. Each relation is marked by one of the five family relation markers; relations with the same family marker are sorted together. This accounts for the major feature of Fig. 14.1, the arrangement of relations into five major groups. The organization of the families by similarity is not explained, nor is the organization of relations within each family. The family marker position would have to view the similarities between and within families as spurious products of post hoc interpretation of a random arrangement of families and relations within families.

The Relation Element Account of Relation Similarity

The sorting data are consistent with semantic analyses of the relations (Leech, 1974; Lyons, 1968, 1977). It remains to be seen whether a detailed account of the relational components of the 31 relations can provide a good account of the way that the relations were sorted. This was the goal of a recent study by Theresa Stasio (Stasio, Herrmann, & Chaffin, 1985).

Relation elements were derived from the literature for the 31 relations in the previous sorting study. The similarity of each pair of relations was computed as the proportion of shared elements. The ability of this measure of element similarity to account for the sorting data was then compared with that of family markers.

Semantic relations can be characterized by a structured set of elements. The *contrary* relation can serve as an example. The contrary pair hot–cold has at least five elements. First, contraries are on a common dimension, such as "temperature state" for hot–cold. Pairs that are not on a common dimension, (e.g., hot–infallible) are not antonyms. Second, the two concepts are on opposite sides of the midpoint of the dimension; pairs on the same side of the midpoint, (e.g., hot–warm), are dimensional similars, not contraries. Third, the dimension must involve the denotative meaning of both terms. For example, flaming–cold are opposed because flaming connotes "hot," which is the contrary of "cold," but flaming–cold are pseudocontraries because their opposition occurs through their connotative meaning. Fourth, the two concepts must be symmetrically positioned about the midpoint. Hot–cool are asymmetrical contraries, not true contraries, because they are not symmetrical. Fifth, contraries are opposed on a continuous dimension, one that admits gradation. Alive-dead are contradictories rather than contraries because their dimension is dichotomous.

The elements of the *contrast* relation form a hierarchical structure. Two concepts must be on a common dimension before they can be located unilaterally or bilaterally, and they must be located bilaterally before they can be positioned symmetrically or asymmetrically about the midpoint. The two elements that are basic to the hierarchy for contrast relations, common dimension and bilateral position, are common to all contrast relations. They form the family component of the relation which defines membership in the contrast family. Other elements are unique to the specific relations within the family. These form the specific component of each relation which serves to distinguish one relation within a family from another.

To determine whether relation elements can provide an explanation of the sorting data, it will be necessary to describe the elements of each of the 31

TABLE 14.2
Thirty-one Semantic Relations with Relation Elements Organized
According to the Five Families of Empirical Taxonomy

Relation Families	Example	Relation Elements
I. CONTRASTS		
Contrary	old–young, happy–sad	DIM(BIP(Sym),Cont)
Contradictory	alive–dead, male–female	DIM(BIP(Sym),Dich)
Reverse	attack–defend, buy–sell	DIM(BIP,Dich,Vec)
Directional	front–back, left–right	DIM(BIP,Dich,Top)
Incompatible	happy–morbid, frank–hypocritical	DIM(BIP)
Asymmetrical contrary	hot–cool, dry–moist	DIM(BIP),Cont)
Pseudoantonym	popular–shy, believe–deny	DIM(BIP,Con)
Attribute similar	rake–fork, painting–movie	INT(Over(Att,Dis))
II. SIMILARS		
Synonymity	car–auto, buy–purchase	INT(Inc(Bil))
Dimensional similar	smile–laugh, annoy–torment	INT(Over),Dim(Unip)
Necessary attribute	bachelor–unmarried, tower–high	INT(Over(Att,Poss))
Invited attribute	food–tasty, cut–knife	Inc,Poss,Con
Action subordinates	talk–lecture, cook–fry	INT(INC(UNIL))
III. CLASS INCLUSION		
Perceptual subord.	animal–horse, flower–rose	INT(INC(UNIL))
Functional subord.	furniture–chair, tool–hammer	INT(INC(UNIL))
State subord.	disease–polio, emotion–fear	INT(INC(UNIL))
Activity subord.	game–chess, crime–theft	INT(INC(UNIL))
Geographical subord.	state–New Jersey, country–Russia	INT(INC(UNIL))
Place	Germany–Hamburg, Asia–China	INC(PARTIVE(Poss,Loc))
IV. CASE RELATIONS		
Agent–action	artist–paint, dog–bark	EVT(Act,Obj)
Agent–instrument	farmer–tractor, soldier–gun	EVT(Agent, Inst)
Agent–object	baker–bread, sculptor–clay	EVT(Agent, Obj)
Action–recipient	sit–chair, hunt–prey	EVT(Act,Obj)
Action–instrument	cut–knife, drink–cup	EVT(Act,Inst)
V. PART–WHOLE		
Functional object	engine–car, tree–leaf	INC(PARTIVE (At-tach,Comp, Prop,Poss))
Collection	forest–tree, fleet–ship	INC(PARTIVE (Homo,Prop,Poss))

TABLE 14.2 (*Continued*)

Relation Families	Example	Relation Elements
V. PART–WHOLE		
Group	choir–singer, faculty–professor	INC(PARTIVE (Homo,Prop, Poss,Soc))
Ingredient	table–wood, pizza–cheese	INC(PARTIVE (Comp,Prop, Poss,Loc))
Functional location	kitchen–stove, house–dining room	INC(PARTIVE (Attach,Comp, Prop,Poss))
Organization	college–admissions, army–corps	INC(PARTIVE (Attach,Comp, Prop,Poss,Soc))
Measure	mile–yard, hour–minute	INC(PARTIVE(Homo))

Note: The order of relations is the same as in Table 14.1 except where change was required to conform to empirical taxonomy.

relations in the sorting study. The description is summarized in the third column of Table 14.2, which lists the elements for each relation used in Stasio's (1985) study, and in Table 14.3, which gives a brief description of each element. The elements were assigned on the basis of an a priori analysis based on the linguistics literature. This was done because the purpose was to determine how well relation elements derived from linguistic analyses accounted for the sorting data. The elements listed in Tables 14.2 and 14.3 are not a definitive set, but provide a preliminary demonstration of the feasibility of decomposing relations into relation elements.

Contrast.   Contrast relations are those in which the meaning of one term contrasts, opposes, or contradicts the other term (Bolinger & Sears, 1981; Cruse, 1976; Groves, 1973; Kempsen 1977; Leech, 1974; Lyons, 1968; Ogden, 1932). The family is defined by the elements *dimension* and *bilateral position*, which are common to all contrast relations. The abbreviations for these family elements occur in capitalized letters in Table 14.2. All the relations in the table involve the *denotative* meaning of both words and so this element of the relations is not listed. The specific contrast relations are distinguished by additional relation elements. For contraries (e.g., old–young) the dimension of opposition is *continuous*, whereas for contradictories (e.g., alive–dead) the dimension is *dichotomous*. The dimension for reverse terms (e.g., attack–defend) is a vector, i.e., the nature of the relation depends on the direction. For directional contrasts (e.g., front–back) the dimension involves a spatial or temporal dimension. For

TABLE 14.3
Relation Elements and Their Definitions

Relation Elements	Description

I. Elements of Intensional Force

Denotative (Den)	W_i and W_j share denotative meaning
Connotative (Con)	W_i connotes W_j

II. Dimensional Elements

Dimension (Dim)	W_i and W_j share a single dimension
Unilateral Position (UniP)	W_i and W_j are on same side of midpoint
Bilateral Position (BiP)	W_i and W_j are on opposite sides of midpoint
Symmetrical Position (Sym)	W_i and W_j are equidistant from midpoint
Continuous (Cont)	W_i and W_j can be qualified; dimension is gradable
Discrete (Dis)	W_i and W_j cannot be qualified; dimension is nongradable
Dichotomous (Dich)	If W_i then not W_j; W_i and W_j are mutually exclusive
Spatial (Spa)	W_i is spatially opposite W_j
Vector (Vec)	W_i is directionally opposed to W_j

III. Elements of Agreement

Inclusion (Inc)	W_i is included in W_j semantically or physically
Overlap (Over)	Meanings of W_i and W_j overlap; W_i and W_j are semantically similar
Intersection (Int)	W_i is semantically included in W_j
Unilateral Inclusion (Unil)	W_j includes all of W_i but W_i does not include W_j
Bilateral Inclusion (Bil)	W_i and W_j include each other; $W_i = W_j$
Attribute (Att)	W_j is an attribute of W_i; W_i "is" W_j

IV. Propositional Elements

Event (Evt)	W_i and W_j related by an event
Action (Act)	W_i and W_j related by an action
Agent (Agt)	W_i is the agent of an action
Object (Obj)	W_j is the object of an action
Instrument (Inst)	W_j is the instrument used for an action

V. Elements of Part–Whole Inclusion

Partive Inclusion (Partive)	W_j is physically included in W_i
Locative Inclusion (Loc)	W_j is "in" W_i
Attachment (Attach)	W_j is attached to W_i
Social (Soc)	W_j is part of W_i by agreement
Homogeneous (Homog)	W_j's are interchangeable
Component (Comp)	W_j is a "component" of W_i
Property	W_j is a property of W_i
Possession (Poss)	W_i "possesses" a property or attribute

Note: Relation elements are from Stasio et al. (1985). To facilitate exposition changes have been made in the descriptions and in the order in which the elements are listed, and elements of part-whole inclusion are listed separately.

pseudoantonyms (e.g., popular–shy), opposition occurs on a dimension that involves *connotative* meaning—the contrary of "popular" is "unpopular," which connotes "shy."

The hierarchical relationship of the elements is indicated in the third column of Table 14.2 by parentheses. Elements that require the presence of another element are placed in parentheses after the required element. Elements that can occur independently of one another are separated by commas. For example, the elements for contraries are represented as DIM(BIP(Sym),Cont). The element of bipolarity (BIP) requires the presence of a dimension (DIM). In turn, symmetry (Sym) requires the element of bipolarity (BIP). Continuity (Cont) can occur independently of bipolarity or symmetry, and so is separated from "BIP(Sym)" by a comma, but requires the presence of a dimension of opposition and so is placed within the parentheses following "DIM."

Similarity.   Similarity relations are those that overlap in denotative or connotative meaning or both. Overlap of meaning can be represented by Euler's diagrams. Fig. 14.2 represents four configurations of meaning that must be distinguished. The three cases in which the areas of the two circles intersect represent three cases in which the meaning of A and B are similar because they share some features of meaning. In each case, we say that the meanings of A and B intersect, the element of *intersection* (Int). Figs. 14.2(a) and 2(b) represent situations in which the meaning of one term is totally included within the meaning of the other, the element of *inclusion* (Inc). Inclusion can be *unilateral* (Unil), as in Fig. 14.2(a) or bilateral, as in Fig. 14.2(b). Unilateral inclusion occurs when the meaning of A is totally included within the meaning of B, but the meaning of B extends beyond that of A. This situation occurs with class inclusion where the meaning of the category member includes that of the category name and the member has additional properties that distinguish it from other category members (e.g., vehicle–auto). *Bilateral* inclusion (Bil) occurs when the meaning of A is totally included in the meaning of B and vice versa; this occurs with synonyms (e.g., car–auto). Intersection can occur without inclusion, as in Fig. 14.2(c), if part of the meaning of each word intersects that of the other and part does not. We will say in this case that the meanings of two terms *overlap* (over). This occurs with dimensional similars, (e.g., smile–laugh).

The family element common to the similarity relations is intersection of meaning. The best known relation in the similarity family is synonymity (e.g., car–auto) (Herrmann, 1978; Naess, 1953), in which the denotative meaning of each term totally includes the other, INT(Inc(Bil)). Dimensional similars (e.g., smile–laugh) have overlapping meanings, but the relation also has elements that are characteristic of contrast relations. The two terms are on a common dimension but are on the same side of the midpoint. The relation of two terms that have similar attributes (e.g., rake–fork) also has elements of similarity and contrast. The two terms have overlapping meanings and also involve contrast on a nominal

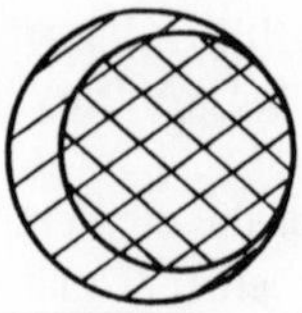

Intersection, Inclusion, Unilateral

3-a

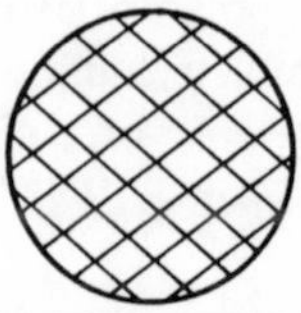

Intersection, Inclusion, Bilateral

3-b

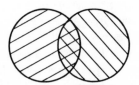

Intersection, Overlap

3-c

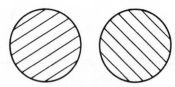

No Intersection

3-d

FIGURE 14.2. Euler's circles illustrating the relational elements of intersection, unilateral or bilateral inclusion, and overlap.

scale that has discrete values. Overlap of meaning is also present in the relation of an object to an attribute. The object can be said to "possess" (Poss) the attribute. An attribute may be essential to the nature of the object (e.g., bachelor–unmarried). An attribute that is nonessential but typical of an object (an "invited" attribute) is part of the connotation (Con) of the object (e.g., food–tasty). The *invited attribute* relation was assigned elements of a similarity relation even though it was classified as a case relation in the a priori taxonomy for the sorting study. This a priori classification was incorrect because there is no plausible way to assign it elements that are common to other case relations that are described below.

Class Inclusion. The class inclusion relation is the relation between two classes when one subsumes the other (Lyons, 1977; Miller & Johnson–Laird, 1976). The meaning of the two categories intersect, so that the meaning of the superordinate is included in the meaning of the subordinate term (INC). The subordinate also has additional features that distinguish one exemplar from another. These three elements, INT(INC(UNIL)), are common to all class inclusion relations and are hierarchically organized. There are differences in the kind of information that forms the basis for recognizing a member of the category (Wierzbicka, 1984). Some are principally characterized by visible, physical properties (e.g., animal–horse), some by their function (e.g., tool–hammer). States are identified by attributes (e.g., emotion–fear), activities and actions by intentions (e.g., game–chess and cook–fry). Geographical terms (e.g., country–Russia) represent a relation that is distinct form of the inclusion relation, that between an individual and the set it belongs to. This relation was, nevertheless, assigned the same elements as class inclusion relations in the Stasio et al. (1985) study.

Case Relations. The family of case relations includes relations between the arguments in the complex knowledge structures call "frames" or "scripts" that have been postulated to account for knowledge of the everyday world (Minsky, 1975; Rumelhart & Ortony, 1977; Schank & Abelson, 1977). An important aspect of this knowledge is that it includes expectations that result from experience with everyday events. These expectations can be represented by "default values," which give typical values for the arguments. For example, a tractor is typically used by a farmer for plowing; the agent–instrument relation was represented by pairs such as "farmer–tractor."

The family of case relations differs from the families we have considered so far in that *case relations* do not depend simply on the meaning of the two words in the relation. The two terms in a case relation are embedded in a knowledge structure that mediates the relationship. Without this structure, the relation does not exist. For example, it would be possible for someone to know of tractors as machines for mowing grass in the city and to know of farmers as people who plow with oxen to raise crops. This person could have a correct understanding of the meaning of "farmer" and "tractor" but would lack the knowledge structure that places the two in an agent–instrument relation for people in the U.S.A. In contrast, it would be difficult for a person to know the meanings of "animal" and "horse" without knowing that they are in a class inclusion relation.

What case relations have in common is that they are related through a common core which we will call an *event*. A description of an event typically involves an action or state that can take a variety of arguments. The arguments represented are the agent who is seen as the instigator of the action, the object that is affected by the action, and the instrument or force causally involved in the action or state (Fillmore, 1968). The five combinations of these elements represented in Table 14.2 were selected to represent the most general of the case relations.

Other important relations that might fall into this family include cause–effect relations (e.g., virus–disease), and location (e.g., artist–studio). Some of the examples that were selected to represent general case relations can also be viewed as illustrating important but more restricted relations. The pair "drink–cup," which was selected to exemplify the action–instrument relation, is also an instance of an object–function relation (Whitely, 1976). "Baker–bread" is an example of the provenience relation (Casagrande & Hale, 1967), "carpenter–lumber" of possession. The event through which arguments are related can place restrictions on relations that make them very specific, for example, the common elements of "flood–dike" and "invasion–fortification."

Part–whole. There are a number of distinct part–whole relations (Cruse, 1979; Lyons, 1977; Markman & Seibert, 1976; Miller & Johnson–Laird, 1976; Nagel, 1961). Part–whole relations, like class inclusion, have the element of inclusion. The inclusion of part–whole relations, however, is physical (INC(PARTIVE)) rather than an inclusion of the meaning of one term in another, as is the case with class inclusion (Herrmann, Chaffin, & Winston, 1986).

Part–whole relations have a relatively large number of elements that combine to produce a wide variety of part–whole relations (Winston, Chaffin & Herrmann, in press). Some parts are attached to the wholes of which they are a part (e.g., tree–leaf), whereas others are not (e.g., forest–tree). The relation of "forest–tree" is similar to that of "faculty–professor" except that the latter is based on a social contract rather than physical inclusion. For some types of part–whole relations, the parts are homogeneous so that one part can be readily substituted for another (e.g., forest–tree), whereas for others each part is distinct (e.g., car–engine). Distinct parts that play a role in the function of the whole (e.g., kitchen–refrigerator) are called components.

Many parts can be viewed as properties (Prop) of the whole, an element that finds expression in the sentence frame, "Ws have Ps" (e.g., Cars have engines). Parts of measures and places (e.g., hour–minute, Asia–China) are not properties in this sense. Many parts can be said to "belong to" the whole, i.e., to be a possession of the whole (e.g., tree–forest), but this is not true of units of measure (e.g., mile–yard). For some of the relations, the second term can be said to be "in" the first term; this is indicative of locative (Loc) inclusion (for example, Asia–China and table–wood). These two relations are not strictly part–whole relations. Like part–whole relations, they involve physical constituency, but are more accurately expressed by "China is in Asia" and "A table is made of wood" than by "part of".

Adequacy of the Relation Element Account

How well do the relation elements we have described account for the similarities between relations? Stasio's study addressed this question by using the relation elements to try to account for the similarities between relations in the sorting tasks, which are shown in Fig. 14.1. First, the similarity of each of the 31 relations to each other was computed as the proportion of common elements for each pair of relations. This measure was adopted for the sake of simplicity; it does not take into account the structure of the elements. The proportion of common elements was entered into a 31×31 matrix of element similarity. The element similarity matrix was then correlated with the 31×31 sorting matrix already described to determine how well element similarity accounted for the frequency with which relations were sorted together. The correlation was substantial, $r (463) = 0.71, p<.001$, indicating that the relation elements proposed accounted for nearly half the variance in the sorting frequencies.

To determine how well family markers accounted for the sorting data, a new matrix was constructed to represent the similarity of the 31 relations as determined by their family markers. Each cell of the 31×31 matrix was filled with a "1" if two relations were in the same family, or "0" if they were in different families. The correlation of this family-marker similarity matrix with the sorting matrix was $r (463) = 0.69, p<.001$. A high correlation was to be expected because family markers account for the major feature of the sorting data, the organization of the relations into five major clusters.

The question to be answered is whether family markers account for all of the variance accounted for by relation elements. They did not. A partial correlation of the relation element and sorting matrices with the family marker matrix partialed out was still highly significant, $r (461) = 0.35, p<.001$. Relation elements thus account for variance in the sorting data that is not accounted for by family markers.

There are two sources of similarity between relations that is not accounted for by family markers. One is the similarity of families to one another. For example, class inclusion and similarity relations were grouped more closely to each other than to part–whole relations. Second, relations within a family vary in similarity.

For example, within the part–whole family, measure (pound–ounce) and ingredient (pizza–cheese) relations were grouped more closely to each other than to functional object–component (car–wheel) relations. Neither type of similarity is accounted for by family markers which represent each family by a unitary marker and all relations within a family by the same marker.

The success of relation markers in accounting for similarity between and within families was evaluated by correlating the relevant portions of the element similarity and sorting matrices. The ability of relation elements to account for similarity between families was assessed by correlating those cells representing relations in different families. The correlation, r (378) = 0.40, $p<.01$, indicated that relation elements did account for some of the similarities of the families. Similarities within families were evaluated separately for each family by correlating the cells for relations in the same family. The relation elements for contrast relations were most successful in accounting for similarities within the family, ($r(28)$ = 0.75, $p <.05$), followed by class inclusion, ($r(15)$ = 0.53, $p<.05$). Correlations for the other three families were lower and did not reach significance: For similars $r(10)$ = 0.52, $p<.07$; for case relations $r(10)$ = 0.45, $p<.10$; for part–whole relations $r(21)$ = 0.33, $p<.08$.

Thus, relation elements account for the organization into families and also account for similarities between and within families. Family markers are able to account for the grouping into families, but do not account for similarities between and within families. The success of the relation element account of the sorting data is limited by two factors. First, the linguistic and logical analyses of the relations that were used to select the elements, while they provide a fairly good account of how our subjects viewed the relations, could undoubtedly be improved upon. Second, the sorting may have been influenced by factors other than the properties of the relations. For example, as noted previously, the sorting of the place relation was affected by the similarity of the concepts involved.

THE JUDGMENT OF ANALOGIES

Analogy problems also require judgments to be made about the similarities of relations. The subject must choose from among several choice relations the one that matches a standard relation most closely. According to the relation element hypothesis, the subject identifies the elements of the standard and each of the choice relations and decides which choice (relation) matches the standard most closely. The unitary marker position would maintain that a marker is retrieved for each word pair and the choice pair is selected that has the same marker as the standard.

The elements that make up a relation can be divided into two components, of which the relation element theory and the two unitary marker positions give different accounts. The family component consists of the elements that are common to all members of the family (i.e., the capitalized components in Table

TABLE 14.4
Examples of Three Types of Analogy Problems from the
Semantic Relations Test
(Select the choice pair whose relation matches the relation of the
target pair.)

Target Pairs		Choice Pairs	
a. inside	hammer	upstairs	wheel
outside	nail	downstairs	bicycle
b. top	office	vegetable	life
bottom	desk	apple	death
c. front	entrance	absence	poverty
back	exit	presence	wealth

14.2). The specific component consists of the elements that distinguish one relation in a family from another (because elements are hierarchically arranged, family elements are more basic in the hierarchy than specific element). The two unitary marker theories differ in the component used to mark links between concepts. The family marker hypothesis maintains that information about the family component, but not the specific component, is represented in memory. The specific marker hypothesis maintains that markers represent the specific but not the family component. The relation element position maintains that information about both the family and the specific components is represented. The three positions thus differ in their predictions about the kind of analogy items that people are able to solve.

To compare the three hypotheses, analogy items were developed on the basis of the taxonomy of semantic relations in Fig. 14.1 by Julie Ross (Ross, Herrmann, Vaughan, & Chaffin, 1987). This test, called the Semantic Relations Test (SRT), required subjects to solve analogy items, each consisting of a standard pair and three choice pairs. Three sample items are shown in Table 14.4 in the form in which they were presented to subjects. The task is to select the choice pair whose relation most closely matches that of the target pair. The reader may wish to attempt the three items at this point, because the answers are given subsequently.

Design of the SRT

The items in Table 14.4 illustrate the three types of item that were created for each family. The three items each test knowledge of contrast relations, but each tests different components of relation knowledge. For heterogeneous–same items (a), the correct choice can be selected on the basis of either the family or specific component of relations. For heterogeneous–different items (b), the correct choice can only be selected on the basis of the family component. For homogeneous items (c), the correct choice must be selected on the basis of the specific component. The three types of item thus test for the presence of different components of relation knowledge.[1]

This is made more clear in Table 14.5, which presents the three items from Table 14.4 again, giving the family and specific components of the relation of each pair. This time, the word pairs are listed in a column on the left of the table with the relation components for each pair on the right. The answer for each item is indicated by an asterisk after the correct choice. The correct choice is the pair whose family and specific components best match those of the target pair: The components of the correct choice that match are underlined. We describe each item of table 14.5 in turn beginning at the bottom with the third item. This is an example of a "homogeneous" item, so-called because the target and three choice pairs are from the same family. The correct choice is the same specific relation, while the distractors are other specific relations from the same family. For homogeneous items, (c), the target and the correct choice match only on the specific component. Knowledge of the specific component is therefore required for a correct choice to be made. Knowledge of the family component alone will not allow a correct choice to be made. The first two items we call "heterogeneous" because the incorrect choices are from different families than the correct choice and the target. For heterogeneous–same items (a) the correct choice is the same specific relation as the standard. For heterogeneous–same items (a), the correct choice is distinguished by both family and specific components; knowledge of either component would allow a correct choice to be made. For heterogeneous–different (b) items the distractors are again from a different family than the target. The correct choice is from the same family as the target but is a different specific relation from that family. For heterogeneous–different items, knowledge of the family component is required for a correct choice; knowledge of the specific component will not suffice.

According to the unitary marker position, only one component of relation knowledge is represented in memory. In the family marker version, the family component is represented but the specific component is not; chance level responding is therefore predicted for homogeneous items. The unitary specific marker version represents the specific component but not the family component of relation knowledge; chance level responding is therefore predicted for the heterogeneous–different items. The relation element hypothesis represents both family and specific components of relation knowledge; responding above chance level is therefore possible for all three types of items.

Both the unitary and the relation element hypotheses allow for the possibility that subjects may be better at some relation families than others. According to the

---

[1]Copies of the SRT and a scoring key can be obtained from D.J. Herrmann, Department of Psychology, Hamilton College, Clinton, NY 13323.

TABLE 14.5
Family and Specific Components of Relation Definitions for Three
Types of Analogy Item

		Components	
		Family	Specific
1.	Heterogeneous–same. Family and Specific Components Match.		
Target	Inside Outside	Contrast	Directional
Choices	Hammer Nail	Case	Instrument/ Object
	Upstairs Downstairs*	*Contrast	*Directional
	Wheel Bike	Part–whole	Functional
2.	Heterogeneous–different. Family Components Match		
Target	Top Bottom	Contrast	Directional
Choices	Office Desk	Part–whole	Locational
	Vegetable Apple	Class inclusion	Collateral
	Life Death*	*Contrast	Contradictory
3.	Homogeneous. Specific Components Match		
Target	Front Back	Contrast	Directional
Choices	Entrance Exit*	Contrast	*Directional
	Absence Presence	Contrast	Contradictory
	Poverty Wealth	Contrast	Contrary

Note: Underlining indicates target pair, correct choice, and the components on which they match. Asterisks indicate the correct choice and the component(s) on which the selection of the correct choice is based.

TABLE 14.6
Examples of Relations on the SRT with the Names of their Family
and Specific Components

Family	Specific Relation	Example
Contrast	Contrary	poverty–wealth
Contrast	Contradictory	life–death
Contrast	Directional antonym	inside–outside
Similar	Synonym	middle–center
Similar	Dimensional similar	smile–laugh
Similar	Attribute similar	ball–orange
Class inclusion	Superordinate	bird–robin
Class inclusion	Coordinate	table–couch
Class inclusion	Collateral	vegetable–apple
Case relation	Agent–object	king–crown
Case relation	Instrument–object	hammer–nail
Case relation	Agent–instrument	artist–paintbrush
Part–whole	Functional object	wheel–bicycle
Part–whole	Membership	singer–choir
Part–whole	Functional location	desk–office

unitary view, however, accuracy above chance level for a particular relation family should not differ by item type. A marker for a particular relation is either present or absent. If present, its availability should not differ by type of item. The relation element position, in contrast, allows for the possibility that the level of accuracy for a relation family may vary with item type because each item type depends on a different component of relation knowledge. It is quite possible, for example, for subjects to be good at identifying the family component but poor at identifying the specific components of relations in a family.

Ross constructed 60 analogy items, six homogeneous, three heterogeneous–same and three heterogeneous–different items for each family. Each family was represented by three specific relations, which are listed in Table 14.6. Each specific relation was used four times as a target relation for an item. The words selected were all frequently used nouns ($\bar{x} > 20$; Kucera & Francis, 1967). The SRT was given to 83 students at Hamilton College.

Results of the SRT

Ross's results are shown in Fig. 14.3, which gives the mean percentage correct as a function of relation family and item type. Responding was above chance level for all item types for each of the five relation families, with one exception. With this exception, the prediction of the relation element position was supported. For four of the five families, subjects did have knowledge of both the family and the specific components of relations. Knowledge of the family com-

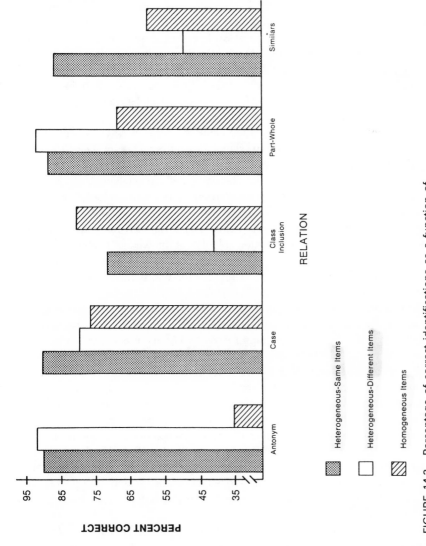

FIGURE 14.3. Percentage of correct identifications as a function of relation and item type.

241

ponent was required to respond accurately to heterogeneous–different items; knowledge of the specific component was required for homogeneous items. The prediction of the unitary marker view of chance level responding to one item type was thus not supported.

For homogeneous–contrast items, responding was at chance level, as predicted by the unitary family marker view. The results for the other four families suggest that these results should also be explained in terms of relation elements. Other research suggests that subjects are initially unable to distinguish specific antonym relations from one another, but improve rapidly when given explicit instruction (Conti, 1978). Apparently, knowledge of the specific component of contrast relations is lacking in the Hamilton College undergraduate population tested by Ross and by Conti.

The second prediction of the relation element approach was also supported. The different item types did differ in accuracy within each *family*. The difference in difficulty can be explained in terms of differences in the ease with which the family and specific components of relations could be recognized. When the family component was more readily recognized, accuracy was higher for heterogeneous items. When the specific component was recognized more easily, accuracy was higher for homogeneous items. The difference in difficulty is not readily explained by a unitary position. If relation knowledge is unitary, a distinction between family and specific components of a relation cannot be made. A relation is either present or absent; if present for one item type, it should be present for another.

The relation element view, in contrast, allows conclusions to be drawn about the relative discriminability of a family and specific components for each family. For contrast items, accuracy was high for the two kinds of heterogeneous items and at chance level for the homogeneous items. Heterogeneous items involve the family component; homogeneous items only the specific component. The family component was accurately distinguished. This is not surprising because the sorting study showed that contrast relations are the most distinct of the five families.

The subjects' ability to pick out the family component contrasts sharply to their inability to distinguish the specific component of contrast relations. This is indicated by the chance level performance for the homogeneous items which involve only the specific component. The distinction between contrast relations (e.g., between contraries and contradictories) is not one which most people are familiar with and was apparently not one that could be constructed on the spot from the examples that appeared in each item.

The *part–whole family* showed a similar pattern to the *contrast family:* Accuracy was higher for heterogeneous than for homogeneous items. Unlike the contrast relations, accuracy for the homogeneous items was well above chance. This pattern of results indicates that the family component was more readily distinguished than the specific component, but that subjects had some knowledge of both. Unlike contrast relations, the specific components of part–whole relations are reflected in numerous common terms for various part–whole relations, e.g., "section," "member," "portion," "piece" (Winston, Chaffin, & Herrmann, in press). Familiarity with these relational concepts may account for subjects' accuracy on the homogeneous part–whole items.

The pattern for case relations was similar to that for the part–whole family, except that the difference between omogeneous and heterogeneous items was smaller. The family and specific components were equally distinct.

The pattern of results for *class inclusion* was quite different. Accuracy was lowest for the heterogeneous–different items which depend on the family component, and higher and approximately equal for heterogeneous–same and homogeneous items which both involve the specific component. The family component for class inclusion was not readily recognized. This may be because the coordinate (e.g., table–chair) and collateral (e.g., vegetable–apple) relations were used. These require the generation of a superordinate (furniture and fruit respectively). If the superordinate is not generated, the two words may be seen as similars.

For the similarity relations accuracy was low for both heterogeneous–different and homogeneous items. Performance was good only for the heterogeneous–same items for which knowledge of both family and specific components can be used together. This may be due to the fact that similarity is characteristic of most relation families. The family elements for similarity may, therefore be hard to distinguish from those of other relation families, except when other specific elements are present.

In summary, the predictions of the relation element view were supported, those of the unitary view were not. Subjects performed with above chance accuracy on all three item types, and item types differed in difficulty within the same family. The SRT has thus provided evidence that when subjects solve analogy problems they decompose relations into at least two components.

CONCLUSION

The evidence for the use of relation elements has come from tasks in which subjects make judgments based on the similarity of relations. We have shown that people can make graded similarity judgments about the similarity of semantic relations, and that this ability may be based on a comparison of the elements of which relations are composed. The sorting study showed that people's judgments about the similarity of relations yielded a coherent taxonomy of relations that was better explained by relation elements than by unitary relation markers. The SRT showed that people solve analogies by decomposing the standard and choice relations into at least two components, a family and a specific component; these components can be described in terms of the family and specific elements that make up each relation. Unitary marker theories of relations, in contrast, allow only all-or-none judgments about relations; they do not account for the ability to make graded similarity judgments about relations.

Variants of current network theories might be devised to account for the ability to make graded similarity judgments by representing each relation by multiple markers. Such a modification would be to abandon the unitary relation position in favor of the relation element approach proposed here (see also Johnson–Laird et al., 1984; Klix, Hoffman, & van de Meer, 1983). Standard relations would no longer function as the primitive explanatory elements of the theory, but would themselves be described in terms of more fundamental relation elements. Relation elements would be the new primitive terms in the theory.

Relation similarity judgments are involved in most of the tasks that are commonly used to study relation comprehension. Performance in these tasks may also be based on the evaluation of relation elements. For example, relation similarity is evaluated in semantic decision tasks in which subjects are asked to decide whether pairs of words represent a particular semantic relation (e.g., ''Is A a type of B?'' ''Is A part of B?''). This judgment requires the subject to evaluate the similarity of the relation between stimulus words to the target relation that they are asked to identify. This is indicated by the effect of relation similarity on the latency and probability of correct decisions. For example, when subjects are asked to decide if pairs of words are antonyms, response times for a stimulus pair are a function of the degree to which the relation of the pair typifies or is similar to antonymy. In one study (Herrmann, Chaffin, Conti, Peters, & Robbins, 1979) *yes* decisions were faster for good examples of antonymy (e.g., hot–cold) than for poor examples (e.g., clear–foggy), and *no* decisions were faster for pairs that have none of the characteristics of antonymy (e.g., salty–gentle) than for pseudoantonym pairs that have some elements of the antonym relation (e.g., popular–shy). This effect of relation similarity, like the other relation similarity effects we have examined, indicates that the target and stimulus relations were decomposed into elements for comparison.

Relation similarity has parallel effects on the latency of decisions about other semantic relations (Herrmann & Chaffin, 1986). The effects are similar to the typicality and similarity effects commonly reported for class inclusion decisions (e.g., McCloskey & Glucksberg, 1979; Smith, Shoben, & Rips, 1974). It is probable, therefore, that relation similarity plays a role in these effects. A model of semantic decisions about relations is described in another paper (Herrmann & Chaffin, 1986).

The view that relations can be decomposed into elements requires a shift in the way that we view psychology's oldest theoretical construct, the association. Unlabelled associations account for the fact that ideas are connected; they do not explain the nature of the connection (Clark, 1970; Miller, 1969). Unitary relation markers remedy this by labelling the associations with a unitary label; but the composition of the relation is still not explained or even described. Unitary markers are, therefore, unable to provide a full account of relation phenomena.

Relation elements represent both the connection between ideas and also the nature of the connection. The nature of the connection must be represented in order to account for people's ability to judge the similarity of relations. To account for the perception of relation similarity, it is necessary to represent more than the simple fact that an association exists, or event that a labelled relation exists. It is necessary to account for its character. Relation elements provide such an account and are thus a more powerful explanatory tool than either unlabelled associations or unitary markers.

Once relation elements are recognized, further questions are raised. How are elements acquired? Is their number limited? Are they universal? What is their role in other cognitive operations? Although the importance of relations has long been recognized, basic questions about their nature and function have yet to be answered. These questions involve many different areas of psychology. The relation element approach to semantic relations has its origin in linguistics (Leech, 1974; Lyons, 1968, 1977) but has implications for all areas of psychology in which relations are used as explanatory constructs. Language and cognitive development, comprehension, inference, problem solving, and reasoning are among the abilities for which relation elements may provide a more powerful explanatory tool than either unlabelled associations or unitary relation markers.

ACKNOWLEDGMENTS

We thank the students of Hamilton College who contributed to this work: Theresa Stasio for her work on relation elements, and Julie Ross for her work on the SRT, which was done as part of a senior fellowship. We also thank our colleagues: Jonathan Vaughan for his work on the SRT and for numerous discussions of all the issues discussed here, and Morton Winston for discussion of part–whole relations and other issues. The writing of this chapter was supported in part by a grant from Trenton State College to the first author.

15

Beyond Associationism: Comments on the Chapters by Reder and by Chaffin and Herrmann

Sam Glucksberg
Princeton University

These two chapters share a common theme: beyond associationism. However, the nature of the *beyond* differs. For Reder, *beyond* associationism refers to multiple retrieval strategies from a single type of memorial representation, an associative network. For Chaffin and Herrmann, *beyond* involves multiple representations with a single mode of retrieval. Aside from this superficial commonality, the two chapters address quite different issues, and appropriately so. Reder is concerned with specific memories. In contrast, Chaffin and Herrmann are concerned with semantic memory, or more precisely, knowledge of semantic relations. Reder's "beyond" is therefore still within the Ebbinghaus tradition; Chaffin and Herrmann's work grows out of a quite different tradition.

Reder goes beyond the Ebbinghaus approach in two ways. First, the pattern of associations is more sophisticated than Ebbinghaus' pair-wise connections, in keeping with the development of associationism within the framework of modern cognitive psychology (See Estes, this volume, on the development of associationism from Ebbinghaus to the present). Second, the operations on such associations are also more complex, consisting of at least two processes: direct retrieval via a search among associative connections, and indirect retrieval via a familiarity or plausibility judgment.

As Reder suggests, adding this retrieval strategy to Ebbinghaus' conception of storage permits one to reconcile the traditional Ebbinghaus position with that of Bartlett. Ebbinghaus provides the form of representation and the idea of verbatim retrieval from memory; Bartlett provides the notion of a reconstructive memory. Reder's "plausibility judgment strategy" can be viewed as one variant of a reconstructive memory process.

Appealing as this view might be, it may be an oversimplification of both Ebbinghaus and Bartlett. As Hoffman, Bringmann, Bamberg, and Klein (this volume) point out, Ebbinghaus was not so naïve as to think that what is remembered is a verbatim record of experience. To begin with, associations themselves are not a record of events, but a construction of the mind. The temporal relations among events determine the formation not only of direct associations, but of remote associations as well, as reflected in Ebbinghaus' use of derived lists. His use of such lists was a precursor of contemporary experiments on part–whole transfer effects. Not only are records of events constructed by the mind, those records are not necessarily available to awareness. Indeed, Ebbinghaus' most commonly known invention, the method of savings, was expressly designed to reveal the existence of memorial records that were not directly accessible.

In short, Ebbinghaus' view of memory was constructive at least in the sense that associations were constructed on the basis of temporal relations among stimuli. But more than that, Ebbinghaus was well aware of the more cognitive forms of constructive memory, so that in addition to mere temporal contiguity, the formation of associations is affected by such factors as meaning, imagery, grouping, and other mnemonic mediators (Hoffman et al., this volume). That Ebbinghaus chose to focus on "bare" remembering—albeit with rhythmic grouping to facilitate learning—should not lead us to conclude that he was ignorant of more complex remembering.

Similarly, that Bartlett chose to focus on the more complex memorial processes, emphasizing constructive recall, should not lead us to conclude that memorial records do not exist. In order to reconstruct, one needs some residue of experience on which to build—this residue may be in the form of associations, images, or schemas, but whatever it might be, it is a record of experience of the kind Ebbinghaus strove to isolate.

In this sense, Ebbinghaus and Bartlett do converge. They each explicitly recognized that memories are not verbatim records of what is experienced, and both developed experimental paradigms to answer questions about memory. Their questions were, however, of different kinds. Ebbinghaus tried to devise methods that would illuminate the nature of the memorial record. Bartlett, in turn, took the fact of such a record as a given—it was partial and incomplete. With this as a given, the questions for the memory theorist involved retrieval mechanisms. And, like Reder, both Ebbinghaus and Bartlett assumed that there was one basic form of memory representation, with multiple ways to interrogate that representation.

In contrast, Chaffin and Herrmann argue for multiple rather than unitary memorial representations, if not in kind, at least in content. They argue that associative links are insufficient to account for a variety of cognitive abilities, including the ability to solve certain kinds of analogy problems, as in their Semantic Relations Test. Their major claim is that people have more than just one component of relational knowledge stored in memory. Their multiple representation view argues that people have specific relational knowledge directly represented in memory, and this, in turn, involves a decompositional view of semantic memory. For example, not only do people have such relational elements as "part–whole" represented in memory, they also have more specific versions of such a relation, e.g., section, member, portion, piece.

There is no doubt, given what we know of people's abilities to perceive analogies and relations, that such concepts can be used. I would like, however, to propose an alternative to Chaffin and Herrmann's relational element account of semantic memory. To begin with, the term "semantic memory" is a metaphor that implies a store with things contained in that store. Accordingly, semantic relations, such as class inclusion relations, are believed to be directly represented in memory. An alternative account (cf., McCloskey & Glucksberg, 1979) argues that such relations need not be directly represented in memory, but are instead computed (inferred). Thus, to answer the question, "*Is an aardvark a mammal?*" one would use one's knowledge of the characteristics and properties of aardvarks and of mammals to infer the answer, "yes."

This nonrepresentational, computational position has several distinct advantages over the complete-representation-and-retrieval position. For one thing, it can handle our ability for limitless cross-classifications. Aardvarks are not only mammals, they are also rare animals, furry animals, a source of protein, could be expensive pets, belong to the category of zoo animals, and could belong to any number of other categories, some natural, some ad hoc (cf., Barsalou, 1983; Barsalou & Sewell, 1984). With respect to part–whole relations, aardvarks have ears (part-of relation), spleens (part-of relation?), specific needs and motivations (what relation is that?), and could have any number of other "parts" and properties. It is difficult to imagine that each of these relations is always directly stored and retrieved when needed. It seems more plausible that we usually infer the answers to such questions about relations on the basis of our world knowledge, whether these questions are in the form of class-inclusion questions, property questions, or analogies of the kind used in the Semantic Relations Test.

As an example, consider the limitless bases for analogy problems. Some require knowledge of a specialized domain, such as musical instruments, as a *Violin: Cello:: Piccolo: _____?*

(a) Scriabin
(b) Trumpet
(c) Flute
(d) Pasta

The relation within the musical instrument domain is relative pitch within an instrument family. *Trumpet* would be an acceptable answer, but *flute* is a better one. Are such relational elements always directly stored? Perhaps. But consider the following, which I dimly recall from the Miller Analogies Test, which I took some 30 years ago:

*Yesterday: Finaly::   Today:*_____

(a) rubber
(b) Willfuly
(c) Tomorrow
(d) Noon

The answer in this case is (b), willfuly. The relation? Spelled correctly: spelled incorrectly. Is this a relational element that we want to have directly represented in semantic memory?

The effects of context on the interpretation of analogy terms also argue for a computational rather than a direct memorial representation view. Consider the analogies:

Front: back

(a) Black:White
(b) Yellow:Green
(c) Yellow:Brave
(d) Blue:Red
(e) Blue:Pink

The general relation is "opposites." Which are the better concluding terms? If no context is specified, most people would, I think, choose (a), black–white. If the context were to be "bananas," then (b) would be more suitable (ripe:unripe); if personality traits, then (c), if color terms, then (a), (b) or (d), but if babies' gender, then (e). How many of such specific relations must we directly represent in semantic memory? The problem is clear. We are capable of too many different classifications, too many different ways of perceiving relations, for them all to always be directly represented and still be manageable. It may well be that the direct representational view is too cumbersome, and that instead of semantic elements, or relational elements, we have a different kind of semantic primitive: knowledge of the world, from which we can derive knowledge of relations.

On the basis of this nonrepresentational view, the questions posed by Chaffin and Herrmann at the end of their chapter become different questions. The question, "How are elements acquired?" becomes, "How is world knowledge acquired?" Is the number of elements limited? Obviously not, if by elements we now mean world knowledge. Are "the" elements universal? This question now becomes meaningless. Presumably, world knowledge has commonalities among cultures, but there are also differences. And finally, the suggestion that relational elements may provide an explanatory tool for inference and problem solving may be reversed: Inference and problem solving—in short, thinking—may provide the explanatory tool for the abilities that Chaffin and Herrmann attribute to relational elements that are directly represented in memory.

The suggestion in Reder's work, that remembering may involve thinking, can, I suggest, be extended to semantic memory as well: The judging of relations requires thinking, and not merely accessing prestored knowledge representations. Both Ebbinghaus and Bartlett acknowledged this in the domain of episodic memory. Perhaps we should consider acknowledging this in the domain of semantic memory as well.

ACKNOWLEDGMENT

Preparation of this comment was supported in part by grant No. BNS 85–19462 from the National Science Foundation.

16

What is Conscious in the Control of Action? A Modern Ideomotor Theory of Voluntary Control

Bernard J. Baars
The Wright Institute
Berkeley, California

INTRODUCTION

Ebbinghaus is known to us mainly as a pioneer in the study of associative memory, but this reputation surely reflects our own biases and predilections. He was interested in a great range of topics. His doctoral dissertation of 1873, for example, was an exploration of the concept of the unconscious, a most difficult and pressing issue for all 19th century psychology (Baars, 1986; Murray, 1983).

Today we find ourselves rediscovering the crucial role of both conscious and unconscious events. In that sense, this chapter owes a debt not just to Ebbinghaus but to his whole generation, which asked questions and gave some answers that we cannot ignore today. Fortunately, the intervening hundred years have yielded some advances, so that we may be able to interpret the insights of the Ebbinghaus generation in ways that are a little more precise and adequate.

This chapter explores a convergence between two streams of my work, one empirical and the other theoretical. On the empirical side, it builds on a decade of research in collaboration with others on experimentally elicited slips of the tongue (e.g., Baars, 1980a,b; Baars, forthcoming, b). On the theoretical side, I approach the issue of conscious experience through a "Global Workspace" model, which has so far proved extremely fruitful in integrating large amounts of evidence and generating new testable hypotheses (Baars, 1983, 1985a, b, and forthcoming, a). In principle these empirical and theoretical programs must somehow be related: After all, slips of the tongue are *involuntary* speech acts—in commonsense terms, they are not under "conscious control." But what does that really mean?

Part of the answer can come from the Ebbinghaus generation, which thought so deeply about these issues, but not all: The late 19th century had great philosophical difficulties with the foundations of psychology, difficulties that seem less problematic today. William James, for example, was committed to the position that all psychological phenomena must be reducible to conscious events (James, 1890, chapters 1, 6, and 7). Further, for James there are no unconscious psychological events. Chapter 6 of his great book explores ten persuasive arguments for unconscious processes, each followed by a "refutation." These are of two kinds: first, James maintains that many allegedly unconscious processes result from very fast, conscious "flashes" that cannot be recalled and reported. Second, he argues that all true unconscious processes are physiological, and therefore not really in the psychological domain of discourse.

These difficulties with unconscious processes are quite typical for that time. In the 19th century, with major exceptions such as Freud and Janet, most psychologists found it hard to believe in complex, functional, or intelligent unconscious processes. Today however, with so many examples of intelligent information processing, both biological and mechanical, we can no longer deny the importance of unconscious events, nor must we reduce all psychological events to conscious processes. Within the cognitive framework we are free to infer both conscious *and* unconscious events when they seem warranted by the evidence (Baars, 1986). Nonetheless, as we shall see, the generation of James and Ebbinghaus is still a major source of insights.

This chapter is organized into three main sections. First, I list a set of constraints on action control, based on various sources of evidence. Next, I consider William James' ideomotor theory of voluntary control, which suggests a role for unconscious components in the control of action. And finally, I interpret both the constraints and James' theory in terms of a global workspace model, which suggests that conscious experiences correspond to representation in a global workspace, widely broadcast to many unconscious specialized processors, including goal systems, actions schemas, and effectors. Conscious goals, I suggest, become involved when some nonroutine aspect of action must be controlled, whereas the unconscious processors correspond largely to the routine, predictable, and presupposed components of action.

I begin by listing constraints on theory. How shall we view actions and intentions, and their relation to conscious experience?

SOME CONSTRAINTS ON ACTION SCHEMA AND INTENTIONS

The study of errors provides a revealing window into the organization of action. For instance, many spontaneous action errors collected by Reason (1984) involve the insertion, deletion, or exchange of coherent subunits of an overall action. Consider the following errors:

1. "I went into my room intending to fetch a book. I took off my rings, looked in the mirror and came out again—without the book" (deletion error).

2. "As I approached the turnstile on my way out of the library, I pulled out my wallet as if to pay—although no money was required" (insertion error).

3. "During a morning in which there had been several knocks at my office door, the phone rang. I picked up the receiver and bellowed '*Come in*' at it" (substitution error).

4. "Instead of opening a tin of Kit-E-Kat, I opened and offered my cat a tin of rice pudding" (component exchange—"behavioral spoonerism").

5. "In a hurried effort to finish the housework and have a bath, I put the plants meant for the lounge in the bedroom, and my underwear in the window of the lounge" (component exchange).

In all five errors, action components are inserted, deleted, and exchanged in a smooth, normal, seemingly volitional fashion.

Action Schemas

This suggests that normal action may be organized in terms of subunits, i.e., actions may be made up of modular parts. The fact that complex actions tend to decompose into meaningful components has been known for some time from linguistic errors. In speech, the elements that are deleted, inserted, or exchanged are almost invariably well-formed linguistic units, such as phonemes, syllables, morphemes, words, or even syntactic constituents (Baars, 1980a; Fromkin, 1973).

Reason (1984) calls these modules the "action schemas", which "can be independently activated and behave in an energetic and highly competitive fashion to try to grab a piece of the action" (p. 34). That is to say, action schemas seem to be active: They seem to compete for the privilege of participating in an action, to the point where activated action schemas tend to enter into the wrong context, as in errors (2) through (5). This claim is consistent with a widespread conviction that the detailed control of action is decentralized or "distributed," so that much of the control problem is handled by local processes (Arbib, 1982; Baars, 1980b, 1983; Gel'fand et al., 1971; Greene, 1972). It is also consistent with findings about the autonomy of highly practiced skills which have become automatized and largely unconscious (Shiffrin & Schneider, 1977). Normal actions, of course, combine many highly practiced skills.

Action schemas seem to be composable and decomposable. It makes sense to think that a complex action schema can often be called on as a whole to perform its function. In the act of leaping on a bicycle we cannot wait to gather the separate components of spatial orientation, motor control, balance control, and vision. Instead, we seem to call in an instant on a single "bicycle-riding sche-ma," one that will organize and unify all the components of bicycle riding. However, in getting off the bicycle it makes sense to decompose the bicycle-riding schema, so that parts of it become available for use in standing, walking, and running. Those actions also require general skills, such as spatial orientation, motor control, balance, and vision. It makes sense to adapt general skills for use in a variety of similar actions. Moreover, if something goes wrong while we are riding the bicycle—if we lose a piece of the left pedal—we must be able to decompose the action as a whole, in order to find the part of the bicycle-riding skill that must be altered to adapt to the problem.

Evidently we need two abilities that seem at odds with each other: the ability to call on complex functions in a unitary way, and also the ability to decompose and reorganize the same complex functions when task or context changes. Action schemas are rather like Chinese puzzle boxes. They are defined recursively, so that a schema may consist of a coalition of schemas, which in turn may also be a member of a larger set of schemas that can act as a single chunk. We should not expect to define an action schema independent of task and context, although some tasks may be so common that they need generalized, relatively invariant schemas.

This kind of flexible, recursive organization does not make life simpler from a theoretical point of view, but it is suggested by artificial intelligence systems that simulate complex human functions (e.g., Winograd, 1972). It also appears in analyses of patients with brain damage, such as aphasia and apraxia. In some cases, large functional units seem to "drop out," whereas in others, only parts of the larger skill are affected (e.g., Geschwind, 1979).

Because such action schemas are unconscious and automatic, they appear to act in the service of goals that are sometimes consciously accessible. Indeed, action schemas can be labeled most naturally by the goal or subgoal which they appear to subserve. Error (1) in the list given is a failure of a goal that may be called "fetch book." Error (2) is an inappropriate execution of the goal "pull out wallet," and so on. Each of these actions could be described in many different ways; for example, in terms of physical movements, in terms of muscle groups, etc. But such descriptions would not capture the error very well. Thus, action schemas appear to be *goal-addressable*. However, in any given action, the goals are not necessarily conscious.

Further, effector control is rarely accessible to conscious introspection. Try wiggling your little finger. What is conscious about this? The answer seems to be, "remarkably little." We may have some kinesthetic feedback sensation, some sense of the moment of onset of the action, perhaps a fleeting image of the goal a moment before the action occurs. But there is no clear sense of command-ing the act, no clear planning process, and certainly no awareness of the details of the action. Wiggling a finger seems simple enough, but its details are not conscious in the same way in which we are conscious of perceptual events, such as the sight of a pencil or the sound of a spoken word. Few people know where the muscles that move the little finger are located (they are not in the hand, but in the forearm). No normal speaker of English has conscious knowledge of the movement of the jaw, tongue, velum, glottis, and vocal cords that are needed to shape a single spoken syllable. It is remarkable how well we get along without conscious retrievable knowledge of our own routine actions. Greene (1972) calls this "executive ignorance," and maintains that it applies to many distributed control systems.

In technical language, we can sum up all these considerations by saying that: (a) Actions are organized *modularly;* (b) They may be composed and decomposed *recursively* in a context-sensitive way; (c) Control of detail is widely *distributed* or decentralized; (d) Executive processes are relatively *ignorant* of effector control; (e) Action schemas seem to be *goal-addressable;* and (f) For any given action, only some of the goals will be conscious.

So much for the organization of action schemas. What about intentions, or the goals that guide our actions? How are we to think about intentions?

Intentions as Non-Qualitative Goal States that Dominate Central Limited Capacity: The "Tip-of-the-Tongue" Phenomenon.

Consider William James' (1890/1983) well-known observations about the state of attempting to recall a forgotten word. Is such a state truly conscious or not, asks James?

> Suppose we try to recall a forgotten name. The state of our consciousness is peculiar. There is a gap therein; but no mere gap. It is a gap that is intensely active. A sort of a wraith of the name is in it, beckoning us in a given direction, making us at moments tingle with the sense of our closeness, and then letting us sink back without the longed-for term. If wrong names are proposed to us, this singularly definitive gap acts immediately so as to negate them. They do not fit into its mold. (p. 286)

Something is clearly going on—we are consciously involved in some sort of definite state, because if soemone suggests the wrong word to us, we know immediately that it is wrong and we instantly recognize the right word when it comes to mind. In modern terms, we can successfully match and mismatch the forgotten word. This ability implies that the tip-of-the-tongue state involves a representation of the target word that must be complex because words can vary along many dimensions, just like mental images or percepts.

Furthermore, the tip-of-the-tongue state resembles a mental image or a percept in that it seems to compete with other conscious contents. We cannot search for a forgotten word and at the same time contemplate a picture, or think of yesterday's breakfast, or do anything else involving conscious experience or mental effort. The tip-of-the-tongue state occupies central limited capacity.

In one major respect this state differs from mental images, bodily feelings, inner speech, and perceptual experiences. These conscious events all have qualitative properties, such as size, color, warmth, or flavor, but the tip-of-the-tongue state does not have such experienced qualities (viz. Baars, 1985a; Natsoulas, 1982). Different tip-of-the-tongue states are not experienced as different, even though the words they stand for may sound different. In some ways, therefore, this state resembles conscious experiences such as percepts and images; in other ways, it is very different.

James suggests that the tip-of-the-tongue state itself triggers a memory search that yields the words to clothe the intention. That is, it is active; it triggers a conscious display of candidate words and "it welcomes them . . . and calls them right if they agree with it, it rejects them and calls them wrong if they do not" (p. 287).

These observations apply generally to intentions and expectations. To create experiences like this for *any* action, we need only ask someone to perform the action and then delay the moment of execution. To have a runner experience a "tip-of-the-foot" experience, we need only say "GET READY," "GET SET," and then delay "GO." At that point, the runner is poised to go, the "intention" is at its highest pitch, and yet the action is not executed. There may be no sensory experience of the "intention to run," but the runner's concentration will still be impaired by interfering conscious events. The "intention to run" takes up limited capacity just as the tip-of-the-tongue state does. For that reason, I refer to this state as a *current intention,* or just "intention" for short.

A Modern Interpretation of Intentions

Although James could make these deep observations, he was not free to follow up their implications because he was deeply committed to the position that all psychological facts must be reducible to conscious experiences. For James, there were no truly unconscious psychological facts. Yet, the intention to retrieve a word seems to reveal just such a fact! We can restate James' observations in modern terms:

1. The intention to retrieve a word involves a complex representation of the missing word, as shown by the fact that one can accurately match and mismatch candidate words.

2. The intention restricts central limited capacity, like conscious experiences do. Witness the fact that it excludes incompatible conscious events.

3. The intention helps to trigger word retrieval processes, so that candidate words come to consciousness as long as this state dominates our limited capacity.

4. The intention to retrieve the word serves to evaluate each conscious candidate word, and it only stops dominating our central limited capacity when the matching word is found, or when the search is given up.

5. The intention does not have experiential qualities such as color, warmth, flavor, location, intensity, etc. It is therefore different from other conscious experiences, such as images, feelings, inner speech, and percepts.

If it is true that intentions do not have qualitative conscious contents, then a current controversy about the ability to report intentions begins to make more sense. Nisbett and Wilson (1977) cite a number of social psychological studies showing that the intentions people attribute to themselves can often be quite incorrect. However, we also know that under optimal conditions people can report their own mental processes quite accurately (e.g., in mental imagery, explicit verbal problem solving, rehearsal in short-term memory, etc.; see Ericsson & Simon, 1980). Nevertheless, the evidence is still strong that people often make surprising mistakes in reporting their own intentions, their reasons for doing things. One possible explanation of this conflict is that intentions are complex, nonqualitative events that are difficult to report in detail. To become reportable, intentions must be converted into an introspectible form, such as inner speech, visual images, or perhaps bodily feelings—and these may be easier to report accurately. This is not to say that intentions are entirely nonqualitative: There may be qualitative images, inner speech, etc., associated with the intention. However, such conscious contents are not the same as the intention itself. I argue below that consciously experienced goals are important parts of any intention, although the bulk of any intention is not qualitatively conscious. But first, I specify the notion of "intention" in more detail.

Intentions as Multi-Leveled Goal Structures

Intentions involve goals. They represent future states of the system which serve to recruit and activate processes that are able to reach those future states. Intentions are not simple goals. They must be multi-leveled goal structures, consisting of numerous nested goals and subgoals. Even a single spoken sentence is constrained by many simultaneous goals, including goals and criteria that specify the desired loudness and rate of speech, voice quality, choice of words, intonation, dialect, morphology, syntax, choice of rhetorical style, semantics, discourse relations, conversational norms, and communicative effectiveness. Each of these levels of organization can be described in terms of general goals, which the action can match or mismatch. Each of these levels can go astray, and errors at each level of control are often detected and corrected immediately.

Beyond these linguistic criteria, we use language to gain a multitude of pragmatic ends, many of which combine to constrain any single speech act. Thus we may routinely want to appear educated in our speech, but not stuffy; tolerant, but not undiscriminating; we usually want to capture the listener's attention, but not to the point of screaming for it. All such pragmatic goals simultaneously constrain any speech act.

Once established, linguistic and pragmatic goal systems rarely become conscious as a whole. Thus at the minimum, an "intention to say something" must involve a many-leveled goal structure, in which each major goal can activate numerous subgoals to accomplish its ends. At any one time, most of the components of such goal structures are not qualitatively conscious.

We now have some constraints on theory. Actions appear to be modular, recursively organized in a variable way, distributed, and goal addressable, yet executive processes seem to be ignorant of the details of action control. Intentions seem to be multi-leveled goal systems that dominate central limited capacity as long as they are active. Is there experimental evidence in support of these assertions?

EXPERIMENTAL EVIDENCE FOR PRIMING AND EDITING IN ACTION CONTROL

Some experimental evidence from the study of speech errors bears on these ideas. There are now a number of techniques for eliciting such errors experimentally, with predictable content (Baars, 1980a). These techniques can elicit errors that are generically correct, or they can violate generic rules. Rule-violating slips are marked with asterisks (*). Thus:

(1). *barn door—darn bore* (true lexical items)

(2). *bad goof—gad goof* (nonlexical) (*)

(3). *nery vice—very nice* (syntactically correct)

(4). *vice nery—nice very* (nonsyntactic) (*)

(5). *lice negs—nice legs* (sexual comment)

(6). *reel fejekted—feel rejected* (depressed comment)

Likewise, we can elicit word-exchange slips such as:

(7). *She touched her nose and picked a flower.—She picked her nose. . .* (socially embarrassing) (*)

(8). *She hit the ball and saw her husband.—She hit her husband. . .* (aggressive affect) (*)

(9). *The teacher told the myths and dismissed the stories.—The teacher dismissed the myths. . .* (hard to pronounce) (*)

(10). *She looked at the boy and talked softly.—She talked at the boy and looked softly.* (semantically anomalous) (*)

(11). *Is the gray sea below the blue sky?—No, the blue sky is below the gray sea.* (false) (*)

Errors (1) through (6) can be elicited by priming the speaker with previous word pairs that resemble the error. Thus, the slip *barn door—darn bore* can be elicited by showing the subject a series of pairs such as *dart board, dark bowl, dot bone,* etc. Subjects do not know ahead of time which word pair they must say, so they must prepare to say each one out loud. This need to be ready apparently primes the system to articulate the error when the phoneme patterns is switched (Baars, 1980a).

The sentential errors (7) through (11) are triggered by creating uncertainty about the order of two phrases in a sentence. Thus, if people are unsure about whether to say, *She touched her nose and picked a flower,* or *She picked a flower and touched her nose. . . ,* they will tend to switch nouns or verbs between the phrases. There are several ways to create this uncertainty, the easiest being to present the stimulus sentences, and after each one simply signal the subject either to repeat the previous sentence exactly, or to reverse the phrases of this sentence. This technique produces predictable slips at an adequate rate.

Materials can be designed so that we can elicit almost any involuntary statement from the subjects (Baars, 1980a, forthcoming, b). Two general phenomena have been observed. First, the likelihood of a slip is increased by priming with verbal material that is related to the slip in sound, form, or meaning. The speaker's physical and social environment can also prime particular slips. Thus, Motley, Camden, and Baars (1979) showed that subjects who were led to expect the possibility of an electric shock made more slips like *shad bok—bad shock,* whereas male subjects who were run by an especially attractive female experimenter were more likely to make slips like *lake muv—make love.* Recently, we have found preliminary evidence that an induced depressed mood can increase the rate of slips like *deel fown—feel down,* and *juzza werk—was a jerk.*

Priming usually involves the influence of a conscious content on subsequent unconscious processes, which can be assessed by tasks such as reaction time or threshold measurement. In these studies, the priming stimulus was either a synonym of the slip, an attractive member of the opposite sex, or a series of "depressing" sentences. These priming stimuli presumably induced some largely unconscious mental "set," which was reflected in the greater frequency of related slips. Thus, conscious events can lead to unconscious mental states that behave much like intentions. Priming phenomena may simulate the relationship between a conscious event or goal, and the creation of an intention to act.

In addition to priming, there is evidence for anticipatory editing of the speech plans, and that, too, can lead to slips. By designing slips that violate some level of control and comparing them with matching, rule-governed slips, we have found a number of cases where the rate of rule-violating slips drops precipitously, sometimes even to zero (e.g., Baars, 1980a; Baars, Motley, & MacKay, 1975; Motley, Camden, & Baars, 1979). All starred (*) slips listed above violate such linguistic or pragmatic regularities and show lower rates than matched slips that obey the rules.

The drop in the rate of rule-violating slips may reflect a mismatch editing capability. Ordinarily we think of "editing" as a review process in which one person (such as newspaper editor) checks the output of another (a reporter, perhaps) with respect to a set of criteria—of linguistic adequacy, conformance to editorial policy, and the like. The editor is always monitoring for matches and mismatches with respect to his or her criteria.

To show that editing in this sense occurs in normal speech production, we must demonstrate that people in the act of speaking can detect mismatches between a speech plan and prior criteria. Motley, Camden, and Baars (1979) report that for a task that elicits sexually expressive slips (*lake muv—make luv, bice noddy—nice body*), there is a large and rapid rise in the electrical skin conductivity on sexual-slip trials even if the slip is not actually made. On neutral control items there is no such effect. Because the Electro-Dermal Response (EDR) is a predictable physiological concomitant of surprise, novelty, and mismatch with expectations—these results suggest that a mismatch was detected and the slip was successfully avoided. Thus egregious errors can be detected even before they are made overtly, and suppressed. This is the notion of editing that we have suggested.

We cannot be sure in these experiments that the edited speech plan was conscious, but we do know that conscious speech plans can be edited by largely unconscious criteria. Not all errors in spontaneous speech are detected, not even all overt errors (MacKay, 1980). However, once speakers become conscious of an error they are likely to correct it. In fact, normal speech is marked by a great number of overt self-corrections or "repairs" (Clark & Clark, 1977). In any case, only part of the process of error detection and correction is conscious and reportable. Certainly the slip itself is often so, but detailed mechanisms of detection and correction are not. Therefore, even though we do not know for sure that the edited slips in the experiments cited were conscious, we can suggest that unconscious editing of conscious errors occurs quite commonly.

We now have a set of ideas about the organization of actions and intentions, summarized in Table 16.1. This list includes the ability of actions to be primed by conscious events, and the ability of conscious goals to be edited by many unconscious criteria.

TABLE 16.1
Constraints on Theories of Action

---

1. Properties of Action Schemas:
a. Modularity—components can be combined and decomposed
b. Distributed—relatively autonomous action schemas control the local details of action.
c. Goal—addressability
d. Executive ignorance

2. Properties of Intentions:
a. They are multileveled goal structures
b. Current intentions constrain central limited capacity
c. Unlike percepts or images, intentions are nonqualitative

3. Evidence from Experimentally Elicited Slips:
a. Slips can be primed by related conscious material
b. Internal errors that lead to slips can be edited

4. James' Ideomotor Theory Suggests that People are Conscious of:
a. Novel goals
b. Conflicts between goals
c. The moment of onset of a nonrepetitive action

THE ROLE OF CONSCIOUS GOALS IN THE CONTROL OF ACTION: JAMES' IDEOMOTOR THEORY

What then, is the role of conscious experiences in the control of action? We can find strong hints of an answer in William James' ideomotor theory of voluntary control. These ideas were not articulated in the kind of detail expected of modern theories, but the basic components are quite clear. James suggested that a conscious goal or "idea" is inherently "impulsive," so that it tends to trigger spontaneous action. But the action itself—the "motor" component of ideomotor control—was purely physiological for James, and as such, he was willing to consider it unconscious.

However, it is obvious that not all conscious "ideas" are executed automatically. We are not so impulsive that we will leap off a tall building just because we have the conscious thought of doing so. James explained this by suggesting that some conscious goals encounter contrary ideas or intentions, which block execution if they arrive before the action is executed. That is, in terms of our previous discussion, some conscious goals are edited by multiple unconscious criteria, which can act to block execution of the wrong goals. If editing is circumvented, conscious goals tend to execute unconsciously "by default."

To illustrate the main ideas of the ideomotor theory, James begins with a homely example of a conscious conflict about getting up from bed on a cold morning (1890/1983):

> We know what it is to get out of bed on a freezing morning in a room without a fire, and how the very vital principle within us protests against the ordeal. Probably most persons have lain on certain mornings for an hour at a time unable to brace themselves to the resolve. We think how late we shall be, how the duties of the day will suffer; we say, "I *must* get up, this is ignominious," etc; but still the warm couch feels too delicious, the cold outside too cruel, and resolution faints away and postpones itself again and again just as it seemed on the verge of bursting the resistance and passing over into the decisive act. . .
>
> Now how do we *ever* get up under such circumstances? If I may generalize from my own experience, we more often than not get up without any struggle at all. We suddenly find that we *have* got up. A fortunate lapse of consciousness occurs; we forget both the warmth and the cold; we fall into some revery connected with the day's life, in the course of which the idea flashes across us, "Hollo, I must lie here no longer"—an idea which at that lucky instant awakens no contradictory or paralyzing suggestions, and consequently produces immediately its appropriate motor effects. . .
>
> It was our acute consciousness of both the warmth and the cold during the period of struggle, which paralyzed our activity then and kept our idea of rising in the condition *wish* and not *will*. The moment these inhibitory ideas ceased, the original idea exerted its effects. . .
>
> This case seems to me to contain in miniature form the data for an entire psychology of volition. (pp. 524–525)

This commonsense example has many profound implications. It begins with a state of conflicting conscious goals and intentions, which is resolved *not* when one side drives the other from consciousness, but simply when the conflict is forgotten, and the impulse to stand up suddenly becomes conscious without contradiction. At that point, the action of standing up is performed largely unconsciously. The ideomotor theory is consistent with the constraints I have listed. It suggests that we have executive ignorance, in the sense that we do not give a conscious "command" to carry out an action. We do not have conscious control over action details. Competing intentions can create conflicting conscious impulses, and action proceeds only when such a conflict is resolved. Finally, James suggests that we are generally conscious of the moment of onset of a nonrepetitive action, which he calls the "fiat." Thus, we are conscious of some goals, conflicts between goals, and the onset of action. I now suggest that these three conscious components correspond to novel, or "underdetermined," elements of action control, and that this property of novelty is the key issue in determining what will become conscious in the control of action.

THE IDEOMOTOR THEORY INTERPRETED IN TERMS
OF A GLOBAL WORKSPACE MODEL

In a series of recent papers, I have pointed to cognitive, functional, and neurophysiological evidence in favor of a "global workspace architecture" to model the limited-capacity component of the nervous system and conscious experience. I will illustrate the theory here; for further details and experimental predictions, the reader is referred to work published elsewhere (Baars, 1983, 1985a,b, forthcoming a).

A global workspace (or "blackboard") is basically a working memory that permits one processor in a large collection of specialized processors to "broadcast" a message to all the others. This architecture was first used in computer simulations of speech perception, which required the interaction of multiple knowledge sources—having to do with acoustics, lexicon, syntax, and the like—in order to resolve otherwise underdetermined ambiguities in speech recognition (Erman & Lesser, 1975; Reddy & Newell, 1974). But it has much broader application (e.g., Hayes–Roth, 1984). From a psychological and neuropsychological point of view, Global Workspace theory claims that the nervous system can be viewed largely as a collection of highly specialized processors (Baars, 1983). Conscious experiences correspond to mental representations that are globally broadcast, coherent, and able to trigger widespread adaptive processing in the nervous system, as shown in Fig. 16.1. For simplicity, I deal here only with the property of global broadcasting, by assuming that all global representations are conscious, and all other events are not conscious.

The simplest illustration of this architecture is an auditorium filled with human experts, each with a specialized domain of expertise in which he or she can solve problems very efficiently. Precisely because of this specialization, each expert finds it difficult to solve novel problems that may require information from other experts. To solve problems that no single expert can solve, the group of experts requires a public information exchange (a blackboard or global workspace), which can make information available to the whole audience. Each expert decides by his or her own criteria whether the information broadcast is important, so that "the processing initiative" is local and widely distributed. However, to communicate with and control other systems, a specialized processor must gain access to the blackboard in the face of competition from others. Once a system gains access to the global workspace it can broadcast a global message in order to activate, recruit, and control numerous other processors. As Fig. 16.1 shows, all the theoretical entities discussed—the action schemas, effector controllers, and goal systems—can be considered to be specialized processors in such a system. This forms a model of all constraints on a theory of action that has been described, including the ideas in James' ideomotor theory.

I can only summarize here the fit between the global workspace architecture and the constraints on action theory: relatively autonomous modules, distributed

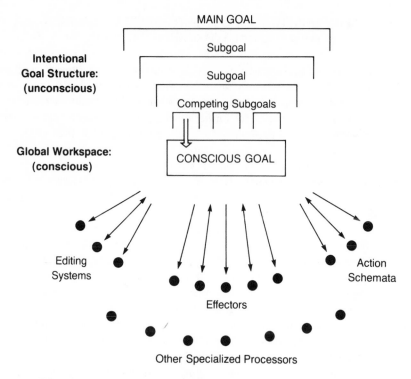

FIGURE 16.1.   The Global Workspace theory applied to the control of action. Effectors, action schemats, and intention goal systems can all be considered to be specialized processors, or coalitions of specialized processors. For the sake of simplicity only representations in the global workspace are assumed to be conscious.

control, etc. Other constraints follow from the functioning of this architecture. Thus, specialized processors are assumed to act to reduce mismatches between their predictions about global contents, and those contents. When global messages are goals, the specialized processors that can carry out the goals detect such a mismatch, and attempt to act to carry out the goals to reduce the mismatch. That is, the action schemas and effector systems are goal-addressable. The ability of multiple expert systems to compete for global access provides a broad-based editing capability because any global representation can be erased by sufficiently strong competing systems.

Fig. 16.1 shows how Global Workspace theory represents intentions, in the sense I have defined them in this chapter: as complex, multilevel systems of goals that can constrain limited capacity but that have only a few conscious components. Intentional systems can be treated as one set of specialized processors. It is useful to think back to the "intention to say so-and-so" in James' discussion of the tip-of-the-tongue experience, and to consider the "conscious goal" as the mental image of the candidate words that come to mind, matching or mismatching the intention. The graphic "frames" that stand for intentions in Fig. 16.1 are not themselves messages on the global workspace. Rather, they are collections of specialized processors that can cooperate and compete with others to constrain global messages. If we walk on a narrow suspension bridge overhanging a steep gorge, there will be multiple unconscious intention systems making sure that the goal of stepping the wrong way does not enter conscious experience, at least not long enough to trigger the effectors needed to leap off the bridge.

Several other current models argue in favor of distributed competition between action schemas for access to limited-capacity mechanisms (e.g., Anderson, 1983; Norman & Shallice, 1985; Reason, 1984; and Shallice, 1978). These authors agree that the bulk of detailed processing is unconscious. However, these theories do not explain the *function* of a conscious action schema. The global workspace theory offers a reason why it would be advantageous for goal systems to control the limited-capacity component: Because global goals are broadcast to all modules in the system, they can recruit effectors, intention goal structures, and action schemas to carry out their goals. In this view, without access to global broadcasting, no new goal is likely to gain control over the appropriate effectors.

Notice that this point only applies to novel components of action. The theory suggests that conscious involvement is required primarily in cases of novelty. In fact, most actions have at least some novelty. For example, decisions between alternative goals may require novel input. Even in routine actions, the moment of onset is often not entirely predictable. Errors are unplanned and unpredictable by definition. Feedback from actions may be conscious, especially if the feedback is surprising or unplanned. Unexpected resistance to the achievement of a routine goal tends to be conscious. In general, if some uncertainty must be resolved using sources of knowledge that are not known ahead of time, the global workspace is useful because it allows novel interactions between different expert systems. Those are also the cases in which consciousness is required, including the ones that James suggested are conscious in the control of normal actions. More formally, this suggests that the pre-eminent function of consciousness is to allow multiple knowledge sources to act upon a point of indeterminacy in a many-to-one fashion.

An Illustration

The tip-of-the-tongue phenomenon can be used to show the way in which Global Workspace theory works, because the phenomenon clearly involves some things that are conscious and reportable, and others that are not. Following are illustrations of six hypotheses emerging from this approach.

1. Conscious contents can activate unconscious goal structures. Suppose we ask the reader: What are two names for the winged dinosaurs that lived millions of years ago? The reader is conscious of the question, and this experience initiates an intention to retrieve a word with certain known parameters (at least three syllables, likely to end in "saurus," etc.). Because the words are rare, the momentary intention is likely to be prolonged into a tip-of-the-tongue state—which involved, by the arguments we have made, a goal structure.

2. In combination with a capacity-limiting goal structure (intention), conscious contents can recruit a coherent system of action schemas and effectors. Now let us suppose that the reader has recalled the name "pterosaurus" (or "pterodactyl") as an answer to the question that has been posed. This is a conscious representation of a word. Now, how do we recruit the largely unconscious systems that control pronunciation of this difficult word? It is useful to remember here how complex and fast moving the speech apparatus really is, and how little of it is accessible to awareness at any single time. It seems plausible that the conscious word, in combination with a capacity-limiting intention, can recruit and organize the complex effector system in order to pronounce the word.

3. Given a compatible current intention, a conscious goal tends to execute automatically. Once "pterosaurus" becomes conscious, something rather magical happens: We suddenly notice that our mouth has begun to pronounce the conscious word. The intervening steps of motor control are simply not conscious. In James' words, "consciousness is impulsive"—unless, of course, other goal systems begin to compete for access to consciousness.

4. Conscious contents can be edited by multiple unconscious goal systems. Suppose the reader first retrieves "tyrannosaurus" instead of "pterosaurus." Clearly, we do not want to execute this incorrect goal image. Various knowledge sources should interfere with its execution by signaling a mismatch: Some may remind us that "tyrannosaurus" is too long, or that it has a different meaning. Such contradictory knowledge should have access to the global workspace, to compete against the incorrect conscious goal image. There is empirical evidence for anticipatory editing of speech plans, as has been discussed. The global workspace theory suggests that editing is not some "added-on" capacity, but an integral aspect of the architecture of the cognitive system.

5. Conscious feedback can reveal success or failure of an action to many unconscious goal systems, which may then develop corrective measures. When we notice a speech error consciously, we often "repair" it immediately (Clark & Clark, 1977; MacKay, 1980). But we are rarely conscious of details of the repair. Responding to overt errors is similar to anticipatory editing of covert errors, except that editing takes place before the action is executed. Correction of overt errors is useful in preparing for a more successful action the next time around.

6. Sufficiently long-lasting conscious contents can be acted upon or described by specialized language systems. Any adequate theory of consciousness must explain how a conscious experience can be reported—how highly specialized linguistic systems can gain access to conscious content. Global Workspace theory suggests that linguistic experts constitute another set of distributed processors, which can receive the globally broadcasted information. In turn, they can gain access to the blackboard, in order to recruit and control effectors that are themselves able to put out their own messages.

However, like other distributed specialists, linguistic systems require time to respond, especially if the message they react to is not routine. Thus, the global message that linguistic processors act upon must be available for some minimum period of time. The Sperling effect provides one case in which apparently conscious events may fade before they can be reported (Sperling, 1960). In this case, the visual image may be displayed in the global workspace only very briefly, long enough to trigger practiced and hence well-prepared responses, but not long enough to activate linguistic mechanisms that are needed to report on the momentary global event. There may thus be global goal images that last long enough to trigger prepared routine effectors, but not long enough to enable novel recall and linguistic description. It is in this sense that James argued that some apparently unconscious events are momentary conscious "flashes" that are difficult to retrieve and report (James, 1890, Chapter 6).

SUMMARY AND CONCLUSIONS

I have briefly sketched a set of empirical constraints on action theory, emphasizing the great number of things that are not conscious in normal voluntary action—the action schemas, intentional goal systems, and the effectors themselves. But this does not mean that action control involves no conscious experience at all. There is reason to think that consciousness becomes involved at underdetermined choice points in the control of action.

Several current models can explain aspects of this process (Anderson, 1983; Baars, 1983; Norman & Shallice, 1985; Reason, 1984). Global Workspace theory suggests that conscious messages are made globally available throughout a nervous system that consists of numerous specialized processors (Baars, 1983, 1985a,b, and forthcoming, a). Action schemas, effectors, and goal systems can be treated as such specialized processors. The advantage of global broadcasting of conscious contents is that multiple systems can cooperate and compete through the global workspace in order to solve novel problems, such as are posed by underdetermined choice points in action control. The competition for global access creates a limitation of processing capacity. Conscious events are capacity-limited but flexible, because multiple knowledge sources can interact to solve novel problems. Unconscious processes are less limited in capacity, but they are inflexible in the face of novelty. Optimal control of action requires a smooth blend of both conscious and unconscious processing modes.

My colleagues and I are currently developing a more detailed model of these concepts, and generating additional experimental hypotheses to test the approach.

ACKNOWLEDGMENTS

I am grateful for useful comments by Donald A. Norman, James Reason, David Galin, Anthony Marcel, Ray Jackendoff, Arthur Reber, Bob Kunzendorf, Benjamin Libet, and Bob Hoffman. This work was completed while the author served as Visiting Scientist at the Program for the Study of Conscious and Unconscious Processes, directed by Mardi J. Horowitz, Langley Porter Neuropsychiatric Institute, University of California, San Francisco, supported by the John D. and Catherine T. MacArthur Foundation. This support is gratefully acknowledged.

17 Comments on the Chapters by Baars and Ceraso

Richard Dolinsky
University of Toledo

In the latter part of his book *Thought and Language*, Vygotsky (1962) deals with the issue of "inner speech" and what he calls the "semantic peculiarities" that constitute it. He writes that the basic pecularity is:

> The preponderance of the sense of a word over its meaning. . . The sense of a word . . . is the sum of all the psychological events aroused in our consciousness by the word. It is a dynamic, fluid, complex whole, which has several zones of unequal stability. Meaning is only one of the zones of sense, the most stable and precise zone. A word acquires its sense from the contexts, it changes its sense. Meaning remains stable throughout the changes of sense. The dictionary meaning of a word is no more than a stone in the edifice of sense, no more than a potentiality that finds diversified realization in speech. (p. 146)

Vygotsky continues:

> A word in a context means both more and less than the same word in isolation: More because it acquires new context; less, because its meaning is limited and narrowed by the context. . . In inner speech, the predominance of sense over meaning, of sentence over word, and of context over sentence is the rule. (p. 146–147)

Although the chapters by Baars and by Ceraso are on different topics and appear in different sections in this volume, it seems that they both relate to the kind of thing that Vygotsky was writing about. Even though Vygotsky, like Paulhan who influenced him, views the sense of a word as something that arouses consciousness, the implication from the chapter by Baars is that this is not necessarily the case. Certainly there seems no reason to deny the unconscious a role in conceptualization, perhaps even a major note. In fact, Ceraso suggests that "the idea of the learning and recall of more general aspects of material has implications for studies which deal with the processing of words without awareness."

From a methodological view, both chapters provide some excellent lessons in the value of looking at error data. The data that Ceraso presents are clear. It is apparent that as learning progresses, the nature of the errors change. The learner zeros in on the relevant dimension and the more general errors are excluded. Presumably, in Vygotsky's view, the context becomes more specific and the sense of the word becomes more limited. With delayed recall, the situation reverses and the sense of the word, in Vygotsky's terminology, means more. For this argument to work, it is necessary to think of the paired associate list as providing the context: This is probably different from what Vygotsky had in mind, but it doesn't seem to produce major problems in interpretation.

In the Baars chapter, errors in the form of slips act as benchmarks, or undetermined choice points. The chapter by Baars recognizes the importance of the distinction between conscious and unconscious factors in behavior. It also addresses the executive functions inherent in this type of behavior. Two of the major functions deal with the behavior at "undetermined choice points" and the role of the "global workspace."

An undetermined choice point seems to act as a node where conscious and unconscious processes in intentional behavior converge. Here, again, is Baars' list of conscious undetermined choice points:

- choosing the original goal of a novel action,
- internal errors,
- conflicts between plans and goals,
- feedback from actions that mismatch goals,
- selection of the moment of execution of an action.

It appears as if these conscious choice points shift actions from one process to another. This is not all they do, but it seems to be a major role. Some of the undetermined choice points are novel or unpredictable, such as mismatches, and others seem to be critical, such as the choosing of original goals. These functions trigger the conscious action. Yet novelty and unpredictability seem to be insufficient for an action to become conscious.

In discussing errors, Baars notes that "errors are unpredictable by definition, but not all errors become conscious." And it is noted that perhaps only egregious ones do. But what determines when a choice point error is egregious? Is it when the thought is shifted to another path? That is, is the error something different that "derails" the intention for a short time—but only for a short time? Pulling out one's wallet at the library turnstile is inappropriate—an error on the physical action level—but the main intention, getting out of the library, has not been altered. That is, there is a short-term, temporary, derailment in the straight-line path toward the goal. Nevertheless, this short-term derailment is great enough to result in consciousness intruding into an automatic sequence.

In some of his other work, Baars has found that when "subjects were made to monitor their speech for possible errors, the rate of semantically anomalous slips dropped to zero without affecting the rate of semantically acceptable slips." An example of such a slip is "She talked at the boy and looked softly" instead of "She looked at the boy and talked softly." There is an interesting experimental issue here. Could one switch the kinds of slips and the conscious perception of these slips if the subject was told to switch main intentions at some point during the experimental task?

As Baars notes, many factors are responsible for speech and language errors. This suggests that manipulations in the laboratory might be difficult to produce reliably, and with something apparently as sensitive as the kind of errors discussed here, there are distinct implicit demand characteristics in the task itself. The psychological laboratory is not the same as the everyday environment and it is likely that phonemic, articulatory errors would be less likely to occur. This underlines Baars's contention that conscious contents can be edited by multiple unconscious rule systems. Some of these can be social and essentially outside the task itself.

It is also noted that "the ability of multiple expert systems to interact almost without limit provides a broad-based editing capability for the (global workspace) architecture." This, of course, is consistent with the executive role of global conscious experience. And as intentions change, so does the strength of the plans that compete for the limited capacity available.

Baars has presented the beginning of an ideomotor theory relating conscious and unconscious events. The proposal of a global workspace attempts to direct many unconscious (and presumably conscious) processes in a "many-to-one" fashion. The idea is that this convergence will allow novel problems to be solved. Further, because the global workspace is conscious, the individual can receive feedback regarding the success or failure of the venture.

To Baars, one negative consequence of the "many-to-one" convergence is that processing capacity will be limited and processing speed will be retarded.

In principle, this model is logical and testable. The evidence presented, however, has come from other areas and, at this point, there is little integration with the model. As is well known, slips of the tongue provide convincing evidence of unconscious planning. What remains unclear is how these errors will help in understanding a complex, integrative, mechanism like the "global workspace."

V TOPICS IN MEMORY RESEARCH

18 Serial-Order Effects in a Distributed-Memory Model

Bennet B. Murdock, Jr.
University of Toronto

Serial learning was first studied experimentally by Ebbinghaus 100 years ago. In this chapter I discuss the general topic of serial-order effects because this was one of his major contributions. We have learned a great deal about serial-order effects in the last 100 years, and they form a large and important part of our experimental data on human memory.

I first present some of the main serial-order effects in the literature. I then briefly list the major theoretical explanations and some of their problems. Next I consider a distributed-memory model based on convolution and correlation and show how it can contribute to our understanding of serial-order effects. I present the basic assumptions of the model and illustrate its application and end by mentioning some problems and possible solutions.

OVERVIEW OF SERIAL-ORDER EFFECTS

The serial-order effects we consider are serial-position effects in learning and memory, partial-report effects, whole-report effects, delayed recall, chunking, and repetition.

Learning and Memory

Serial learning was first studied by Ebbinghaus, and his most general finding was that performance improves with practice. This result, and many others, may be found in his classic monograph (Ebbinghaus, 1913), and has been amply documented by many students of verbal learning since then. The U-shaped serial

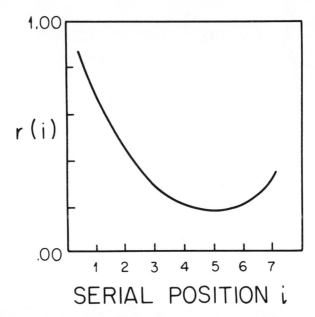

FIGURE 18.1.   Recall probability $r(i)$ as a function of Serial Position i.

position curve that is always obtained in serial learning antedated even Ebbinghaus. It was apparently first reported by Nipher (1878) (see Stigler, 1978). Also in that century, Binet and Henri (1894) studied the memory-span function, which can be described by saying that the perfect recall of a short list of items becomes less likely as list length increases.

Figs. 18.1 and 18.2 show stylized drawings of the serial-position function for serial recall and the memory-span function, respectively. The serial-position curve shows recall probability $r(i)$ as a function of serial position i, and the memory-span function shows the cumulative probability $p(L)$ that the entire list will be recalled correctly as a function of list length L. The exact shapes of these two functions are dependent on experimental details, but the main points are obvious: The serial-position curve shows extensive primacy and little recency whereas the memory-span function is a reverse S-shaped curve that decreases as list length increases.

Research on verbal learning flourished in the first half of this century, and the importance of retroactive interference was firmly established as a significant cause of forgetting (McGeoch, 1932). Competing material interspersed between the end of learning and the time of recall interferes with attempted recall of the original material. The greater the similarity of the interfering material to the original material, the greater the retroactive interference (RI). Proactive interference (PI), on the other hand, was brought to our attention by Underwood (1957) who showed that the more lists learned before a target list, the worse the

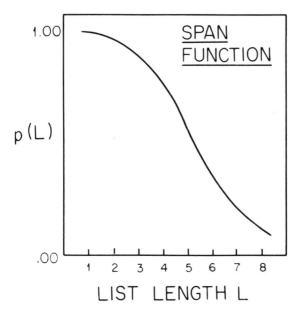

FIGURE 18.2. Probability of correct recall $p(L)$ as a function of List Length L.

recall of the target list. Interference theory, then, had two sources of forgetting to contend with, RI and PI, and as recently as 1960 interference theory was the dominant approach to the study of memory (Postman, 1961).

Partial Report Effects

The partial report effect refers to the fact that, following a single brief presentation, more can be remembered than can be recalled. This was convincingly demonstrated by Sperling (1960) in an iconic-memory study and by Anderson (1960) in serial recall. In both cases, partial report was used. It is now commonly called a *probe* technique where the probe specifies the subset of the material to be recalled. The fact that partial report effects lead to superior performance relative to whole report procedures implies that there is output interference. Recalling one thing interferes with the potential recall of something else, thus the inferiority of whole report.

Probe serial-position effects were demonstrated by Waugh and Norman (1965). A list of digits was presented followed by a single "probe" digit; the subject was to recall the digit that had followed the probe. This was a sequential probe; one is probing for Item $i + 1$ with Item i as the probe. As they found,

$$r(i) = f(i). \tag{1}$$

That is, probability of recall $r(i)$ is a function of Serial Position i. This point was illustrated in Fig. 18.1, though that was more for serial recall than probe recall.

Various types of probes may be used, and this was investigated by Murdock (1976). I compared sequential probes, as used by Waugh and Norman, with positional probes (e.g., What was the item in Serial Position i?), and reverse probes (e.g., Given Item i, what was its serial position?). Although there were clear differences between serial recall and probe recall (more primacy and less recency in the former than in the latter), the differences as a function of probe type were minimal.

The importance of intrusions (responses transposed from other serial positions or other lists) was stressed by Conrad (1960), and this was a harbinger of things to come. In probe recall, intrusions display a marked asymmetry (Murdock, 1976) in that they are more likely to come from later serial positions. This asymmetry could reflect the existence of criterion effects, and criterion effects imply that the amount of primacy and recency one would find in a probe-recall task would depend on the measures used. In fact, with standard probability measures there is more recency than primacy, but with a posteriori probability measures there is more primacy than recency. This pattern of results is just what a criterion interpretation would suggest.

A persisting puzzle has been the existence of probe modality effects. They have been reported for probe (or probe-like) serial tasks by Buschke (1962) and by Murdock (1967). As is now well known, recall following auditory presentation is superior to recall following visual presentation. This effect also occurs in serial recall (Drewnowski & Murdock, 1980), and the literature is now very extensive. (For a review of the first decade of work on this problem, see Penney, 1975.)

Whole-Report Effects

Various types of recall may be required when the complete string is to be recalled; these include serial recall, constrained or positional recall, and free recall. These represent variations in the instructions given to subjects. By serial recall, I mean the subject must recall the items in order starting with the first and ending with the last. In constrained or positional recall, the presentation order must be reconstructed, but the order of reporting the items is up to the subject. In free recall, both presentation and reporting order are free. Sometimes a free-recall scoring criterion may be used even though serial or positional recall was requested.

The exact serial-position curves one obtains depend on the type of recall and the method of scoring. Sample data from Drewnowski and Murdock (1980) for serial recall are shown in Fig. 18.3. The important point to notice is the extensive primacy effects under all conditions. This is one of the basic phenomena any serial-order model must explain.

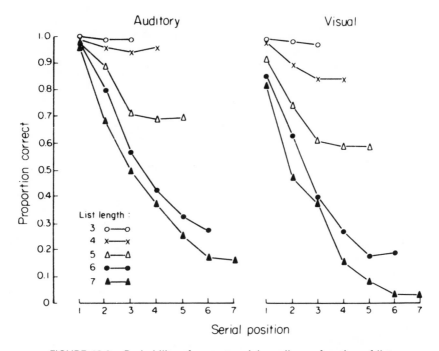

FIGURE 18.3. Probability of correct serial recall as a function of list length and mode of presentation (Drewnowski and Murdock, 1980, reproduced with permission).

The memory span function can be obtained directly from serial (or positional) recall data. Specifically,

$$p(L) = \prod_{i=1}^{L} \pi r(i) = f(L). \qquad (2)$$

that is, the probability of correctly recalling an entire list of list length L is simply the product (π) of the separate probabilities. It is this product $p(L)$ which declines with L. The so-called "memory span" (Watkins, 1977) is commonly defined as the value of L at which $p(L) = 0.5$. Typical curves for two different presentation modalities are shown in Fig. 18.4.

Delayed Recall

Active research on short-term memory began about 1960 and was greatly facilitated by the methodology of Peterson and Peterson (1959). They presented consonant trigrams and had the subjects count backwards during the retention interval to prevent rehearsal. Typically, one finds very rapid forgetting over a

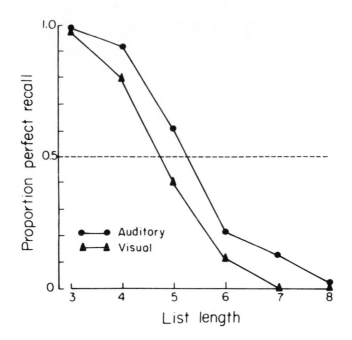

FIGURE 18.4. Span Functions for auditory and visual presentation
(Drewnowski & Murdock, 1980, reproduced with permission).

short period of time. As noted by Blumenthal (1977), a very similar method had
been reported by Daniels (1895) many years earlier. This technique has been
widely used for many purposes.

Varying the delay of recall gives us a way of tracing out forgetting curves, and
these have been of interest in the study of forgetting since the time of Ebbinghaus. The Peterson distractor technique gave us a powerful method to obtain
forgetting curves for individual subjects for subspan lists; we could now study
forgetting for "single" items over short periods of time. Without this technique,
our understanding of short-term memory would be very limited today.

The type of interpolated task (distraction) makes some difference (Posner &
Konick, 1966), though the effects are not large. This first seemed damning to an
interference-theory interpretation, but other types of interference have surfaced.
Originally, the forgetting was attributed to decay, but that seems less important
now. Without rehearsal some decay occurs (Reitman, 1974), but the effect is not
large.

One type of interference that is clearly manifest in the Peterson distractor
paradigm is the buildup of PI over trials (Keppel & Underwood, 1962). On the
first trial there is little forgetting, but by Trial 3 or 4, considerable forgetting
occurs. This is comparable to the buildup of PI in long-term memory, first
reported by Underwood (1957). This has been an important argument for the

continuity position; i.e., that short-term and long-term memory are not fundamentally different (Melton, 1963).

Many other findings have been reported; they cannot all be chronicled here. Two in particular, however, should be mentioned. They are "release" from PI and differential forgetting rates for item and order information.

First, changing taxonomic category after several trials produces release from PI (Wickens, Born, & Allen, 1963), but other types of changes may not (Wickens, 1970, 1972). This suggests that semantic factors must be involved even in simple short-term recollection. The fact that recall is typically used is not critical because the buildup and subsequent release from PI also occur with recognition (Gorfein & Jacobson, 1972).

Second, item information and order information may be experimentally separated (Murdock & vom Saal, 1967). Retention of item information is better with Same-category trigrams but retention of order information is better with Different-category trigrams. In addition, item and order information are forgotten at different rates (Lee & Estes, 1981; Shiffrin & Cook, 1978). These are important results to be explained by the various item-and-order models.

Chunking

A different line of development has been the work on chunking, much of which was inspired by the seminal "magic number seven" paper of Miller (1956). Given that the capacity of the memory span is limited by the number of items ("chunks") and not by the number of bits (binary digits required for an information-theory representation), the obvious way to increase capacity is by enriching the chunks. Extension to serial learning and serial organization is an obvious application of the chunking notion, and the importance of chunking has been clearly demonstrated (e.g., Johnson, 1970, 1972; Martin, 1974; Martin & Noreen, 1974). Work on serial structures can be viewed as studying the organization of chunks into a larger framework (Restle, 1970, 1975).

A stylized version of a chunk curve is shown in Fig. 18.5, which shows the retention curves for chunks of size one to seven. The figure is taken from Melton (1963). The chunk curves show how the probability of correct recall for chunks of different size falls off with time. One parameter that would be important is the type of material (see Miller, 1956, or Crannell & Parrish, 1957). Another important parameter is the acoustic similarity of items within a list (Conrad, 1964). Not only does acoustic similarity affect the span function but it also affects order information (transpositions). That is, similarity produces confusions in serial-order tasks, and the most important similarity dimension is acoustic similarity.

Performance can be improved by grouping (Ryan, 1969; Wickelgren, 1964), and groups of three to four seem optimal. As in probe recall, intrusions are instructive in serial recall. There is a marked tendency for interlist intrusions to come from the same serial position (Conrad, 1959, 1960); the percentage can be

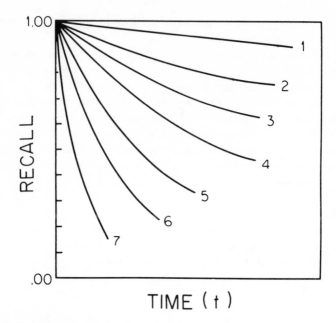

FIGURE 18.5.   Recall of chunks of size one to seven as a function of time (adapted from Melton, 1963).

quite high. Intralist intrusions are generally symmetrical around the target loca-tion, as revealed by the distance functions of Estes (1972). Finally, prefix and suffix items can affect overall performance (Conrad, 1960) as well as perfor-mance on the terminal item (Crowder & Morton, 1969).

Repetition

These are single-trial effects, and I now discuss repeated presentations. As mentioned at the outset, the effects of repetition on memory were part of the classic Ebbinghaus monograph. He studied such variables as number of repeti-tions, length of list, type of material, and length of the retention interval. Of particular theoretical importance is how the serial-position curve changes with repetition; typical data (from Robinson & Brown, 1926) are shown in Fig. 18.6. As can be seen, the serial-position curve is like a catenary (the curve formed by a heavy cord suspended from two points of unequal height). The point of max-imum difficulty stays remarkably constant as the cord shortens.

Another variable of considerable historical interest is massed-versus-spaced practice. At one point it was thought to be an important variable (Hovland, 1951), but this view has been revised (Underwood, 1961; Slamecka, this vol-ume). Unlike the learning of perceptual-motor skills, the distribution of practice is probably not very important in serial learning. Any postulated inhibition must therefore be somewhat different in the two cases.

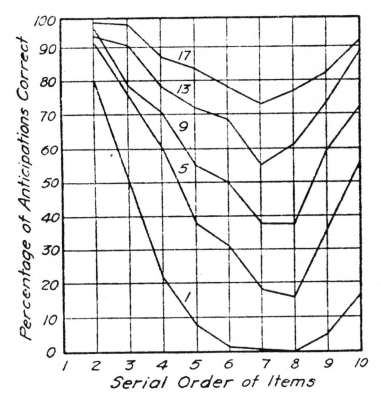

FIGURE 18.6.   Correct recall as a function of serial position for anticipation Trials 1, 5, 9, 13, and 17. Data are from Robinson and Brown
(1926).

By contrast, chunking and organization are of very great importance in learning. The literature on this topic is vast. For some early work, one could consult
Johnson (1970, 1972) or Restle (1970, 1975), but this aspect of cognitive psychology is changing rapidly today. Current models of semantic memory (e.g.,
Anderson, 1983) indicate some of the directions.

In summary, I have reviewed some of the major empirical serial-order effects.
I now discuss the theoretical explanations of these phenomena.

THEORETICAL EXPLANATIONS

There have been a number of attempted theoretical explanations of these serial-
order effects, and I would categorize them as interference models, decay models,
non-associative models, item-and-order models, organizational-type models,
and distributed-memory models. Interference models take pairwise associations

as the basic building block for serial-order effects and assign an interference process to produce forgetting. Decay models rely on temporal decay rather than interference as the basic cause of forgetting. Non-associative models do not specify what the exact associative linkage is, so they are "non-associative" by default. Item-and-order models separate forgetting of item information from forgetting of order information whereas organizational-type models stress the development or utilization of chunking or serial organization. Distributed-memory models are, in a sense, orthogonal to all of these; they assume that the memory store contains a pooled representation of items or associations rather than a localized representation in separate "bins," storage registers, or nodes.[1]

Interference-Based Models

Although not actually suggested as a theory or model, the chaining notion of Ebbinghaus may be considered the original interference hypothesis. Each item in the list is associated to the next item much as the links in a chain attach the beginning to the end. Following Herbart, Ebbinghaus extended this notion to remote associations wherein the associations spanned one or more items. Remote associations became the basis for the Hull–Lepley hypothesis (Hull, Hovland, Ross, Hall, Perkins, & Fitch, 1940), and the monograph of Hull et al. was an early attempt at formal mathematical modelling of serial-order effects in learning.

Early in this century it seemed as if sequential associations, or chaining, were not enough to explain the data. Positional associations were suggested as an additional factor. These are associations of items to positions, absolute or relative. For specifics and the historical development of these ideas, see Woodworth (1958) or Crowder (1976). Later, sequential and positional associations formed the basis for an interference theory of forgetting (McGeoch, 1932, 1946).

To explain forgetting, interference theories assume that both PI and RI may be operating to interfere with, or weaken, the associative bond (sequential or positional association). An early version by Foucault (1928) was a simple additive model, but quantitatively its predictions were quite bad (see Murdock, 1974, for details). The role of PI and RI was extensively investigated at the experimental level (see Underwood, 1983, for details), and there is little doubt that both PI and RI are important determinants of forgetting. However, the theoretical integration of PI and RI was somewhat more troublesome (Postman, 1976). As a result, theorizing has turned in other directions.

Decay Models

An early competitor to interference theory was a decay model, where associative processes were essentially nonexistent and forgetting was produced by the pas-

---

[1]A different approach to serial-order effects is that of Grossberg (1971, 1978a; Grossberg & Pepe, 1971), which does not readily fit into any of these five categories. It will not be discussed here.

sage of time. The important filter theory of Broadbent (1958, 1971) was one of the first information-processing models. It represented serial order as a single file of items where the sequence was preserved by the processing mechanisms involved. In a mechanical version, this was a Y-shaped tube (Broadbent, 1957). Conrad (1965) suggested a fixed address or bin model where information was stored in a sequence of registers like those in a computer. Information could decay within each bin, but no change of position was possible.

A more detailed specification of the processes may be found in the phonemic model of Sperling and Speelman (1970). Although different from the Broadbent and Conrad models in many ways, it too makes forgetting contingent on temporal decay even though the decay is at the feature level and not the item level.

Decay models (particularly those of Broadbent & Conrad) were tested and found wanting by Waugh and Norman (1965). They observed little difference in their probe-digit task as a function of rate of presentation, whereas they observed large effects as a function of RI. Their conclusion has not gone unchallenged (e.g., Baddeley, 1976), but the majority view today seems to weight interference more heavily than decay.

Non-Associative Models

Non-associative models assign the locus of serial-order effects to other processes. An explanation based on distinctiveness (Murdock, 1960) suggested a perceptual basis for serial-order effects. According to this model, end items in a list should be most distinctive or salient, middle items least distinctive, and the serial-position effects should mirror those found in studies of absolute judgment of unidimensional stimuli.

From a rather different orientation, the EPAM (Elementary Perceiver And Memorizer) model of Feigenbaum and Simon (1963; 1984) attributed serial-order effects to associations developing inward from end anchors. Learning was seen as a slow, gradual process. From a still different orientation, Wickelgren (1969) suggested serial ordering occurs on the basis of context-sensitive allophones. Much like pieces of a jigsaw puzzle, $_xA_b$, $_aB_c$, and $_bC_y$ as an unordered set may be formed into the triplet ABC by matching interlocking triples.

Item-and-Order Models

Perhaps the first explicit item-and-order model was the random address model of Crossman (1961). In an attempt to rescue an information-theory approach to memory from the findings of Miller (1956), he suggested that a measure of the retention of item information alone was incomplete. A more adequate accounting required measurement of item *and* order information, and together these might be invariant over type of material. McNicol (1975) has referred to this as a "random address" model in contrast to a "fixed address" model, such as that of

Conrad (1965). A finite-state version that is similar in the separation of item-and-order information was suggested by Fozard, Myers, and Waugh (1971).

The perturbation model (Estes, 1972; Lee & Estes, 1981) has been one of the more influential item-and-order models over the past decade. Not only are item and order information separated, but retention of item information is dependent on retention of order information. In the original version, a recycling process was envisaged, and place changes leading to transposition errors in recall were ascribed to variability in the timing process. An extension of this model, with emphasis on different features and their forgetting characteristics, has been proposed by Drewnowski (1980).

A pattern model for the short-term retention of spatial location has been suggested by Healy (1978). Although her model deals with spatial location rather than temporal position, temporal and spatial information should be integrated in any complete account of serial-order memory (Metcalfe, Glavanov, & Murdock, 1981; O'Connor & Hermelin, 1978). A multicomponent model for the retention of digit triples was developed by Schmidt and Vorberg (1979), where different item-and-order states occurred with differing probabilities at different retention intervals in a Peterson distractor technique.

The relational model of Shiffrin and Cook (1978) differed from the perturbation model of Estes in that item-to-item as well as explicit positional associations were assumed. It is a decay model in that temporal decay is assumed to occur, but I am reporting it here because the item-and-order aspect seems more crucial. This model, like some of the other models in this section, yielded quantitative fits to data, but so far few comparative tests have been made.

Organizational-Type Models

One of the more influential of the organizational-type models is the chunking model of Johnson (1970, 1972). Long strings of items are assumed to be broken into shorter strings or chunks, and to some extent each chunk is autonomous. Errors in recall are more likely to occur at chunk boundaries than within a chunk, and internal changes in a chunk are more disruptive if they occur at the beginning of a chunk than at the middle or end. This latter result is consistent with the "reallocation" hypothesis of Bower and Winzenz (1969), which proposed that repetition was only effective if the initial part of the chunk was preserved.

The perturbation model is also a hierarchical model and so in principle it can accommodate organizational effects. I proposed a nesting model (Murdock, 1974) where chunks were embedded in an onion-like fashion, and errors could occur during encoding or unpacking. Network models such as ACT (Anderson, 1983) can deal with hierarchical organization because they were designed with that in mind.

At a still higher level, theories have utilized serial structures, such as the structural trees of Restle (1970) and the cognitive representations of serial patterns (Jones, 1974). This in turn leads to language, and a network model specifically aimed at representation of serial order in speech has recently been suggested by Dell (1984). Language is a serial-order problem par excellence, but it is far beyond the scope of this chapter. However, we should be reminded of the Lashley caveat in his famous paper on serial order (Lashley, 1951); namely, chaining is inadequate to cope with the fluency of highly skilled acts such as language.

Distributed-Memory Models

The last models to be considered are of a somewhat different genre. These are the distributed-memory models, such as those proposed by Kohonen (1977, 1984), Murdock (1983), and Pike (1984). They differ from all of the above in that items or pairs of items are stored in a common memory store (a memory matrix or a memory vector, depending on the model). The models discussed use local storage in that each item or each association is stored in a separate memory register, bin, terminal node, or whatever. To access an item, search is required. Distributed-memory models, on the other hand, use direct access; no search is required.

As a metaphor, one can think of the ripples caused by throwing a number of pebbles into a pond. Each pebble has a different size and shape, so the waves produced by each pebble are different. However, thay all combine to form a single pattern of wave activity. So the ripples, or waves, form a distributed memory, and all of the waves are stimultaneously present on the surface of the pond. Although a number of such distributed-memory models have been proposed (see Hinton & Anderson, 1981; Pribram, 1971), the three mentioned previously have been explicitly formulated to include the serial-order problem. The Kohonen model stores associations (digrams based on overlapping pairs of items) along with feedback in a common memory matrix. The Pike model stores a serial chain in a higher-order, outer-product matrix defined to be the cumulative product of item vectors, so it is an extension of matrix models, such as those of Kohonen (1977) or Anderson (1970).

I have suggested a "convolution–correlation" model whereby associations are formed by convolution and retrieval is effected by correlation (Murdock, 1982, 1983). Convolution is a way of combining two vectors into a single vector of higher dimensonality. Correlation is a way to operate on the combined vector with one of the original vectors to retrieve an approximation to the other vector. (For more detailed descriptions of convolution and correlation, see Eich, 1982, 1985; or Murdock, 1979, 1982.)

In the remainder of the chapter, I will focus on the convolution–correlation model as it applies to serial-order effects. However, to justify this selection it is necessary to detail some of the problems of the competing models.

PROBLEMS

There are conflicting data, otherwise there would not be such a plethora of models. The chaining notion has been cast into doubt, if not completely discredited, by the data on serial to paired-associate transfer (Harcum, 1975; Young, 1968). If serial learning were mediated by a chain of associative links (AB, BC, CD, . . .) then one would think that the learning of subsequent paired-associate lists containing such pairs as A–B and C–D would be facilitated. Usually it is not, at least when trials-to-criterion is the measure of paired-associate learning.

Remote associations have undergone the same fate. That is, if remote associations were formed during serial learning, then the learning of derived lists that make use of such associations should be facilitated. It is in Ebbinghaus' data, but the savings were quite small and were hard to come by. This issue has a long history involving extensive experimentation. For a detailed account, as well as a recent position statement, the interested reader is referred to Slamecka (1985).

Decay theories have been tested by varying the presentation rate, but presentation rate turns out to be a surprisingly weak variable in serial-order memory (Murdock, 1974; Waugh & Norman, 1965). This is not to say that decay effects do not exist (e.g., Shiffrin & Cook, 1978), but there and elsewhere they are generally small in magnitude. On the other hand, when interference effects are so large (e.g., Waugh & Norman, 1965) it is rather hard to make a convincing case for temporal decay as the main vehicle for forgetting.

Quite apart from conflicting data is the lack of generality of some models. If we consider "lower-level" models as those which deal with simple memory-span and list-learning data, and "higher-level" models as those which deal with chunking and organization, then some of the lower-level models cannot easily explain (or reasonably be extended to) higher-level effects and vice versa. For instance, although it might once have been thought that simple pair-wise chains would be sufficient to explain all of language, such a view would find few adherents today. Conversely, for all the enthusiasm for chunking and organization-type models, it is often not clear how they could make detailed predictions about serial-position and list-length effects.

Some of the earlier models are too simple to have much explanatory power. At least in retrospect this seems to be the case. If serial-order phenomena were simple, perhaps simple models might suffice, but neither seems to be the case. On the other hand, rejection of some of these earlier models may be premature. Although simple versions may be inadequate, more sophisticated versions might not be so easily rejected. As an example, consider the chaining notion, which is in ill repute today. I have argued elsewhere (Murdock, 1985b) that it might not be that chaining is wrong, but that the view of the associations which formed the chain is too simple.

Some of the models are descriptive not explanatory. An example of such a model is the distinctiveness model of Murdock (1960). As pointed out by Bower (1971), to characterize the bowed, serial-position curve in a quantitative fashion is not to explain how it came to be. Still, if one wanted to test a particular model, then the quantitative formulation would bring the target into focus.

Some of the models are complex or difficult to work with. Simulation models (e.g., EPAM, Estes' perturbation model, Drewnowski's attribute model, and the Shiffrin & Cook relational model) can be difficult to fit to data. Distributed memory models may also be considered complex and hard to work with. To those who are unfamiliar with their approach, such models may seem formidable. In fact, they are not difficult, even though the typical exposition (mine included) often does little to dispel their mysteries. Once one has worked with a distributed-memory model for a while, it seems quite simple and natural.

The final problem is perhaps the most serious of all. I could say that many of the models are qualitative not quantitative—which is true—but that does not quite make the point. I am convinced that we have not brought sufficient quantitative sophistication to our modeling efforts to have much chance of success. If one accepts the view that memory traces in general (or associations in particular) vary in strength, and that it is these variations in strength that produce serial-position effects, list-length effects, RI, PI, learning, and forgetting, then we must take the next obvious step: We must develop models that permit explicit expressions for the moments of the strength distributions in terms of the parameters of the model, and then apply the model to data. Although some of the models offered here are in principle capable of this, the actual work has not yet been done. I have attempted this with the convolution–correlation model and I discuss it next.

CONVOLUTION–CORRELATION MODEL

I shall list the basic assumptions of the convolution-correlation model and then indicate how it can be applied to data.

Basic Assumptions

1. Items can be represented as N-dimensional random vectors. This simply means that items can be represented as vectors in an N-dimensional space and the elements of each vector are independent random variables.

2. The N elements of each item vector are random samples from a normal distribution with mean zero and variance P/N (P stands for "power," and generally $P = 1$). This is a standard assumption of most distributed memory

models, though sometimes binary elements are used instead. This normal distribution is the feature distribution of the item, although "feature" is an abstract concept whose relation to the physical or semantic characteristics of an item is not specified.

3. Associations are formed by convolution (an operation denoted by "*"). Convolution is a particular way of combining two vectors into a single vector. A mathematical analogy would be the multiplication of two polynominals to form a third polynominal.

4. The equation describing the storage of serial-order information is:

$$\mathbf{M}_j = \alpha \mathbf{M}_{j-1} + \gamma_j \mathbf{f}_j + \omega_j \mathbf{f}_j * \mathbf{f}_{j-1} \qquad (3)$$

where $\mathbf{M}_j$ is the memory vector after item j has been stored and $\mathbf{M}_{j-1}$ is the memory vector before it was stored. Also, α is the forgetting parameter, γ_j is the weighting parameter for item information, and ω_j is the weighting parameter for associative information. The parameters γ and ω are subscripted because they may vary over serial position or trials. The current item $\mathbf{f}_j$ is associated with the prior item $\mathbf{f}_{j-1}$ so this is a simple chaining model.

5. Retrieval occurs through correlation: $\mathbf{f}_{j-1} \#\mathbf{M} = \mathbf{f}_j'$ where $\mathbf{f}_{j-1}$ is the probe from serial position $j-1$, $\mathbf{M}$ is the memory vector at the time of test, and $\mathbf{f}_j'$ is the retrieved information. Again, correlation is the appropriate retrieval operation when vectors are combined by convolution[2].

6. Assuming $P = 1$, then the probability of successful recall $r(i)$ at Probe Position i is given by:

$$r(i) = \int_a^b \phi_i(s) \prod_{k=1}^m [1 - \int_{1-s}^{1+s} \phi'_k(x)dx]ds. \qquad (4)$$

This the probability that $\mathbf{f}_j'$ is similar enough to $\mathbf{f}_j$ to be recalled (map into $\mathbf{f}_j$) and more similar to (the expected value of) $\mathbf{f}_j$ than any of the m possible competitors. (By "similar enough" I mean that the similarity falls between a and b where a and b are the tolerance limits.) The possible competitors might be, say, $\mathbf{f}_{j+1}$ and $\mathbf{f}_{j+2}$. In this equation $\phi_i(s)$ is the probe-target similarity distribution for a probe at Serial Position i, and the $\phi'_k(s)$ distributions are the comparable similarity distributions for the m possible competitors.

7. Similarity between any two vectors $\mathbf{f}$ and $\mathbf{g}$ is assessed by the dot product $\mathbf{f} \cdot \mathbf{g}$ where $\mathbf{f} \cdot \mathbf{g} = \sum_{i=1}^N f_i g_i$. If one thinks of vectors in N-space as geometric ob-

---

[2]Actually, $\mathbf{f}_{j-1} \#\mathbf{M}$ results in both $\mathbf{f}_{j-2}'$ and $\mathbf{f}_j'$. In all probability $\mathbf{f}_{j-2}'$ can be filtered out since subjects almost never repeat an item they have just recalled.

jects (which we can't visualize unless $N = 2$ or $N = 3$) then the dot product of two vectors is an inverse function of the angle between them. Thus, the more similar they are, the closer they are together.

8. Recall probability $r(i)$ can be represented graphically as shown in Fig. 18.7, where the cross-hatched area shows the probability of correct recall $r(i)$. This figure is a "picture" of Equation 4, except that the cross-hatched area must be reduced by all possible intrusions. Here, $f_O(s)$ denotes the probe-target similarity distribution while $f_N'(s)$, $f_N''(s)$, and $f_N'''(s)$ denote three "new-item" similarity distributions (i.e., possible competitors).

9. For serial recall, the number of competitors (m) is typically a function of the number of unrecalled items. The exact functional relation may vary with conditions. This is not true of a probe test, where m has the same value for all probe positions.

10. Information is added to the memory vector **M** during output (the test phase) as well as during input (the study phase). It must be because otherwise subjects could not remember their earlier responses. The same storage rule (Equation 3) applies to test as to study.

If chaining is the basis for serial learning, it is reasonable to ask why the serial-to-paired-associate transfer data are so negative. One way these data could be interpreted is that chaining is not the basis for paired-associate learning. The data do not rule out the possibility that chaining is the basis for serial learning.

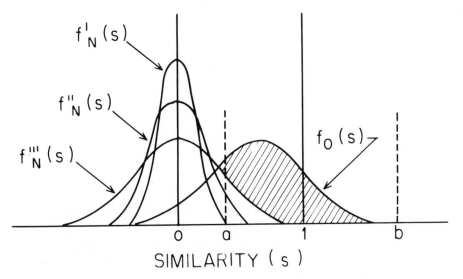

FIGURE 18.7. Similarity distributions for old and new items. The cross-hatched area corresponds approximately to probability of recall $r(i)$; a and b are the tolerance limits.

Also, the data are not completely negative. Positive transfer usually does occur on the first trial, and some studies (e.g., Postman & Stark, 1967) even show positive transfer when the dependent variable is trials to criterion. Many studies, of course, do not (Young, 1968).

Of course it is possible that there are two systems, an "A" system for associations and an "S" system for seriation. The S system would operate during serial learning and the A system would operate during associative learning. Not only would this explain the transfer data, but also there is evidence in support of two systems (Murdock & Franklin, 1984). However, before I advocate two separate systems I want to be quite sure that a single system will not suffice. Therefore, in this chapter it is assumed that there is only a single system for the storage of serial-order information.

In the next section I discuss the probe-response variance matrix: what it is, why it is necessary, how it is computed, and how one uses it to predict recall probability. This covers the detailed working of the model and how the model is applied to data. By necessity, it is somewhat technical, and the reader who is not interested in the details can skip to the section on Applications.

Probe-Response Variance Matrix

The trickiest step in applying the model to data is the computation of the probe-response variance matrix. The probe-response variance matrix gives the variance of the similarity of all list responses to all list probes. It is an $L \times L$ square matrix for the L possible probes and the L possible responses whose entries are the variances of the distributions shown in Fig. 18.7. The diagonal elements (Response i to Probe i where i denotes serial position) are not defined because the probe is not given as a response to itself. The superdiagonal ($j = i+1$) elements are the variances of the correct responses, and all other elements in each row are the variances of the possible competitors.

In serial-anticipation learning there is a different variance on each learning trial for each probe position and for each response position. We use the triple subscript nij to denote Trial n, Probe Position i, and Response Position j. Then the variance σ^2_{nij} is given by

$$\sigma^2_{nij} = (I_{nij} + A_{nij})/N \qquad (5)$$

where I_{nij} is the item component on Trial n for Response j to Probe i and A_{nij} is the associative component on Trial n for Response j to Probe i. Thus, the probe-response variance is the sum of two components, an item component and an associative component. Also, it is inversely related to N, the number of elements in the item vectors.

The item component I_{nij} is given by

$$I_{nij} = \mathbf{a}_{ni} \cdot \mathbf{p}_{ij} \qquad (6)$$

which is the dot product ("similarity") of two vectors $\mathbf{a}_{ni}$ and $\mathbf{p}_{ij}$ where $\mathbf{p}$ is the same for all trials and $\mathbf{a}$ is the same for all response positions. The associative component A_{nij} is given by

$$A_{nij} = \mathbf{b}_{ni} \cdot \mathbf{q}_{ij} \tag{7}$$

which is the dot product ("similarity") of two vectors $\mathbf{b}_{ni}$ and $\mathbf{q}_{ij}$ where $\mathbf{q}$ is the same for all trials and $\mathbf{b}$ is the same for all response positions. These dot products are purely computational, and they could equally will be represented in summation notation.

The vectors $\mathbf{p}$ and $\mathbf{q}$ are the vectors of weighting coefficients which reflect the relation between the probe and the response (i.e., i and j) and each of the L engrams (single items) and L (pairs of items) digrams in the memory vector. For the L engrams, the kth element of $\mathbf{p}$ is $7/4$ if $k = i$ or if $k = j$; otherwise, the kth element of $\mathbf{p}$ is $3/4$. For the L digrams, the kth element of $\mathbf{q}$ is $16/3$ if both the probe and the response match the digram. If one matches and one does not then the kth element of $\mathbf{q}$ is $5/3$. If neither match then the kth element of $\mathbf{q}$ is $2/3$. The values of the weighting coefficient come from the derivations, and they are summarized in Table 1 of Murdock (1985a). (The numerical values of the coefficients given here are approximations which involve only the highest-order N term in the polynomials, but for large N little is lost by disregarding the lower-order terms).[3]

Let me give an example. For $L = 6$ the engrams in the memory vector are assumed to be **X, A, B, C, D,** and **Y.** Thus, L denotes the number of list items (**A, B, C, D**) plus a start signal **X** and an end signal **Y.** These engrams are represented by independent random vectors, and each one is added to the memory vector as specified in Equation 3. It is assumed that there is no basic difference between list items (**A, B, C, D**) and end items (**X** and **Y**). Each is an independent random vector of dimension N.

The digrams (associated pairs) in the memory vector are assumed to be $\mathbf{X} * \mathbf{M}_0, \mathbf{A} * \mathbf{X}, \mathbf{B} * \mathbf{A}, \mathbf{C} * \mathbf{B}, \mathbf{D} * \mathbf{C},$ and $\mathbf{Y} * \mathbf{D}$ where $\mathbf{M}_0$ denotes the memory vector at the start of list presentation. Each digram is the association (convolution) of the current item with the prior item, and each digram is added to the memory vector according to Equation 3. There are as many digrams as engrams in the memory vector. The numerators of the elements of the $\mathbf{p}$ vectors and the numerators of the elements of the $\mathbf{q}$ vectors for all rows (probes) and responses (columns) for a probe test for $L = 6$ are shown in Table 18.1.

We have, in effect, two three-way crossed classifications: Probe × Response × Engram and Probe × Response × Digram. What Table 18.1 does is to represent these three-way classifications as two-way Probe × Response classifi-

---

[3]There was a slight error in the original derivation. The last term in the associative component of the probe-target pair (Appendix B, Murdock, 1983) should have been $16N^3$ not $14N^3$, also in the last line of Table 1 (Murdock, 1985a).

TABLE 18.1
The Numerators of **p** and **q** for Each Probe (Row) and Each
Response (Column) for $L = 6$. For **q**, $X = 16$

p
Response

	X	A	B	C	D	Y
Probe						
X		773333	737333	733733	733373	733337
A	773333		377333	373733	373373	373337
B	737333	377333		337733	337373	337337
C	733733	373733	337733		333773	333737
D	733373	373373	337373	333773		333377
Y	733337	373337	337337	333737	333377	

q
Response

	X	A	B	C	D	Y
Probe						
X		5X5222	555522	552552	552255	552225
A	5X5222		25X522	255552	255255	255225
B	555522	25X522		225X52	225555	225525
C	552552	255552	225X52		2225X5	222555
D	552255	255255	225555	2225X5		22225X
Y	552225	255225	225525	222555	22225X	

cations whose entries are the **p** and **q** vectors. This representation is convenient because we must sum over all engrams and all digrams to get a single entry (namely, the variance) for each row (probe) and each column (response) for the probe–response variance matrix.

The vectors **a** and **b** (Equations 6 and 7) reflect the parameter values α, γ, and ω. The elements of **a** are $\alpha\gamma$ products while the elements of **b** are $\alpha\omega$ products. For a probe test, the kth element of **a** is $(\alpha^{L-k}\gamma_{1,k})^2$ and the kth element of **b** is $(\alpha^{L-k}\omega_{1,k})^2$. Products are involved because both α and γ operate on the item information in multiplicative fashion and both α and ω operate on the associative information in multiplicative fashion. Note that both these terms involve the square of a product. The reason that these products are squared is because $\text{Var}[cz] = c^2\text{Var}[z]$.

I have already indicated (Equation 3) that α and ω may be functions of serial position. We assume that $\gamma_k = 1 - \gamma_1\exp(-\kappa k')$ and $\omega_k = \omega_1\exp(-\lambda k')$ where $k' = k-1$. Thus, γ increases in a negatively accelerated fashion over the study list with a starting value of $1-\gamma_1$, and a rate constant of κ. By contrast, ω decreases exponentially (geometrically) over the study list with a starting value of ω_1 and a

TABLE 18.2
Values to Compute the Item Variance Component I_{12} for a Probe
Test for Selected Parameter Values
($a(k)$ and $p(k)$ denote the kth elements of the vectors **a** and **p**.)

k	Engram	α^{L-k}	γ_k	$p(k)$	$a(k)\,p(k)$
1	X	.815	.800	7/4	.744
2	A	.857	.819	7/4	.862
3	B	.903	.836	3/4	.427
4	C	.950	.852	3/4	.491
5	Y	1.000	.866	3/4	.562
					a·p = 3.086 = I_{12}

rate constant of λ. These are about the simplest assumptions that one could reasonably make, and they specify the functional relations between the parameters and serial position implied by Equation 3. In general I assume that $\gamma_j = 1-\omega_j$ but here I separate γ and ω to illustrate the computations.

To illustrate how to compute σ^2_{nij} for a probe test, an example for $i = 1$ and $j = 2$ for $L = 5$ is shown in Tables 18.2 and 18.3. For $L = 5$ the list would be $XABCY$ where X is the start signal and Y is the end signal. Since $i = 1$ and $j = 2$ the probe would be X and the response would be A. To illustrate the computations assume $\alpha = .95$, $\gamma_1 = .2$, $\kappa = .1$, $\omega_1 = .9$, $\lambda = .2$, and $N = 50$. Table 18.2 shows the values needed to compute I_{12} and Table 18.3 shows the values to compute A_{12}. (I am dropping the subscript n since for a probe test there is only a single presentation.) The kth element in the vector **a** is the $\alpha\gamma$ product squared and the kth element in the vector **b** is the $\alpha\omega$ product squared.

Because $I_{12} = 3.086$ and $A_{12} = 3.775$ then by Equation 5 it follows that $\sigma_{12}{}^2 = 0.137$ and $\sigma_{12} = 0.370$. This value of 0.370 would be the standard deviation of $f_O(s)$ as shown in Fig. 18.7. To compute the m new-item distributions $f_N(s)$, one would repeat this procedure with the same values of **a** and **b** but different values of

TABLE 18.3
Values to Compute the Associative Variance Component A_{12} for a
Probe Test for Selected Parameter Values
($b(k)$ and $q(k)$ denote the kth element of the vectors **b** and **q**.)

k	Digram	α^{L-k}	ω_k	$q(k)$	$b(k)q(k)$
1	X*M$_0$	.815	.900	5/3	.897
2	A*X	.857	.737	16/3	2.128
3	B*A	.903	.603	5/3	.494
4	C*B	.950	.494	2/3	.147
5	Y*C	1.000	.404	2/3	.109
					b·q = 3.775 = A_{12}

p and **q**. Which vectors **p** and **q** were used would depend on which response competitor was being considered. In this example the three possibilities would be $j = 3$, $j = 4$, and $j = 5$.

This example assumes that there is no probe interference. That is, the probe X is not associated with the prior item Y or added to the memory vector before retrieval occurs. This assumption is probably wrong, but it simplifies the computations and probably does not affect the results very much. As I have mentioned, the start signal X is associated with the memory vector $\mathbf{M}_0$ where $\mathbf{M}_0$ is the memory vector at the start of list presentation.

For the anticipation method and serial recall, I assume that there is probe interference (i.e., the probe is encoded) and that the stored information is cyclical and continuous. When we get to the point in Trial 2 where the subject has been presented with or has recalled A and B and is using B as the probe for the recall of C, the information in the memory vector is as shown in Table 18.4. Thus, the assumption is made that each item vector ($\mathbf{X}$, $\mathbf{A}$, $\mathbf{B}$, $\mathbf{C}$, $\mathbf{Y}$, $\mathbf{X}$, $\mathbf{A}$, and $\mathbf{B}$) and each digram ($\mathbf{X}*\mathbf{M}_0$, $\mathbf{A}*\mathbf{X}$, $\mathbf{B}*\mathbf{A}$, $\mathbf{C}*\mathbf{B}$, $\mathbf{Y}*\mathbf{C}$, $\mathbf{X}*\mathbf{Y}$, $\mathbf{A}*\mathbf{X}$, and $\mathbf{B}*\mathbf{A}$) is stored with no breaks in the chain. This assumption not only makes computation easier but also extends naturally to the multitrial situation. Also, it is assumed that storage (of the probe item) precedes retrieval (of the next item). As shown in Table 18.4, the α values illustrate the repeated application of Equation 3 to the information in the memory vector. The γ and ω values depend on the numerical values of the parameters γ_1, κ, ω_1, and λ.

In computing the values of σ_{nij}^2 for both I_{nij} and A_{nij}, the $\alpha\gamma$ and the $\alpha\omega$ values are summed over trials before they are squared. More specifically, the kth element of $\mathbf{a}_{ni}$ is:

$$a_{ni}(k) = \left(\sum_{j=1}^{n'} \alpha^x \gamma_{j,k} \right)^2 \tag{8}$$

and the kth element of $\mathbf{b}_{ni}$ is:

$$b_{ni}(k) = \left(\sum_{j=1}^{n'} \alpha^x \omega_{j,k} \right)^2 \tag{9}$$

where $x = (n' - j) L + i - k$ and

$$n' = \left\{ \begin{array}{ll} n, & k \leq i \\ n-1, & k > i \end{array} \right\} \tag{10}$$

These equations are simply a formalization of the pattern shown in Table 18.4, but they make the programming easier because the notation is explicit. Here as always, one simply follows Equation 5; compute the $\alpha\gamma$ and the $\alpha\omega$ vectors for each probe position for each trial using Equations 8 and 9. The $\mathbf{p}_{ij}$ and $\mathbf{q}_{ij}$ vectors are as described before, except that one must take the cyclical nature of the presentation into account (see Table 18.4).

TABLE 18.4
The Engrams and the Digrams in the Memory Vector on Trial 2
when B is Being Used as the Cue for the Recall of C

Engrams:	X	A	B	C	Y	X	A	B
Digrams:	$X*M_0$	$A*X$	$B*A$	$C*B$	$Y*C$	$X*Y$	$A*X$	$B*A$
α values	α^7	α^6	α^5	α^4	α^3	α^2	α^1	α^0
γ values	$\gamma_{1,1}$	$\gamma_{1,2}$	$\gamma_{1,3}$	$\gamma_{1,4}$	$\gamma_{1,5}$	$\gamma_{2,1}$	$\gamma_{2,2}$	$\gamma_{2,3}$
ω values	$\omega_{1,1}$	$\omega_{1,2}$	$\omega_{1,3}$	$\omega_{1,4}$	$\omega_{1,5}$	$\omega_{2,1}$	$\omega_{2,2}$	$\omega_{2,3}$

As an example, the calculated old-item variances using the same parameter values are given in Table 18.5 for Trials 2 and 3 for serial learning using the anticipation method. To simplify the programming, I assumed that $M_0 = Y$ but that would be easy to change. A memory-span or study-test procedure would simply be the first two trials of the anticipation method where Trial 1 is the study trial and Trial 2 is the test trial.

Given the probe-response variance matrix we also need the mean of the old-item (probe-target) distribution on Trial n for Probe i. The old-item mean μ_{ni} is:

$$\mu_{ni} = \sum_{x=1}^{n-1} \alpha^{(n-x)L-1}\omega_{x,i+1} \tag{11}$$

Thus, μ_{ni} is simply the convolution of the α vector appropriate for Trial n with the ω vector appropriate for Response $i + 1$ and Trial n. Since the α vector depends on trials but not on serial position, we see that the changes in the old-item mean are due to changes in ω rather than α.

Given the probe-response variance matrix and the old-item mean, we can compute probability correct $r(i)$ by numerical integration. That is, Equation 4 does not have an explicit solution, but its value can be approximated. This is like the standard signal detection algorithm for an m-alternative forced choice situation. Because the absolute magnitude of the dot product is not important, "closer to" substitutes for "greater than." Probability correct $r(i)$ is $A \cap B$ where if x is the probe-target similarity then $A = Pr(a < x < b)$ (Fig. 18.7) and $B = Pr(|1-x| < |1-y|)$ where y is the comparable (nontarget) response similarity for all

TABLE 18.5
Old-item Variances on Trials 2 and 3 of
Serial-anticipation Learning for Selected
Parameter Values

Probe	2	3
X	.250	.575
A	.256	.548
B	.263	.533
C	.307	.589

m possible intrusions. We average the m new-item variances and do the numerical integration only once for each probe position, but to be more accurate, the numerical integration could be done separately for each possible competitor.

APPLICATIONS

In the following section I give some applications of the model to data. These include serial-position effects, experimental separation of primacy and recency, and learning. For the benefits of those readers who skipped the previous section, I shall summarize the procedure. We assume that item and associative information is stored in the memory vector both during presentation and recall according to Equation 3. For each probe position, recall probability is computed according to Equation 4, whose solution is the numerical value of the area under the similarity distributions depicted in Fig. 18.7. The means and variances of these similarity distributions are computed in terms of the parameters of the model (N, α, γ_j, ω_j. and m). One can derive the expressions for the entries in the probe-

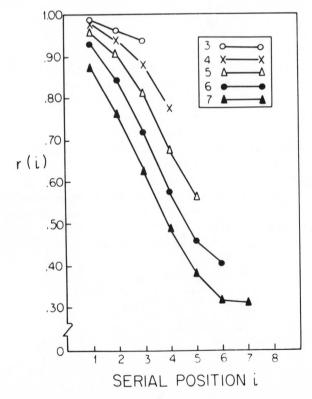

FIGURE 18.8.   Theoretical serial-position curves for L = 1–8.

response variance matrix from the basic assumptions of the model, but these derivations will not be presented here.

Serial-position Effects

An example of serial-position effects is given in Fig. 18.8. This shows the serial-position curves for serial recall (memory span or study test) for lists of 3–7 items. The parameter values were $N = 500$, $\alpha = 0.85$, $\omega_1 = 0.98$, $\lambda = 0.25$, $\gamma_j = \omega_j$, and the tolerance range was 6 so $a = -2$ and $b = 4$. The value of m, the number of competitors to the correct item (target) was equal to one more than the number of unrecalled list items. Subjects seldom repeat items they have correctly recalled (if the list is not too long), so this implements a sampling-without-replacement process. These curves seem to show the right pattern of results (cf. Fig. 18.3).

Experimental Separation of Primary and Recency

Some very striking evidence for experimental separation of primacy and recency has been provided by Watkins and Watkins (1977). Their data are shown in Fig. 18:9. As can be seen, word frequency affects primacy but not recency, whereas mode of presentation affects recency but not primacy.

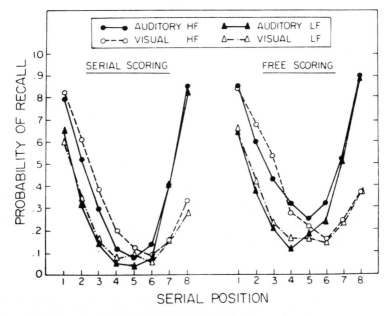

FIGURE 18.9.   Experimental separation of primacy and recency. (Data from Watkins & Watkins, 1977, reproduced with permission.)

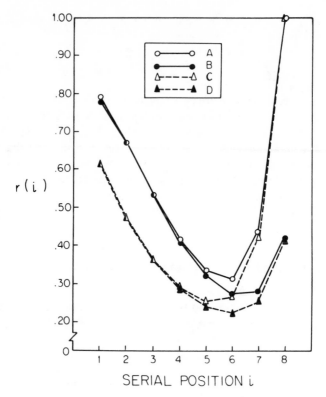

FIGURE 18.10.   Theoretical curves to illustrate the separation of primacy and recency.

It was not hard to mimic these results, at least the pattern if not the exact values. The results are shown in Fig. 18.10. To vary primacy, I set the ω starting value ω_1 to 0.98 (*A* and *B*) or to 0.68 (*C* and *D*). To vary recency, I added 0 (*A* and *C*) or 1 (*B* and *D*) to the value of *m*. This equivalent to saying there is one more competitor to the target item for visual presentation than for auditory presentation. In other respects, the parameters were the same as in Fig. 18.8. As can be seen, ω_1 affects primacy but not recency while the value of *m* affects recency but not primacy. The model's separation seems about as sharp as in the original Watkins and Watkins data.

Learning

The model accounts for learning by saying that more information is added to the memory vector with each repetition. Previously (Murdock, 1982), I said that

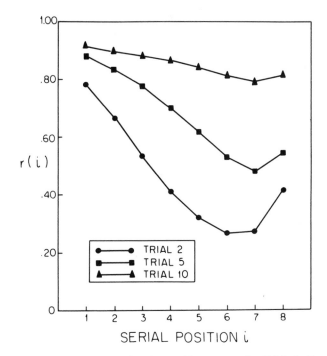

FIGURE 18.11.   Theoretical serial-position curves for Trials 2, 5, and 10 of the anticipation method.

learning might be a problem for the model because simply adding the same items to the memory vector was not enough. However, as shown in Fig. 18.11, learning does seem to occur. This was accomplished simply by letting λ decrease (exponentially) over trials. Thus, on each trial the starting value of ω was the same (i.e., ω_I) but the rate (λ) at which it decreased over serial position decreased over trials. Otherwise, the parameters were the same as in the previous fits. Thus, improvement with repetition no longer seems to be a serious problem. The convolution–correlation model can generate reasonable catenaries that characterize the change in serial position over trials.

Figs. 9–11 are not "fits" in the usual sense of the word. No formal parameter-estimation program was used. Rather, it was an informal trial-and-error procedure, and the parameter values selected seemed to give reasonable results.[4] We are currently trying to fit data quantitatively with the model, but it is too early to tell how it will turn out.

---

[4]I would like to thank Steve Lewandowsky for fitting the model to many different sets of data. I have used some of his results to select these particular parameter values.

EXPLANATORY VALUE

The convolution–correlation model may help us to better understand serial-order effects and how they could arise. It also provides some possible insights into more general aspects of memory.

Direct Access

The model explains how direct access can occur (correlation). The probe vector is correlated with the memory vector to retrieve the target item. As has been noted, no "search" process is necessary.

Associations

The model suggests that an association is not simply a connection or link between two items, but instead the fusing or melding (convolution) of two separate item vectors into a single common associative vector.

Temporal-to-spatial Mapping

The model shows how sequential information could be stored without a temporal-to-spatial mapping. It has often been assumed that some sort of temporal-to-spatial mapping must occur to store order information (e.g., Milner, 1961), but this is not necessary. Sequential information can be preserved and reconstructed from a distributed memory.

Forgetting

The model describes how forgetting can occur (adding information to a common memory vector). Adding additional information both decreases the mean strength of the target information (by α) and increases the variance by virtue of the fact that all information is stored in a common pool.

Input interference

The model explains why input interference occurs (Equation 3). As each new item comes along, both item and associative information are added to the common memory store.

Output interference

The model explains how output interference occurs. Since information is added to the memory vector during both study and test, both the mean strength (of the

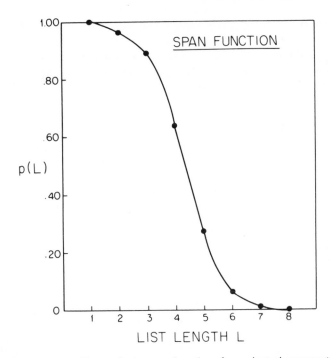

FIGURE 18.12. Theoretical span function for selected parameter values.

unrecalled items) decreases and the variance increases as recall proceeds. Both are consequences of the basic assumptions of the model—so output interference falls directly out of the model.

Memory span

The model explains the origin of memory span. Performance deteriorates as list length increases because both input and output interference increases. A span function obtained from the model is shown in Fig. 18.12. It was derived directly from the data of Fig. 18.8 simply by computing the running product as in Equation 2.

Backward Memory Span

Backward memory span is the memory span when items must be recalled in reverse, or backward, order. I think the model can explain why backward memory span is worse than forward memory span. It seems to depend on the particular parameter values, and I do not know whether the parameter values that give the right result are reasonable. However, when it does work it may be a small *tour de force* for the model. I originally thought that the model could not handle backward memory span because convolution is commutative ($\mathbf{f}*\mathbf{g} = \mathbf{g}*\mathbf{f}$). However, the variances do the trick. As concisely as possible, $\mathrm{Var}[\alpha^3 x + \alpha^2 y + \alpha x + y] \neq \mathrm{Var}[\alpha^3 x + \alpha^2 y + \alpha y + x]$, and with the right values of x and y the backward variance will be greater than the forward variance.

Positional Probe

How can a subject respond to the positional probe if only sequential association exist? One possibility is that the memory vector is unpacked from the beginning and from the end. By counting the number of steps, the subject could respond to a positional probe using only sequential associations. For some suggestive data from studies of judgments of recency, see Muter (1979) or Hacker (1980).

The Hebb Repetition Effect

The Hebb repetition effect (Hebb, 1961) refers to the fact that a repeated list of digits in a memory-span experiment shows gradual improvement over the course of the session when compared with control lists. Because the model can handle repetition, it seems quite likely that it can handle the Hebb repetition effect as well. However, I have not computed this explicitly. Also, I suspect it can show that the benefits vary with spacing (Melton, 1963), although again the same caveat applies.

Reallocation Hypothesis

The reallocation hypothesis of Bower and Winzenz (1969) says that the benefits of repetition require the leading element(s) of the string to be preserved. Given the serial nature of the model, this seems like a reasonable outcome to be expected.

Free and Serial Recall

There is a very close relation between serial recall and free recall as free recall is explained in Metcalfe and Murdock (1981). In the Metcalfe and Murdock model, associations are formed by associating the current item with a prior item. The associative mechanism (convolution) and the retrieval scheme (correlation) is the same in the two cases. The major difference between free recall and serial recall would then seem to be in the rehearsal distributions employed. In free recall, the distributions are approximately geometric, whereas in serial recall the item rehearsed is always the prior item so it is a "point" distribution with no variability. This synthesis of free recall and serial recall would seem to be a real plus for the convolution–correlation model: It can handle serial recall and free recall within the same conceptual framework.

DIFFICULTIES

In the final section I briefly consider some difficulties for the model and suggest some possible answers. These difficulties are primacy and recency, proactive inhibition, saturation, intrusions, chunking, and organization.

Primacy and Recency

As noted in Murdock (1983), the primacy and recency flip-flop is a major problem for any quantitative model of serial-order effects. How can the same processes give rise to extensive primacy and little recency under one set of conditions but extensive recency and little primacy under another set of conditions? One can always adjust parameter values to give the desired pattern of data, but that is not a very satisfactory explanation. It does not seem to add much to our understanding of the processes that are involved.

There is an answer to this problem, at least at a qualitative level. In serial recall, output interference destroys the recency effect that one would otherwise observe, and this interference results from adding the retrieved information to the memory vector. This can explain the dominance of primacy over recency, but what about the reverse? In a probe test, there should be considerable primacy because otherwise serial recall would not be so successful. The answer may be that there are marked criterion effects that considerably reduce the observed primacy. Evidence for this possibility has already been mentioned, and may be found in Murdock (1968). When the a posteriori probability or d' curves were plotted, the primacy effect was considerably greater than the recency effect. Thus, the problem is not in the model but in the way that the data are analyzed, and the stylized serial-position curve of Fig. 18.1 may indeed characterize probe recall as well as serial recall.

Proactive Inhibition

How does PI occur? This may be handled by reusing the same start vector ($\mathbf{X}$) on successive trials. Alternatively (or in addition), we may have to bring in the role of context. Although context is an important concept, it has several different uses (see Wickens, this volume) and the issue of how to model it is not immediately clear.

Saturation

Saturation refers to the overloading of the elements of the memory vector because new information is continually being presented. How can saturation (see Grossberg, 1978b) be prevented? Perhaps it can be handled by α; at this point I am not sure. Or perhaps some version of a closed-loop model (Sutton & Barto,

1981) will be necessary. Saturation, like context effects, is a matter for further theoretical development.

Intrusions

How can serial order (interlist) intrusions occur? Positional associations may be necessary. As mentioned, we could have two memory systems, an A system for associations and an S system for seriation. If the S system functioned by Equation 3 and the A system stored item-to-position associations, then recency effects, PI, and serial-order intrusions could be explained. Details of an associative model have been worked out (Murdock, 1982), and there is some experimental evidence (Harcum, 1975; Young, 1968) suggesting the need for positional associations. However, this extension would greatly complicate the model; hopefully it will not be necessary.

Chunking

How can chunking occur? If we stored engram (item), digram (associative), and trigram (relational) information, then:

$$M_j = \alpha M_{j-1} + af_j + bf_j{}^*f_{j-1} + cf_j{}^*f_{j-1}{}^*f_{j-2} \qquad (12)$$

where a, b, and c are the parameters for the three types of information. This could lead to the formation of chunks and higher-order units.

Suppose we had a nine-item string **A, B, C, D, E, F, G, H,** and **J.** With variable weighting coefficients a, b, and c we could highlight **A, B*A, C*B*A, D, E*D, F*E*D, G, H*G,** and **J*H*G.** This could be done if abc followed the pattern 100, 010, 001, 100 . . . . as each new item came along. Then we could chunk into propositions (**P**) so

$$P_1 = A + A^*B + A^*B^*C$$
$$P_2 = D + D^*E + D^*E^*F$$
$$P_3 = G + G^*H + G^*H^*J$$

Not only would this break the string into three groups or chunks, but it would reverse the temporal direction so that the backward direction appropriate for storage was mapped into the forward direction appropriate for retrieval. Some such "time reversal" seems necessary; one associates the current item with earlier items for storage, but the current item must lead to later items for retrieval.

Organization

To be useful, chunks must be stored as units and be retrievable on demand. How can they be organized? One possibility is:

$$M_j = \alpha M_{j-1} + P_j{}^*P_{j-1}$$

so that each proposition is associated with the prior proposition and

$$P_j = A_j + A_j{}^*B_j + A_j{}^*B_j{}^*C_j.$$

Thus, a proposition contains engram, digram, and trigram information in a forward temporal order. Then to retrieve a proposition, we could have

$$P_{j-1}\#M = P'_j \rightarrow P_j$$

so that one proposition retrieves the next. It is possible to unpack the proposition ABC into its separate components (see Liepa, 1977, reviewed in Murdock, 1979). Then to retrieve the next proposition:

$$P_j\#M = P'_{j+1} \rightarrow P_{j+1}$$

and the process continues. If we relax the contiguity restriction, we can replace $P_j{}^*P_{j-1}$ with P^*Q so

$$M_j = \sum_j P_j{}^*Q_j$$

and we have the association of ideas.

CONCLUSIONS

The convolution–correlation model as it now stands can handle many of the basic serial-order phenomena. Not unreasonable extensions will give it even greater power. Although it has some difficulties, at least solutions to these difficulties exist in principle. Whether they are the correct ones remains to be seen.

Chaining as a mechanism for seriation was rejected by Lashley (1951) in a very influential paper. I think he may have been wrong. At a simple level, chaining must be the basis of seriation just as associations must be the building block for learning. How skilled acts run off certainly involves additional complexities (see Baars, this volume), but this by no means precludes chaining at a lower level.

To understand in detail the operation of chaining as a basic mechanism for serial-order effects will require the development and testing of quantitative models. This conclusion would not displease Ebbinghaus. He was a pioneer in the formal analysis of data on memory and learning, and this approach still holds the most promise for broadening and deepening our understanding of human memory.

ACKNOWLEDGMENTS

Preparation of this chapter was facilitated by Research Grant APA 146 from the Natural Sciences and Engineering Research Council of Canada and a Killam Research Fellowship from the Canada Council. I would like to thank Steve Lewandowsky for many helpful comments.

19 Discussion of the Chapter by Murdock

Joan Gay Snodgrass
New York University

Let me preface this chapter by emphasizing that I am not an expert on distributed memory models. A man I once knew described an expert as someone who, when he discovers he is unaware of a finding in the area, feels embarrassed. By that criterion, I am not an expert, because I felt little embarrassment as I discovered all the things I did not know about distributed memory models. However, as a nonexpert, the steps I took in the exploration of this topic may be of help to other nonexperts.

WHAT, WHY, AND WHERE

The questions that I asked may be divided into a *what* question, a *why* question, and a *where* question. As a nonexpert, the first question I asked myself was: "What are distributed memory models?"

A distributed memory model may be contrasted to a discrete or localized memory model. In a localized system, a particular location contains information about only a single item or a single relationship between a pair of items. As an example, the Collins and Loftus (1975) network model of semantic memory contains information about individual items at the nodes and information about relationships at the labeled links between nodes. In models of short-term memory of the Sternberg (1966) type, items are stored in discrete locations, and the label of the location (or possibly the spatial relationship between the locations) contains the order information.

In contrast, a distributed memory model stores information from a particular item in several locations, and often combined with information from other items.

311

Thus, no particular location (or, as it is usually instantiated, value of a memory vector) contains all the information in the to-be-remembered stimulus. In Murdock's model, the information from a single list is contained in a single memory vector in which the middle N elements of the memory vector contain both item and pair-wise associative information, while the N-1 flanking items contain only associative information generated by pair-wise convolutions.

The second question I asked myself was: "Why distributed memory models?" The impetus for distributed memory models comes from two sources: neuroscience and artificial intelligence. We learn from neuroscience (e.g., Anderson & Hinton, 1981) that brain functioning, particularly that of the cortex, shows the following two properties: (a) *Parallelism*, as exhibited by multiple connections among neurons, simultaneous activation, and topographical organization. Parallelism seems to be universally agreed on as a property of neural tissue by neuroscientists. (b) *Distributed storage*, as exhibited by the fact that more than one neuron or set of neurons participates in the storage of information. However, there is less agreement here, with some functions appearing to be very specifically stored (e.g., the "monkey hand" cell) or very generally stored (e.g., Lashley's "engram").

I will argue that a memory model can incorporate either or both distributed (parallel) processing and distributed storage. A distributed memory does not necessarily imply parallel processing, and a discrete or local memory system does not rule out parallel processing. For example, the Sternberg (1966, 1975) short-term memory scanning model has properties that contradict both parallel processing and distributed storage: First, it has seriality at a macro-level, in that the four stages proposed by Sternberg are assumed to occur in serial order—the stage of probe encoding precedes the stage of memory scanning, which precedes the stage of decision, which precedes the stage of response organization and execution. Thus there is seriality in stage sequencing. Second, there is seriality at a micro level, in that the memory-scanning stage itself consists of a series of substages that are carried out sequentially. Third, there is discete or localized memory storage of the memory set.

Each of these three properties can be modified to produce distributed processing, distributed storage, or both.

(1) At the macro-level of stages, the cascade model of McClelland (1979) postulates a quasiparallel operation for sequencing stages. Specifically, his model assumes that one stage can begin before the second finishes. Partial information from one stage is sent to the second throughout the processing of the first. This cascade model is consistent with, although it does not particularly require, the possibility of distributed processing.

(2) The results of Townsend (Snodgrass & Townsend, 1980; Townsend, 1972; Townsend & Ashby, 1983) show that serial scanning in the memory-scanning stage can be mimicked by parallel scanning. Thus, parallel scanning

can occur in the memory scanning stage without affecting either the macro-seriality of stages or the localized storage of memory set items.

(3) The memory set items can have distributed storage, as in Murdock's model. Here, for the probe recognition task of the Sternberg experiment, changing the form of the memory storage from discrete to distributed does affect the scanning stage—using the recognition mechanism from Murdock's model produces a parallel scan of short-term memory. Thus, for this situation, changing the form of the memory storage also changes the form of the scanning (although the macro-seriality of the stages need not be affected). Another example that illustrates the use of distributed processing without distributed storage is Fahlman's (1981) network model of semantic memory which employs discrete memory storage but parallel access and retrieval.

Evidence from both cognitive psychology and artificial intelligence points to several aspects of human memory that may require the particular properties of distributed storage models. The human's ability to retrieve information from partial cues seems to be extraordinarily good, and this ability does not seem capable of duplication with present-day serial computers. For retrieval by recognition, we are able to recognize a voice we haven't heard for years, recognize a face we haven't seen for years, or recognize familiar persons out of the corner of our eye or from down the street. Our phenomenal ability to retrieve in recall may be illustrated by our ability to use partial cues in solving crossword puzzles. An eight-letter word such as ASSASSIN can be recalled from such partial cues as its definition (e.g., murderer), an example (e.g., Lee Harvey Oswald), or word fragments (e.g., __ S S __ S S __ __).

The third question I asked myself about Murdock's model is a *where* question—where is the distributed memory placed and, more importantly, where is it not placed? The model seems to be very finicky about exactly where it puts the distributed memory. The only explicit distribution occurs in the construction of the memory vector, whereas both feature memory and response memory would appear to be localized. Before exploring the *where* question in more detail, I briefly summarize the salient features of Murdock's model.

MURDOCK'S CONVOLUTION-CORRELATION MODEL

The model uses the operation of convolution to store items and pair-wise associations, and the operation of correlation to retrieve items for recall.

In Murdock's model, a list of to-be-remembered items is stored into a memory vector, M, which keeps track of both individual items (A,B,C, etc.) and of adjacent pairs (AB, BC, CD, etc). Individual items are themselves N-dimensional vectors, and associations between adjacent items are computed by the operation of convolution (*). The resulting memory vector is of dimension 2N-1 because only adjacent item associations are stored (i.e., not all possible associations are made).

Retrieval is accomplished in two different ways depending on whether the task is recognition or recall. In recognition, similarity is computed between the probe (which can either be a single item or a series of test items) and the memory vector by the dot product computation ($\cdot$). For a single item, A, this is denoted as A$\cdot$M, and for a set of items denoted as $M_1 \cdot M_2$. If the similarity is above a "yes" criterion, the subject responds positively; if below a "no" criterion, he responds negatively; and if in between, he defers the decision.

In recall, the operation of retrieval is correlation, denoted #. Recall proceeds in serial order from the first item on the list to the last item on the list or the last item retrievable. The subject enters the memory vector with the δ-vector (delta-vector) which is obtained by correlating the start signal with itself, producing a vector with a 1 in the middle position and all flanking zeros. Correlating the δ-vector with the memory vector produces the middle N values of the memory vector, M, which is usually close to the first item, A's vector. A is retrieved by comparing the retrieved vector A' with a list of possibilities in the output response box, R, and picking the one with the highest similarity (by computing the dot product). The correct vector A (rather than the retrieved vector A') is then used to correlate with the memory vector to retrieve B, and so on until the process fails. In the present version, which is explicitly designed for a task in which both item and order information are to be tested, the memory vector is constructed by the operations of convolution and addition.

However, there are several uses of other memory stores which appear not themselves to be distributed. Thus, the model is distributed in only a small aspect of its functions. Let me spell out in detail those aspects of the model in which distributed memory is not assumed, and indeed, in which perfect nondistributed memory has apparently been assumed in generating predictions for the model.

Memory for Features:

Each item consists of a list of N features, which are assumed to be generated by the subject, in an unspecified manner, on presentation of a study item. These features presumably must be retrieved from long-term memory, but what is the nature of this retrieval? Is long-term memory itself distributed? If it is, then the feature values will be noisy because retrieved information from a distributed memory store will contain noise. Furthermore, subsequent retrieval of features will not give the same vector because of such noise. The nature of the features is left undefined in Murdock's papers of 1982 and 1983, although he points out that if N is on the order of 100 to 1000, these are clearly not semantic features as they are usually understood. Yet, in simulations, N is often considerably lower—usually on the order of 15 to 60.

Eich (1985) has proposed a similar distributed memory model for cued recall. She gives the following illuminating examples of the features that might be generated and stored to the two names Bill and Bob: aggressiveness, first phoneme of name, hair color, age, and attractiveness. Most of these must obviously be retrieved from some long-term semantic or episodic memory. My point here is that feature retrieval will be noisy if this memory is distributed, yet absolute reliability of feature values is assumed.

A second property of features which makes their use somewhat problematic is that features must be "center-justified." That is, the feature at the ith location of A's vector must be the same as the feature at the ith location of B's vector. This is because similarity of the memory trace to the probe, or of the retrieved information to one of the candidates for recall, is computed by the dot product. The dot product computes the sum of the products of the ith features of the two vectors, and this dot product would be uninterpretable if center justification could not be guaranteed. On the other hand, the fact that two memory vectors may have to be "jiggled" until they fit (that is, until they generate a dot product which bears some criterion similarity to another dot product) may also make the model more attractive (even through this process of "jiggling" is not a feature of the model). It is possible that our long latencies in retrieving information, and the sudden emergence of such information, is due to something very much like this "jiggling" process.

Memory in the R-System:

Another place where an apparently nondistributed and error-free memory system is used by the model is in the response (R) system. The R-system contains the primed items from the list that must be compared with the retrieved vector A'. However, the retrieved vector, A', is compared with the intact vector, A, which itself must be error-free and also must be stored in R in a discrete or localized (rather than distributed) fashion. Otherwise, the similarity values, computed by the dot product between A' and all candidates (including A), would not yield the desired result. The R-system may contain all of long-term memory, but for the purposes of the model it contains only the candidates for recall, which are the m list items reduced by the items already recalled.

In order to recall the first item, an N-element vector is retrieved from M, and a candidate is selected on the basis of the dot product of the retrieval vector and each of the m candidates in turn. However, this similarity computation is made against an error-free representation in R, which means that items in R are not distributed but discrete.

To retrieve the second item, the first item's error-free vector is used, and so on. Thus, an undistributed memory list (in R) supports a distributed memory list (in M). The only information R seems to lack is the order information, but why bother with M when you have R?

Murdock (1982) is obviously aware of this problem with the R-store, because he wrote:

> From this description it might seem as though each competitor somehow existed in memory waiting, as it were, to be compared. In fact, nothing like this is intended. There is the retrieved information g' and nothing more. The comparison with all competitors is for the experimenter's benefit—that is, to predict performance—but the subject only has the single vector g' as the basis for producing the target item g. (p. 616)

But then we are left with the problem of how the subject retrieves the correct alternative g, including exact replicas of each of its N feature elements.

The Problem of Learning:

A final undesirable property of the model as described in the 1982 and 1983 papers is that learning is not possible. And if there is one fact we can be sure of from this conference it is, as Slamecka has pointed out, that the "law of frequency" can be reified as the "Law of Frequency." Probability of recognition or recall does increase as frequency of presentation increases, so any model that cannot predict this perhaps uniquely incontrovertible fact of memory is in trouble. To quote Murdock (1982):

> If more than a single presentation is used, it seems reasonable to assume simply that additional representations are added to the memory vector. In fact, this idea must be wrong. If one works out the predictions, one finds that although the expected values increase, so do the variances. In the cases I have examined, the variances increase so as to offset exactly the increases in the means. As a result, learning would not be expected. (p. 625)

In his chapter, Murdock suggests several ways in which the model can accommodate learning effects. The initial value of the weighting parameter for the associative information (ω_0) can be increased over trials, or the value of N (the number of features stored for each item) can be increased over trials. Apparently, both of these modifications were incorporated in the model to predict recall as a function of serial position and trial number shown in Figure 18.12 of Murdock's chapter. Thus, reasonable modifications of the model would appear to solve the learning problem.

The performance of the model in accounting for standard results in the serial-order literature is quite impressive. The model accounts for forgetting, input and output interference, serial-position effects, experimental separation of primacy and recency effects, and the advantage of forward over backward memory span, among others.

In summary, there is important neurological and cognitive evidence to support the notion of distributed memory systems. However, I am not convinced that this particular instantiation of a distributed memory system is the best one. Specifically, there are a number of hidden assumptions in the model that seem to force reliance on undistributed memory systems. However, as one of the few extant memory models to have been developed so extensively for the classic verbal learning and memory paradigms, the model does represent a rather breathtaking accomplishment.

20 On Generic Recall

John Ceraso
Institute for Cognitive Studies
Rutgers University, Newark, NJ

INTRODUCTION

The phenomenon I consider is what Brown and McNeill (1966) have called *generic recall*. Generic recall occurs when accurate recall fails but some aspect of the desired material is still available. In trying to remember a name one may be able to recall its first letter, the number of syllables it contains, and that it designates someone of a particular ethnic background. For example, I have been called Caruso, Sorroso, Cesaro, and so on.

I believe that generic recall is the result of the way material is encoded when it is first learned. I discuss evidence which indicates that the more general attributes of material are learned before the specific attributes, and that these attributes are forgotten in the reverse order. In addition, I suggest that the act of remembering recapitulates learning in that, at the point of recall, general features are recovered before specific features. These factors make it likely that when one cannot remember the desired item, some general attributes of the item will be available to mediate generic recall.

Generic recall is an instance of the larger phenomenon of generalization and should, therefore, be looked at in that broader context. Generalization has been treated in one of two ways: One conception is that generalization is the result of the spread of excitation from one specific entity to another. The other conception regards generalization as the result of the arousal of general attributes. In what follows I present a brief survey of these two positions with special focus on their relevance to generic recall.

319

THEORIES OF SPECIFIC ACTIVATION

Pavlov and Stimulus Generalization

The original specific activation theory is Pavlov's theory of stimulus generalization (1928). It was intended to explain the fact that a stimulus similar to the original conditioned stimulus could, without prior training, evoke the conditioned response. Basic to Pavlov's explanation is the idea that the cortex is a sensory analyzer surface and that a particular stimulus will activate a particular cortical locus. When a conditioned stimulus is presented it activates its own cortical locus but the excitation also irradiates to neighboring cortical loci. If a cortical point is activated by the excitation spreading from the conditioned stimulus at the time that the unconditioned stimulus is presented, then it too becomes associated with the unconditioned stimulus, and its corresponding external stimulus also acquires the capacity to evoke the conditioned response. The role of similarity in stimulus generalization was accounted for by the assumption that stimulus similarity corresponded to cortical proximity.

Thus, starting from a theory which involves the activation of specific cortical points, Pavlov evolved a theory which can account for generalization. In order to do this he invoked the construct of the spread of excitation from one specific point to another.

Response Generalization

An everyday instance of stimulus generalization would be to call a stranger by the name of someone you know, when it is the case that the stranger resembles the person you know. The example of generic recall I gave earlier, however, is that you mistakenly call the person you know by a name which resembles the correct name; and that sort of error is called *response generalization*.

Investigators of verbal learning have studied response generalization in the context of studies of transfer and false recognition. For example, in a transfer study where the degree of first list learning, and the degree of similarity of meaning of first and second list responses were varied, Underwood (1951) found that ease of learning the second list was positively related to those two variables. The explanation Underwood (1951) offered for his findings is very similar to the Pavlovian theory described earlier. Underwood proposed that at the point of learning the first list A–B association, the B item would evoke other specific responses which were associated to it, and these would then also become associated with the A term. These implicit responses would lead to positive transfer if they were the response terms required in the second list, or they could serve as mediators for the second list responses.

The theory proposes, then, that the activation of a specific response will spread to, and activate other responses similar to it. The major difference between this theory and the theory of Pavlov is that similarity is related to cortical nearness by Pavlov and to associative linkage by Underwood.

Another phenomenon which can be subsumed under the heading of response generalization is false recognition. Underwood (1965), for example, showed that in a continuous recognition task subjects might falsely recognize new words if the new words were similar in meaning to the old. The explanation offered is the same as the one described previously; old words when first seen will, via associative linkage, arouse related words. Because of that arousal those related words might subsequently be falsely recognized.

Priming and Spreading Activation

The most popular current account of the effect of similarity of meaning on recall is the theory of spreading activation (e.g., Collins & Loftus, 1975). Perhaps the main evidence for this sort of theory is the priming phenomenon (Meyer & Schvaneveldt, 1971). If two words are presented successively and the second word is to be judged as to whether it is a real word or not, then the judgment will be made more quickly if the first word (the prime) is related in meaning to the target word. To account of this phenomenon, the assumption is made that the first word activates its representation in a semantic network of associated entities, and that the excitation spreads along the associative pathways from the node representing the original word to excite the representations of other words. In a priming task, reaction time will be faster to a target word if its representation has already been excited by the spread of excitation from the priming word. Spreading activation is quite similar to Pavlov's irradiation, except that the spread is along associative pathways (as with Underwood's theory) rather than over the cortical surface.

GENERAL ACTIVATION THEORIES

Lashley and Wade

In a very well-known paper, Lashley and Wade (1946) argued that the fact of generalization had been misinterpreted by Pavlov and his followers. One needs to postulate an active process of "generalization" or "spread" only if one also postulates that something very specific is activated at the point of original learning. But suppose that when a tone of 220 cps is presented at learning, all that an animal learns is that "tone" precedes shock. The subsequent response to a tone of 280 cps would not mean that anything had spread or generalized, but simply that the animal was responding to the "same" stimulus to which it had been conditioned, namely, "tone." Furthermore, Lashley and Wade argued that the so-called gradient of stimulus generalization was an artifact of the method of testing for it. That is, the procedure involved in generating the gradient forced the subjects to discriminate between the original stimulus and the generalized stimuli, and the farther apart stimuli are along a sensory dimension the easier it will be to discriminate between them; these factors generate the gradient.

It would not be appropriate at this point to discuss the large experimental literature associated with the ideas of Lashley and Wade, except to say that some of it was confirmatory and some not, but, in my opinion, much of their thesis has been accepted. For example, the notion that the important stimulus is not the specific physical stimulus presented by the experimenter, but the stimulus as interpreted by the subject, now seems to be universally accepted. I offer as evidence for this statement the current ubiquitous use of the term "encoding."

Brown and McNeill:TOT

Perhaps the work that comes most readily to mind when one thinks of the phenomenon of generic recall is the study by Brown and McNeill (1966). In that study these investigators were trying to get at that subjective state, tip of the tongue (TOT), where you feel that you are on the threshold of recalling something. Subjects were given a definition and asked to recall the word that fit the definition. Of special interest were the attempts at recall of the subjects who claimed that were in the TOT state. Brown and McNeill found that these subjects could often recall aspects of the word even though they could not recall the word itself. Thus, they might recall the first letter of the word, or they might recall another word that sounded like the target word, or had the same number of syllables, or was accented in the same way, etc. The incorrectly recalled words were similar to the intended word, but Brown and McNeill did not invoke the notion of spreading excitation to account for them. Rather, they suggested that a word has many properties and that only some of these properties might be available at the point of recall. The words that the subjects selected were words that matched the generic properties which were available to them.

Further Studies of False Recognition

Following Underwood's (1951) demonstration of false recognition some investigators suggested that the phenomenon was mediated by the arousal of more general properties of the target words when they were originally seen, rather than by the arousal of specific associations to those words. Kimble (1968), for example, pointed out that the number of words which can be potentially falsely recognized following the presentation of a target word is enormous. Rather than imagining that all of those words were aroused at the time of original presentation Kimble suggested that false recognition is mediated by the implicit evocation of a concept of which all these specific words are exemplars.

Grossman and Eagle (1970) repeated Underwood's (1951) false-recognition study with certain added controls, and by and large they replicated Underwood's results. An interesting feature of their design, however, was that they had a measure of the associative strength of the relation between the old items and the distractor items. They found no relation between associative strength and false recognition. If false recognition has to do with the implicit evocation of associates to the target item upon its initial presentation, then one would except associate strength and false recognition to be related. Grossman and Eagle concluded that their results supported Kimble's conjecture that a word evoked a more general concept during presentation, rather than a host of specific implicit associates.

In another study of false recognition, Eagle and Ortof (1967), had subjects listen to words with focal attention, or with distraction (subjects performed a digit-coding task while listening to the words). A recognition task was then given in which the original word was presented along with semantically related, acoustically related, and unrelated, new words. The main result of the experiment was that the distraction condition, as compared with the focal attention condition, showed a drop in the recognition of old words, and an increase in the false recognition of acoustically related distractors. These results suggest that with divided attention there was a tendency for subjects to store only the sound of a word and not its meaning.

Eagle and Ortof were influenced by the earlier work of Treisman (1964), and they anticipated the levels of processing hypothesis of Craik and Lockhart (1972). The theme that runs through all these investigations is that the apprehension of a word is a temporally extended event that follows a defined course, so that, for example, the acoustical properties of a word are available before its meaning. The levels of processing hypothesis, like the Lashley–Wade hypothesis, allows us to understand false recognition as due to the encoding of general features of an item rather than as being the result of spreading activation.

General Effects in Priming Studies

The fact that a category name can prime a word that is a member of that category, or that a word can be primed by another word that is related in meaning is both explained by, and used as evidence, to support the notion of spreading activation. In a recent study, however, Lorch (1982) has presented evidence which questions this interpretation of the priming effect. Lorch started with the fact that a prime will activate some items faster than others. For example, when primed by a category name, words strongly associated to that category name will be responded to more quickly than will less strongly associated words. That fact has typically been taken to mean that the distance in the semantic network between the prime and the target is smaller in the case of the highly associated words. To test this assumption, Lorch performed an experiment in which subjects saw a category name followed by another word which was to be judged for category membership.

In other experiments, the subjects were asked merely to read the second word. The two variables of interest were, (a) the strength of the association between the category name and the exemplar and (b) the time between the prime and the probe (i.e., the stimulus onset asynchrony; SOA). If a prime activated the probe via spreading activation, and if excitation reached the probe more quickly in the case of highly associated items, then one should expect that as the SOA was increased the items of low associative strength would "catch up" with the high associates, and differences in response latency should decrease. Lorch found no such effect; high associates retained a constant advantage over low associates over the range of SOAs employed. Lorch concluded from his results that the presentation of a prime activates the whole concept network at once. This work indicates that priming, the chief evidence for specific spreading activation, may actually be better interpreted by the concept of general activiation.

General Effects in Learning: Dinnerstein and Egeth

Incremental and all-or-none theories of learning have differed on whether a specific item is learned incrementally or all or none. Dinnerstein and Egeth (1962) took a different approach to this question and presented evidence to suggest that a trace develops along a general to specific dimension rather than a weak to strong dimension. The following items were given to subjects in a paired-associate experiment:

Mab–July
Vid–△
Biv–▽
Dak–Five
Cep–□
Bem–June
Hax–Four
Kes–▯

Note that the responses can be grouped at different levels and form a hierarchy of: (a) words or figures, (b) the subcategories of month or number, and triangle or rectangle, (c) and finally, the eight specific items required for a correct response. Subjects saw the list once and were then asked to give the response to each stimulus. The critical result of the experiment came from the analysis of the subjects' errors (excluding blanks and extra-list errors). These errors can be of three kinds, which I will illustrate with the Hax–Four. If triangle or rectangle is offered as the response to Hax then that would be an error at the most general level. An error by definition excludes the correct response and, in this case, could be any one of the seven remaining alternatives. We call an error at this most general level, a category error, and it can be expected to occur by chance four out of seven times (57%). If the subject offered *June* or *July,* then that response would be correct at the category level, but incorrect at the subcategory level. An error of that kind would be expected by chance two out of seven times (29%).

Finally, the subject could give *five* as the response which would be correct at the category and subcategory level but incorrect at the item level. An error at the item level would be expected one out of seven times (14%). Dinnerstein and Egeth found that 34% of the errors (less than the 57% expected by chance) were category errors, 29% were subcategory errors (about chance), and 38% were item errors (or about twice that expected by chance). These results indicate that even when the subjects made an error, they had, nevertheless, learned something about the item they could not recall, that is, they often learned about the category or subcategory to which the item belonged.

Recently, Richard Coll (1985) completed a doctoral dissertation at Rutgers in which he followed up on the Dinnerstein and Egeth experiment. Coll used the same pairs of items they had used. He modified the experiment in that he gave the subjects five presentation trials, each followed by a recall trial. In addition, he gave two delayed recall trials, one a week after the last recall trial, and one three weeks after the last recall trial. If the trace develops from general to specific, as Dinnerstein and Egeth had argued, then one should be able to plot the course of that development over the five learning trials. Coll also wanted to know if the process would reverse itself over time and go from specific to general. Table 20.1 shows his data plotted for the percentage of the three kinds of error over the five learning trials and over the two delayed recall trials.

Notice that over the learning trials there is a steady decrease in the category error, which is the most general error, and an increase in the item error, the most specific form of error. These trends reverse themselves with delayed recall.

The subcategory errors do not show a clear pattern over trials, presumably because category errors become subcategory errors and subcategory errors become item errors as learning progresses. To get at this, Coll undertook an item by item analysis to determine if the history of each item showed the same pattern as indicated in the group data. His analysis showed that more than 65% of the items underwent a progression through the levels of error without a reversal of level. For example, an item might show a pattern of being correct at the subcategory level on the first trial, then show two trials of being correct at the item level, and finally the item might be completely correct on the last two trials. The delayed recall trials showed similar patterns but in the direction from specific to general. What about the 35% that showed a reversal of direction? Those cases may be explained, at least in part, as being due to guessing, or to forgetting from trial to trial.

TABLE 20.1
Percentage of Total Error for Category, Subcategory, and Item
Errors, for Learning Trials and Delayed Recall Trials

	Learning Trials					Delayed Recall	
Type of error	1	2	3	4	5	1 week	3 week
Category	41	38	22	17	3	25	29
Subcategory	26	27	19	17	28	22	26
Item	33	35	59	67	69	53	46

In short, Coll's results confirmed the hypothesis put forth by Dinnerstein and Egeth that the trace develops in an order from general to specific. In addition, his results showed that forgetting follows the reverse order, going from specific to general.

DISCUSSION

I began with a discussion of the phenomenon of generic recall, that is, erroneous recall that resembles correct recall. I take the Dinnerstein and Egeth (1962), and the Coll (1984) studies to show that the phenomenon can be explained by postulating that at the point of recall the subject has only general information, and uses that general information to select a response. So, for example, the subject may remember that Hax went with a number. Given that the list is fairly short the subject may remember both numbers that appeared on the list and then select one of the two. Similarly, in attempting to recall my name someone may only have available certain general features of the name and select, from a set of similar names which come to mind easily, one that matches the features available. What is perhaps more likely is that the recaller will construct a name given the information available, or will just give up and say that the name was an Italian name which started with a "C." This account of generic recall is similar to that given by Brown and McNeill (1966), but it adds the idea that the available generic features are likely to be those that are learned first and forgotten last.

The findings that support the levels of processing hypothesis raise the interesting possibility that the processing of a word may go through stages that recapitulate the original order of learning. Thus, with divided attention a word might be processed only as far as its more general meaning, that is, the meaning that it has in common with its synonyms. This more general meaning, as Kimble (1968) and Grossman and Eagle (1970) suggest, may be the mediator of false recognition.

It seems to me that the ideas of general learning and general activation have implications for studies that deal with the processing of words without awareness. For example, in a study by Lewis (1970), it was shown that an unattended word can influence the processing of an attended word. That finding, and others like it, have been taken to mean that the unattended word is registered below the level of awareness. The levels of processing experiments suggest, instead, that the unattended word may have been processed only to a general level, and it is this general level of meaning that mediates the analysis of the attended word. Thus, the fact that unattended words can be shown to prime other words need not mean that the unattended words are completely analyzed below the level of awareness.

Finally, I emphasize the point that the idea of general activation poses the same challenge to the theory of spreading activation as Lashley and Wade's arguments did to the theory of the irradiation of excitation. That is, it raises the possibility that the idea of spreading activation might not be necessary to account for the data for which it was developed.

21 Comments on the Chapter by Ceraso

David S. Gorfein
Adelphi University

A few years ago it became the policy of a number of the journals of our field to announce that in order to achieve publication one needed a paper containing two, three, or more related studies with the implication that such quantity was necessary to achieve theoretical significance. Although such policy, fortunately, seems to be changing, it is still remarkable that such a small study as Coll's, as reported by Ceraso, can make such large points. Ceraso uses the study by Coll (1984) and the much earlier paper by Dinnerstein and Egeth (1962) to raise questions about the nature of "spreading activation" and support a strong form of the "levels of processing" hypothesis. Both theoretical views have won a great number of adherents in recent years.

The view Ceraso offers is certainly consistent with the data. A number of things must be done, however, before the form of "levels of processing" advocated by Ceraso can be established. Most notably some direct evidence for some ordered hierarchy of processing must be established. If this is not done, what we have left is strong support for the argument that what is easier to learn is harder to . forget.

22 Criteria for the Identification of Memory Deficits: Implications for the Design of Memory Tests

Herman Buschke
Saul R. Korey Department of Neurology and Rose F. Kennedy Center for Research in Mental Retardation and Human Development
Albert Einstein College of Medicine, New York

The identification and analysis of memory deficits is an important application of cognitive psychology. Accurate assessment of learning and memory is a significant part of clinical neuropsychological evaluation and is needed for analysis of clinical syndromes and for correlation of neuropsychological findings with neurophysiological, neurochemical, and neuropathological findings. It is needed to evaluate procedures for cognitive rehabilitation and attempts to improve learning and memory by neuropharmacological treatments. It is also needed if neuropsychological findings are to be useful for suggesting and testing models of normal learning and memory. However, it can be difficult to identify genuine memory deficits because learning and memory depend on other kinds of cognitive processing. Genuine memory deficits must be distinguished from apparent memory deficits due to impairment of other kinds of cognitive processing. If other kinds of cognitive processing are impaired, such limitations must be circumvented in order to assess learning and memory. The aim of this chapter is to invite consideration of the assumptions we make when we claim that a patient has a memory deficit, so that we can formulate criteria for the identification of memory deficits and the design of memory tests. Formulation of criteria for the identification of memory deficits is an important issue that has not yet received the explicit discussion it needs, and this chapter is intended to stimulate further consideration of this issue.

This discussion focuses on verbal learning and memory of the sort involved when patients are tested by presentation of items such as words, pictures, or sentences to test learning and memory by subsequent free recall, cued recall, or recognition. As outlined in Fig. 22.1, this kind of test requires the patient to process each item and achieve a mental representation that corresponds appropri-

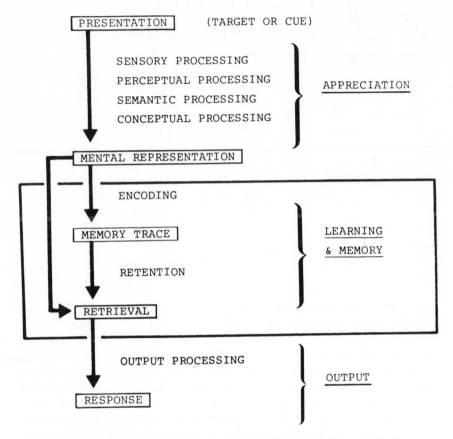

FIGURE 22.1. Simplified outline of cognitive processing in verbal learning and memory.

ately to the item. Such processing depends on attention, perception, semantic analysis, access to the lexicon and permanent knowledge, and other cognitive processes, to reach what may be referred to as an "appreciation" of the item to be remembered. Based on the mental representation that embodies the appreciation, some kind of memory trace must be encoded, retained, and retrieved. At the time of retrieval, any cues used for retrieval also must be processed so that features of their mental representation can be used to retrieve the target memory trace. Finally, the patient must be able to produce some kind of output that accurately indicates retrieval of that memory trace.

Although encoding, retention, and retrieval depend on the processing that leads to appreciation of the items to be learned and the cues used to retrieve those items, the identification of memory deficits is generally meant to refer just to limitations of encoding, retention, or retrieval as in Fig. 22.1. The present discussion will focus on the identification of such genuine memory deficits, and criteria that might help us to identify such deficits.

IDENTIFICATION OF MEMORY DEFICITS

What assumptions do we make when we claim that a patient has a memory deficit? How can we be sure that our assumptions have been satisfied? The following assumptions are not exhaustive but seem to be a reasonable initial consideration of assumptions made and criteria to be used.

The Deficit is a Memory Deficit

A memory deficit is supposed to be shown by impaired performance on a memory test due to limitations of memory, rather than limitations of other factors affecting the use of memory processes. These other factors fall into three classes. The first includes the specific cognitive processes involved in the appreciation of the items to be remembered, and those involved in the generation of an appropriate response. These include sensory processing, attention, perceptual processing, semantic processing, and any other kinds of cognitive processing necessary to achieve appropriate mental representation of those items and to generate appropriate responses.

The second class includes control processes and processing capacity. Control processes are needed to organize the sequence of subprocesses involved in various kinds of cognitive processing, so that the results of earlier processing will be available when needed for later processing. Processing capacity limits the ability to carry out several processes concurrently. The effects of both of these factors are not necessarily limited to learning and memory processes.

The third class deals with the selection and use of appropriate and efficient strategies. Different strategies can be used to carry out what is supposed to be the same memory task. For example, in free-recall learning, subjects may use an alphabetical strategy, or group items on the basis of semantic relatedness, or create a story incorporating the items, or they may use other strategies. Unless patients and control subjects are induced to use the same strategies, it may be difficult to interpret apparent memory deficits, since better performance by control subjects may be due to use of more efficient strategies. Failure to select and use optimal strategies may itself be due to other cognitive deficits, but such impairment is not the same as a deficit in performance on a memory task when the subject is using optimal strategies.

One approach often used to determine whether apparent memory deficits are due to these other factors is to evaluate them separately by appropriate cognitive tasks. This approach is of limited usefulness because many patients will have other cognitive deficits in addition to any memory deficits they may have. In that case it is necessary to circumvent such difficulties by restructuring the memory task in ways that permit patients to show their memory abilities despite such additional cognitive deficits. Generally it is necessary to structure memory tests in such a way that the patient does process the items to be remembered and can provide some evidence that each item was properly processed and appreciated.

A Specific Kind of Memory is Impaired

Memory is not a unitary phenomenon. Distinctions can be made between sensory, primary, secondary, and tertiary memory; episodic and semantic memory; declarative and procedural memory; modular and conceptual memory; verbal and nonverbal memory; anterograde and retrograde memory; and others, such as automatic or effortful encoding, and incidental or intentional learning. It is necessary to specify the type of memory which is supposed to be impaired, since it appears that some kinds of memory may be preserved in patients who have other types of memory deficits (Brooks & Baddeley, 1976; Parkin, 1982). For instance, procedural memory may be intact in amnesic patients who have deficits of declarative memory, as shown by amnesic patients who still can learn to read inverted text at a normal rate (Cohen, 1984; Cohen & Squire, 1980).

Much clinical testing of learning and memory in patients is concerned with intentional, verbal, declarative, episodic, conceptual, secondary, anterograde memory. This requires relevant kinds of sensory and modular memory needed to appreciate the information presented for learning. Conceptual memory implies retention of information in a form that is accessible to various modular systems (Fodor, 1983). In general, testing is intended to identify deficits of conceptual memory that are not due to limitations in initial processing (such as hearing or vision) or to limitations in output mechanisms that are needed to show retrieval (such as speech or writing). The identification of such conceptual memory deficits would seem to require the use of more than one mode of presentation and more than one mode of output.

The Best Performance of Patients is Deficient

The performance of patients, as well as normal subjects, may vary when the same test is used on different occasions. Although it may not be possible ever to be certain that a patient's best performance has been obtained, it would seem necessary to obtain more than one sample of their performance on a memory test to determine that their best performance is deficient.

Because performance can be limited by use of inefficient strategies, best performance can only be obtained when the learner is induced to use an optimal strategy. Therefore it is necessary to identify optimal strategies and to control cognitive processing in ways that induce the use of specific optimal strategies. The use of particular strategies can be induced either by training or by structuring the test in a way that essentially compels the use of a particular strategy (Belmont & Butterfield, 1977). Since some assurance is needed that the intended kinds of processing have been carried out, it would seem necessary to design tests that induce a particular kind of processing and show that the intended processing has been carried out.

Because the evaluation of learning and memory depends on retrieval, maximum retrieval will be needed to obtain the maximum estimates of encoding, retention and retrieval necessary to measure best performance. Although recall depends on encoding, there can be retrieval failures as well as encoding failures (Tulving, 1974). Such retrieval failures have been shown by spontaneous free recall without continuing presentation (Buschke, 1974), by cued recall (Tulving & Pearlstone, 1966), and by recognition after prior recall failure. Free recall alone may not result in retrieval of all of the items that were encoded and retained (Tulving & Pearlstone, 1966). Therefore, free recall should be supplemented by cued recall and recognition to obtain maximum retrieval.

Encoding and Retrieval are Coordinated

Encoding and retrieval must be coordinated to obtain maximum retrieval because encoding and retrieval are interdependent (Schacter & Tulving, 1982). Encoding can only be shown by retrieval, but successful retrieval will depend on encoding that is appropriate for the kind of retrieval to be used. The "encoding specificity principle" (Thomson & Tulving, 1970; Tulving & Thomson, 1973) states that: "Specific encoding operations performed on what is perceived determine what is stored and what is stored determines what retrieval cues are effective in providing access to what is stored" (Tulving & Thomson, 1973, p. 369). Maximum retrieval will require encoding of information that is needed for retrieval of the memory trace. The memory trace can be regarded as a: "collection of features or a bundle of information . . . which is determined at least by three classes of variables (a) characteristics of the focal element or elements of the event, (b) the conditions and general context of its occurrence, and (c) specific operations performed on the elements-in-context" (Tulving & Bower, 1974, p.269). Subsequent retrieval depends on the correspondence between features of the cue used for retrieval and features of the memory trace.

It may be useful to consider the memory trace as containing at least two kinds of information, "cue-specific" features which are necessary for the cue to access the memory trace, and "target-specific" features which are necessary to identify the target item or event to be remembered. The principle of encoding specificity means that optimal performance will be achieved by processing the cue together with the target item at the time of encoding so that relevant cue-specific and target-specific features will be encoded in the memory trace.

The mental representation of an item presented for learning, and thus its memory trace, will be specified by the context in which it is presented. Reinstatement of that context at the time of retrieval will help one to think about a cue and its target trace in the same way as at the time of encoding. Such specification of context is needed to minimize the effects of "encoding variability" (Bower, 1972; Martin, 1968) in which "over nominally identical presentations of the same stimulus event, the learner sometimes perceives one subset of component features and at other times, other subsets" (Martin, 1971, p. 324). It is because of such encoding variability that a patient may fail to retrieve "*lion*" when cued by "*animal*" if "*animal*" is thought of as "*farm animal*" rather than "*jungle animal.*"

Effective cueing can be achieved by specifying the context at the time of encoding and by later reinstating the same context to obtain maximum retrieval. Controlled processing is needed to achieve such coordination of encoding and recall. An illustration of effective cueing achieved by controlled processing is shown in Fig. 22.2 (Buschke, 1984, p. 435). An array of 12 line drawings was presented to patients who were asked to search the array and name each item when given its category cue (such as "*animal*" for "*elephant*"). After all 12 items had been identified, the patients attempted free recall, followed by cued recall of any items that were not retrieved by free recall. Before the next trial of free recall, the array was searched again, but only for items that were not retrieved by cued recall. The addition of cued recall to free recall provides a measure of total recall on each trial.

Fig. 22.2 shows perfect total recall of all items as well as good free-recall learning by 10 normal older adults. The patients with mild dementia of the Alzheimer's type (SDAT) or Alzheimer's disease (AD), as well as patients with amnesia due to other causes, showed very good total recall, due to the addition of effective cued recall. However, their free-recall learning was clearly limited. Although the total recall by patients and controls cannot be compared because total recall was limited by ceiling effects (Schacter & Tulving, 1982), the coordination of encoding and retrieval achieved by use of the same cues during encoding and retrieval did result in effective cued recall that showed encoding and retention that were not apparent from free recall alone. It is clear that free recall alone may underestimate learning and retention.

The use of this procedure illustrates how processing can be controlled to induce patients to carry out specific kinds of processing in a way that coordinates encoding and retrieval. The identification of each item on the basis of its category cue during the array search also shows that the processing was carried out and that each item was appreciated at least well enough to name it. The data in Fig. 22.2 indicate that both free recall and cued recall are needed to evaluate learning and memory. Cued recall is needed to obtain recall of items not retrieved by free recall, and free recall is needed to show impairment of learning when cued recall or recognition are still intact. Multitrial free-recall learning is needed to assess free recall because free recall on the first trial may be within the normal range even when free-recall learning is impaired (panels E and H in Fig. 22.2).

Failure of cued recall, resulting in lower total recall even when encoding and retrieval were coordinated, has been found in testing more severely demented patients (Grober & Buschke, in press). Failure of cued recall despite successful processing of cues and targets during encoding (shown by correct identification of targets in the initial search) may provide the most convincing demonstration of a genuine memory deficit.

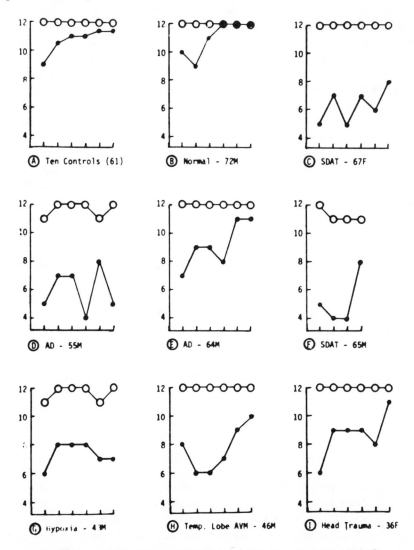

FIGURE 22.2.   Free recall (closed circles) and total recall (open circles) obtained by the addition of cued recall to free recall (from Buschke, 1984; reprinted with permission).

Learning and Memory are Measured Accurately

To identify a memory deficit we must have some way of measuring learning and memory. The main measures of memory in verbal learning tests of the sort under discussion here are the number of items recalled, speed of recall, and amount of work required for recall. While the number of items recalled on a single trial may provide a single measure of memory, in multitrial recall several measures of learning can be used (Buschke, 1973; Kraemer, Peabody, Tinkleberg, & Yesavage 1983; Tulving, 1964), so that appropriate measures must be selected and justified. Speed of recall can be measured most easily by latency of cued recall or recognition, and should be measured when processing is controlled to obtain the patient's best performance when using an optimal strategy (Macht & Buschke, 1984). Additional tests will be needed to identify slowing due to memory impairment rather than to slowing of other kinds of cognitive processing (Madden, 1985; Welford, 1984). An increase in the amount of cognitive effort required for recall can be measured by evaluation of processing capacity through the use of "secondary" tasks performed concurrently with the "primary" memory task (Macht & Buschke, 1983; McDowall, 1984). Performance on a secondary task can be used to estimate the amount of processing capacity used to carry out the primary task. The present discussion is limited to measurement of learning and memory by the number of items retrieved by free recall, cued recall, or recognition.

Generally we assume that there is a correspondence between the number of items presented for learning and memory, the number of memory units that are encoded, retained, and retrieved, and the number of items recovered by recall or recognition. That is, we assume that the number of items recalled reflects the amount of learning and memory. We assume that each item in the presentation is treated as a separate memory unit and that encoding, retention, and retrieval of each unit is independent of the encoding, retention, and retrieval of other units. These assumptions will not necessarily hold in free-recall learning, when subjects who group individual items into multi-item units may recall more items by retrieving fewer memory units (Buschke, 1977; Tulving, 1962). Furthermore, in free-recall retrieval of items is not independent because earlier recall can limit later recall (Nickerson, 1984; Roediger, 1974, 1978).

Cued recall and recognition test the retrieval of each item separately, so that their use is more likely to satisfy the assumptions that each item is encoded and retrieved independently. Both cued recall and recognition should be added to free recall to obtain maximum evidence of encoding and retention. Cued recall can be used after each trial of free recall in order to obtain maximum total recall on each trial, providing a more accurate assessment of learning rates. Recognition can be used after multitrial free and/or cued recall have been completed, but cannot be used on each trial because the presentation of foils would interfere with learning the target items. Thus cued recall can be used to assess multitrial learning but recognition cannot. Multitrial learning should be assessed because recall on a single trial may not show impaired learning. Therefore it appears that cued recall is more useful.

Because apparent recognition may be due to guessing, it is necessary to have some kind of correction for guessing or analysis of overall recognition by methods such as signal detection analysis. It is difficult to evaluate recognition of an individual item, but this may be needed to assess memory for particular items that were not recovered by either free or cued recall. Furthermore, the need to correct for possible guessing in recognition makes it difficult to appreciate the true recognition of small numbers of items when recognition appears to be at or below chance level. However, it is possible that a patient may truly recognize a small number of items. The possibility of correct responses due to guessing does not necessarily mean that correct responses were in fact due to guessing.

It may be possible to overcome this limitation of recognition. True recognition not due to guessing may be identified by consistent choice of a target item in repeated tests of forced-choice recognition when the same targets and foils are presented on each test. In situations where it is appropriate to use foils that are related to the targets (such as another item from the same category as the target), it also may be possible to identify true recognition by the joint recognition of a target and independent rejection of its related foil when targets and related foils are presented separately for yes–no recognition. Such target-specific recognition can then be confirmed by consistent recognition when the same targets and foils are retested by additional forced-choice recognition testing.

Memory Deficits are Shown by Diminished Recall

The assessment of memory requires that at least some items be recalled because it would otherwise be unclear whether the subject understood the task properly. When nothing is recalled, the results cannot be interpreted. When a normal number of items are recalled, there is no apparent memory deficit. Memory deficits are usually identified by failure to recall as many items as are recalled by the normal control subjects. But if a patient can recall some items, why can't he or she recall the other items, since the successful recall of some items shows that the patient can learn and remember? Recall of some items seems to indicate that the processing necessary for appreciation, encoding, retention, and retrieval can still be carried out, but not consistently. Is such inconsistency (or decreased probability) of encoding or retrieval due to impairment of learning and memory, to impairment of other cognitive processes, to impaired control processes, to decreased processing capacity, or to inconsistent application of appropriate strategies? Although such causes for recalling fewer items indicate cognitive impairment, they do not necessarily indicate genuine memory deficits. One kind of memory deficit that could lead to an increased number of recall failures is failure to encode as many features in a memory trace as normal subjects. This could cause two kinds of problems at the time of retrieval.

The first involves the encoding of two kinds of features in the memory trace, cue-specific features needed to access the memory trace, and target-specific features needed to identify the target item that is to be recalled. If the memory trace does not contain or cannot accommodate enough information, there may be sufficient cue-specific information for access to the trace by the cue, but too little target-specific information to identify (or even to recognize) the item. If the memory trace contains sufficient target-specific information but not enough cue-specific information, the trace cannot be accessed by that cue (but it may be possible to recognize the item).

A second difficulty is due to encoding variability, in which the learner perceives different features of the cue at different times. Encoding variability may not limit retrieval if the memory trace contains sufficient cue-specific information to allow retrieval of the target trace by using different features of the cue at different times. However, if the memory trace contains a more limited amount of cue-specific information, there may not be sufficient correspondence between those features of the cue perceived at the time of retrieval and those features of the cue encoded in the target memory trace, resulting in failure to access the target trace on some attempts.

Even if the memory trace can accommodate enough cue-specific and target-specific features, retrieval could be limited by failure to encode sufficiently specific features of the target or cue. Impaired ranking of semantic attributes according to their importance in specifying well-known concepts has been found in some patients with dementia (Grober, Buschke, Kawas, & Fuld, 1985). If the memory trace does not contain important specific features of either the cue or the target item, retrieval may fail. Memory traces containing insufficient or insufficiently specific information also may be more vulnerable to interference by competing traces.

Some rationale is needed to justify the identification of memory deficits by the failure to recall some items when other items are encoded and recalled. If retrieval depends on the amount or quality of target-specific and cue-specific information in the memory trace and in the mental representation of the cue, then it would appear that the number of items retrieved may be an indirect and not entirely clear measure of learning and memory, and that some more direct measure of information in the memory trace may be useful (Tulving & Bower, 1974; Tulving & Watkins, 1975; Watkins, 1979). Even successful recall shows only that some minimum amount of information necessary for retrieval was encoded, but not how much. For example, successful cued recall by patients with impaired free recall only shows that sufficient information for retrieval by that cue was encoded; it is possible that the memory traces of normal subjects might contain additional information which could permit retrieval by other cues as well. The same limitation also applies to recognition, which requires only the retention of "more" target-specific than foil-specific information.

Even if the existence of a memory deficit can be identified by significantly decreased recall, it is not clear how the amount or severity of the deficit should be measured. Estimates of the amount of deficit are needed to evaluate progression or recovery, to assess the effects of neuropharmacological treatment or rehabilitation, to relate degree of memory deficit to neurological impairment, and to compare memory deficits with other kinds of cognitive impairment. Perhaps surprisingly, at present there does not appear to be any satisfactory way to estimate the magnitude of the deficit, to determine how much underlying memory processes are impaired, or how much residual memory capability remains. Neuropsychological analysis of cognition will be severely limited unless some way can be found to measure the magnitude of cognitive deficits.

The relative severity of a memory deficit cannot be measured simply by the percentile in which the scores fall. Defective scores will all fall in the tail of the distribution of normal scores, where the percentiles will not discriminate adequately between different defective scores. Tulving (personal communication, 1985) suggests that this problem may be resolved by the use of two stages of testing. In the first stage, the patient is tested in the usual way by comparing the patient's performance with that of normal control subjects to determine whether there is a memory deficit. In the second stage, patients with memory deficits are tested by an "easier" test that results in ceiling performance by normal controls but will elicit a range of performance from patients. The severity of a memory deficit then may be estimated by where it falls in the distribution of scores obtained from persons with memory deficits on this second easier test. Thus, the first stage of testing would show that there is a memory deficit and the second stage of testing would assess the severity of the deficit. It might also be possible to achieve the same resolution by use of an easier test in the first place, in which normal controls would perform at ceiling but patients with memory deficits would show a range of scores. In this case, the existence of a memory deficit would be shown by anything less than perfect performance and the distribution of those imperfect scores could be used to assess the severity of the memory deficit.

Patient and Control Subjects are Properly Matched

Different subjects (or the same subject at different times) can carry out what appears to be the same memory task, but in different ways using different strategies or different cognitive processes. In order to compare performance by patients and control subjects it is not sufficient to match patients and control subjects only in terms of those well-known variables that may be expected to affect their performance (such as age, education, premorbid IQ, health, and presence or absence of depression, among others). It is also necessary to induce patients and control subjects to use the same strategy, to carry out the same kinds of cognitive processing, and to encode and retrieve the same memory units.

Because the identification of memory deficits means that the best performance by the patient is worse than the best performances by the control subjects, it is also necessary to obtain the best performance from the control subjects. It is not sufficient that performance by control subjects is not limited by ceiling effects (Schacter & Tulving, 1982) because performance below ceiling will not necessarily be the best of which control subjects are capable. At least two tests would be needed to obtain their best performance, since there is no way to determine whether any single performance represents their best performance, even when optimal strategies are used.

Although patients and control subjects should be tested in the same way, some patients may not be able to use certain strategies if other cognitive processes that are needed for a particular strategy are impaired. In that case, it may be necessary to compare the performance of control subjects and patients when both are using some less than optimal strategy that requires only those kinds of cognitive processing which still can be carried out by the patients, even if that does not result in the best possible performance by the control subjects.

The Deficit is not Due to Erroneous Learning

Decreased recall is usually assumed to be due to failure of normal encoding or retrieval. However, apparent limitations of learning and memory also can be due to erroneous learning or erroneous unlearning (Brown & Packham, 1967). It is not uncommon for patients with cognitive deficits to recall the same incorrect item repeatedly despite correction and repeated opportunities to learn the correct item. It appears as if a correct item was replaced by an erroneously learned incorrect item. Even if a memory trace was encoded for both a correct item and a related incorrect item (as shown by recognition of the correct item), the trace for the incorrect item may be more accessible, perhaps because of its more recent recall. It is not clear how to deal with such repeated incorrect recall: The repeated recall seems to show learning and memory, but it is recall of an incorrect item generated by the patient.

Such "perseverative" errors can be due to either faulty encoding or erroneous retrieval, indicating impairment of learning and memory. They can also be due to perceptual deficits leading to incorrect appreciation, or to other cognitive deficits, such as those associated with frontal lobe pathology (Goldberg & Bilder, in press; Goldberg & Tucker, 1979; Oscar–Berman, 1971; Oscar–Berman, Sahakian, & Wikmark, 1976; Parkin, 1984; Sandson & Albert, 1984; Squire 1982). Whatever their cause, such erroneous learning may interfere with learning and retrieval of correct items and should be minimized by control of perceptual processing designed to achieve an adequate mental representation of the items to be remembered. It may even be necessary to replace such items with new items in order to assess learning and memory fully by circumventing such perservation.

Erroneous unlearning also can interfere with learning and memory when an item is retrieved, but the patient decides incorrectly that it is not a target item and therefore excludes it from overt recall (Brown & Packham, 1967). This would be difficult to demonstrate because such items would not be reported, but might be detected by incorrect rejection on subsequent recognition testing.

CRITERIA FOR MEMORY TESTS

This brief discussion of some assumptions that seem to underlie the identification of memory deficits suggests some criteria for the design of memory tests:

1. Obtain the best performance from both patients and control subjects,

2. When both patients and controls are induced to use the same optimal strategies,

3. Under conditions of experimentally controlled processing,

4. Which show that other kinds of cognitive processing which are necessary but not sufficient for encoding and retrieval have been carried out,

5. Using accurate measures of learning and memory,

6. When encoding and retrieval are coordinated,

7. For well-specified kinds of memory.

The further development of such criteria, and the design of memory tests that satisfy such criteria, seems necessary. Although there are some memory tests that meet at least some of these criteria, many tests commonly used in clinical evaluation of learning and memory do not (Erickson & Scott, 1977; Erickson, Poon, & Walsh–Sweeney, 1980; Schacter & Tulving, 1982).

Because neuropsychological analysis depends on the identification of specific cognitive deficits (of which memory deficits are only one class), similar criteria are needed for the identification of other kinds of cognitive deficits. Most of the present criteria also apply to the identification of other kinds of cognitive deficits. Therefore the assumptions underlying the identification of cognitive deficits should receive further consideration in order to formulate criteria for the design of tests intended to assess specific cognitive functions.

Control of cognitive processing is needed to meet such criteria. Controlled processing is needed to show that an apparent memory deficit is not due to other specific or general cognitive or ''production'' deficits (Belmont & Butterfield, 1977; Flavell, 1970) and that the other kinds of cognitive processing that are a prerequisite for encoding and retrieval have been carried out. Controlled process- ing is needed to induce the use of optimal strategies for encoding, retrieval, and optimal coordination of encoding and retrieval; to induce patients and control subjects (or the same patient at different times) to carry out the same kinds of processing and obtain the best performance of patients and control subjects; to obtain measurements of learning and memory that accurately reflect the amount of learning and memory; and to specify the type of learning and memory tested.

Control of cognitive processing is needed to identify memory deficits because clinical memory tests are experiments. Although clinical memory tests may be done for different purposes and the results analyzed differently than other kinds of memory experiments, the design and execution of memory tests should satisfy the same criteria as any other experiment dealing with learning and memory.

This discussion has been concerned with the cognitive processing carried out by patients and control subjects in tests of verbal leaning and memory. Other important statistical and methodological considerations have been discussed elsewhere (e.g., Branconnier, Cole, Spera, & DeVitt, 1982; Chapman & Chapman, 1973, 1978; Erickson & Scott, 1977; Schacter & Tulving, 1982). The reason for emphasizing the design of memory tests, the processing carried out by the patient, and the need to control cognitive processing in order to identify memory deficits, is that elegant statistical design and analysis can be useful only when tests have been carried out in a way that provides a test of what is supposed to be tested. Because tests of memory require other kinds of cognitive processing before encoding or retrieval can be carried out, it is necessary to circumvent any limitations of such other kinds of cognitive processing in order to identify memory deficits. This will require more experimental control of memory testing than has been customary, but tests of learning and memory that satisfy the assumptions and criteria for identification of memory deficits can be designed by careful application of the principles, findings, theoretical formulations, and methods of experimental cognitive psychology.

ACKNOWLEDGMENT

Preparation of this chapter was supported by USPHS grants AGO–4623, NS–03356, HD–01799, AGO–3949, and NS–19234.

23
Comments on the Chapter by Buschke

Murray Glanzer
New York University

The chapter by Professor Buschke has two characteristics that make it appropriate for this meeting. (1) It has an Ebbinghausian concern with finding evidence of memory traces when there may at first glance be little evidence of such traces; (2) It marks the distance we have come in the field since 1885. Instead of a simple, unitary memory function we are now concerned with a group of complexly interrelated processes.

Much of the chapter is concerned with the listing of six requirements in evaluating memory deficits.

1. When an investigator claims that a patient has a memory deficit, he should show that the deficit is not due to other factors, for example, attention. There is no disagreement likely on this point.

2. When an investigator claims there is a deficit, he should define the specific kind of memory impaired. Usually when we talk about a memory deficit we mean that the individual does not remember a story told a short while before, or does not remember what he had for lunch; we mean what is labeled declarative, secondary, episodic memory. It certainly would not do any harm to be clear about this.

3. When an investigator claims there is a deficit he should elicit the patient's best performance. This requirement reflects Professor Buschke's special focus on diagnosis and therapy. What is recommended is a full sampling of the patient's performance. This sampling is not done to develop a probabilistic picture of the performance, but to define the range and limits of performance. Knowledge of that range is useful for both diagnosis and therapy. To define the top of the range, the retrieval techniques developed in standard experimental studies of

memory in normal subjects are recommended, such as cueing and reinstatement of context.

4. When an investigator claims there is a deficit learning and memory should be measured in a way that reflects the amount of learning and memory. There are several different concerns expressed here. One concern is that we are not misled by the presence or absence of special skills (such as grouping or chunking) in comparisons of normal and impaired subjects. This seems related to the first requirement. Another concern is that each failure and each success be examined separately and in detail. This is not what would be done in a standard experimental study, but it does make sense in the framework of diagnosis and therapy. This approach rejects the standard picture of memory as a probabilistic affair. In this connection, there is a passage in Professor Buschke's chapter that I found striking: "if a patient can recall some items, why can't he or she recall the other items, since the successful recall of some items shows that the patient can learn and remember." I found this statement odd and I started on the following argument to reduce it to an absurdity.

Given this assertion, why do not all subjects remember all items in any list of any size? Because they remember some, why do they not remember the others? A probabilistic view does not answer that question. What is really being called for is a statement about why memory is described probabilistically. Instead of an absurdity, I ended up with a stimulus for speculation. The speculation concerns the role of limited attentional resources, limited congruence of successive list items to an encoding schema, and limited congruence of registered items to a retrieval schema.

5. When an investigator claims there is a deficit, he or she should show that the patient is doing the same things as control subjects on the test; in Professor Buschke's wording, that they "were tested by the *same* memory test." This condition can be striven for, but it is very difficult to demonstrate that it holds. It is difficult to show that two normal subjects are doing the same thing on a test even when they are restricted by encoding tasks. I remember a heated discussion over a study in which different groups of subjects were given a presumably equalizing encoding task, lexical decision, before their incidental recognition memory was tested. The heat of the discussion came from the question "How do you know that they are doing lexical decision the same way?"

6. When an investigator claims there is a deficit, he should show that the subject has not done erroneous learning or unlearning. This is the most specific of the requirements. Evidence of such effects does change the analysis of the deficit. It does not, however, remove the deficit.

The distinctions and techniques that come out of standard experimental work may continue to be of use to Professor Buschke in his special mission of diagnosis and therapy. I hope that they will be because their application would be of value both in the clinic and the laboratory. In the active and growing communication between clinical and experimental workers, valuable information is transmitted both ways. The impact of the clinical work on the experimental literature is seen in the appearance of studies involving clinical groups, and the appearance of studies involving distinctions and operations that arise form the study of such groups. Within the last year there were six memory studies involving clinical groups in the *Journal of Experimental Psychology: Learning, Memory and Cognition* and the *Journal of Experimental Psychology: General.* This count does not include a number of studies on normal subjects that arise, in part, from problems raised in the study of clinical groups: for example, studies of priming effects and studies of the dissociation of memory functions. This number will surely increase to the benefit of both the investigation of memory in normal and clinical subjects.

24 Retrieval Modes Produce Dissociations in Memory for Surface Information

Henry L. Roediger, III
Purdue University

Teresa A. Blaxton
BDM Corporation, McLean, Virginia

Rereading *Über das Gedächtnis* reminds one of Ebbinghaus' many contributions: his clever methods, his careful (even compulsive) experimentation, his remarkably systematic findings, and his crisp, economical writing style. However, a contemporary reading leads to the more surprising insight that not only did Ebbinghaus make the many discoveries for which he is justly celebrated, but that other, overlooked, passages also seem important today (Hoffman et al., this volume; Roediger, 1985; Slamecka, 1985).

One such surprise is that Ebbinghaus clearly distinguished among different forms of remembering. The idea that there are various modes of expressing retention has received little attention by experimental psychologists in the 100 years since publication of his book, except for the relation between recall and recognition. However, this issue has become a prime concern for some contemporary workers and is the focus of the research to be reported in this chapter.

In the first two pages of his 1885 monograph, Ebbinghaus distinguished between voluntary and involuntary remembering. In the former, one must make an effort at recollecting the events in question. In the latter, the memories of the events come to the rememberer unbidden, or "automatically." Furthermore, and importantly for present concerns, Ebbinghaus noted that involuntarily produced memories may or may not carry with them any direct feeling of familiarity. Sometimes we are aware that these involuntarily produced states of mind refer to memories of past experience through such feelings of familiarity, but on other occasions we can only infer this indirectly. Finally, Ebbinghaus pointed up a third possibility and he reckoned that it represented a "large group" of memories. These are memories that "remain concealed from consciousness and yet produce an effect which is significant and which authenticates their previous experience'' (1885/1964, p. 2).

The use of what Ebbinghaus (p.8) called introspection—or measures of recall or recognition, as we would say today—fails to capture these distinctions. Almost all such memories produced by the rememberer are of the voluntary kind. Perhaps a few are involuntary; sometimes memories seem to occur spontaneously during lengthy repeated tests for reasons that subjects cannot articulate (e.g., Erdelyi & Becker, 1974; Roediger & Payne, 1982), and occasionally an event seems familiar but no specific experience can be identified as giving rise to this feeling. However, Ebbinghaus' third class of "unconscious retention" must, by definition, escape notice by methods of recall, recognition, or similarly derived measures that depend on conscious recollection (e.g., feelings of knowing, frequency judgments).

Ebbinghaus' relearning and savings methods overcame some of the drawbacks of introspection because savings for material could be shown even when it could not be voluntarily reproduced. As Hilgard (1964) remarked in his introduction to the Dover reprint of *On memory:*

> Ebbinghaus took the fact of ease of relearning something once known—a fact so plausible that it must have been often observed—and made it part of science by developing the quantitative saving score, in which the saving in relearning is scored as a per cent of the time (or trials) required in original learning. This is a genuine scientific advance, although once accomplished it is so easily comprehended that one wonders why nobody else thought of it. (p. viii)

Today we might wonder why so few researchers use it.

In analysis of one experiment (Chapter 5), Ebbinghaus asked whether the ability to recollect a series played a role in relearning. He relearned some lists that had previously been learned very well and that he had recognized during relearning, as well as other lists that had not been so practiced and which he did not recognize during relearning. Although the overlearned series were more easily relearned, he found no evidence in the savings scores to indicate that conscious recollection affected relearning in any way. That is, no discontinuity occurred in the savings function for the overlearned lists that were recognized during relearning. Although the issue was not explored systematically, this finding might be said to be the first experimental demonstration of dissociation between states of awareness and performance (Tulving, 1985a), the topic of the present chapter.

Savings in relearning is a useful measure, for it can potentially show retention even when the subject lacks conscious knowledge of the material (Kolers, 1976; Nelson, 1978). However, without additional measures the savings score cannot differentiate among the various forms of retention that Ebbinghaus described. Most modern researchers approach the issue by examining performance across different tasks, only some of which require conscious awareness of the learning episode for successful performance (e.g., Jacoby & Dallas, 1981).

The aim of the present chapter is to discuss dissociations between measures of conscious recollection (recall and recognition) and other measures of transfer or priming in which conscious recollection of studied events is not necessary for successful performance. The purposes of the present chapter are to (a) add some information to the empirical data base showing these dissociations, and (b) provide observations that, in our opinion, bear strongly on their proper explanation. In the next section, we review selected studies that are critical to our own experimental research. To anticipate, we examine the effects of presenting information in various surface forms (such as visual or auditory, or drawing or word) on retention as measured in various ways. In the third major section, we discuss theoretical accounts of the empirical findings and suggest that one approach is currently more promising than its competitors as an explanation of dissociations among measures of retention. We conclude with a few remarks about this approach and suggest some directions for future research.

MODES OF KNOWING

The concern with forms of knowing and performance has been raised in many papers over the past few years, and only a few studies will be described here to set the stage for the present research (see Jacoby & Witherspoon, 1982; Kolers & Roediger, 1984, for more extensive reviews). Of primary interest, as with some parts of Ebbinghaus' work, is the relation between consciousness and performance. Modern work on this problem springs from at least two related lines of work. First, studies of densely amnesic patients have shown that although they perform dismally in recalling or recognizing recently presented information, their performance on more subtle transfer or priming measures indicates that they have processed and stored the information. For example, Warrington and Weiskrantz (1970) compared performance of amnesic patients with normal patients at the retention of word lists. The amnesics performed much worse than normals when tested for recall or recognition of recently presented information. However, they also tested patients with another task in which they had to name severely degraded words that could not be identified unless recently presented. The amnesic subjects exhibited normal amounts of priming when they were given fragmented words and asked to name them.[1]

---

[1]Throughout this chapter *priming* refers to the benefit on a task accruing from presentation of an item. For example, in a task of completing fragmented words, if subjects correctly identify 50% of the items after studying them and the completion rate for the nonstudied words is 30%, then the priming effect is 20%. Priming refers to the difference between studied items and nonstudied (unprimed) items on a task.

Many other studies have confirmed the conclusion that amnesics show performance just as good as that of normals, even when tested on verbal materials, as long as the test does not require conscious recollection (e.g., Graf, Squire, & Mandler, 1984; Jacoby & Witherspoon, 1982; Shimamura & Squire, 1984). These patients then obviously have no difficulty encoding or storing some type of representation of the material; the difficulty is in gaining conscious access to it. Put another way, they are "amnesic" on only some tests of retention, apparently those involving conscious recollection. These studies show that such patients' knowledge of what they know can be dissociated from their actual performance.

These phenomena might only be regarded as curiosities to researchers interested in normal memory functioning if it were not for a related line of research that is also relevant to present concerns. This second line of research demonstrates in normal adults the same phenomena found in amnesics. That is, normal subjects also show dissociations between conscious recollection (as assessed by recall or recognition) and retention as measured in ways that do not require conscious awareness of the prior learning experience. For example, Kolers (1976) required subjects to read passages presented in an unusual inverted typography until they became proficient at it. A year later the subjects were unexpectedly retested and asked to read the same inverted passages intermixed with new ones from the same source. Subjects showed savings in reading speeds for the previously read passages relative to the new ones and, further, these benefits were uncorrelated with recognition judgments as to whether or not the sentences were ones they had previously read.

Many similar dissociations have been reported by Larry Jacoby and his colleagues (e.g., Jacoby, 1983; Jacoby & Dallas, 1981; Jacoby & Witherspoon, 1982) in memory for presentations of individual words. Typically, subjects in the experiments were presented with words under various study conditions and then tested on one of two tests. Some subjects were given a standard yes/no recognition test in which old and new words were mixed together and the task was to pick out the previously studied words. The other test was one of perceptual identification in which words were tachistoscopically presented for about 30 milliseconds and the subjects' task was simply to read them aloud. In the latter task, the dependent measure of interest is priming, or how much benefit having recently studied the words produces in naming them, relative to the case when they were not previously studied.[2] Jacoby and Dallas (1981) showed in their Experiment 1 that when words were presented with questions entailing attention to their graphemic, phonemic, or semantic features, a standard "levels of processing effect" was found in recognition. Semantic encoding produced the best

---

[2]Jacoby and Dallas (1981) refer to this task as perceptual recognition, but here we prefer to call it perceptual identification so as better to distinguish it from recognition memory in describing the experiments.

recognition, followed by phonemic and then graphemic encoding. However, on the perceptual identification test these conditions produced equal amounts of facilitation relative to nonpresented control words. This pattern, like that of Kolers (1976), represents a dissociation between performance on a test of conscious recollection (recognition) and performance on a second test in which conscious recollection is not required, in this case perceptual identification.

An even more dramatic dissociation is found in Jacoby's (1983) experiments in which subjects studied antonyms, such as *cold,* as target items in one of three contexts. The context in which the antonyms were placed caused them to be processed in three different ways across conditions. In the No Context Condition three Xs appeared to warn subjects that an item was about to be presented; in the Context condition the antonym (*hot*) preceded the target word; and in the Generate condition, subjects saw *hot* followed by three question marks and had to generate *cold.* In all three study conditions, subjects read the context word (if any) silently and spoke the target word aloud.

Two different forms of test were given, which produced opposite patterns of results, as shown in Table 24.1. In a recognition test, subjects performed best in the Generate condition, next best in the Context condition and worst in the No Context condition. This pattern replicates the "generation effect" (Slamecka & Graf, 1978) in that generated items are remembered better than those read in the No Context condition. However, on the perceptual identification test, in which words were flashed and the subjects' task was simply to name them, the pattern of results was exactly opposite that of recognition. Note that No Context items were best identified and Generate items identified least often. In fact, across Jacoby's (1983) experiments the Generate items showed little (Experiments 2

TABLE 24.1
Results of Jacoby's (1983) Experiment 2.
The Proportion of Items Identified or Recognized
in Each Condition

	Type of Test	
	Yes/No Recognition	*Perceptual Identification*
No Context (XXX–COLD)	0.56	0.82
Context (HOT–COLD)	0.72	0.75
Generate (HOT–???)	0.78	0.67
Nonstudied	——	0.60

(Reproduced with permission.)

and 3) or no priming (Experiment 1) relative to nonstudied items. The generation effect is thus test-dependent.

We should briefly summarize our interpretation of Jacoby's (1983) results in order to introduce concepts that we use to describe our own results. Jacoby's findings can be interpreted as illustrating the principle of "transfer appropriate processing": Different study conditions and types of test require various kinds of processing, and performance on a test will depend on the overlap between the type of processing engendered by the encoding condition and that required by the test (Morris, Bransford, & Franks, 1977). In Jacoby's (1983) terms, reading the word without context (xxx-COLD) involves data-driven (bottom–up) processing, whereas generating a word when given its antonym (hot–???) requires conceptually driven (top–down) processing. That is, in the No Context condition there is no other means for the person to produce *cold* than for the data (the letters forming the word) to be "driven through" the cognitive system, bottom–up. In the Generate condition, on the other hand, the visual features (the letters) specifying the response *cold* are absent, and it must be produced by inference from the related concept *hot* and the rule to produce opposites. Presumably, subjects in the Context condition (*hot–COLD*) used a mixture of these two forms of processing. With regard to the tests, recognition memory is assumed to depend heavily on conceptually driven processing, whereas perceptual identification is assumed to require data-driven processing (Jacoby, 1983).

Given these assumptions, the pattern of results in Table 24.1 can be explained. Items produced during study in the Generate condition required the greatest amounts of conceptually driven processing, so they should be better recognized than items in the other two conditions, as was the case. On the other hand, items produced in the No Context condition required data-driven processing and thus they should be better identified from a brief presentation than items in the other two conditions. The results in Table 24.1 show exactly this pattern. The general point is that Jacoby (1983) and others (e.g., Kolers & Roediger, 1984; Morris et al., 1977), explain interactions among study and test conditions by appealing to the kinds of processing required during study and test manipulations. However, a very different form of explanation has been used to account for the next pattern of data to be described.

Another example of dissociation between tasks requiring different forms of remembering was reported by Tulving, Schacter, and Stark (1982). They presented subjects with 96 words for study and then tested them both 1 hour and 1 week later on two different tests. One was a standard yes/no recognition test and the other was a modification of a word fragment completion test that had been used previously in testing amnesics (Warrington & Weiskrantz, 1970, Woods & Piercy, 1974). In the Tulving et al. (1982) version, subjects were given word frames with letters omitted and asked to complete the word To perform as a subject in the unprimed condition, complete the following fragments. (Allow 20 seconds each): __ EX __ __ NT, FL __ __ __ EL, __ REV __ CE,

_ G _ O _ T _ C, _ OYH _ O _, SW _ H _ _ I, _ _ F _ _ NO,
B _ _ D _ NN _, HYAC _ N _ H, _ ISS _ _ TAT _ _ _.[3]

Tulving et al.'s (1982) findings showed independence between recognition and fragment completion performance in two different ways. First, over the week delay, recognition performance dropped markedly, but priming in fragment completion (i.e., the benefit in completing fragments for studied relative to nonstudied words) did not decline at all, as shown in Fig. 24.1. (The completion rate for nonstudied words was .31 so performance in the fragment completion test was considerably enhanced by the study of the words.) Second, when recognition was tested within a session prior to fragment completion, fragment completion performance was stochastically independent of recognition performance. That is, subjects completed the fragments as well when they had previously judged a recognition item to be old as when they had judged it to be new. Tulving et al. (1982) interpreted this pattern of results as generally supporting the notion of separate memory systems (episodic and semantic), although they acknowledged some difficulties with this dichotomy and thought the results might implicate a third system, too.[4] The important point is that dissociations among measures of retention are explained by appeal to different memory systems (see Tulving, 1983, Chapter 4, for description of the logic for postulating memory systems.

AIMS OF THE PRESENT RESEARCH

The forgoing research has indicated a consistent pattern showing dissociations among measures of retention. Independent variables often affects conscious recollection in one way, but exert no effect or even an opposite effect on other (transfer) measures that assess retention indirectly. The proper account of such dissociations among measures of memory is, to our minds, a central task facing cognitive psychologists today.

We turn first to the basic issues motivating the experiments. The major empirical aim of our studies is an examination of the effect of various surface features of information on its representation in memory and performance on

---

[3]The words completing the fragments are SEXTANT, FLANNEL, CREVICE, AGNOSTIC, BOYHOOD, SWAHILI, INFERNO, BANDANNA, HYACINTH, DISSERTATION.

[4]Episodic memory refers to the system that is thought to underlie experience for personal memories in which one must recollect the time and place of occurrence for an event to be remembered. Semantic memory is the system thought to be responsible for general knowledge in which one need not recall the time or place of occurrence to perform accurately. Tulving (1972, 1983, 1985b) spells out the distinction in greater detail. Within the context of Tulving et al.'s (1982) experiment, recognition memory taps the episodic memory system, since subjects must decide whether or not the test words belong to the studied list. Word fragment completion is a semantic memory task because subjects need not recollect previous occurrence of a word in the list to perform accurately.

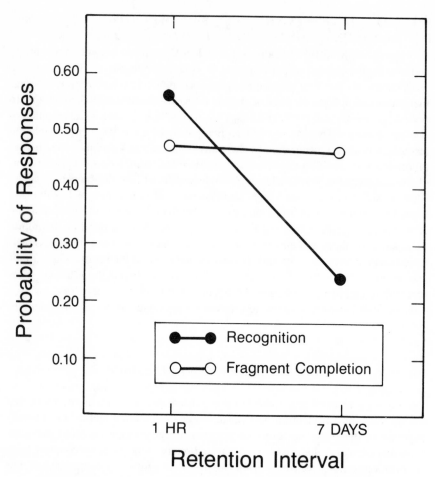

FIGURE 24.1.   Results of Tulving, Schacter, and Stark's (1982) experiment. Recognition dropped sharply over the retention interval, but fragment completion performance did not. However, word fragment completion was not simply insensitive, because studied words were completed better than nonstudied words. (Reproduced with permission.)

various memory tests. Fifteen years ago researchers had reached the conclusion that various media by which information was presented played little role in its long-term memory representation. Factors such as modality of presentation (auditory or visual), the typeface in which information was presented, or even the syntax (say, active or passive constructions) were believed to form no part of the trace in long term retention. Important studies by Sachs (1967), Bransford and Franks (1972), Kintsch and Monk (1972) and others bolstered this point, for these researchers found little effect of various surface characteristics on long-term recall or recognition. These studies led to the conclusion, which is still prevalent in some quarters today, that incoming information is quickly coded into abstract representations (schemas, scripts, deep structures, logogens, or networks of associative connections). The medium seemed to play no role in the message coded in long-term memory.

These claims are, of course, challenged by many more recent findings, particularly those of Paul Kolers and his associates (e.g., Kolers, 1975, 1978; Kolers & Ostry, 1974; see Kolers & Roediger, 1984, for a review). Various surface features, such as modality of presentation or orientation of typeface (normal or rotated), are shown to have important consequences for performance on retention tests. One important difference between studies that have found no effect of form of presentation and those that have shown an effect is the dependent measures used. Typically, researchers showing that mode of presentation plays little role have measured recall or recognition, whereas Kolers' studies have often measured speed of reading or other measures less dependent on conscious recollection (however, Kolers & Ostry, 1974, reported effects on recognition memory, too). It seems possible, if not likely, that the type of test is critical as to whether effects of surface form are revealed in performance. Jacoby's (1983) studies reviewed previously are consistent with this claim.

In the experiments, we presented subjects with a list of items in a list and then tested their memories in various ways. We varied the modality (auditory or visual), typography (typed or handwritten, and upper- or lower case), language for bilinguals (Spanish or English), and form of referent (word or picture). The tests employed were free recall, yes/no recognition, and word fragment completion, although not all these tests were used in all experiments. Of primary interest is how these variables affect word fragment completion performance, a task that does not require conscious recollection. We show, as have Kolers and Jacoby, remarkable specificity in forms of presentation on certain retention tests. To anticipate, variables that have large effects on free recall exert no effect or even opposite effects on word fragment completion.

The general theoretical framework within which our experiments were designed was that of transfer appropriate processing (Morris, et al., 1977), in which improvements in test performance are expected to the extent to which the types of processing required on the test were acquired during the study episode. To state the same ideas in terms of processing operations (Kolers & Roediger, 1984), performance will benefit to the extent that procedures used in an acquisition phase are reinstituted during a test phase. We later describe why we prefer these accounts of dissociations to others imputing various memory systems (e.g., Tulving, 1983).

VARIATION IN MODALITY AND TYPOGRAPHY

The effects of modality of presentation on recall have been examined in many experiments. The generally accepted conclusion, at least until lately, has been that mode of presentation has an effect only on recently presented information (Crowder, 1976, Chapter 3). The conclusion aptly summarizing dozens of experiments on free and serial recall is that performance on the last few times is better if the information is presented auditorily rather than visually, but that very little or no effect of modality can be determined in long-term recall for information not recently presented (but see Gardiner & Gregg, 1979, and Glenberg, this volume, for a curious exception). Under conditions employed in our experiments to be described, modality has no effect on free recall (Blaxton, 1985).

To our knowledge, no studies of the effects of typography on free or serial recall exist, but data collected by Blaxton (1985) indicate that typography (uppercase elite type versus lowercase italic) has little effect in free recall. The case of modality and typography effects on single item recognition is somewhat different. Kirsner (1974) reported small effects of modality and typography on recognition, such that subjects performed better if the test form matched the surface form in these cases. Kolers, of course, has shown impressive effects of the orientation of print on the recognition of sentences (e.g., Kolers & Ostry, 1974)

Jacoby and Dallas (1981, Experiment 6) compared the effects of modality of presentation on yes/no recognition of visually presented test items and on their identification from brief displays. They reported a sharp dissociation, with modality having no effect on recognition but a large effect on perceptual identification. In the latter measure, performance was much improved if the item had been presented visually, but no benefit occurred for items presented auditorily (relative to nonstudied items). Winnick and Daniel (1970) and Clarke and Morton (1983, Experiments 1 and 2) have reported similar findings. This pattern can be accounted for by assuming that perceptual identification is a data-driven task (and thus should be highly sensitive to the way "data" are presented at study), whereas recognition is largely a conceptually driven task and is thus less affected by the form of presentation. However, according to Jacoby (1983), recognition also involves a data-driven component. Subjects may judge an item to be familiar when it is rapidly processed—when it seems to "jump off the page" (see Mandler, 1980 for a similar assumption). Thus, to the extent that recognition judgments are affected by such perceptual fluency factors, one can account for the effects of surface features such as found by Kirsner (1974) and Kolers and Ostry (1974) in recognition. Johnston, Dark, and Jacoby (1985) provide evidence for the operation of a data-driven component of recognition judgments under some conditions.

In the first of our experiments described here, (described in part in Roediger & Blaxton (1987) as Experiment 1), we presented subjects with 96 words, half visually and half auditorily. The items were presented under one of four conditions, in blocked fashion. Half of the 48 visually presented items were typed on an IBM Selectric typewriter in lowercase letters; the other 24 visually presented items were printed by hand in uppercase letters (all visually presented items were shown to subjects via a slide projector). Twenty-four other items were presented auditorily; 24 more were also presented auditorily, but subjects were told to form an image of the word as it would appear typed (subjects were given prior experience with the typeface). Across subjects, all items appeared equally often in each study condition and were presented at a 5-second rate.

These various study conditions were manipulated within subjects, but type of test was a between-subjects factor. One set of subjects received a standard yes/no recognition test in which the 96 old items were randomly intermixed with 96 new items on a sheet with instructions to circle items they recognized as being old. Each test typography was used for half the items in each study condition. Subjects who received the word fragment completion test received exactly the same sort of form as did recognition subjects (i.e., half old and half new items, etc.), but now only fragments of the words were presented and the subjects' task was to fill in the missing letters to complete the word correctly. (Examples of our materials were provided earlier.) The design appears in Fig. 24.2.

The word fragment completion test results are presented in Table 24.2. Note first that, relative to the nonstudied completion rate, items presented under all study conditions primed their later completions. Thus, unlike Jacoby and Dallas's (1981) finding with perceptual identification (their Experiment 6), we obtained cross-modal priming in fragment completion, in that completion rates averaged 0.43 in the auditory condition and only 0.27 in the nonstudied condition. However, priming from visual presentations was greater than for auditory presentations (0.52 versus 0.43), showing that same-mode priming exceeded cross-modal priming. In addition, within the visual mode, a slight but significant effect of typography was obtained. When the typography at test matched that of the study episode, performance was better than when the two mismatched (0.55 and 0.50 completions, respectively; most of this effect is due to superior performance in the Handprinted–Handprinted case). Finally, when subjects were presented words auditorily but told to image what the word would look like typed, fragment completion performance improved about 5% relative to the case of auditory presentation, (0.48 to 0.43), but this increase was not specific to the mode of test (i.e., the increase also appeared when subjects were tested with the handprinted fragments, contrary to expectation). This last finding seems to argue that subjects encoded more information when instructed to image the word, but that this effect was not specific to the typeface imagined. Nonetheless, it is interesting that when subjects were instructed to image the word typed, word fragment completion performance was equivalent to that of items actually presented typed (see Jacoby & Witherspoon, 1982, for a similar result).

Recognition results for the experiment are shown in Table 24.3, where the trends found in fragment completion are largely absent. That is, visual presentation was not reliably superior to auditory presentation, nor was there a reliable effect of typeface. Whereas visual presentation produced the best performance in fragment completion, auditory presentation with instructions to image the words

Roediger & Blaxton (1987)
Design of Experiment 1

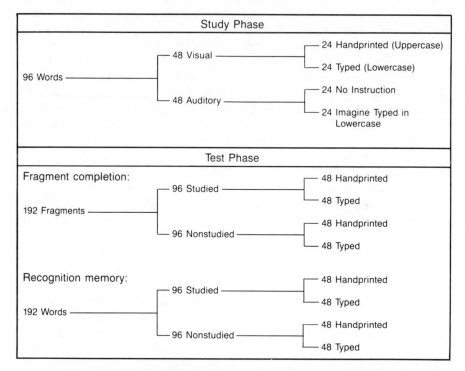

FIGURE 24.2. The design of Roediger and Blaxton's (1987) Experiment 1. The study phase manipulation is represented at the top, with the test phase manipulations below.

TABLE 24.2
Proportion of Fragments Completed in Each Condition of
Experiment 1

| | Study Condition | | | | |
| | Visual | | Auditory | | Nonstudied |
Test Condition	Handprinted	Typed	No Instruction	Image–Word Instruction	
Handprinted	0.59	0.48	0.44	0.49	0.27
Typed	0.52	0.51	0.42	0.48	0.27

TABLE 24.3
Recognition Performance (d') for the Conditions in Experiment 1

| | Study Conditions | | | |
| | Visual | | Auditory | |
Test Condition	Handprinted	Typed	No Instruction	Image–Word Instruction
Handprinted	2.49	2.32	2.15	2.80
Typed	2.40	2.46	2.40	2.52

yielded best recognition. A slight tendency existed, within the visual presentation conditions, for compatible typographies to produce better performance than mixed typographies, but this trend was not statistically reliable. Although some dependency may exist across conditions between the recognition memory and fragment completion tests, its magnitude seems small.

We performed a second experiment on the issue of effects of typography and modality on fragment completion, this time including delay of recall. Subjects were tested either a few minutes or one week after studying the list. In general, the main results of the first experiment were replicated at both testing intervals. Priming occurred in all study conditions, with visual presentation leading to greater priming that auditory presentation, and matched typographies at study and test producing better performance than mismatched typographies. Notably, we found significant priming on the word fragment completion task after a 1-week retention interval, although performance declined in all conditions during the delay. Subjects completed 10% fewer fragments in the primed conditions after the week delay. Tulving et al. (1982) found no such loss in priming over a week, but their "initial" test occurred an hour after presentation whereas ours was given shortly after study. This procedural difference may account for the discrepancy.

In sum, the results of these experiments indicate that fragment completion is highly sensitive to the correspondence between features of the study and test presentations for both modality and typography. Recognition is less sensitive to typography in our experiments and, if anything, the effect of modality on recognition was opposite that for fragment completion (i.e., a slight tendency existed for auditory presentations to exceed visual in recognition).

Our results agree with those of Graf, Shimamura, and Squire (1985, Experiment 1), who reported cross-modal priming for both amnesics and normals in a word stem completion task in which subjects received three letters of a word with instructions to provide the first completion that came to mind. Same-mode priming was also greater than cross-mode priming. Our results and those of Graf et al. (1984) show that priming can occur across modality boundaries, unlike results obtained by others using perceptual identification (Jacoby & Dallas, 1981, Experiment 6) or threshold measures (Clarke & Morton, 1983; Winnick & Daniel, 1970). Our results on the effects of typography also provide tentative support for specificity of visual features in priming, unlike the results of Clarke and Morton (1983; see also Jackson & Morton, 1984).

THE EFFECTS OF LANGUAGE OF STUDY

The next experiment we discuss was conducted by Aydin Durgunoğlu in collaboration with the first author and tested how language of presentation affects performance in bilingual subjects (Durgunoğlu and Roediger, 1987). The subjects were Spanish–English bilinguals, mostly graduate students at Purdue whose native language was Spanish but who were also fluent in English. All subjects were presented 115 words to remember in six study conditions and then received one of three types of test: free recall, yes/no recognition, or word fragment completion. Only some of the study conditions need be described for present purposes; these are illustrated in Table 24.4. The study conditions were varied within subjects, while the type of retention test was a between-subjects factor. Sets of words were rotated through the study conditions across subjects and were presented individually at an 8-second rate.

The study conditions shown in Table 24.4 indicate that during the 8-second study period, subjects either read the words (a) twice in Spanish or (b) twice in English, or (c) once in each language. The first presentation appeared on a screen via a slide projector and the second was given on a sheet before the subject. Items in these study conditions were presented in blocks, prefaced by the appropriate instructions. One set of items was not presented but was used to assess base line

TABLE 24.4
Results of Durgunoğlu and Roediger (1987)
(Reproduced with permission.)

	Type of Test		
Study Condition	Free Recall	Yes/No Recognition*	Word Fragment Completion*
Read Spanish caballo, caballo	0.23	0.62	0.44
Read English horse, horse	0.17	0.79	0.66
Read Spanish & English caballo, horse	0.39	0.95	0.68
Nonstudied	——	0.05	0.42

performance on the fragment completion and recognition tests. On these latter tests, subjects received words (for recognition) or word frames (for fragment completion). Recognition subjects were told to circle words they recognized as having occurred in the list and were explicitly told to circle words referring to concepts that may have occurred in the alternate language. Fragment completion subjects were simply told to write the first word that came to mind to complete the fragment. All items in the fragment completion and recognition tests were given in English, a fact impressed on the subjects through instructions just before the test. For the free-recall test, subjects were instructed to recall as many words as possible from the study list in whichever language they came to mind.

The results are presented in Table 24.4. First, consider free-recall performance. Items presented in Spanish were somewhat better recalled than those given in English, probably reflecting the fact that our subjects were mostly Spanish-dominant bilinguals (however, the difference was of borderline significance). Interestingly, recall was better when subjects read the word in both languages during study rather than twice in the same language, even when this was Spanish. This may reflect an effect of encoding variability (Madigan, 1969), and replicates a finding of Glanzer and Duarte (1971) with massed presentation. In Jacoby's (1983) terms, free recall is a conceptually driven task because no "data" are given in the task to guide performance. In line with his findings, the condition that encouraged coding of conceptual information (variable encoding) produced better performance than the two conditions that simply required subjects to read information in one language.

Turning to the word fragment completion results on the far right of Table 24.4, a very different pattern emerges. Relative to the completion rate for new items (0.42), studying the word twice in Spanish produced no reliable priming (0.44) (Watkins & Peynircioğlu, 1983, Experiment 2 reported similar findings). However, reading the word in English, or reading it in both Spanish and English, produced sizable priming of roughly equal magnitude. Thus, fragment completion acts as a data-driven task. Subjects use the fragments as "data" to construct words. If similar data had been presented at study (i.e., words in English), performance was facilitated.

According to Jacoby (1983), recognition involves a mixture of both conceptual and data-driven processing. To use Mandler's (1980) terms, there is both activation or integration of the surface features of the item, and the elaboration of concepts. Thus, recognition should show a mixture of the features of free recall and word fragment completion, depending on whether study conditions emphasized processing of surface features or the elaboration of concepts. This is true in our experiment on bilinguals. Several lines of evidence for conceptual aspects of recognition are present. First, recognition shows better than chance responding in all conditions (unlike fragment completion), presumably reflecting conceptually driven processing. Second, subjects recognized words better after the elaborative processing involved in the varied encoding condition (presentation in both languages, 0.95) than when the items were presented twice in the same language (0.62 and 0.79). However, evidence also exists for a data-driven component to recognition. In recognition (unlike free recall), presentation of the items in English (0.79) led to better performance than their presentation in Spanish (0.62). This presumably reflects the fact that the test was all in English and thus with English presentation there was a greater match between the data at study and test.

In sum, a reasonable story can be made from results of the present experiment indicating that free recall is conceptually driven, fragment completion is largely data-driven, and recognition memory involves a mixture of the two types of processing. The data are thus in line with the proposals of Jacoby (1983), as well as related ideas of Graf and Mandler (1984).

PRIMING BY PICTURES AND BY WORDS

The next experiment to be discussed under the general rubric of effects of surface aspects of media on retention involves a comparison of memory for pictures and words. The general finding from a huge body of literature is that pictures are recalled and recognized better than their labels (Paivio, 1969, 1971). Free recall shows a substantial picture advantage and so does recognition. In free recall, the picture advantage occurs despite the fact that subjects are actually recalling words (labels of the pictures) after studying pictures, a factor which might be expected to favor word recall. Interestingly, the advantage of pictures in recognition also occurs even when the test items are presented as words. That is, if the word *horse* were presented during the test, subjects would recognize it better if they had previously studied a drawing of a horse rather than the word itself. Even though the data at test better match those studied in the word–word case then in the picture–word case, recognition is better in the latter (see Madigan, 1983). The usual interpretation of these findings is that pictures are encoded into a richer or more elaborate representation in memory and therefore are better recognized and recalled than are words (e.g., Nelson, Reed, & McEvoy, 1977; Paivio, 1971).

The question motivating the present research was whether or not the usual picture superiority effect could be eliminated or even reversed when the word fragment completion test was used to assess retention. Assuming that fragment completion is a data-driven task, then medium of presentation should play a larger role in determining fragment completion than it does in recognition or recall. The experiment described here is the first in a series conducted by Mary Susan Weldon in collaboration with the first author (Weldon & Roediger, 1987). Thirty-three items were selected from the Snodgrass and Vanderwart (1980) picture norms and prepared in two forms, either as simple line drawings or as the labels for the drawings. Twenty-two items were presented to subjects, half as

TABLE 24.5
Results from Weldon and Roediger (1987)
(Reproduced with permission.)

	Test	
	---	---
Study	Free Recall	Word Fragment Completion
Drawing	0.35	0.45
Word	0.28	0.64
New	——	0.38

drawings and half as words, in the midst of a number of buffer items. All subjects received list presentation under the same conditions, but half were given a free-recall test and the other half received a word fragment completion test. In the fragment completion test, subjects completed 33 fragments representing 11 items studied as drawings, 11 as words, and 11 that were not studied. Items were counterbalanced across the study conditions over subjects. The primary results are shown in Table 24.5, in which the proportion of items recalled and completed in each of the conditions is given. As usual, pictures were better recalled than words (0.35 to 0.28). However, this pattern was reversed in the word fragment completion test. Relative to the base line, pictures produced only a seven percent priming effect, but study of words led to a 27% priming effect. The interpretation, which should be familiar now, is that the word fragment completion test, being data-driven, is facilitated by a match between mental operations engendered by processing the data in the study and test phases. Free recall, which depends on elaborative processing, reveals the alleged "richer" encoding of drawings than words.

The reversal of the usual picture superiority effect with word fragment completion as the measure of retention is not due simply to a perceptual match between the data (cues) given at test and those studied earlier, but must also be due to the type of retrieval operations subjects perform on the data provided during testing. The reason for this assertion is a comparison between our findings and those described earlier employing recognition of words (Madigan, 1983). Surely the perceptual match between the word studied and the test cue is greater when recognition memory is tested (e.g., *birdhouse* at study and test), than when the subjects' task is word fragment completion (*birdhouse* at study and b __ __ d h __ __ __ e at test). In recognition, pictures are recognized better than words, but in fragment completion words are identified better than pictures. Thus the task demands, and not simply the completeness of the cues, helps determine performance. Presumably, on a recognition test, subjects call conceptual operations into play that are largely absent on the word fragment completion task. We say "largely" and not "completely" absent, for we did find modest but reliable priming from pictures on word fragment completion (see Table 24.5). Of course, this effect may be explained by covert labeling of pictures during study, but in later experiments (Weldon and Roediger, 1987, Experiments 2 and 3) we found no change in primed fragment completion levels from pictures when we varied instructions designed to encourage or discourage labeling. Thus the priming effect of pictures on word fragment completion may be conceptually mediated, a point to which we will return.

REPRISE: MEDIA AND RETENTION

A few years ago the commonplace assumption was that the medium of presentation had little to do in most cases with the underlying message retained in long-term memory. The present results add to those of others (Jacoby & Dallas, 1981; Kolers, 1975; Kolers & Ostry, 1974) in showing that this conclusion is false. Although some tests are insensitive to changes in surface representation, others reveal large effects. Typography, modality, and even language of presentation for fluent bilinguals are all variables that have no effect on long-term free recall in most situations, and little effect on recognition. However, all these variables yield large effects on word fragment completion as seen in the present experiments, and they also affect other measures of implicit retention such as perceptual identification (Jacoby & Dallas, 1981) visual duration thresholds (Winnick & Daniel, 1970), word stem completion (Graf et al., 1985), and reading speed (Kolers, 1975).

These recent results also add new information about word fragment completion as a measure of retention. Presented in Fig. 24.3 is a graph showing the amount of priming obtained from studying items in various forms. Constructing this graph takes a certain amount of daring because different sets of items were used across the experiments reviewed here. However, each of these experiments (and one other, not yet described) includes a condition involving repetition priming (same mode and typography at study and test). The amount of repetition priming across five experiments was 0.24, 0.26, 0.27, 0.28, and 0.31 for an average of about 0.27. These values seemed stable enough to warrant the construction of Fig. 24.3.

The data in Fig. 24.3 provide a reasonable ordering of influences, convincing us that word fragment completion does indeed represent a ''data-driven'' test of retention, in Jacoby's (1983) terms. The magnitude of the priming effect generally accords with expectations based on similarities between data processed at study and the fragment provided at test. Performance is best when presentation is visual and the typography matches that used at test (0.27), and is next best with visual presentation and mismatched typography (0.23) (this effect of typography was larger in Experiment 1 of Roediger & Blaxton, when materials were held constant; the diminution here occurs from averaging across experiments to obtain

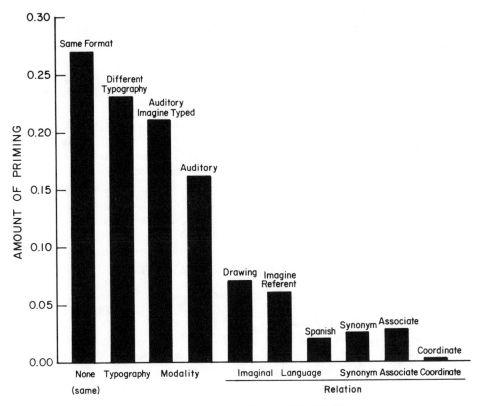

CHANGE BETWEEN STUDY AND TEST

FIGURE 24.3.   Amount of priming in word fragment completion from various manipulations of medium of presentation.

the estimate of repetition priming). When words were presented auditorily, less priming occurred (0.16), although this effect is accentuated slightly if subjects are told to image the appearance of the word. Performance was worst when the presentation of the item occurred in a very different format or medium from the fragment––pictures produced a 0.07 priming effect, forming an image to a word presented in a different language led to a 0.06 priming effect, and presenting the item in an alternate language produced essentially no priming effect (0.02).

The failure to find substantial priming effects in these latter three cases cannot be attributed to subjects' not encoding the list items, since free-recall tests actually showed better performance in these three conditions than in the appropriate control conditions. The conclusion is that fragment completion does not rely on elaborative or conceptually driven processing, but instead on data-driven processing.

The three conditions at the far right of Fig. 24.3 come from an experiment conducted in collaboration with Valerie Ludwick and Bradford Challis that has not yet been described. Briefly, subjects studied a list of words and then received a word fragment completion test similar to those described earlier. The words in the list bore various relations to the items represented in the word fragments. Besides repetition priming (study *horse* and tested with h __ r __ e, for example), studied items could bear other relations to the fragments such as being synonyms (*stallion*), associates (*saddle*), or category coordinates (*cow*). As can be seen in the figure, these types of studied items produce very little priming on the word fragment completion test. Synonyms and associates produced about a three percent effect, relative to the nonstudied base line, and coordinates produced no priming at all. Again, the standard word fragment completion test seems largely data-driven, because when items are given that are meaningfully related to the fragment but whose appearance is quite different, little or no priming occurs.

THEORETICAL ALTERNATIVES

Throughout our description of the above research, we have employed a procedural view (Kolers & Roediger, 1984) in which performance on a retention or transfer test is assumed to be a function of the similarity of processing operations engendered between study and test, with further assumptions added about the types of processing required by different tests (Jacoby, 1983; Mandler, 1980). We will defend this view, but will first consider our results as they might be interpreted by other theories.

Strength Theory

At the considerable risk of flogging a long-deceased *caballo*, let us consider the implications of these results for strength theory. A simple strength theory would maintain that experiences leave memory traces as their mental residue and that these vary in strength along a single dimension. Different levels of performance reflect varying strengths in these traces. The assumption that remembering is determined only by a trace dependent factor, such as strength, makes the obvious prediction that the ordering of performance in various study conditions should generalize across memory tests. That is, if Trace A is stronger than Trace B on a free-recall test, then this ordering should be preserved on all other tests. Obviously, the present results and many others falsify this hypothesis. Any study showing opposing effects on memory tasks as a function of independent variables, as in the Weldon and Roediger (1987) experiment described earlier, can be so considered. Other examples include Balota and Neely (1980), Fisher and Craik (1977), and Morris et al. (1977).

Logogens and Nodes

Priming effects in tasks such as lexical decision or naming latency are often attributed to the activation of a logogen or node that is effected by external experiences. Such hypothetical entities are usually postulated to be relatively abstract, and do not incorporate surface features of the medium by which the information is conveyed. For example, according to Morton's (1969) theory, the same logogen would be aroused if one saw the word *horse*, or heard someone say it.

Many recent results challenge the logogens view, including those of Morton (1979). These experiments replicate and extend the earlier work of Winnick and Daniel (1970), showing that prior visual presentation of a word produced greater facilitation in reducing visual duration thresholds than did auditory presentation. Morton (1979) postulated separate visual and auditory logogen systems to account for the results. Experiments by Jacoby and Dallas (1981) and Jacoby (1983) raise similar problems and even extend them, for Jacoby and Dallas (1981) found substantial priming in a perceptual identification task after a 2-day retention interval. The activation of logogens is usually thought to be short-lived, on the order of seconds, and thus priming after a 2-day interval stretches the concept beyond recognition.

The present results also discredit the logogen/node account of repetition priming, although in fairness the idea was never put forward to encompass situations such as those investigated here. In order to account for priming in word fragment completion, the logogen account would have to postulate (a) activation lasting up to a week; (b) different logogen systems not only for modality of presentation, but also for different typographies, for presentations in alternate languages, and for presentation of an "item" as a word or picture. The attractiveness of the idea of abstract logogens as an explanatory device is reduced if a new logogen system must be invented for every variable that affects priming, and if one of the concept's basic properties—activation that decays rapidly—is removed. Simpler alternatives that would provide a more parsimonious account are therefore preferred.

Memory Systems

The results reported above reveal several dissociations between independent variables and performance on the various memory tests. Tulving (1983, Chapter 5) has interpreted similar dissociations as evidence for separate memory systems, episodic and semantic. The former is believed responsible for recollection of personal experiences requiring retrieval of time and place, whereas the latter underlies permanent knowledge. Most dissociations in the evidence reviewed by Tulving took the form of independent variables affecting an episodic memory task (such as recognition), but having no effect on a semantic memory test (such as fragment completion or perceptual identification). For example, Jacoby and Dallas (1981) manipulated the "level of processing" of presented words by having subjects attend to their appearance, sound, or meaning and then provided either a perceptual identification or a yes/no recognition test. They found that level of processing had the usual large effect on recognition, but no effect on perceptual identification. Tulving (1983) argued that such results support the distinction between episodic and semantic memory, because a variable is shown to affect a task tapping one type of memory (episodic recognition) but not the other (perceptual identification).

Our own experiments reviewed earlier reveal several dissociations that can be similarly interpreted. Modality and typography were shown to affect word fragment completion, but not recognition. This outcome is different from virtually all those reviewed by Tulving (1983) in showing variables that exert greater effects on a semantic memory task than on an episodic memory task. Two other variables studied here produced opposing effects on recall and fragment completion, a more powerful dissociation similar to that of Jacoby (1983). For bilinguals, words presented in Spanish were better recalled than words given in English, but the opposite was true in word fragment completion (with English fragments). Similarly, pictures were free recalled better than words, but words primed fragment completion more than pictures. Again, these interactions can be interpreted as evidence for different memory systems, with one system assumed to underlie free recall (episodic memory) and the other to underlie word fragment completion (semantic or, perhaps, procedural memory; see Tulving et al., 1982).

The use of dissociations to support the episodic/semantic distinction has been questioned on several occasions (Hintzman, 1984; McKoon, Ratcliff, & Dell, 1986; Roediger, 1984). One argument is that the theory is not specific enough to predict the form of the interaction in a given experiment. The general form of Tulving's argument (1983, Chapters 4 and 5) can be paraphrased as "my theory predicts interactions between study and test conditions; interactions are found; therefore the theory is supported." Reasons are rarely given as to why some variable should affect an episodic but not a semantic memory task, or vice versa. In fairness, in an enterprise so new as trying to distinguish among various memory systems, perhaps Tulving's logic of simply looking for interactions is the best possible without further knowledge. However, it is only persuasive if some other framework or theory cannot provide a better account of these interactions. As we have argued throughout, we believe an alternative is available, a matter to which we now turn.

Transfer Appropriate Procedures

We have argued against the ideas of separate memory traces with varying strengths as an explanation of our results; we argue too against the ideas of separate logogens or nodes that are activated, and against proliferating memory systems. Instead we opt for a more process-oriented view, emphasizing the mental operations people perform in accomplishing tasks and the information these require. The ideas represent an amalgamation of those from Kolers and Roediger (1984), Jacoby, (1983), and Morris et al. (1977; see also Bransford, Franks, Morris, and Stein, 1979). In addition, they are similar in spirit to the encoding specificity hypothesis (Flexser & Tulving, 1978; Tulving and Thomson, 1973), although the latter emphasizes mental contents more than processes. Here we first state the ideas rather abstractly, and then will use them to interpret data from the experiments which have been described. Third, we describe data from another experiment that we believe supports this view over Tulving's (1983) postulation of separate memory systems.

When one is exposed to information, the instructions given, the type of material, its expected future use, and individual proclivities combine to emphasize certain types of mental operations (Jenkins, 1979). To take familiar examples, subjects' attention can be directed at various features of words, as in the "levels of processing" experiment; or subjects can be told to form mental images; or they can be led to expect recall, recognition, or some other type of test. The processing activities so engendered affect the type of information learned about an experience—what is coded—and that in turn affects how information can be expressed on some particular test. In general, the more similar the processing activities required by the test to the encoding activities, the better will be performance on the test. This restates the ideas of many others, (e.g., Bransford et al., 1979; Kolers, 1975; Kolers & Roediger, 1984; Tulving & Thomson, 1973), although in somewhat more general form.

We find particularly useful the additional idea, applied by Jacoby (1983) to remembering, of data-driven (bottom–up) and conceptually driven (top–down) processing. Some study and test conditions will emphasize attention to presented information (the data), whereas others will emphasize concepts—elaborations, associations, etc. (see also Mandler, 1980, and Graf & Mandler, 1984). Examples of these ideas as applied to study activities would be judgments of appearance versus judgments of meaning in the levels of processing experiment; reading versus generating in the generation effect experiment; and rote repetition of words versus forming images of their referents in experiments on mental imagery (e.g., Bower, 1972). In each case, the first activity emphasizes data more than concepts and the second does the reverse.

Turning to the various memory tests, free recall is the paradigmatic "conceptually driven" test, for no data are presented as cues. Rather, subjects must "drive" their performance by using mental concepts. Other tests such as perceptual identification and word fragment completion are more data-driven. That is, subjects are given data at test and must process it as rapidly as possible in performing some task. When used as tests of retention, the data in these tasks are provided in no particular context, and thus conceptually driven processing is difficult (especially in perceptual identification).

The distinction between data-driven and conceptually driven processing should not be considered a strict dichotomy, we believe, but rather as endpoints on a continuum. For example, a word fragment completion test could be made more conceptually driven if subjects were given associative cues (DAGGER — A _ _ A _ _ IN). Similarly, recall is made more data-driven if one provides cues that resemble the targets in terms of their appearance (Blaxton, 1985) or sound (Fisher & Craik, 1977). Recognition memory tests are argued to be affected both by data-driven and conceptually driven components (Jacoby, 1983), or by activation of features and elaboration of meaning (Mandler, 1980). However, in most standard yes/no recognition memory tests, with their leisurely pace, conceptually driven processing is probably more important (see Johnston et al., 1985).

Having provided these rather abstract distinctions and assumptions, how might they apply to our data? In these experiments we manipulated the medium of presentation—modality (auditory or visual), typography (uppercase and hand-printed, lowercase and typed), language (Spanish or English), and form of representation (drawing or word). In general, our results fit well with the ideas outlined here. Variation in modality and typography affected the data-driven word fragment completion test, but not the recognition test that is believed to have a greater conceptually driven component. (Others have found slight effects of these variables on single word recognition, e.g., Kirsner, 1974.) However, Blaxton (1985) found no effect of typography on free recall, and a large literature on modality effects reveals no effect on free recall in long-term memory under conditions similar to those employed here (Crowder, 1976; Murdock & Walker, 1969). Thus the effects of typography and modality fall in line with what one would expect—largest effects on data-driven tasks, small effects on recognition with its small data-driven component, and no effect on free recall.

Language of presentation (Spanish or English) and form of representation (drawing or word) provide more interesting manipulations of media, because in both cases one can make a reasonable assumption that one mode of presentation produces a richer, more elaborate encoding than does the other. For our Spanish-dominant bilinguals, words in Spanish may be expected to be more richly encoded than words in English; similarly, drawings are assumed by many to be more elaborately encoded than their verbal labels (e.g., Paivio, 1969). In line with this assumption, the relevant experiments reported here showed slightly greater free recall for Spanish than English words by our bilinguals, and for pictures than words. However, on the word fragment completion test, performance reversed in both cases. In this case, bilinguals completed the words better than had been presented in English than those presented in Spanish (the fragments were presented in English). For our other subjects, presenting items as words produced greater priming in word fragment completion than presenting them as pictures. In both cases, these outcomes were predicted by the theory emphasizing transfer appropriate processing, since the data-driven fragment completion test should benefit most from conditions in which similar data are processed during study, viz. English words.

A COMPARISON OF THEORIES

We have shown that the transfer appropriate procedures approach can account well for the dissociations in our data. But so can theories that ascribe these dissociations to different memory systems, as we have outlined. How can we decide which approach is best? Or are both approaches so vague that no distinctive, testable consequences can be derived from them?

We believe that the transfer appropriate processing approach is clearly better, and that testable differences can be derived. Consider first some data from our own experiments. In the Durgunoğlu and Roediger (1987) experiment, some items were studied only in English and others only in Spanish, among the other conditions. In free recall, Spanish words were slightly better remembered than English words, but in recognition (which gave test words only in English) words that had been presented in English were better recognized. How can the memory systems approach explain this finding? Both recognition and recall are episodic memory tests, so the same pattern of results is to be expected in both tasks. Presumably, dissociations should not occur within tasks tapping the same system. On the other hand, the view emphasizing transfer appropriate procedures has no trouble with this finding. Recognition, unlike free recall, has a data-driven component and thus on a test in which English words are given, having studied English words should be better than having studied words in another language.

A critic of our logic might complain, somewhat justifiably, that we stacked the deck in this experiment by giving these test items in English. All Tulving (1983, 1985b) would need to do is add something like transfer appropriate processing to the multiple systems idea to account for the results. That is true enough, but such a course then raises the interesting question of why the notion of memory systems need be added at all to explain the results. The transfer appropriate procedures idea accounts for the data without requiring the addition of separate systems.

Also, the switch between Spanish and English in our experiment does not affect the form of the argument, since the same point can be made from other data. For example, if word frequency is manipulated in recognition and recall experiments, the consistent finding is that high-frequency words are better recalled than low-frequency words, but that low-frequency words are better recognized than high-frequency words (e.g., Balota & Neely, 1980). Once again, there is a dissociation within two episodic memory tasks, which is difficult to encompass in Tulving's (1983) system. On the other hand, if we make the common assumption that high-frequency words are more richly or elaborately encoded than low-frequency words (Anderson & Bower, 1972), but that low-frequency words are more distinctive and receive more data-driven processing, then the explanation from the transfer appropriate procedures view assumes its familiar form.

In brief, Tulving's (1983) view distinguishing among various memory systems does not provide a straightforward account of dissociations within tasks believed to tap the same system. This problem usually does not arise in experiments showing dissociations between measures of retention (see Tulving, 1983, Chapter 5), because researchers have typically employed only two tests of retention—one episodic and one semantic—when examining dissociations (Roediger, 1984). For example, Jacoby and Dallas (1981) looked at how various independent variables affected perceptual identification and yes/no recognition, and Tulving et al. (1982) examined the effects of retention interval on word fragment completion and yes/no recognition. With only two measures in an experiment—one thought to tap semantic memory and one episodic—any interaction obtained can be taken as support for the distinction between memory systems. On the other hand, the failure to obtain an interaction is not necessarily evidence against the distinction, because no one would argue that all variables should affect the two systems differently.

In most experiments showing dissociations between memory tests reviewed by Tulving (1983, Chapter 5), a confounding exists between the system the task is to tap and the type of task, according to Jacoby's (1983) typology. Shown in Fig. 24.4 is a 2×2 representation crossing memory systems (episodic and semantic) with task type (data-driven and conceptually driven). Most experiments to date have involved only two cells—the episodic memory tasks have been con-

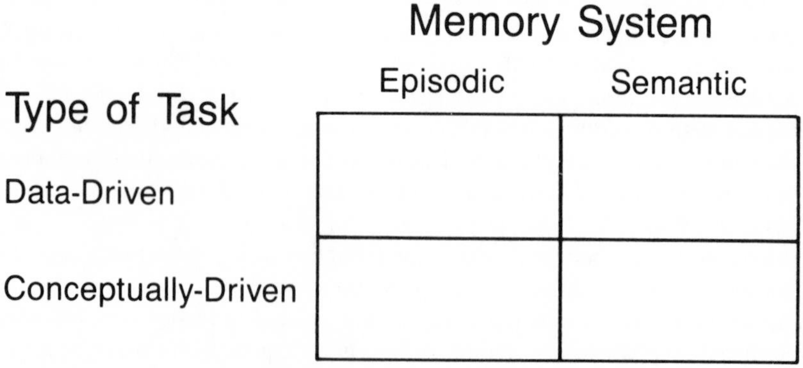

FIGURE 24.4.   Crossing of two memory systems with types of processing. Most previous experiments have involved a comparison of conceptually driven episodic memory tests with data-driven semantic memory tests, the lower left and upper right cells.

ceptually driven (recognition, recall) and the semantic memory tasks have been data-driven (perceptual identification, word fragment completion).

The design of experiments needed to distinguish the memory systems approach to explaining dissociations from the transfer appropriate procedures view is to use all four tasks, as suggested by Fig. 24.4. That is, tests involving episodic and semantic memory should be varied orthogonally to the type of processing the task requires. Assume that two tasks can be reasonably classified as episodic and two as semantic; also that two of these can be classified as data-driven and two as conceptually driven. If these dimensions are uncorrelated, it should be possible to vary study conditions and assess performance on the four different tasks to determine whether the results better conform to an interpretation in terms of the memory system that each task involves or the type of processing each requires. Blaxton (1985) has used this general logic in a series of experiments designed to determine the adequacy of these two approaches to explaining dissociations. Here we will describe only one of her experiments that makes the general point. In addition, we will simplify our discussion of the design slightly to make our points more clearly.

Subjects in Blaxton's (1985) Experiment 1 studied a list of words under three conditions analogous to those in Jacoby's (1983) experiment. On some occasions subjects received items such as XXX–COPPER (no context); on others they received items in context, in the form of a semantic associate (tin–COPPER); and in still other cases they had to generate the word (TIN–C _ _ _ _ _). This manipulation was intended to affect the relative amounts of data-driven and conceptually driven processing during study, with data-driven processing decreasing across the no context, context, and generate conditions, but with conceptually driven processing increasing across these conditions. These conditions were varied within-subjects, in blocks of 21 items. Thus subjects studied 63 words altogether before receiving a test, the nature of which was not specified beforehand.

Four different tests were given, as can be seen in Fig. 24.5. Test type was manipulated between subjects. Free recall is considered a conceptually driven episodic memory test. The data-driven episodic memory test created by Blaxton (1985) was cued recall with words that looked like the target words (e.g., CHOPPER for COPPER.) Subjects taking this test were carefully instructed that they were to try to recall words that looked like the cue words and were told that the meaning of the cues was irrelevant to the task. The data-driven semantic memory task was word fragment completion, on which these subjects told simply to think of the first word possible to complete the word fragment. Half the fragments given were for studied words and half for nonstudied words, with the two sets counterbalanced across subjects. The conceptually driven semantic memory test was a test of general knowledge (Nelson & Narens, 1980), e.g., "What metal makes up ten percent of yellow gold?" For half the questions given

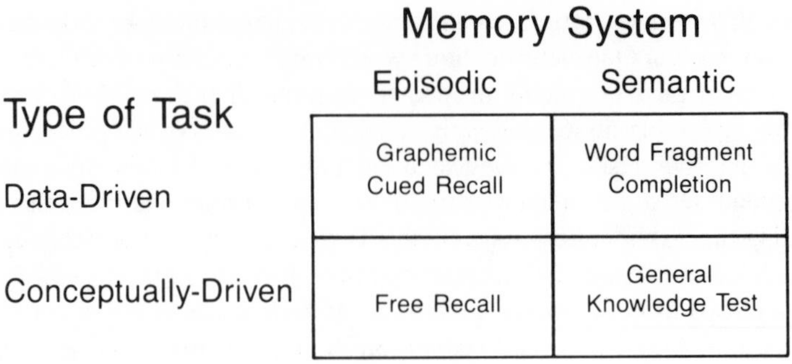

Memory System

Episodic   Semantic

Type of Task

	Episodic	Semantic
Data-Driven	Graphemic Cued Recall	Word Fragment Completion
Conceptually-Driven	Free Recall	General Knowledge Test

1. Graphemic Cued Recall: CHOPPER
2. Free Recall: No cues given
3. Word Fragment Completion: C __ P__ E__
4. General Knowledge Test: What makes up 10% of yellow gold?

FIGURE 24.5.   Test conditions used in Blaxton (1985, Experiment 1).

on the test, the correct answer was a previously studied word and for half it was not. Thus, for the two semantic memory tests, a base line of nonstudied words was included to assess priming from prior study.

The results are presented in Table 24.6. If the memory systems approach to explaining dissociations between study and test conditions is accurate, then we should expect to see performance similar in the two episodic tasks (free recall and cued recall with graphemic cues), and different from that in the two semantic tasks (word fragment completion and accessing general knowledge). On the other hand, if the transfer appropriate processing view is more accurate, we should expect to see similar performance in the tasks emphasizing data-driven

TABLE 24.6
Results of Blaxton (1985) Experiment 1
(Reproduced with permission.)

	Study Condition			
Task	No Context	Context	Generate	Nonstudied
Free recall	.19	.16	.30	——
General knowledge	.33	.38	.50	.25
Graphemic cued recall	.45	.40	.34	.06
Word fragment completion	.75	.62	.46	.27

processing for their completion (word fragment completion and graphemic cued recall) and a different pattern in the tasks requiring conceptually driven processing (free recall and accessing general knowledge). As is apparent from Table 24.6, the data support the transfer appropriate processing view. As expected, generated items produced better performance than those read without context in both the free recall and general knowledge tests. These are both supposed to involve conceptually driven processing, although they tap different memory systems. However, for word fragment completion and graphemic cued recall (the data-driven tests), this pattern is reversed. Here, items studied in the No Context condition transferred better to the test than those in the Generate condition. Performance in the Context condition is generally intermediate between the other two conditions, except in free recall. Thus, these data suggest that the transfer appropriate processing approach provides the better interpretation of dissociation experiments than does the postulation of memory systems.

CONCLUDING COMMENTS

The argument put forward here is that dissociations among measures of retention can be best interpreted within a framework emphasizing the transfer appropriate procedures between study experiences and test occasions (Kolers & Roediger, 1984; Morris et al., 1977). Further, the distinction between data-driven and conceptually driven processing (Jacoby, 1983) is useful in describing differences among retention tests. Because these ideas are relatively new, some criticisms and qualifications are in order, as well as descriptions of future research that would be useful in testing these ideas.

First, how can one distinguish between data-driven and conceptually driven memory tests? What converging operations can be proposed? In these initial stages of inquiry a bootstrapping operation has been employed; that is, tasks that are sensitive to changes in surface features of information at study (modality, language, etc.) are said to be data-driven, whereas tasks that are relatively insensitive to such manipulations are classed as conceptually driven. A converging operation *can* be specified: Conceptually driven tasks should be greatly affected by study manipulations that vary elaborative processing, such as generating rather than reading items, or generating images to words rather than their rote repetition, etc. These same manipulations should have little effect, or even an opposite effect, on data-driven tests (depending on how the materials are presented at study). Thus, two converging operations can be proposed to distinguish data-driven from conceptually driven memory tests. The former should be greatly affected by changes in the surface form of studied information, but little affected by elaborate operations, and conversely for conceptually driven tests.

A second refinement, to expand on a remark made earlier, is that the data-driven/conceptually driven distinction should properly be considered as end-points on a continuum rather than a strict dichotomy. Most memory tests will likely have components of each type of processing. For example, some theorists believe that recognition can be accomplished either by a fast-acting judgment process or a slower, more reflective deliberation usually called "memory search" (e.g., Atkinson & Juola, 1974; Mandler, 1980). In Jacoby's (1983) terms, the former would be aligned with data-driven and the latter with concep-tually driven processing. However, the balance between these two can be changed by test manipulations (Johnston, et al., 1985).

The same combination of influences is likely to be found on other tasks. The primary tasks that have been used to measure "retention without awareness" are (a) perceptual identification, (b) visual or auditory thresholds, (c) word fragment completion, (d) word stem completion, and (e) reading inverted text. These measures show priming effects in amnesics of roughly the same magnitude as found in normal subjects (except [b], which has not been examined to our knowledge). We would class all these as primarily data-driven tasks, but dif-ferences among them are found as a function of input modality. For example, auditory presentation of material produces no priming on measures of perceptual identification (Jacoby & Dallas, 1981, Experiment 6) or visual thresholds (Mor-ton, 1979; Winnick & Daniel, 1970), but does produce facilitation in word stem completion (Graf, et al., 1985), word fragment completion (Roediger & Blax-ton, 1987) and the reading of inverted text (Kolers, 1975).

Obviously, then, using cross-modal priming as an index of how data-driven a task is leads to the conclusion that perceptual identification and visual duration thresholds are more data-driven than are word stem completion, word fragment completion and reading inverted text. It would be of interest to see if these tasks order themselves the same way in detecting other changes in form of presenta-tion, such as language of presentation for bilinguals, or verbal and pictorial representations. As yet, data are not available, even across experiments, to make meaningful comparisons on these dimensions. However, from our own experi-ments we can see indications that word fragment completion, when used as a memory test, is not completely data-driven. Besides cross-modal priming (Roediger & Blaxton, 1987), pictures produce reliable (if small) priming effects (Weldon & Roediger, 1987), as do instructions to form images of words' refer-ents (Blaxton, 1985). The large cross-modal priming effect seems to indicate the role of a lexical representation (on fragment completion) that is shared by items presented visually and auditorily. The effects from other modes of presentation may indicate small amounts of conceptual priming.

A further clarification is in order in describing tasks as data-driven. The meaning attached to this statement is that they are data-driven when used as tests of retention for recent episodes by presenting isolated items. We do not mean that no conceptual processes are ever used in perceptual identification, fragment completion, or (certainly) reading inverted text. For example, if appropriate contexts are given, visual duration thresholds for words can be increased or decreased (Tulving & Gold, 1963). Surely similar conceptual manipulations would affect the other measures, whether these were used to measure retention for recently presented episodes or for "semantic memory" information. Unpublished data collected by the first author in collaboration with Bradford Challis and Valerie Ludwick show that this assumption holds true for word fragment completion, because modification of fragments by synonyms, associates and the like greatly enhances subjects' ability to complete the fragments, relative to the condition in which fragments are presented without context.

Another important facet of these tasks that measure retention without awareness is the instructions given to the subjects. Following the tradition of research with amnesics, these tasks are often not presented as retention tests. Rather, because subjects can potentially complete each task without recourse to memory for the episode, they are simply told before the test phase to identify the words or to complete the fragments, etc., as well as possible. In fact, different effects may be found when subjects are told to use the cues given at test to produce previously studied material, as Graf and Mandler (1984, Experiment 3) have shown in the case of word stem completion. Another obvious direction for future research is to see how sensitive these tasks are to manipulation of subjects' expectancies.

Other classifications have been proposed to account for differences in tasks that measure retention with and without awareness. These include the episodic/semantic distinction (Tulving, 1983), the procedural/declarative distinction (Cohen & Squire, 1980), and the description of the tasks as measuring implicit versus explicit memory (Graf & Schacter, 1985). These typologies partly overlap those of data-driven and conceptually driven processing as described by Jacoby (1983) and developed here. A primary task for future research is to discover which of these distinctions is most useful for understanding the dissociations among measures of retention. The ideas put forward here have the advantage of (a) emphasizing processing components of tasks rather than metaphysical systems lurking in the mind, (b) permitting operationalization of the terms, and (c) providing relatively straightforward means of falsification of the ideas if converging operations do not bear out the ordering of tasks in terms of their data-driven and conceptually driven components.

ACKNOWLEDGMENTS

We would like to thank Robert R. Hoffman, James H. Neely, Endel Tulving, and Mary Susan Weldon for their comments on a prior draft of the manuscript. The research reported here was supported by Grant RO1 HD15054 from the National Institute of Child Health and Human Development.

25

Functional Dissociation: Comments on the Chapter by Roediger and Blaxton

David S. Gorfein
Adelphi University

Roediger and Blaxton have developed the justification for their theorizing on the basis of the functional dissociation in performance of several memory tasks following a common learning experience. Their work on free recall, recognition and word fragment completion shows differing patterns of performance as a function of orienting tasks. The authors offer a framework—transfer appropriate procedures—to interpret the outcome of these several studies as well as the other literature reviewed. In essence, this analysis is similar to that of Kolers (1975) in suggesting that the amount of intertask transfer obtained is a function of the similarity in operations required by the tasks in question.

In commenting on their chapter I focus on the utility of "functional dissociation" in theorizing rather than on specific content. Two specific instances of functional dissociation came to mind as having lead to considerable theoretical controversy in the relatively recent history of the psychology of memory. One was concerned with the serial position effect, i.e., in free recall wherein a variable (e.g., delay) that influenced one portion of the free-recall list (recency) had no apparent effect on other portions of the list (cf., i.e., Glanzer & Cunitz, 1966). The other dissociation was between two memory tasks, i.e., list memory as opposed to short-term memory. Where it was generally agreed that list memory was strongly influenced by the learning of other lists (retroactive and proactive inhibition) cf., Postman, 1961, the early reports with respect to the distractor paradigm (Brown, 1958; Peterson & Peterson, 1959) suggested that forgetting in that task was due to decay of the memory trace over time.

The current views of both of these controversies suggest that the postulating of new theoretical mechanisms to account for dissociations can often be premature.

Specifically with respect to the serial position effect in free recall, early attempts to explain the dissociation postulated theoretical mechanisms as short-term store or working memory with a "dump" of that store prior to retrieval from long-term store, creating the recency effect (cf., e.g., Atkinson & Shiffrin, 1968). There were some early nonbelievers in the two-store theory, including Tulving (1968) who wrote:

> I prefer the view that all input information is stored in the same unitary storage system, whatever its nature, and the differences in recall of early, middle, and late input items reflect primarily differences in the accessibility of these items. (p. 15)

The majority bought the need to postulate two separate stores (cf., the text of Klatzky, 1975). In the ensuing years, however, a number of lines of thought and investigation, including the levels-of-processing framework (Craik & Lockhart, 1972), the work of Baddeley and Hitch, (1974), and the demonstration of long-term recency, (Bjork & Whitten, 1974) have lead to a rejection of the two-store model in favor of more sophisticated versions of a single-store theory. (The reader is referred to Glenberg's chapter in this volume for discussion of some of the current trends.)

In the case of the short-term memory distractor procedure, the apparent dissociation between that procedure and list memory was quickly assimilated into the interference theory framework of the time by some well-conceived experiments (i.e., Keppel & Underwood, 1962; Wickens, Born, & Allen, 1963) and a brilliant overview paper by Melton (1963). Nevertheless, the two-process view (decay versus interference) continued to maintain support, as shown by the development of several new theories including Posner's (1966) imaginative acid-bath model. Bennett's 1975 paper offered compelling reasons to reject most decay models. A current view of the problem can be found in chapter 10 of this volume.

In their chapter, Roediger and Blaxton are responding to the position taken by Tulving (1983) that postulates multiple memory systems. In focusing on transfer appropriate procedures, we believe the authors are on solid ground and are taking a position consistent with the history of other recent functional dissociations in the memory literature (i.e., by not finding additional memory stores necessary). It should be noted that Hintzman (1984) makes a similar argument against the episode-semantic memory distinction of Tulving. It is ironic that Tulving, who is quoted previously for his early stand against the two-storage model, appears now as the champion of the multiple memory systems view (Tulving, 1983).

What then can we conclude from recent work on functional dissociation? It seems that such dissociations will tend to be powerful stimuli to the researchers in the field, and justly so. However, we tend to the intemperate in our response to such dissociations. On each occasion we have had the current theoretical view rejected as a consequence of the newly discovered dissociation, only to have the theory reinstated by further experimentation and thought. Perhaps it is time, in the 100th year after Ebbinghaus, that our field showed the maturity to attempt to incorporate a new finding into its abiding viewpoint before offering a proliferation of additional memory stores to account for a few new data points.

VI OVERVIEW

26 Functional and Cognitive Memory Theory: An Overview of Some Key Issues

Harry F. Bahrick
Ohio Wesleyan University

INTRODUCTION

I confess that I approached the task of summing up this book without a proper appreciation of its challenges. Ideally, an overall summary should provide an integrative and objective account of the various chapters and the discussions which followed them. My comments are perhaps better described in the words Underwood (1966) used when he undertook a similar task 20 years ago. He referred to his observations as a "varied, perhaps even a ragged lot." Of course, Underwood was inappropriately modest in his self-assessment, but I now know that success in identifying unifying themes is limited by the great diversity of issues discussed at this conference, and by my own ignorance of some of the issues. Moreover, my own biases necessarily affect my selections and interpretations. I agree with Wertheimer (1979) who said:

> There is no such thing as a definitive, correct history of anything. What is fished out of the stream of events as worth paying attention to, and how what is selected is to be interpreted, depends ultimately on the idiosyncratic, subjective biases of the historian. (p. 9)

However, awareness of subjectivity will not stop us from trying to make sense out of the history of memory research.

The issues that I raise are not new, and they are not limited to the chapters presented here, or even to memory research. But I believe that they are particularly relevant to the recent evolution of theories of memory, and they are well illustrated by the chapters in this book. I raise three interrelated issues; they deal with (a) the language of memory theory, (b) the extent to which memory theory stipulates specific cognitive processes, and (c) the extent to which memory theory is organizational rather than associative.

THE NEW TERMINOLOGY OF MEMORY THEORIES

Psychologists have had frequent occasion to debate the rules that govern the formulation of theory. One area of agreement that emerged from these discussions concerns the desirability of avoiding ambiguity and the need to establish clear relations between the concepts used and the phenomena to which the concepts refer. The dangers of ambiguity first became apparent during the early introspective era of psychology. The frustrations engendered by irresolvable theoretical controversies led American psychologists to adopt a narrow behavioristic paradigm. Later, more sophisticated guidelines for developing an appropriate language of science emerged under the tutelage of an empirically oriented philosophy of science (Feigl, 1943; Stevens, 1939). Dissatisfaction with the restrictions of behavioristic research increased, and the availability of computer science methods for analyzing processes of encoding, transforming, and retrieving information led to the emergence of a new, and less-restrictive cognitive psychology. This new paradigm has enlarged the scope of inquiry, and recovered the option of extending psychological research to a variety of mental processes. Psychologists again explore the relations of cognitive processes (both conscious and non conscious) to other phenomena. Most of the chapters in this volume illustrate this domain of cognitive psychology.

Clearly we are once again trying to find out more about the way in which the world of objects relates to the world of ideas. However, history does not ever quite repeat itself, or science would be a futile endeavor. We must go about our business differently from the way we did 100 years ago, and the changes must reflect the lessons learned the first time around.

Herrmann and Chaffin point out that introspection is once again viewed as an appropriate method for certain problems. Baars makes the point that cognitive psychologists have found it necessary over the past two decades to bring back almost the entire vocabulary of psychological common sense into scientific psychology, and he is not critical of this development. Slamecka agrees that this has happened, but he clearly disapproves. He quotes a long list of cognitive terms from "accepting," "activating," "adding," to "transforming," "understanding" and "using," and sides with those who consider the new vocabulary to be one of speculative abandon. He points out that Ebbinghaus' approach to specifying cognitive processes was a great deal more disciplined 100 years ago, and he might have added that psychology was mentalistic at that time and had not yet sustained penalties for developing theories that extended far beyond the capacity of available methods of verification. I wish that Slamecka had pursued this theme further because it is so central in relating the present to the past, but he devotes the rest of his chapter to the status of specific empirical issues.

I defer discussing changes in the focus of memory research during the past 100 years, and at this point address only the matter of maintaining an appropriate theoretical language. I believe this matter to be of great importance and to require constant discipline. The contributors to this volume vary widely with regard to their self-imposed discipline, and their diversity reflects current practices of the field.

Cognitive psychologists have advanced the field by imaginative investigations that reveal how the mind functions when engaged in a variety of tasks. We are no longer required to treat the mind as if it were a black box; rather, the methods of cognitive psychology give information about processes inside the box. Historians of psychology have said that psychology first lost its soul, and then its mind, and in the future they will surely report that the mind was recovered during the cognitive era. However, these gains reflect the skillful applications of new methods and the inferences they yield about mental processing; they do not only or merely reflect the reintroduction of common-sense vocabulary into psychological theorizing. We all admire William James' literate descriptions of consciousness, but his rhetoric was far ahead of his data, and his legacy is one of beautifully expressed, insightful ideas, not one of empirically verified conclusions. This conference celebrates the contributions of Ebbinghaus, not of James, and Slamecka is surely correct in his view that Ebbinghaus did not permit his conclusions to get far ahead of his data. I agree with Baars that psychologists have brought back most of the common sense psychological vocabulary, but I fear that this has happened frequently without observing Baars' injunction that it be done legitimately, by anchoring each common sense term to distinct and reliable empirical phenomena.

Manuscripts I have recently reviewed for the *Journal of Experimental Psychology* use constructs such as the "overall meaning of one's life" or the "autobiographical self-knowledge system." Such global abstractions cannot be tied closely to the observations of experiments; therefore the data cannot serve to document theory, they can be illustrative at best. The absence of close ties between observations and theory seriously restricts the testability of theory, and limits the basis on which alternative positions can be evaluated. The discipline of closely linking our theoretical language to empirical phenomena requires continuing thought and research, and if we fail to keep our house in order we will surely end with an accumulation of untestable theory and irresolvable problems comparable with those that lead to the abandonment of introspective psychology early in this century.

FUNCTIONAL VERSUS COGNITIVE EMPHASIS

My second, and related theme contrasts functional and cognitive approaches in memory theory. By functional approaches I refer to theories that attempt to establish parsimonious relations between manipulated variables and memory performance without necessarily attempting to reach conclusions about internal processing. In contrast, cognitive approaches focus on the nature of the mental processing, the stages, the strategies, and the nature of the mental representation. The major purpose of the empirical work from this approach is the ability to draw inferences about what is going on inside the head. I do not mean to suggest that current theorizing can be neatly classified into a dichotomy. The dominance of the cognitive *Zeitgeist* has led most investigators to be concerned about internal processing, but there exists much variation in emphasis, and it is possible to distinguish between investigations that directly address cognitive questions, and investigations that have primarily functional goals and treat cognitive questions as secondary.

Applying this distinction to the papers presented at this conference, it would seem to me that several contributions have a clear cognitive emphasis. Reder, for example, attempts to determine to what extent the recognition decisions of individuals are based on plausibility judgments and to what extent they are based on familiarity judgments. Chaffin and Herrmann wish to establish whether associations are represented in the form of specific components, or as unitary phenomena. Baars' chapter deals most directly with the nature of conscious content in a variety of tasks.

In contrast, the chapters that deal with context effects are generally more functional in nature. Their aim is to give a parsimonious account of the effects of various aspects of the environmental context on memory performance. Inferences about processing are relatively secondary—Wickens' contribution, for example, sorts out two distinct, but previously insufficiently differentiated uses of the term "context." He proposes that "context alpha" refers to aspects of the experimental environment not intrinsically related to the task, and "context beta" to those aspects that help to define the meaning of target items or the task. The data he reviews have cognitive implications. Although a particular context is intrinsically unrelated to the meaning of a task, and would therefore clearly be type alpha, other aspects of context may gradually define meaning as the individual acquires relevant knowledge. Accordingly, such context would change from context alpha to context beta as the individual becomes aware of previously ignored contingencies. My point is that Wickens' chapter makes significant contributions to the functional analysis of memory performance. The chapter has implications for the nature of cognitive processes, but such implications are relatively independent of the functional contribution.

It seems to me that Gorfein's distinction between environmental and semantic context addresses similar points. The PI release paradigm provides a method for determining semantic encoding and for demonstrating the extent to which semantic release depends on the prior knowledge of the individual. Gorfein's chapter certainly involves considerations of cognitive processing, but the major thrust is functional.

The same is true of Glenberg's discussion of temporal context and context discrimination. He shows that this dimension can be used to account for recency effects. The temporal context can become an important retrieval cue when other aspects of the retrieval environment are impoverished.

Slamecka reviews the effects on recall of variations of local context (i.e., the sequence of words within which a particular target item is embedded during learning). The context words are sometimes related and sometimes unrelated to the target words. Therefore this study involves variations of both context alpha and beta, following Wickens' terminology. Slamecka finds that neither type of variation has important overriding effects on experiments that test the law of frequency. In multitrial learning, the principle of encoding specificity becomes trivial in import in relation to the law of frequency.

The chapters dealing with various aspects of context all contribute knowledge about the way in which internal and external environmental conditions affect retrieval. We have known for some time that retrieval is optimal when the retrieval environment mirrors the encoding environment, but a more analytical approach is needed to determine the relative importance of various aspects of the experimental environment in a variety of tasks and situations. The chapters by Glenberg, Gorfein, Roediger, Slamecka, and Wickens all contribute significantly to this end.

It seems to me that functional and cognitive orientations in theory development are complementary, and that progress of both types is needed for the development of psychological science. Reliable inferences concerning cognitive processes must be based on a parsimonious, functional analysis of independent and dependent variables. Inference about cause–effect relations will remain the primary method of cognitive psychology unless we develop more satisfactory methods for obtaining direct knowledge of cognition. Systematic introspection and verbal reports are used again in cognitive research, but introspection cannot play the role it did 100 years ago (i.e., it cannot provide the primary basis for establishing the nature of cognitive content or process). The reasons for this are that cognitive processes may or may not be represented in our awareness, (see Baars' chapter and that of Roediger & Blaxton), and that strong inferences based on empirical findings may be counterintuitive (i.e., they may yield conclusions contrary to our introspections). The existence of memory without awareness was already discussed by Ebbinghaus, and this evidence has been reviewed by Roediger and Blaxton, who point out that the savings method measures retention without being limited to content that is introspectively familiar to the subject (see also Nelson, 1985).

I believe that the attention of our metatheorists must be directed at establishing more rigorous guidelines for drawing inferences about cause–effect relations in cognitive processes and contents. This is not the first time we have debated the merits of stipulating explicit cognitive processes that are not directly observed. During the 1940s and 1950s psychologists debated the comparative merits of hypothetical constructs and intervening variables in theory construction. The former assert the existence of entities and the occurrence of events not reducible to the observable whereas the latter refer to relations among variables without hypothesizing the existence of nonobserved entities or the occurrence of unobserved processes (MacCorquodale & Meehl, 1948). This distinction is also involved in my present differentiation between functional and cognitive approaches to memory theory.

Methodological advances based on accomplishments of the computer sciences may now provide a firmer basis for cognitive inference. The hypothetical constructs of cognitive psychology are built on this foundation. The new constructs are not directly observed, but they are not merely plausible, functional analogies. They are the product of inference. There is now widespread agreement that psychologists can and should seek to make such inferences, but it is imperative that progress be monitored, and that sources of error be identified and contained, so that we can profit from experience. I would like to contribute to that effort by suggesting two sources of errors of cognitive conclusions. I refer to them as the "semantic gap" and the "inferential gap."

THE SEMANTIC GAP

The semantic gap is created when we give a name to a cognitive process or representation. The name, particularly if it is used in ordinary language, may have a broad range of meanings; and ambiguities or metaphors that are inherent in that usage are likely to become a liability in establishing the desired close relation between the phenomenon of interest and the label of reference. The term "context" is a good example. It has a variety of meanings, and Wickens found it necessary to develop a more precise psychological taxonomy to accommodate the diversity of empirical findings obtained when variables are grouped in accordance with the common-sense usages of the term.

The semantic gap derives not only from the ambiguities of using commonsense vocabulary in psychology, it also reflects the potential error of overgeneralizing from the indicant used in a study to the conceptually broader label used to refer to the observations. For example, in my own recent investigation of the retention of Spanish language learned in school (Bahrick, 1984a), I used a subtest of Spanish recall vocabulary, and my conclusions about the retention of Spanish recall vocabulary are based on this test. Theoretical interpretations relating the loss of Spanish recall vocabulary to various independent variables may lose sight of the fact that the data are based on a specific test. Erroneous conclusions are likely if the subtest used is too easy, too difficult, or in other ways not representative of the total Spanish vocabulary of the individuals who were tested. Interval and ratio comparisons are justified on the basis of test scores, but they are no longer justified for the generalized construct. Thus, one individual's score on my test may be twice as large as another individual's, but it would not be legitimate to conclude that the Spanish vocabulary of these individuals stood in the same ratio.

To some degree all psychological theory involves extrapolations, not just in the statistical sense in which we generally assess the risk of quantitative generalization, but also in the semantic domain in which we have no sound basis for estimating error due to extrapolation from an indicant to the class of phenomena under investigation (Nelson, 1985). This type of error is particularly prominent when common-sense vocabulary is used in psychological theories, because of the wide range of meanings often associated with common-sense terms.

THE INFERENTIAL GAP

The second source of error is the inferential process that provides the basis for establishing cognitive conclusions. The logic of such inferences can be a source of error to the extent in which a given set of data permits alternative inferences concerning the nature of cognition. The history of cognitive research already shows that virtually every major conclusion has been challenged by subsequent investigators. Such challenges per se do not constitute an indictment of cognitive psychology, but they can and should provide the basis for examining and developing some sort of standards of acceptable inference. Failure to narrow the inferential gap is likely to leave us with an accumulation of unmanageable cognitive theory, reminiscent of our introspective and philosophical past.

In contrast, functional theory is relatively unencumbered by an inferential gap because functional theory does not purport to establish the nature of cognitive phenomena. The semantic gap is also narrower for functional theory because indicants of the phenomena to be named can be directly inspected and ambiguities as well as overgeneralizations are more easily diagnosed. Thus, in the examples given earlier, research can establish the extent to which the term "context" must be redefined to yield parsimonious functional relations with dependent variables; and research with a variety of tests of Spanish vocabulary can establish to what extent the various tests yield consistent inferences with regard to the the total Spanish vocabulary of the individuals who are tested. Such research is far more difficult for cognitive processes, which must be inferred from relations among variables, rather than being directly linked to a particular indicant.

It is not my intention to advocate that we abandon cognitive theorizing and limit ourselves to the functional kind. The major advances of psychological science have occurred when new methods were developed that opened previously inaccessible phenomena to empirical study. Psychophysical methods, Ebbinghaus' methods, conditioning techniques, and electrode implant technology all illustrate such progress. We seem to get into trouble by treating new methods as panaceas, i.e., we apply them to the resolution of questions which do not yield to them. The overextended use of methods has retarded the development of psychological science by prolonging fruitless research and by promoting a *Fachgeist* sustained by polemics, rather than empirical findings. This was true during the "structuralist" era dominated by introspective methods and also during the behavioristic era dominated by conditioning technology.

The cognitive era has already produced a number of important methodological advances and refinements of existing methods, such as Sternberg's (1969) methods of investigating rapid scanning processes, the PI release procedures developed by Wickens and his associates (Wickens, 1970; Wickens, Born, & Allen 1963), and the "levels of processing" framework of Craik and Lockhart (1972). Each yielded valuable inferences regarding the nature of cognitive processing. However, the second and third generation of studies in each domain failed to yield greater certitude, let alone more precision. This was an indication that the methods had been overextended, so that cognitive inferences could not provide definitive answers to the questions being asked. Progress seems to depend on recognizing when existing methods are overtaxed, and on developing new methods in dealing with intractable problems.

ASSOCIATIONIST AND ORGANIZATIONAL THEORY

My remaining comments relate to the distinction between organizational views of memory, pioneered by Bartlett (1932), and the associationist tradition that provided the framework for the contributions of Ebbinghaus. This conference celebrates the work of Ebbinghaus and it is therefore not surprising that most of the contributions reflect an associationist emphasis, either implicitly or explicitly, a for example, the chapter by Chaffin and Herrmann. Hoffman, Bringmann, Bandiey, and Klein have pointed out that Ebbinghaus was quite aware of the importance of interpretive processes in memory, a point that I have also stressed elsewhere (Bahrick, 1984b, 1985) and that his work should not be viewed as the product of doctrinaire associationism. Rather, his contribution was primarily functional. The methods he developed lent themselves to the study of associations, not to the study of organizational principles, and for this reason doctrinaire associationist positions were linked with the Ebbinghaus legacy.

Reder makes the point that associationist and organizational views of memory are complementary. I have also stressed this point elsewhere (Bahrick, 1984b, 1985) and have discussed evidence indicating that individuals will use multiple strategies to retrieve information from memory (Bahrick, 1970, 1979). The same position has also been argued by Jones (1982), and by Ceraso (this volume) who shows how generic recall strategies, based on organizational knowledge, are invoked when accurate recall based on specific associations has failed. Reder makes a significant contribution to the analysis of such multiple strategies and the circumstances under which they are likely to be invoked. Her chapter provides an excellent example of the use of the inferential process in the resolution of questions regarding the nature of cognitive processes.

In contrast, it seems to me that earlier work attempting to demonstrate that all memory processes are organizational rather than associative, illustrates the over-extended use of the inferential process. The inferential method can indicate that specific retrieval performance involves organizational processes, but it cannot demonstrate that *no* associative processes are involved, or that *all* retrieval phenomena are organizational in nature.

Future progress in this area will require a redirection of emphasis toward the resolvable questions. These questions concern the extent of and the nature of organizational processing as a function of the duration of the retention interval, the type of memory content, the age of the individual, the previous knowledge of the individual, motivational variables, etc. Such parametric research will provide the basis for integrating the contributions of Ebbinghaus with the contributions of Bartlett, and lead to the development of models of memory that can do justice to the multifaceted characteristics of the human memory system.

ACKNOWLEDGMENT

This material is based upon work supported by the National Science Foundation under Grant BNS–8417788.

References

Abernathy, E. M. (1940). The effect of change in environmental conditions upon the results of college exams. *Journal of Psychology, 10,* 293–301.

Aquinas, T. (1273/1967). *Summa Theological.* Blackfriars edition. New York: McGraw Hill.

Adams, M. J. (1981). What good is orthographic redundancy? In O. J. L. Tzeng and H. Singer (Eds.), *Perception in Print: Reading Research in Experimental Psychology.* Hillsdale, NJ: Lawrence Erlbaum Associates.

Adams, M. J. (1979). Models of word recognition. *Cognitive Psychology, 11,* 133–176.

Anderson, J. A. (1973). A theory for the recognition of items from short memorized lists. *Psychological Review, 80,* 417–438.

Anderson, J. A. (1970). Two models for memory organization using interacting traces. *Mathematical Biosciences, 8,* 137–160.

Anderson, J. A. and Hinton, G. E. (1981). Models of information processing in the brain. In G. E. Hinton and J. A. Anderson (Eds.), *Parallel models of associative memory.* Hillsdale, NJ: Lawrence Erlbaum Associates.

Anderson, J. R. (1983). *The architecture of cognition.* Cambridge, MA: Harvard University Press.

Anderson, J. R. (1981). Concepts, propositions, and schemata: What are the cognitive units? In J. H. Flowers (Ed.), *Nebraska Symposium on Motivation, 1980: Cognitive Processes, Vol. 28.* Lincoln, NE: University of Nebraska Press.

Anderson, J. R. (1976). *Language, memory, and thought.* Hillsdale, NJ: Lawrence Erlbaum Associates.

Anderson, J. R. (1974). Retrieval of propositional information from long-term memory. *Cognitive Psychology, 5,* 451–474.

Anderson, J. R. (1972). FRAN: A simulation model of free recall. In G. H. Bower (Ed.), *The Psychology of Learning and Motivation: Advances in Research and Theory, Vol. 5.* New York, NY: Academic Press.

Anderson, J. R., and Bower, G. H. (1973). *Human associative memory.* Hillsdale, NJ: Lawrence Erlbaum Associates.

Anderson, J. R., and Bower, G. H. (1972). Configural properties in sentence memory. *Journal of Verbal Learning and Verbal Behavior, 11,* 594–605.

Anderson, N. S. (1960). Poststimulus cuing in immediate memory. *Journal of Experimental Psychology, 60,* 216–221.

Angell, F. (1900). Discrimination of clangs for different intervals of time. *American Journal of Psychology, 12,* 58–79.

Angell, F., and Harwood, M. (1899). Experiments on discrimination of clangs for different intervals of time. *American Journal of Psychology, 11,* 67–79.

Anonymous (circa 100 B. C./1954). *Ad C. Herennium De ratione dicendi.* Translated by Harry Caplan. In *The Loeb Classical Library* (T. E. Warrington, Ed.). London, England: Heinemann. (often incorrectly attributed to Cicero).

Anonymous (c. 500 B.C./1927). *Mnemosyne (Memory)* Edited and translated by J. M. Edwards, Lyra Graeca, Vol. III; The Loeb *Classical Library.* T. E. Page, E. Capps., and W. H. D. Rouse (Eds.) London, England: Heinemann.

Anzai, Y., and Simon, H. A. (1979). The theory of learning by doing. *Psychological Review, 86,* 124–140.

Apreysan, Y. D., Mel'cuk, I. A., and Zolkovsky (1970). Semantics and lexicography: Toward a new type of unilingual dictionary. In F. Kiejer (Ed.), *Studies in syntax and semantics.* Dordrecht, Holland: Reidel.

Arbib, M. A. (1982). Perceptual structures and distributed motor control. In V. B. Brooks (Ed.), *Handbook of physiology, Volume 3.* American Physiological Society.

Aristophanes (circa 423 B.C./1962). *The Clouds,* Translated by B. B. Rogers. *The Loeb Classical Library,* T. E. Page, E. Capps, W. H. Rouse, L. A. Post, and E. H. Warmington (Eds.) London, England: Heinemann.

Aristotle (circa 330 B.C./1928–1952). *The Works of Aristotle,* 12 vols. Edited and translated by J. A. Smith and W. D. Ross. Oxford, England: Oxford University Press.

Ash, M. G. (1982). Reflections on psychology in history. In W. R. Woodward and M. G. Ash (Eds.), *The problematic science: Psychology in nineteenth-century thought.* New York, NY: Praeger.

Asch, S. E. (1968). The doctrinal tyranny of associationism: Or what is wrong with rote learning. In T. Dixon and D. Horton (Eds.), *Verbal behavior and general behavior theory.* Englewood Cliffs, NJ: Prentice-Hall.

Asratian, E. A. (1972). Genesis and localization of conditioned inhibition. In R. A. Boakes and M. S. Halliday (Eds.) *Inhibition and learning.* New York, NY: Academic Press.

Atkinson, R. C., and Juola, J. F. (1973). Factors influencing speed and accuracy of word recognition. In S. Kornblum (Ed.), *Attention and performance, Vol. 4.* New York, NY: Academic Press.

Atkinson, R. C., and Shiffrin, R. M. (1968). Human memory: A proposed system and its control processes. In K. W. Spence and J. T. Spence (Eds.), *The psychology of learning and motivation: Advances in research and theory, Vol. 2.* New York, NY: Academic Press.

Augustine (circa 410 A.D./1955). *Confessions and Enchiridion.* Translated and edited by A. C. Outer. Philadelphia, PA: Westminister Press.

Baars, B. J. (forthcoming, a). *A cognitive theory of consciousness.* London, England: Cambridge University Press.

Baars, B. J. (Ed.) (forthcoming, b). *The psychology of error: A window on the mind.* New York, NY: Plenum Press.

Baars, B. J. (1986). *The cognitive revolution in psychology.* New York, NY: The Guilford Press.

Baars, B. J. (1985a). Can involuntary slips reveal one's state of mind?—with an addendum on the conscious control of speech. In M. Toglia & T. M. Schlechter (Eds.), *New directions in cognitive science.* Norwood, NJ: Ablex Publishing.

Baars, B. J. (1985b). Biological implications of a global workspace theory of conscious experience. In G. Greenberg & E. Tobach (Eds.), *Language, cognition, consciousness: Integrative levels.,* Hillsdale, NJ: Lawrence Erlbaum Associates.

Baars, B. J. (1983). Conscious contents provide the nervous system with coherent, global information. In R. Davidson, G. Schwartz, & D. Shapiro (Eds.), *Consciousness and self-regulation, Volume 3.* New York, NY: Plenum Press.

Baars, B. J. (1980a). On eliciting predictable speech errors in the laboratory: Methods and results. In V. A. Fromkin (Ed.) *Errors of speech and hearing.* New York, NY: Academic Press.

Baars, B. J. (1980b). The Competing Plans Hypothesis: An heuristic approach to the causes of errors in speech. In H. Dechert and M. Raupach (Eds.) *Temporal factors in the control of speech.* Paris, France: Mouton.

Baars, B. J., Motley, M. T., and MacKay, D. G. (1975). Output editing for lexical status in artificially elicited slips of the tongue. *Journal of Verbal Learning and Verbal Behavior, 14,* 382–391.

Bacon, F. (1597–1623/1905). *The philosophic works of Francis Bacon.* Reprinted from translations by Ellis and Spedeling. Edited by John M. Rovertson. London, England: Routledge and Sons.

Baddeley, A. D. (1982). Domains of recollection. *Psychological Review, 89,* 708–729.

Baddeley, A. D. (1976). *The psychology of memory.* New York, NY: Basic Books.

Baddeley, A. D., Cuccaro, W. J., Egstrom, G., and Willis, M. A. (1975). Cognitive efficiency of divers working in cold water. *Human Factors, 17,* 446–454.

Baddeley, A. D. and Hitch, G. J. (1974). Working memory. In G. H. Bower, (Ed.), *The psychology of learning and motivation, Vol. 8,* New York, NY: Academic Press, 83–103.

Baddeley, A. D., and Hitch G. (1977). Recency examined. In S. Dornic (Ed.), *Attention and performance, Vol. 6,* Hillsdale, NJ: Lawrence Erlbaum Associates. 647–667.

Bahrick, H. (1985a). Personal communication based on his conversations with Julius Ebbinghaus. Department of Psychology, Ohio Wesleyan University, Delaware, OH.

Bahrick, H. P. (1985b). *The laboratory and the ecology: Supplementary sources of data for memory research.* The third George A. Talland conference on Memory and Aging. Cape Cod, MA.

Bahrick, H. P. (1985c). Associationism and the Ebbinghaus Legacy. *Journal of Experimental Psychology: Learning, Memory, and Cognition, 11,* 439–443.

Bahrick, H. P. (1984a). Semantic memory content in permastore: 50 Years of memory for Spanish learned in school. *Journal of Experimental Psychology: General, 113,* 1–29.

Bahrick, H. P. (1984b). Replicative, constructive and reconstructive aspects of memory—implication for human and animal research. *Physiological Psychology, 12,* 53–58.

Bahrick, H. P. (1979). Broader methods and narrower theories for memory research: Comments on the papers by Eysenck and Cermak. In L. Cermak & F. I. M. Craik (Eds.), *Levels of processing in human memory.* Hillsdale, NJ: Lawrence Erlbaum Associates.

Bahrick, H.P. (1970). A two-phase model for prompted recall. *Psychological Review, 77,* 215–222.

Bair, J. H. (1903). The practice curve: A study in the formation of habits. *Psychological Review. Monograph Supplements, 4* (Number 19).

Balaz, M. A., Capra, S., Hartl, P., and Miller, R. R. (1980). Contextual potentiation of acquired behavior after developing direct context-US associations. *Learning and Memory, 12,* 383–397.

Barsalou, L. W., and Sewell, D. R. (1984). Constructing representations of categories from different points of view. Emory Cognition Project Report no. 2, Emory University.

Barsalou, L. W. (1983). Ad hoc Categories. *Memory and Cognition, 11,* 211–227.

Baldwin, J. M., and Shaw, W. J. (1895). Memory for square size. *Psychological Review, 2,* 236–239.

Balota, D. A., and Neely, J. H. (1980). Test-expectancy and word-frequency effects in recall and recognition. *Journal of Experimental Psychology: Human Learning and Memory, 6,* 576–587.

Bartlett, F. C. (1932). *Remembering: A study in experimental and social psychology.* Cambridge, England: Cambridge University Press.

Beare, J. I. (1906). *Greek theories of elementary cognition.* London, England: Oxford University Press.

Bellezza, F. J. (1982). Updating memory using mnemonic devices. *Cognitive Psychology, 14,* 301–327.

Belmont, J. M. and Butterfield, E. C. (1977). The instructional approach to cognitive research. In R. V. Kail and J. V. Hagen (Eds.). *Perspectives on the development of memory and cognition.* Hillsdale, NJ: Lawrence Erlbaum Associates, 437–481.

Benjamin, L. (1985). Ebbinghaus and Fechner: Memento. *History of Psychology Newsletter, 17,* 42–43.

Bennet, R. W. (1975). Proactive interference in short-term memory: Fundamental forgetting processes. *Journal of Verbal Learning and Verbal Behavior, 14,* 123–144.

Bennett, R. W., and Bennett, I. F. (1974). PI release as a function of the number of prerelease trials, *Journal of Verbal Learning and Verbal Behavior, 13,* 573–584.

Bentley, I. M. (1899). The memory image and its qualitative fidelity. *American Journal of Psychology, 11,* 1–48.

Bergstrom, J. A. (1893). Experiments upon physiological memory by means of the interference of associations. *American Journal of Psychology, 5,* 356–369.

Bergstrom, J. A. (1894a). An experimental study of some of the conditions of mental activity. *American Journal of Psychology, 6,* 247–274.

Bergstrom, J. A. (1894b). The relation of the interference to the practice effect of an association. *American Journal of Psychology, 6,* 433–442.

Bevan, W., and Dukes, W. F. (1967). Stimulus-variation in recall. *American Journal of Psychology, 80,* 309–312.

Bevan, W., Dukes, W. F., and Avant, L. L. (1966). The effect of variation in specific stimuli on memory for their superordinates. *American Journal of Psychology, 79,* 250–257.

Bever, T. G. (1968). Associations to stimulus-response theories of language. In T. Dixon and D. Horton (Eds.), *Verbal behavior and general behavior theory.* Englewood Cliffs, NJ: Prentice-Hall.

Bigham, J. (1894). Memory. *Psychological Review, 1,* 453–461.

Bilodeau, J. M., and Schlosberg, H. (1951). Similarity in conditions as a variable in retroactive inhibition. *Journal of Experimental Psychology, 41,* 199–204.

Binet, A. (1905). *On double consciousness.* Chicago, IL: Open Court.

Binet, A. (1897). Psychologie individuelle—La description d'un object. *L'Annee Psychologigue,* III, 296–332.

Binet, A., and Henri V. (1894). La memoire des mots. *L'Annee Psychologique, 1,* 1–23.

Bjork, R. A., and Whitten, W. B. (1974). Recency-sensitive retrieval processes in long-term free recall. *Cognitive Psychology, 6,* 173–189.

Blaxton, T. A. (1985). Investigating dissociations among memory measures: Support for a transfer appropriate processing framework. Doctoral dissertation, Purdue University.

Block, R. A. (1982). Temporal judgments and contextual change. *Journal of Experimental Psychology: Learning, Memory, and Cognition, 8,* 530–544.

Blumenthal, A. L. (1977). *The process of cognition.* Englewood Cliffs, NJ: Prentice-Hall.

Bobrow, S. A. (1970). Memory for words in sentences. *Journal of Verbal Learning and Verbal Behavior, 9,* 363–372.

Bolinger, D., and Sears, D. A. (1981). *Aspects of language* New York, NY: Harcourt Brace Jovanovich.

Bolton, F. E. (1896). The accuracy of recollection and observation. *Psychological Review, 3,* 286–295.

Bolton, T. L. (1892). The growth of memory in school children. *American Journal of Psychology, 4,* 362–380.

Boring, E. G. (1929/1950). *A history of experimental psychology.* New York, NY: Appleton-Century-Crofts, Inc.

Bousfield, A. K. (1953). The occurrence of clusterings in the recall of randomly arranged associates. *Journal of General Psychology, 49,* 229–240.

Bouton, M. E., and Bolles, R. C. (1979). Contextual control of the extinction of conditioned fear. *Learning and Motivation, 10,* 445–466.

Bower, G. H. (1981). Mood and memory. *American Psychologist, 36,* 129–148.

Bower, G. H. (1971). Adaptation-level coding of stimuli and serial position effects. In M. H. Appley (Ed.) *Adaptation- Level Theory.* New York, NY: Academic Press, Pp. 175–201.

Bower, G. H. (1972a). Stimulus-sampling theory of encoding variability. In A. W. Melton and E. Martin (Eds.), *Coding processes in human memory.* Washington, DC: Winston & Sons, 85–123.

Bower, G. H. (1972b). Mental imagery and associative learning. In L. W. Gregg (Ed.), *Cognition in learning and memory.* New York, NY: Wiley, 51–88.

Bower, G. H. (1967). A multicomponent theory of the memory trace. In K. W. Spence and J. T. Spence (Eds.), *Advances in learning and motivation, Vol. 1,* New York, NY: Academic Press.

Bower, G. H., and Winzenz, D. (1969). Group structure, coding, and memory for digit series. *Journal of Experimental Psychology Monograph Supplement, 80,* Part 2. Pp. 1–17.

Branconnier, R. J., Cole, J. O., Spera, K. F., and DeVitt, D. R. (1982). Recall and recognition as diagnostic indices of malignant memory loss in senile dementia: A Bayesian analysis. *Experimental Aging Research, 8,* 189–193.

Bransford, J. D., and Franks, J. J. (1972). The abstraction of linguistic ideas: A review. *Cognition, 1,* 211–249.

Bransford, J. D., Franks, J. J., Morris, D. D., and Stein, B. S. (1979). Some general constraints on learning and memory research. In L. S. Cermak and F. I. M. Craik (Eds.), *Levels of processing in human memory.* Hillsdale, New Jersey: Lawrence Erlbaum Associates.

Brett, G. S. (1912/1921). *History of Psychology.* London, England: Allen and Unwin.

Brett, G. S. (1930). Associationism and "Act" psychology. In C. Murchison (Ed.). *Psychologies of 1930.* Worchester, MA: Clark University Press.

Bringmann, W. G. (1977). The European roots of American psychology: Questions of import. In R. Rieber and K. Salzinger (Eds.) *The roots of American psychology: Historical influences and implications for the future. Annals of the New York Academy of Sciences, 291,* 56–65.

Bringmann, W., and Bringmann, N. (1985). Hermann Ebbinghaus: 1875–1879: The Missing Years. Paper presented at *The Internationales Hermann Ebbinghaus Symposium,* Passau University, Passau, West Germany, May 30–June 2, 1985.

Bringmann, W. and King, I. (1985). Ebbinghaus and Cornell University. Paper presented at the annual convention of the Southeastern Psychological Association, Atlanta, Georgia, April.

Broadbent, D. E. (1971). *Decision and Stress.* London, England: Academic Press.

Broadbent, D. E. (1958). *Perception and communication.* New York, NY: Pergamon Press.

Broadbent, D. E. (1957). A mechanical model for human attention and immediate memory. *Psychological Review, 64,* 205–215.

Brooks, D. N. and Baddeley, A. (1976). What can amnesic patients learn? *Neuropsychologia, 14,* 111–122.

Brown, J. (1958). Some tests of the decay theory of immediate memory. *Quarterly Journal of Experimental Psychology, 10,* 12–21.

Brown, J. and Packham, D. W. (1967). The effect of prior recall on multiple response recognition. *Quarterly Journal of Experimental Psychology, 19,* 356–361.

Bruner, J. S., Goodnow, J. J. and Austin, G. A. (1956). *A study of thinking.* New York, NY: John Wiley.

Brown, R., and McNeill, D. (1966). The "tip of the tongue" phenomenon. *Journal of Verbal Learning and Verbal Behavior, 5,* 325–337.

Brown, T. (1858). *Lectures on the philosophy of the human mind.* London: William Tegg & Co.

Burnham, W. H. (1888–9). Memory, historically and experimentally considered. *American Journal of Psychology, 2,* 39–90; 225–270; 431–464; 568–622.

Buschke, H. (1984). Cued recall in amnesia. *Journal of Clinical and Experimental Neuropsychology, 6,* 433–440.

Buschke, H. (1977). Two-dimensional recall: Immediate identification of clusters in episodic and semantic memory. *Journal of Verbal Learning and Verbal Behavior, 16,* 201–215.

Buschke, H. (1974). Spontaneous remembering after recall failure. *Science, 184,* 579–581.

Buschke, H. (1973). Selective reminding for analysis of memory and learning. *Journal of Verbal Learning and Verbal Behavior, 12,* 543–550.

Buschke, H. (1962). Auditory and visual interaction in immediate memory. *Psychiatric Research,* *1,* 229–237.

Buss, A. R. (Ed.). (1979). *Psychology in social context.* New York, NY: Irvington Press.

Calkins, M. W. (1898). Short studies in memory and association from the Wellesley College Psychological Laboratory: I. *Psychological Review, 5,* 451–456.

Calkins, M. W. (1896a). Association: II. *Psychological Review, 3,* 32–49.

Calkins, M. W. (1896b). Association. *Psychological Review. Monograph Supplements, 1* (Number 2).

Calkins, M. W. (1894). Association: I. *Psychological Review, 1,* 476–483.

Capella, M. (circa 430 A.D./1977). *Martianus Cappella and the seven liberal arts: Volume II: The marriage of philology and mercury.* Translated by W. H. Stah, R. Johnson, with E. L. Burges, New York, NY: Columbia University Press.

Carr, H. A. (1925). *Psychology: A study of mental activity,* New York, NY: Longmans, Green and Company.

Casagrande, J. B. and Hale, K. L. (1967). Semantic relations in Papago folk definitions. In D. Hymes and W. E. Bittle (Eds.), *Studies in southwestern ethnolinguistics.* The Hague, Netherlands: Mouton.

Cattell, J. McK. (1890). Mental tests and measurements. *Mind, 15,* 373–381.

Chaffin, R. and Herrmann, D. J. (1984). The similarity and diversity of semantic relations. *Memory & Cognition, 12,* 134–141.

Chapman, L. J. and Chapman, J. P. (1978). The measurement of differential deficit. *Journal of Psychiatric Research, 14,* 303–311.

Chapman, L. J. and Chapman, J. P. (1973). Problems in the measurement of cognitive deficit. *Psychological Bulletin, 79,* 380–385.

Cicero, (51 B.C./1927). *Tusculan Disputation.* Translated by J. E. King. *The Loeb Classical Library,* E. Capps, T. E. Page, and W. H. D. Rouse (Eds.) London, England: Heinemann.

Cicero, (55 B.C./1917). *De Oratore* Translated by E. W. Sutton, *The Loeb Classical Library,* T. E. Page, E. Capps, W. H. D. Rouse, L. A. Post, and E. M. Warmington (Eds.). London, England: Heinemann.

Cieutat, V. J., Stockwell, F. E., and Noble, C. E. (1958). The interaction of ability and amount of practice with stimulus and response meaningfulness (m, m′) in paired-associate learning. *Journal of Experimental Psychology, 56,* 193–202.

Clark, H. and Clark, E. (1977). *The psychology of language.* New York, NY: Harcourt, Brace.

Clark, H. H. (1970). Word associations and linguistic theory. In J. Lyons (Ed.) *New horizons in linguistics.* Baltimore, MD: Penguin Books.

Clarke, R., and Morton, J. (1983). Cross modality facilitation in tachistoscopic word recognition. *Quarterly Journal of Experimental Psychology, 35a,* 789–96.

Cofer, C. N. (1982). Argument and intellectual change: Comments in the context of Arnold's chapter. In W. Weimer and D. Palermo (Eds.) *Cognition and the symbolic processes* (Volume 2. Pp. 147–1534). Hillsdale, NJ: Lawrence Erlbaum Associates.

Cofer, C. N. (1979). Human learning and memory. In E. Hearst (Ed.). *The first century of experimental psychology.* Hillsdale, NJ: Lawrence Erlbaum Associates.

Cofer, C. N. (1968). Problems, issues and implications. In T. Dixon and D. Horton (Eds.) *Verbal behavior and general behavior theory.* Englewood Cliffs, NJ: Prentice-Hall.

Cohen, N. J. (1984). Preserved learning capacity in amnesia: Evidence for multiple memory systems. In L. R. Squire and N. Butters (Eds.), *Neuropsychology of memory.* New York, NY: Guilford Press, 83–103.

Cohen, N. J., and Squire, L. R. (1980). Preserved learning and retention of pattern-analyzing skill in amnesia: Dissociation of knowing how and knowing that. *Science, 210,* 207–210.

Cole, R. A. and Rudnicky, A. I. (1983). What's new in speech perception? The research and ideas of William Chandler Bagley, 1874–1946. *Psychological Review, 90,* 94–101.

Colegrove, F. W. (1899). Individual memories. *American Journal of Psychology, 10,* 228–255.

Coll, R. (1985). *The development of the memory element through storage of progressively finer attributes.* Unpublished doctoral dissertation. Rutgers University, Newark, NJ.

Collins, A. M., and Loftus, E. F. (1975). A spreading-activation theory of semantic processing. *Psychological Review, 82,* 407–428.

Collins, A. M., and Quillian, M. R. (1972). How to make a language user. In E. Tulving & W. Donaldson (Eds.), *Organization of Memory.* New York, NY: Academic Press.

Collins, A. M., and Quillian, M. R. (1969). Retrieval time from semantic memory. *Journal of Verbal Learning and Verbal Behavior, 8,* 240–247.

Conford, F. M. (1934). *Plato's theory of knowledge.* New York, NY: Humanities Press.

Conrad, R. (1965). Order error in immediate recall of sequences. *Journal of Verbal Learning and Verbal Behavior, 4,* 161–169.

Conrad, R. (1964). Acoustic confusions in immediate memory. *British Journal of Psychology, 55,* 75–84.

Conrad, R. (1960a). Serial order intrusions in immediate memory. *British Journal of Psychology, 51,* 45–48.

Conrad, R. (1960b). Very brief delay of immediate recall. *Quarterly Journal of Experimental Psychology, 12,* 45–47.

Conrad, R. (1959). Errors of immediate memory. *British Journal of Psychology, 50,* 349–359.

Conrad, R., and Hull, A. J. (1968). Input modality and the serial position curve in short-term memory. *Psychonomic Science, 10,* 135–136.

Conti, G. (1978). "Quine, meaning, and opposition." Unpublished honors thesis. Department of Psychology, Hamilton College, Clinton, NY.

Craik, F. I. M. (1970). The fate of primacy items in free recall. *Journal of Verbal Learning and Verbal Behavior, 9,* 143–148.

Craik, F. I. M. and Lockhart, R. S. (1972). Levels of processing: A framework for memory research. *Journal of Verbal Learning and Verbal Behavior, 11,* 671–684.

Crannell, C. W., and Parrish, J. M. (1957). A comparison of immediate memory span for digits, letters, and words. *Journal of Psychology, 44,* 319–327.

Crossman, E. R. F. W. (1961). Information and serial order in human immediate memory. In C. Cherry (Ed.) *Information Theory.* London, England: Butterworth.

Crowder, R. G. (1983). The purity of auditory memory. *Philosophical Transactions of the Royal Society of London, 302,* 251–265.

Crowder, R. G., (1976). *Principles of learning and memory.* Hillsdale, NJ: Lawrence Erlbaum Associates.

Crowder, R. G., and Morton, J. (1969). Precategorical acoustic storage (PAS). *Perception & Psychophysics, 5,* 365–373.

Cruse, D. A. (1979). On the transitivity of the part-whole relation. *Journal of Linguistics, 15,* 29–38.

Cruse, D. A. (1976). Three classes of antonym in English. *Lingua, 38,* 281–292.

Crutchfield, R. S. and Krech, D. (1963). Some guides to the understanding of the history of psychology. In L. Postman (Ed.) *Psychology in the making,* New York, NY: Knopf.

Cunningham, T. F., Healy, A. F., and Williams, D. M. (1984). Effects of repetition on short-term retention of order information. *Journal of Experimental Psychology: Learning, Memory, and Cognition, 10,* 575–597.

Da Vinci, L. (circa 1490 A.D./1981). *The literary works of Leonardo Da Vinci.* Compiled and edited by Jean Paul Richter. London, England: Phaidon Press, Ltd.

Dallett, K., and Wilcox, S. G. (1968). Contextual stimuli and proactive inhibition. *Journal of Experimental Psychology, 78,* 475–480.

Daniels, A. H. (1895). The memory after-image and attention. *American Journal of Psychology, 7,* 558–565.

Danzinger, K. (1985). The origin of the psychological experiment as a social institution. *American Psychologist, 40,* 133–140.

Danziger, K. (1979). The social origins of modern psychology. In A. R. Buss (Ed.), *Psychology in social context.* New York, NY: Irvington Press.

Davis, J. C., Lockhart, R. S., and Thompson, D. M. (1972). Repetition and context effects in recognition memory. *Journal of Experimental Psychology, 92,* 102.

Dearborn, G. V. N. (1899). Recognition under objective reversal. *Psychological Review, 6,* 395–406.

Deese, J. (1968). Association and memory. In T. Dixon and D. Horton (Eds.) *Verbal behavior and general behavior theory.* Englewood Cliffs, NJ: Prentice-Hall.

Dell, G. S. (1984). Representation of serial order in speech: Evidence from the repeated phoneme effect in speech errors. *Journal of Experimental Psychology: Learning, Memory, and Cognition, 10,* 222–233.

Dicarie, N. L. (1983). Word repetition effects: The roles of surface and semantic features. Unpublished Masters thesis, University of Toronto.

Dinnerstein, D. and Egeth, H. (1962). On the development of associations. *Psychologische Beitrage, 6,* 544–552.

Dixon, T. R. and Horton, D. L. (Eds.), (1968). *Verbal behavior and general behavior theory.* Englewood Cliffs, NJ: Prentice-Hall.

Drewnowski, A. (1980). Attributes and priorities in short-term recall: A new model of memory span. *Journal of Experimental Psychology: General, 109,* 208–250.

Drewnowski, A., and Murdock, B. B., Jr. (1980). The role of auditory features in memory span for words. *Journal of Experimental Psychology: Human Learning and Memory, 6,* 319–332.

Duncker, K. (1945). On Problem Solving. *Psychological Monographs 58,* (whole No. 270).

Dunlap, K. (1927). The use and abuse of abstractions in psychology. *Philosophical Review, 26,* 462–487.

Durgunoğlu, A., and Roediger, H., L. (1985). *Test differences in accessing bilingual memory.* Unpublished manuscript, Department of Psychology, Purdue University, West Lafayette, IN.

Eagle, M., and Ortof, E. (1967). The effect of level of attention upon "phonetic" recognition errors. *Journal of Verbal Learning and Verbal Behavior, 6,* 226–231.

Ebbinghaus, H. (1908/1922/1932/1973). *Abriss der Psychologie.* Berlin, Germany: De Gruyter. Later editions edited by E. Durr and K. Buehler. Translated as *Psychology: An elementary textbook.* New York, NY: Arno Press.

Ebbinghaus, H. (1897). *Uber eine neue Methods zur Prufung geistiger Fahigkeiten und ihre Anwendung Bei Schulkindern.* Zeitschrift für Psychologie, *13,* 401–459.

Ebbinghaus, H. (1897/1902/1905/1919). *Grundzüge der Psychologie.* Leipzig, Germany: Veit and Company. Later editions edited by E. Durr.

Ebbinghaus, H. (1896). *Über erklarende und beschreibende Psycholoqie.* Zeitschrift für Psychologie, *9,* 161–205.

Ebbinghaus, H. (1893). *Theorie des Farbensehens. Zeitschrift für Psychologie, 5,* 145–238.

Ebbinghaus, H. (1890). *Uber negative Empfindungswerthe. Zeitschrift für Psychologie, 1,* 320–334, 463–485.

Ebbinghaus, H. (1887). *Die Gesetzmassigkeit des Helligkeitscontrastes.* Akademie der Wissenschaften der Berlin, 995–1909.

Ebbinghaus, H. (1885). *Über das Gedächtnis: Untersuchungen zur experimentellen Psychologie.* Leipzig: Duncker and Humblot. Trans. as *Memory: A contribution to experimental psychology* by H. A. Ruger and C. E. Bussenius New York: Teachers College, Columbia University, 1913. Dover Press Edition, 1964.

Ebbinghaus, H. (1880–1971). *Urmanuskript über das Gedächtnis.* Passau, West Germany: Passavia Universitätsverlag.

Ebbinghaus, H. (1873). *Uber die Hartmannsche Philosophie des Unbewussten*. Dusseldorf, Germany: F. Dietz.

Edgell, B. (1924). *Theories of Memory*. Oxford: Clarendon Press.

Egan, J. P. (1958). Recognition memory and the operating characteristic. Technical Note AFCRC-TN-58-51. Bloomington, IN: Hearing and Communication Laboratory, Indiana University.

Eich, J. E. (1980). The cue-dependent nature of state dependent retrieval. *Memory & Cognition, 8*, 157–173.

Eich, J. (1985a). Context, memory, and integrated item/context imagery. *Journal of Experimental Psychology: Learning, Memory and Cognition, 11*, 764–770.

Eich, J. M. (1985b). Levels of processing, encoding specificity, elaboration, and CHARM. *Psychological Review, 92*, 1–38.

Eich, J. M. (1982). A composite holographic associative recall model. *Psychological Review, 89*, 627–661.

Eisler, R. (1904). *Worterbuch der Philosophischen Begriffe*. Berlin, Germany: Mittler und Shon.

Ellenberger, H. F. (1970). *The discovery of the unconscious*. New York, NY: Basic Books.

Erdelyi, M. H., and Becker, J. (1974). Hypermnesia for pictures: Incremental memory for pictures but not words in multiple recall trials. *Cognitive Psychology, 6*, 159–171.

Erdelyi, M. and Kleinbard, J. (1978). Has Ebbinghaus decayed with time? The growth of recall (hypermnesia) over days. *Journal of Experimental Psychology: Human Learning and Memory, 4*, 275–289.

Erickson, R. C., Poon, L. W., and Walsh-Sweeney. (1980). Clinical memory testing in the elderly. In L. W. Poon, J. L. Fozard, L. S. Cermak, D. Arenberg, and L. W. Thomson (Eds.), *New directions in memory and aging*. Hillsdale, N.J.: Lawrence Erlbaum Associates, 379–402.

Erickson, R. C. and Scott, M. L. (1977). Clinical memory testing: A review. *Psychological Bulletin, 84*, 1130–1149.

Ericsson, K. A., and Simon, H. A. (1980). Verbal reports as data. *Psychological Review, 87*, 215–251.

Erman, L. D., and Lesser, V. R. (1975). A multi-level organization for problem solving using many diverse, cooperating sources of knowledge. *Proceedings of the 4th Annual Joint Computer Conference*, Georgia, USSR, 483–490.

Estes, W. K. (1985). Levels of association theory. *Journal of Experimental Psychology: Learning, Memory, and Cognition, 11*, 450–454.

Estes, W. K. (1980). Is human memory obsolete? *American Scientist, 68*, 62–69.

Estes, W. K. (1979). On the descriptive and explanatory functions of theories of memory. In L.-G. Nilsson (Ed.), *Perspectives on Memory Research*. Hillsdale, NJ: Lawrence Erlbaum Associates.

Estes, W. K. (1976). Structural aspects of associative models for memory. In C. N. Cofer (Ed.), *The Structure of Human Memory*. San Francisco, CA: W. H. Freeman.

Estes, W. K. (1975). The locus of inferential and perceptual processes in letter identification. *Journal of Experimental Psychology: General, 104*, 122–145.

Estes, W. K. (1972). An associative basis for coding and organization in memory. In A. W. Melton and E. Martin (Eds.) *Coding processes in human memory*. Washington, DC: Winston and Sons.

Estes, W. K. (1971). Learning and memory. In E. G. Beckenback and C. B. Tompkins (Eds.), *Concepts of Communication: Interpersonal, Intrapersonal and Mathematical*. New York, NY: John Wiley and Sons.

Estes, W. K. (1959). The statistical approach to learning theory. In S. Koch (Ed.), *Psychology: A Study of a Science, Vol. 2*. New York, NY: McGraw-Hill.

Estes, W. K. (1955). Statistical theory of spontaneous recovery and regression. *Psychological Review, 62*, 145–154.

Estes, W. K. (1950). Toward a statistical theory of learning. *Psychological Review, 43*, 94–107.

Estes, W. K., Koch, S., MacCorquodale, K., Meehl, P. E., Mueller, C. G., Jr., Schoenfeld, W. N., and Verplanck, W. S. (1954). *Modern Learning Theory.* New York, NY: Appleton-Century-Crofts.

Evanechko, P. O., and Maguire, T. O. (1972). The dimensions of children's meaning space. *Americal Educational Research Journal, 9,* 507–523.

Evens, M. W., Litowitz, J. A., Markowitz, R. N., Smith, R., and Werner, O. (1983). *Lexical semantic relations: A comparative survey. (Current Inquiry in Language and Linguistics, 34.* Carbondale, IL., and Edmonton, Canada: Linguistic Research Inc.

Fahlman, S. E. (1981). Representing implicit knowledge. In G. E. Hinton and J. A. Anderson (Eds.) *Parallel models of associative memory.* Hillsdale, NJ: Lawrence Erlbaum Associates.

Falkenberg, P. E. (1972). Recall improves in short-term memory the more recall context resembles learning context. *Journal of Experimental Psychology, 95,* 39–47.

Fechner, G. T. (1860/1966). *Elemente der Psychophysik* (2 Vols.) Leipzig, Germany: Breithaus and Hartel. Translated (1966) by H. E. Adler, New York, NY: Holt, Rinehart, and Winston.

Feigenbaum, E. A. (1963). The simulation of verbal learning behavior. In E. A. Feigenbaum and J. Feldman (Eds.), *Computers and Thought.* New York, NY: McGraw-Hill.

Feigenbaum, E. A., and Simon, H. A. (1984). EPAM-like models of recognition and learning. *Cognitive Science, 8,* 305–336.

Feigenbaum, E. A., and Simon, H. A. (1963). Brief notes on the EPAM theory of verbal learning. In C. N. Cofer and B. S. Musgrave (Eds.) *Verbal Behavior and Learning.* New York, NY: McGraw-Hill.

Feigl, H. (1943). Logical empiricism. In D. Runes (Ed.), *Twentieth Century Philosophy.* New York: Philosophical Library.

Fellman, A. C. and Fellman, M. (1981). *Making sense of self.* Philadelphia, PA: University of Pennsylvania Press.

Fernandez, A. and Glendberg, A. M. (1985). Changing environmental context does not reliably affect memory. *Memory & Cognition, 13,* 333–345.

Fillmore, C. J. (1968). The case for case. In E. Bach and R. T. Harmes (Eds.), *Universals of linguistic theory.* New York, NY: Holt, Rinehart and Winston.

Fisher, R. P., and Craik, F. I. M. (1977). The interaction between encoding and retrieval operations incued recall. *Journal of Experimental Psychology: Human Learning and Memory, 3,* 701–711.

Flavell, J. H. (1970). Developmental studies of mediated memory. In H. W. Reese and L. W. Lipsitt (Eds.), *Advances in child development and behavior, Volume 5.* New York, NY: Academic Press, 182–211.

Flexser, A. J., and Tulving, E. (1978). Retrieval independence in recognition and recall. *Psychological Review, 85,* 153–171.

Fodor, J. (1983). *The modularity of mind.* Cambridge, MA: MIT Press.

Foss, D. J., and Harwood, D. A. (1975). Memory for sentences: Implications for human associative memory. *Journal of Verbal Learning and Verbal Behavior, 14,* 1–16.

Foucault, M. (1928). Les inhibitions internes de fixation. *Annee Psychologique, 29,* 92–112.

Fozard, J. L., Myers, J. R., and Waugh, N. C. (1971). Recalling recent exemplars of a category. *Journal of Experimental Psychology, 90,* 262–267.

Franz, S. I., and Houston, H. E. (1896). The accuracy of observation and of recollection in school children. *American Journal of Psychology, 3,* 531–535.

Fromkin, V. A. (Ed.). (1973). *Speech errors as linguistic evidence.* The Hague, Netherlands: Mouton.

Gardiner, J. M. (1983). On recency and echoic memory. *Philosophical Transactions of the Royal Society of London, 302,* 267–282.

Gardiner, J. M., and Arthurs, F. S. (1982). Encoding context and the generation effect in multitrial free-recall learning. *Canadian Journal of Psychology, 365,* 527–531.

Gardiner, J., and Gregg, V. H. (1979). When auditory memory is not overwritten. *Journal of Verbal Learning and Verbal Behavior, 18,* 705–719.

Garrett, M., and Fodor, J. A. (1968). Psychological theories and linguistic constructs. In T. Dixon and D. Horton (Eds.) *Verbal behavior and general behavior theory*. Englewood Cliffs, NJ: Prentice-Hall.

Gartman, L. M., and Johnson, N. F. (1972). Massed versus distributed repetition of homographs: A test of the differential-encoding hypothesis. *Journal of Verbal Learning and Verbal Behavior, 1,* 801–808.

Gel'fand, I. M., Gurfinkel, V. S., Fomin, S. V., and Isetlin, M. L. (Eds.). (1971). *Models of the structural-functional organization of certain biological systems*. Cambridge, MA: MIT Press.

Gentner, D., and Collins, A. (1981). Studies of inference from lack of knowledge. *Memory and Cognition, 9,* 434–443.

Geschwind, N. (1979). Specializations of the human brain. *Scientific American, 241,* 180–201.

Gilmartin, K. J., Newell, A., and Simon, H. A. (1976). A program modeling short-term memory under strategy control. In C. Cofer (Ed.), *The structure of human memory*. San Francisco, CA: W. H. Freeman.

Glanzer, M. and Cunitz, A. R. (1966). Two storage mechanisms in free recall. *Journal of Verbal Learning and Verbal Behavior, 5,* 351–360.

Glaze, J. A. (1928). The association value of nonsense syllables. *Journal of Genetic Psychology, 35,* 255–269.

Glenberg, A. M. (1984). A retrieval account of the long-term modality effect. *Journal of Experimental Psychology: Learning, Memory, and Cognition, 10,* 16–31.

Glenberg, A. M. (1979). Component levels theory of the effects of spacing of repetitions on recall and recognition. *Memory & Cognition, 7,* 95–112.

Glenberg, A. M., Bradley, M. M., Kraus, T. A., and Renzaglia, G. J. (1983). Studies of the long-term recency effect: Support for a contextually guided retrieval hypothesis. *Journal of Experimental Psychology: Learning, Memory, and Cognition, 9,* 231–255.

Glenberg, A. M., Bradley, M. M., Stevenson, J. A., Kraus, T. A., Tkachuk, M. J., Gretz, A. L., Fish, J. H., and Turpin, B. M. (1980). A two-process account of long-term serial position effects. *Journal of Experimental Psychology: Human Learning and Memory, 6,* 355–369.

Glenberg, A. M., and Kraus, T. A. (1981). Long-term recency is not found on a recognition test. *Journal of Experimental Psychology: Human Learning and Memory, 7,* 475–479.

Glenberg, A. M. and Lehmann, T. (1980). Spacing repetitions over a week. *Memory & Cognition, 8,* 528–538.

Glenberg, A. M., and Swanson, N. C. (1986). A temporal distinctiveness theory of recency and modality effects. Journal of *Experimental Psychology: Learning, Memory, and Cognition. 12,* 3–15.

Godden, D. R., and Baddeley, A. D. (1980). When does context influence recognition memory? *British Journal of Psychology, 71,* 99–103.

Godden, D. R., and Baddeley, A. D. (1975). Context-dependent memory in two natural environments: On land and under water. *British Journal of Psychology, 66,* 325–331.

Goldberg, E., and Bilder, R. (in press). Neuropsychological perspective: retrograde amnesia and executive deficits. In L. W. Poon (Ed.), *Handbook of memory assessment of older adults*. Washington, D.C.: American Psychological Association.

Goldberg, E. and Tucker, D. (1979). Motor perseveration and long-term memory for visual forms. *Journal of Clinical Neuropsychology, 1,* 273–288.

Gordon, K. (1903). Meaning in memory and in attention. *Psychological Review, 10,* 267–283.

Gordon, W. C., McCraken, K. M., Dess-Beech, N., and Mowrer, R. R. (1981). Mechanisms for the cueing phenomenon: The addition of the cueing context to the training memory. *Learning and Motivation, 12,* 196–211.

Gorfein, D. S. (1974). Time release from proactive inhibition as a function of amount of proactive inhibition present. *Journal of Experimental Psychology, 103,* 2, 201–203.

Gorfein, D. S., and Jacobson, D. E. (1972). Proactive effects in short-term recognition memory. *Journal of Experimental Psychology, 95,* 211–214.

Gorfein, D. S., and Jacobson, D. E. (1973). Memory search in a Brown-Peterson short-term memory paradigm. *Journal of Experimental Psychology, 9,* 82–87.

Gorfein, D. S., and Spata, A. (in preparation). *Context effects and retrieval in and after short-term memory.*

Gorfein, D. S., and Viviani, J. M. (1981). *What is PI release the release of?* Paper read at the annual meeting of the Psychonomics Society, Philadelphia, PA.

Gorfein, D. S., and Viviani, J. M. (1980). *There are no effects of retention interval.* Paper read at the annual meeting of Psychonomics Society, St. Louis, MO.

Gorfein, D. S., and Viviani, J. M. (1978). The nature of transfer in free recall. *Journal of Experimental Psychology: Human Learning and Memory, 4,* 222–238.

Gorfein, D. S., Viviani, J. M., and Leddo, J. (1982). Norms as a tool for the study of homography. *Memory & Cognition, 10,* 503–509.

Gorfein, D. S., and Schulze, N. (1975). Contextual encoding and recovery from interference in the Brown-Peterson paradigm. *Bulletin of the Psychonomic Society, 6,* 569–571.

Gould, A., and Stephenson, G. M. (1967). Some experiments relating to Bartlett's theory of remembering. *British Journal of Psychology, 58,* 39–49.

Graf, P., and Mandler, G. (1984). Activation makes words more accessible, but not necessarily more retrievable. *Journal of Verbal Learning and Verbal Behavior, 23,* 553–568.

Graf, P., and Schacter, D. L. (in press). Implicit and explicit memory for knew associations in normal and amnesic subjects. *Journal of Experimental Psychology: Learning, Memory and Cognition.*

Graf, P., Shimamura, A., and Squire, L. (1985). Priming across modalities and priming across category levels: Extending the domain of preserved function in amnesia. *Journal of Experimental Psychology: Learning, Memory, and Cognition, 11,* 386–396.

Graf, P., Squire, L. R., and Mandler, G. (1984). The information that amnesic patients do not forget. *Journal of Experimental Psychology: Learning, Memory, and Cognition, 10,* 164–178.

Greene, P. H. (1972). Problems of organization of the motor system. In R. Rosen and F. M. Snell (Eds.), *Progress in theoretical biology, Volume 2.* New York, NY: Academic Press.

Greene, R. L. (1985). Constraints on the long-term modality effect. *Journal of Memory and Language* (in press).

Greene, R. L. and Crowder, R. G. (1984). Modality and suffix effects in the absence of auditory stimulation. *Journal of Verbal Learning and Verbal Behavior, 23,* 371–382.

Greenspoon, J. and Ranyard, R. (1957). Stimulus conditions and retroactive inhibition. *Journal of Experimental Psychology, 53,* 55–59.

Grober, E., and Buschke, H. (1987). Genuine memory deficits in dementia. *Developmental Neuropsychology, 3,* 13–36.

Grober, E., Buschke, H., Kawas, C., and Fuld, P. (1985). Impaired ranking of semantic attributes in dementia. *Brain and Language, 26,* 276–286.

Grossberg, S. (1978a). A theory of human memory: Self-organization and performance of sensory-motor codes, maps, and plans. In R. Rosen and F. Snell (Eds.) *Progress in theoretical biology, Volume 5.* New York, NY: Academic Press.

Grossberg, S. (1978b). Do all neural models really look alike? A comment on Anderson, Silverstein, Ritz, and Jones. *Psychological Review, 85,* 592–596.

Grossberg, S., and Pepe, J. (1971). Spiking threshold and overarousal effects in serial learning. *Journal of Statistical Physics, 3,* 95–125.

Grossman, L. and Eagle, M. (1970). Synonymity, antonymity, and association in false recognition responses. *Journal of Experimental Psychology, 83,* 244–266.

Groves, P. B. (Ed.) (1973). *Webster's new dictionary of synonyms.* Springfield, MA: Merriam.

Hacker, M. J. (1980). Speed and accuracy of recency judgements for events in short-term memory. *Journal of Experimental Psychology: Human Learning and Memory, 6,* 651–675.

Halbwachs, M. (1950/1980). *La Memoire Collective.* Paris, France: Presses Universitaires de France.

Halbwachs, M. (1925; 1952, reprint). *Les Cadres sociaux de la memoire.* Paris, France: Presses Universitaires de France.

Hall, G. S. (Ed.) (1897). *American Journal of Psychology, 1,* p. 4.

Hamilton, W. (1859). Lectures on Metaphysics and Logic.

Harcum, E. R. (1975). *Serial learning and paralearning.* New York, NY: John Wiley.

Harlow, H. F., and Mears, C. (1979). *The human model: Primate perspectives,* Washington, D.C.: Winston and Sons.

Harris, J. E. (1980). Memory aids people use: Two interview studies. *Memory & Cognition, 8,* 31–38.

Hasher, L., and Zacks, R. T. (1979). Automatic and effortful processes in memory. *Journal of Experimental Psychology: General, 108,* 356–388.

Hawkins, C. J. (1897). Experiments on memory types. *Psychological Review, 4,* 289–294.

Hayes-Roth, B. (1984). *A blackboard model of control.* Report No. HPP 83–38, Heuristic Programming Project, Department of Computer Science, Stanford University, Stanford, CA.

Hayes-Roth, B. (1977). Evolution of cognitive structures and processes. *Psychological Review, 84,* 260–278.

Healy, A. F. (1982). Short-term memory for order information. In G. H. Bower (Ed.) *The psychology of learning and motivation.* New York, NY: Academic Press.

Healy, A. F. (1978). A Markov model for the short-term retention of spatial location information. *Journal of Verbal Learning and Verbal Behavior, 17,* 295–308.

Hearst, E. (Ed.). (1979). *The first century of experimental psychology.* Hillsdale, NJ: Lawrence Erlbaum Associates.

Hebb, D. O. (1961). Distinctive features of learning in the higher animal. In J. F. Delafresnaye (Ed.), *Brain mechanisms and learning.* New York, NY: Oxford University Press.

Heidbreder, E. (1933). *Seven psychologies.* New York, NY: Appleton-Century.

Henderson, E. N. (1903). A study of memory for connected trains of thought. *Psychological Review. Monograph Supplements, 5,* (Number 23).

Heraclitus (circa 500 B.C./1888). *Fragments.* In "A further study of Heraclitus." Translated by G. T. W. Patrick and published in the *American Journal of Psychology, 1,* 557–690.

Herbart, J. F. (1834). *Lehrbuch der Psychologie.* Konigsberg, Germany: Unzer.

Herrmann, D. J. (1982). The semantic-episodic distinction and the history of long-term memory typologies. *Bulletin of the Psychonomic Society, 20,* 207–210.

Herrmann, D. J. (1978). An old problem for the new psychosemantics: Synonymity. *Psychological Bulletin, 85,* 490–512.

Herrmann, D. H. and Chaffin, R. (1987). *Memory in historical perspective: The literature before Ebbinghaus.* Washington, D.C., University Press of America.

Herrmann, D. J. and Chaffin, R. (1985). "Comprehension of semantic relations as a function of the definition of relations." *Symposium: In Memoriam Herrmann Ebbinghaus.* Humboldt University, East Berlin, July, 1985.

Herrmann, D. J., Chaffin, R., Conti, G., Peters, D., and Robbins, P. (1979). Comprehension of antonymy and the generality of categorization models. *Journal of Experimental Psychology: Human Learning and Memory, 5,* 585–597.

Herrmann, D. J., Chaffin, R., and Winston, M. E. (1986). "Robins are a part of birds": The confusion of semantic relationships. *Bulletin of the Psychonomic Society, 24,* 413–415.

Hesiod. (c. 700 B.C./1959). *The Theogony.* Translated by R. Lattimore. Ann Arbor, MI: University of Michigan Press.

Heywood, A., and Vortriede, H. A. (1905). Some experiments on the association power of smells. *American Journal of Psychology, 16,* 537–541.

Hicks, R. E., and Young, R. K. (1972). Part-whole list transfer in free recall. *Journal of Experimental Psychology, 96,* 328–333.

Hilgard, E. R. (1977). *Divided consciousness: Multiple controls in human thought and action.* New York, NY: John Wiley.

Hilgard, E. R. (1964). Introduction to the Dover edition. In H. Ebbinghaus (1885). *Memory: A contribution to experimental psychology.* New York, NY: Dover Press.

Hilgard, E. R. (1951). Methods and Procedures in the study of learning. In S. S. Stevens (Ed.), *Handbook of Experimental Psychology.* New York, NY: Wiley.

Hilgard, E. and Bower, G. H. (1975). *Theories of learning, Fourth Edition*, Englewood Cliffs, NJ: Prentice Hall.

Hinton, G. E., and Anderson, J. A. (Eds.) (1981). *Parallel models of associative memory*. Hillsdale, NJ: Lawrence Erlbaum Associates.

Hintzman, D. L. (1984). Episodic versus semantic memory. A distinction whose time has come and gone? *Behavioral and Brain Sciences, 7,* 240–241.

Hintzman, D. L., Block, R. A., and Summers, J. J. (1973). Contextual associations and memory for serial position. *Journal of Experimental Psychology, 97,* 220–229.

Hoffman, R. R., and Senter, R. J. (1978). Recent History of psychology: Mnemonic techniques and the psycholinistic revolution. *The Psychological Record, 28,* 3–15.

Hollingworth, H. L. (1928). General laws of redintegration. *Journal of General Psychology, 1,* 79–90.

Hollingworth, H. L. (1913). Characteristic differences between recall and recognition. *American Journal of Psychology, 24,* 532–544.

Honig, W., and Wasserman, E. A. (1981). Performance of pigeons on delayed simple and conditional discriminations under equivalent training procedures. *Learning and Motivation, 12,* 149–170.

Horton, D. L., and Dixon, T. R. (1968). Traditions, trends, and innovations. In T. R. Dixon and D. L. Horton (Eds.), *Verbal behavior and general behavior theory.* Englewood Cliffs, NJ: Prentice-Hall.

Horton, D. L., and Mills, L. B. (1984). Human Learning and memory. *Annual Review of Psychology, 35,* 361–394.

Hothersall, D. (1984). *History of psychology.* New York, NY: Random House, Inc.

Hovland, C. I. (1951). Human learning and retention. In S. S. Stevens (Ed.) *Handbook of Experimental Psychology.* New York, NY: John Wiley.

Howe, H. C. (1894). "Mediate" association. *American Journal of Psychology, 6,* 239–241.

Huang, S. T., and Glenberg, A. M. (1986). Echoic and retrieval accounts of the long-term modality effect tested using the suffix procedure. *American Journal of Psychology, 99,* 453–470.

Hull, C. L. (1943). *Principles of behavior.* New York, NY: Appleton Century.

Hull, C. L. (1933). Meaningfulness of 320 selected nonsense syllables. *American Journal of Psychology, 45,* 730–734.

Hull, C. L., Hovland, C. I., Ross, kR. T., Hall, M., Perkins, D. T., and Fitch, F B. (1940). *A Mathematico-deductive theory of rote learning.* New Haven, CT: Yale University Press.

Hume, D. (1965). *Treatise on human nature.* L. A. Selby Bigge (Ed.), Oxford, England: Clarendon Press.

Hume, D. (1739–1758/1951). *Hume: A theory of knowledge.* Edited by D. C. Yalden-Thomson, Edinburgh, Scotland: Nelson.

Jacobi, R. (1975). *Social Amnesia.* Boston, MA: Beacon Press.

Jacobs, J. (1887). Experiments on "prehension" *Mind, 9,* 188–205.

Jacobs, J. (1885). Review of *Über das Gedächtnis. Mind, 10,* 454–459.

Jacoby, L. L. (1983). Remembering the data: Analyzing interactive processes in reading. *Journal of Verbal Learning and Verbal Behavior, 22,* 485–508.

Jacoby, L. L., and Dallas, M. (1981). On the relationship between autobiographical memory and perceptual learning. *Journal of Experimental Psychology: General, 110,* 306–340.

Jacoby, L. L., and Witherspoon, D. (1982). Remembering without awareness. *Canadian Journal of Psychology, 36,* 300–324.

Jackson, A. and Morton, J. (1984). Facilitation of auditory word recognition. *Memory and Cognition, 12,* 568–574.

Jaensch, E. R. (1909). Hermann Ebbinghaus. *Zeitschrift für Psychologie, 51,* 3–8.

James, H. (1920). *The Letters of William James* Boston, MA: Atlantic Monthly Press.

James, W. (1890–1983). *The principles of psychology.* Cambridge, MA: Harvard University Press.

James, W. (1885). Experiments in memory. *Science, 6,* 198–199.

Jenkins, J. J. (1979). Four points to remember: A tetrahedral model of memory experiments. In L. S. Cermak and F. I. M. Craik (Eds.), *Levels of processing in human memory.* Hillsdale, NJ: Lawrence Erlbaum Associates.

Jenkins, J. J. (1968). The challenge to psychological theorists. In T. R. Dixon and D. L. Horton (Eds.), *Verbal behavior and general behavior theory.* Englewood Cliffs, NJ: Prentice-Hall.

Johnson, N. F. (1978). Coding processes in memory. In W. K. Estes (Ed.), *Handbook of Learning and Cognitive Processes: Linguistic Functions in Cognitive Theory, Vol. 6.* Hillsdale, NJ: Lawrence Erlbaum Associates.

Johnson, N. F. (1972). Organization and the concept of a memory code. In A. Melton and E. Martin (Eds.) *Coding processes in human memory.* Washington, DC: Winston.

Johnson, N. F. (1970). The role of chunking and organization in the process of recall. In G. H. Bower (Eds.) *The psychology of learning and motivation: Advances in research and theory, Volume 4.* New York, NY: Academic Press.

Johnson-Laird, P. N., Herrmann, D. J., and Chaffin, R. (1984). Only connections: A critique of semantic networks. *Psychological Bulletin, 96,* 292–315.

Johnston, W. A., Coots, J. H., and Flickinger, R. G. (1972). Controlled semantic encoding and the effect of repetition lag on free recall. *Journal of Verbal Learning and Verbal Behavior, 11,* 784–788.

Johnston, W. H., Dark, V. J., and Jacoby, L. (1985). Perceptual fluency and recognition judgments. *Journal of Experimental Psychology: Learning, Memory, and Cognition, 11,* 3–11.

Jones, C. V. (1982). Tests of the dual-mechanism theory of recall. *Arts Psychologica, 50,* 61–72.

Jones, M. R. (1974). Cognitive representations of serial patterns. In B. H. Kantowitz (Ed.), *Human information processing: Tutorials in performance and cognition.* Hillsdale, NJ: Lawrence Erlbaum Associates. 187–229.

Jung, J., and Skeebo, S. (1967). Multitrial free recall as a function of constant versus varied input orders and list length. *Canadian Journal of Psychology, 21,* 329–336.

Kant, I. (1788/1961). *Immanuel Kant's Critique of Pure Reason.* Translated by N. K. Smith. London, England: MacMillan.

Kempsen, R. M. (1977). *Semantic theory.* New York, NY: Harper and Row.

Kennedy, F. (1898). On the experimental investigation of memory. *Psychological Review, 5,* 477–499.

Keppel, G., and Underwood, B. J. (1962). Proactive inhibition in short-term retention of single items. *Journal of Verbal Learning and Verbal Behavior, 1,* 153–161.

Kimble, G. (1968). Mediating associations. *Journal of Experimental Psychology, 76,* 263–266.

Kimble, G. A., and Schlesinger, K. (Eds.) (1985). *Topics in the history of psychology* (2 volumes). Hillsdale, NJ: Lawrence Erlbaum Associates.

Kincaid, J. P., and Wickens, D. D. (1970). Temporal gradient of release from proactive inhibition. *Journal of Experimental Psychology, 86,* 313–316.

Kintsch, W., and Monk, D. (1972). Storage of complex information in memory: Some implications of the speed with which inferences can be made. *Journal of Experimental Psychology, 94,* 25–32.

Kirkpatrick, E. A. (1894). An experimental study of memory. *Psychological Review, 1,* 602–609.

Kirsner, K. (1974). Modality differences in recognition memory for words and their attributes. *Journal of Experimental Psychology, 102,* 579–584.

Klatzky, R. L. (1975). *Human Memory: Structures and Processes,* San Francisco, CA: W. H. Freeman and Company.

Klix, F. (1980). On the structure and function of semantic memory. In F. Klix and J. Hoffmann (Eds.), *Cognition and memory.* New York, NY: North-Holland.

Klix, F., Hoffman, J., and van de Meer, E. (1983). Le stockage de concepts et leur utilisation cognitive. *Bulletin de Psychologie, 35,* 533–543.

Knapp, A. G., and Anderson, J. A. (1984). Theory of categorization based on distributed memory storage. *Journal of Experimental Psychology: Learning, Memory, and Cognition, 10*, 616–637.

Koffka, K. (1935). *Principles of Gestalt Psychology.* New York, NY: Harcourt Brace.

Kohonen, T. (1984). *Self-organization and associative memory.* Berlin, West Germany: Springer-Verlag.

Kohonen, T. (1977). *Associative memory: A system-theoretical approach.* Berlin, West Germany: Springer-Verlag.

Kolers, P. A. (1978). On the representations of experience. In D. Gerver & W. Sinaiko (Eds.), *Language interpretation and communication.* New York, NY: Plenum.

Kolers, P. A. (1976). Reading a year later. *Journal of Experimental Psychology: Human Learning and Memory, 2*, 543–565.

Kolers, P. A. (1975). Specificity of operations in sentence recognition. *Cognitive Psychology, 7*, 289–306.

Kolers, P. A., and Gonzalez, E. (1980). Memory for words, synonyms, and translations. *Journal of Experimental Psychology: Human Learning and Memory, 6*, 53–65.

Kolers, P. A., and Ostry, D. J. (1974). Time course of loss of information regarding pattern analyzing operations. *Journal of Verbal Learning and Verbal Behavior, 13*, 599–612.

Kolers, P. A., and Roediger, H. L. (1984). Procedures of mind. *Journal of Verbal Learning and Verbal Behavior, 23*, 425–449.

Kolodner, J. L. (1983). Maintaining organization in a dynamic long-term memory. *Cognitive Science, 7*, 243–280.

Kraemer, H. C., Peabody, C. A., Tinklenberg, J. R., and Yesavage, J. A. (1983). Mathematical and empirical development of a test of memory for clinical and research use. *Psychological Bulletin, 94*, 367–380.

Kucera, H., and Francis, W. N. (1967). *Computational analysis of present day American English.* Providence, RI: Brown University Press.

Kuhn, T. S. (1962). *The structure of scientific revolutions* Chicago, IL: University of Chicago Press.

Kulpe, O. (1895). *Outlines of psychology.* (E. B. Titchener, Trans.) New York, NY: Macmillan.

LaBerge, D. L., and Samuels, S. J. (1974). Toward a theory of automatic information processing in reading. *Cognitive Psychology, 6*, 293–323.

Lachman, J. L., and Lachman, R. (1980). Age and the actualization of world knowledge. In L. Poon, J. Fozard, L. Cermak, D. Arenberg, and L. Thompson (Eds.), *New directions in memory and aging: Proceedings of the George Talland memorial conference.* Hillsdale, NJ: Lawrence Erlbaum Associates.

Lachman, R., Lachman, J. L., and Butterfield, E. C. (1979). *Cognitive psychology and information processing: An introduction.* Hillsdale, NJ: Lawrence Erlbaum Associates.

Lachman, R., and Laughery, K. R. (1968). Is a test trial a training trial in free recall learning? *Journal of Experimental Psychology, 76*, 40–50.

Ladd, G. T., and Woodworth, R. S. (1911). *Elements of physiological psychology.* New York: Scribner.

Lange, K. (1894). *Apperception. A monograph on psychology and pedagogy.* Boston, MA: D. C. Heath.

Lashley, K. S. (1951). The problem of serial-order in behavior. In L. A. Jeffress (Ed.) *Cerebral mechanisms in behavior.* New York, NY: John Wiley. 112–136.

Lashley, K. S. (1938). Conditional reactions in the rat. *Journal of Psychology, 6*, 311–324.

Lashley, K. S., and Wade, M. (1946). The Pavlovian theory of generalization. *Psychological Review, 53*, 72–87.

Laurence, M. W. (1970). Role of homophones in transfer learning. *Journal of Experimental Psychology, 86*, 1–7.

Lee, C. L., and Estes, W. K. (1981). Item and order information in short-term memory: Evidence for multilevel perturbation processes. *Journal of Experimental Psychology: Human Learning and Memory, 7,* 149–169.

Lee, C. L., and Estes, W. K. (1977). Order and position in primary memory for letter strings. *Journal of Verbal Learning and Verbal Behavior, 16,* 395–418.

Leech, G. (1974). *Semantics.* Baltimore, MD: Penguin Books.

Leeper, R. (1935). The role of motivation in learning: A study of the phenomenon of differential motivational control of the utilization of habits. *Journal of Genetic Psychology, 46,* 3–40.

Lehnert, W. (1977). Human and computational question-answering. *Cognitive Science, 1,* 47–73.

Leuba, J. H. (1893). A new instrument for Weber's Law: With indications of a law of sense memory. *American Journal of Psychology, 5,* 370–384.

Lewis, C. H., and Anderson, J. R. (1976). Interference with real world knowledge. *Cognitive Psychology, 7,* 311–335.

Lewis, J. L. (1970). Semantic processing of unattended messages, using dichotic listening. *Journal of Experimental Psychology, 85,* 225–228.

Liddell, H. S. (1946). The conditioned reflex. In E. A. Moss (Ed.). *Comparative psychology.* New York, NY: Prentice Hall.

Liepa, P. (1977). "Models of content addressable distributed associative memory (CADAM)". Unpublished manuscript, Department of Psychology, University of Toronto, Ontario, Canada.

Light, L. L., and Carter-Sobell, L. (1970). Effects of changed semantic context on recognition memory. *Journal of Verbal Learning and Verbal Behavior, 9,* 1–11.

Littman, R. A. (1979). Social and intellectual origins of experimental psychology. In E. Hearst (Ed.), *The first century of experimental psychology* (Pp. 39–86). Hillsdale, NJ: Lawrence Erlbaum Associates.

Locke, J. (1690/1961). *An essay concerning human understanding.* London: Dent.

Loess, H. (1968). Short-term memory and item similarity. *Journal of Verbal Learning and Verbal Behavior, 7,* 87–92.

Loess, H., and Waugh, N. C. (1967). Short-term memory and inter-trial intervals. *Journal of Verbal Learning and Verbal Behavior, 6,* 455–460.

Loftus, G. R. (1978). On interpretation of interactions. *Memory & Cognition, 6,* 312–319.

Lorch, R. F. (1982). Priming and search processes in semantic memory: A test of three models of spreading activation. *Journal of Verbal Learning and Verbal Behavior, 21,* 468–492.

Lorch, R. F. (1981). Effects of relation strength and semantic overlap on retrieval and comparison processes during sentence verification. *Journal of Verbal Learning and Verbal Behavior, 20,* 593–610.

Luchins, A. (1942). Mechanization in problem solving. *Psychological Monographs, 54,* (Whole No. 248).

Lyons, J. (1977). *Semantics Volume 1.* London: Cambridge University Press.

Lyons, J. (1968). *Introduction to Theoretical Linguistics,* London, England: Cambridge University Press.

MacCorquodale, K., and Meehl, P. E. (1948). On a distinction between hypothetical constructs and intervening variables. *Psychological Review, 55,* 95–107.

Macht, M. L. and Buschke, H. (1984). Speed of recall in aging. *Journal of Gerontology, 39,* 439–443.

Macht, M. L. and Buschke, H. (1983). Age differences in cognitive effort in recall. *Journal of Gerontology, 38,* 695–700.

MacKay, D. G. (1980). Speech errors: Retrospect and prospect. In V. A. Fromkin (Ed.), *Errors in linguistic performance.* New York, NY: Academic Press.

Madden, D. J. (1985). Age-related slowing in the retrieval of information from long-term memory. *Journal of Gerontology, 40,* 208–210.

Madigan, S. A. (1983). Picture memory. In J. C. Yuille (Ed.), *Imagery, memory and cognition: Essays in honor of Allan Paivio.* 65–89. Hillsdale, NJ: Lawrence Erlbaum Associates.

Madigan, S. A. (1969). Intraserial repetition and coding processes in free recall. *Journal of Verbal Learning and Verbal Behavior, 8,* 828–835.

Maki, R. H., and Hasher, L. (1975). Encoding variability: A role in immediate and long-term memory? *American Journal of Psychology, 88,* 217–231.

Mandler, G. A. (1984). *Mind and body.* New York, NY: John Wiley and Sons, Inc.

Mandler, G. (1980). Recognizing: The judgment of previous occurrence. *Psychological Review, 87,* 252–271.

Mandler, G. (1968). Association and organization: Facts, fancies and theories. In T. R. Dixon and D. L. Horton (Ed.), *Verbal behavior and general behavior theory* (Pp. 109–119). Englewood Cliffs, NJ: Prentice-Hall.

Mandler, G., and Dean, P. J. (1969). Seriation: Development of serial order in free recall. *Journal of Experimental Psychology, 81,* 207–215.

Marbe, K. (1909). *Hermann Ebbinghaus: Ein Nachruf. Frankfurter Zeitung,* March 7. p. 7. Frankfurt, Germany: Sonderabdruck.

Markman, E. M., and Siebert, J. (1976). Classes and collections: Internal organization and resulting holistic properties. *Cognitive Psychology, 8,* 561–577.

Marks, L. E. and Miller, G. A. (1964). The role of semantic and syntactic constraints in the memorization of English sentences. *Journal of Verbal Learning and Verbal Behavior, 3,* 1–5.

Marshall, J. C., and Fryer, D. M. (1978). Speak, Memory! An introduction to some historical studies of remembering and forgetting. In M. Gruneberg and P. Morris (Eds.), *Practical aspects of memory.* London, England: Methuen.

Martin, E. (1974). Serial learning: A multilevel access analysis. *Memory and Cognition, 2,* 322–328.

Martin, E. (1971). Verbal learning theory and independent retrieval phenomena. *Psychological Review, 78,* 314–332.

Martin, E. (1968). Stimulus meaningfulness and paired associate transfer: An encoding variability hypothesis. *Psychological Review, 75,* 421–441.

Martin, E., and Noreen, D. L. (1974). Serial learning: Identification of subjective subsequences. *Cognitive Psychology, 6,* 421–435.

Maskarinec, A. S., and Thompson, C. P. (1976). The within-list distributed practice effect: Tests of the varied context and varied encoding hypotheses. *Memory & Cognition, 4,* 741–746.

Massaro, D. W. (Ed.) (1975). *Understanding language: An information-processing analysis of speech perception, reading, and psycholinguistics.* New York, NY: Academic Press.

Mathews, R. C., and Tulving, E. (1973). Effects of three types of repetition on cued and noncued recall of words. *Journal of Verbal Learning and Verbal Behavior, 12,* 707–721.

McClelland, J. L. (1979). On the time relations of mental processes: An examination of systems of processes in cascade. *Psychological Review, 86,* 287–300.

McClelland, J. L., and Rumelhart, D. E. (1981). An interactive activation model of context effects in letter perception, Part 1. An account of basic findings. *Psychological Review, 88,* 354–407.

McCloskey M., and Glucksberg, S. (1979). Decision processes in verifying category membership statements: Implications for models of semantic memory. *Cognitive Psychology, 11,* 1–37.

McDougall, W. (1923). *Outline of psychology.* New York, NY: Charles Scribner's Sons, Inc.

McDowall, J. (1984). Processing capacity and recall in amnesic subjects. In L. R. Squire and N. Butters (Eds.), *Neuropsychology of memory.* New York, NY: Guilford Press, 63–66.

McGeoch, J. A. (1942/1946). *The psychology of human learning.* New York, NY: Longmans, Green and Co.

McGeoch, J. A. (1932). Forgetting and the law of disuse. *Psychological Review, 39,* 352–370.

McGeoch, J. A., and Irion, A. L. (1952). *The psychology of human learning.* New York, NY: Longmans, Green and Co.

McKoon, G., Ratcliff, R., and Dell, G. (in press). A critical evaluation of the semantic/episodic distinction. *Journal of Experimental Psychology: Learning, Memory, and Cognition.*

McNicol, D. (1975). Fixed and random address models for storing order in short-term memory. *Quarterly Journal of Experimental Psychology, 27,* 273–288.

Mechanic, A. (1964). The responses involved in the rote learning of verbal materials. *Journal of Verbal Learning and Verbal Behavior, 3,* 30–36.

Mechanic, A. (1962). Effects of orienting task, practice, and incentive on simultaneous incidental and intentional learning. *Journal of Experimental Psychology, 64,* 393–399.

Melton, A. W. (1970). The situation with respect to the spacing of repetitions and memory. *Journal of Verbal Learning and Verbal Behavior, 9,* 596–606.

Melton, A. W. Implications of short-term memory for a general theory of memory. (1968). *Journal of Verbal Learning and Verbal Behavior, 2,* 1–21.

Melton, A. W., and Irwin, J. M. (1940). The influence of degree of interpolated learning on retroactive inhibition and the overt transfer of specific responses. *American Journal of Psychology, 53,* 173–203.

Merry, R. (1905). The Pains of Memory. In S. Rogers (1905) *The Pleasures of Memory: In two parts to which are added the pains of memory.* Portland, OR: Daniel Johnson.

Metcalfe, J. A., Glavanov, D., and Murdock, M. (1981). Spatial and temporal processing in the auditory and visual modalities. *Memory & Cognition, 9,* 351–359.

Metcalfe, J. A., and Murdock, B. B., Jr. (1981). An encoding and retrieval model of single-trial free recall. *Journal of Verbal Learning and Verbal Behavior, 20,* 161–189.

Meyer, D. E., and Schvaneveldt, R. W. (1971). Facilitation in recognizing pairs of words: evidence of a dependence between retrieval operations. *Journal of Experimental Psychology, 90,* 227–234.

Michon, J. A. (1967). *Timing in Temporal Tracking.* Soesterberg: Institute for Perception RVO-TNO.

Mill, J. (1829/1869). *Analysis of the phenomena of the human mind.* New York, NY: Longmans, Green, Reder and Tyler.

Miller, G. A. (1969). The organization of lexical memory: Are word associations sufficient? In G. A. Talland and N. C. Waugh (Eds.), *The pathology of memory.* New York, NY: Academic Press.

Miller, G. A. (1962). *Psychology: The science of mental life.* New York, NY: Harper and Row.

Miller, G. A. (1958). Free recall of redundant strings of letters *Journal of Experimental Psychology, 56,* 484–491.

Miller, G. A. (1956). The magical number seven, plus or minus two: Some limits on our capacity for processing information. *Psychological Review, 63,* 81–96.

Miller, G. A. and Buckhout, R. (1973). *Psychology: The science of mental life.* New York, NY: Harper and Row.

Miller, G. A., Galanter, E., and Pribram, K. H. (1960). *Plans and the structure of behavior.* New York, NY: Holt, Reinhart and Winston.

Miller, G. A., and Johnson-Laird, P. N. (1976). *Language and perception.* Cambridge, MA: Harvard University Press.

Milner, P. M. (1961). A neural mechanism for the immediate recall of sequences. *Kubernetik, 1,* 76–81.

Minsky, M. (1975). A framework for representing knowledge. In P. H. Winston (Ed.), *The psychology of computer vision.* New York, NY: McGraw Hill.

Mitchell, J. M. (1911). Mnemonics. In the *Encyclopedia Britannica, Vol. 18,* Cambridge, England: Cambridge University Press, Pp. 629–670.

Moeser, S. D. (1979). The role of experimental design in investigations of the fan effect. *Journal of Experimental Psychology: Human Learning and Memory, 5,* 125–134.

Montaigne, M. de (c. 1575/1958). *Essays of Michael deMontaigne.* Translated by J. M. Cohen, Marmondsworth, England: Penguin.

Moore, K. C. (1896). The mental development of a child. *Psychological Review. Monograph Supplements, 1* (Number 3).

Morris, C. D., Bransford, J. D., and Franks, J. J. (1977). Levels of processing versus transfer appropriate processing. *Journal of Verbal Learning and Verbal Behavior, 16,* 519–533.

Morton, J. (1979). Facilitation in word recognition: Experiments causing change in the logogen models. In P. A. Kolers, M. E. Wrolstead, and H. Bouma (Eds.), *Processing of visible language,* New York, NY: Plenum.

Morton, J. (1969). The interaction of information in word recognition. *Psychological Review, 76,* 165–178.

Motley, M. T., Camden, C. T., and Baars, B. J. (1979). Personality and situational influences upon verbal slips: A laboratory test of Freudian and pre-articulatory editing hypotheses. *Human Communication Research, 5,* 195–202.

Muenzinger, K. F. (1957). Introduction. In E. E. Gruber, K. R. Hammond, and R. Jessor (Eds.), *Contemporary approaches to cognition.* Cambridge, MA: Harvard University Press.

Müller, G. E., and Schumann, F. (1893/1894). *Experimentelle Beitrage zur Untersuchung des Gedächtnisses. Zeitschrift für Psychologie und Physiologie der Sinnesorgane, 6,* 81–190, 257–338.

Muller, R., and Van de Kemp, H. (1985). On psychologists's uses of Calvinism. *American Psychologist, 40,* 466–468.

Münsterberg, H. and Bigham, J. (1894). Memory. *Psychological Review, 1,* 34–38.

Murdock, B. B., Jr. (1983). A distributed memory model for serial order information. *Psychological Review, 90,* 316–338.

Murdock, B. B., Jr. (1982). A theory for the storage and retrieval of item and associative information. *Psychological Review, 89,* 609–626.

Murdock, B. B., Jr. (1979). Convolution and correlation in perception and memory. In L.-G. Nilsson (Ed.), *Perspectives in memory research: Essays in honor of Uppsala University's 500th Anniversary,* Hillsdale, NJ: Lawrence Erlbaum Associates.

Murdock, B. B., Jr. (1976). Item and order information in short-term serial memory. *Journal of Experimental Psychology: General, 105,* 191–216.

Murdock, B. B., Jr. (1974). *Human memory: Theory and data.* Hillsdsale, NJ: Lawrence Erlbaum Associates.

Murdock, B. B., Jr. (1968). Serial order effects in short-term memory. *Journal of Experimental Psychology Monograph Supplement,* No. 76, Part 2.

Murdock, B. B., Jr. (1967). Auditory and visual stores in short-term memory. *Acta Psychologica, 27,* 316–324.

Murdock, B. B. Jr. (1961). The retention of individual items. *Journal of Experimental Psychology, 62,* 618–625.

Murdock, B. B., Jr. (1960). The distinctiveness of stimuli. *Psychological Review, 67,* 16–31.

Murdock, B. B., Jr., and Babick, A. J. (1961). The effect of repetition on the retention of individual words. *American Journal of Psychology, 74,* 596–601.

Murdock, B. B., Jr., and Franklin, P. E. (1984). Associative and serial order information: Different modes of operation? *Memory and Cognition, 12,* 243–249.

Murdock, B. B., Jr., and Walker, K. D. (1969). Modality effects in free recall. *Journal of Verbal Learning and Verbal Behavior, 8,* 665–676

Murdock, B. B., Jr., and vom Saal, W. (1967). Transpositions in short-term memory. *Journal of Experimental Psychology, 74,* 137–143.

Murdock, B. B., Jr. (1985a). Convolution and matrix systems: A reply to Pike. *Psychological Review, 92,* 130–132.

Murdock, B. B., Jr. (1985b). The contributions of Hermann Ebbinghaus. *Journal of Experimental Psychology: Learning, Memory, and Cognition, 11.*

Murphy, G. (1929/1949). *An historical introduction to modern psychology.* New York, NY: Harcourt, Brace.

Murray, D. J. (1983). *A history of western psychology.* Englewood Cliffs, NJ: Prentice Hall.

Murray, D. J. (1976). Research on memory in the nineteenth century. *Canadian Journal of Psychology, 30,* 201–220.

Muter, P. (1980). Very rapid forgetting. *Memory & Cognition, 8,* 174–179.

Muter, P. (1979). Response latencies in discrimination of recency. *Journal of Experimental Psychology: Human Learning and Memory, 5,* 160–169.

Naess, A. (1953). *Interpretation and preciseness: A contribution to the theory of communication.* Oslo, Norway: Jacob Dywad.

Nagel, N. (1961). *The structure of science.* New York, NY: Harcourt, Brace and World.

Natsoulas, T. (1982). Dimensions of perceptual awareness. *Behaviorism, 10,* 85–112.

Neely, J. H. (1977). Semantic priming and retrieval from lexical memory: The roles of inhibitionless spreading activation and limited capacity attention. *Journal of Experimental Psychology: General, 106,* 226–254.

Neisser, U. (1982a). *Memory observed: Remembering in natural contexts.* San Francisco, CA: W. H. Freeman.

Neisser, U. (1982b). Memory: What are the important questions? In U. Neisser (Ed.), *Memory observed.* San Francisco, California: Freeman.

Nelson, D. L., and Davis, M. J. (1972). Transfer and false recognitions based on phonetic identities of words. *Journal of Experimental Psychology, 92,* 347–353.

Nelson, D. L., Reed, V. S., and McEvoy, C. L. (1977). Learning to order pictures and words: A model of sensory and semantic encoding. *Journal of Experimental Psychology: Human Learning and Memory, 3,* 485–497.

Nelson, T. (1985). Ebbinghaus' contribution to the measurement of retention: Savings during relearning. *Journal of Experimental Psychology: Learning, Memory, and Cognition, 11,* 472–479.

Nelson, T. O. (1978). Detecting small amounts of information in memory: Savings for nonrecognized items. *Journal of Experimental Psychology: Human Learning and Memory, 4,* 453–468.

Nelson, T. O., and Narens, L. (1980). Norms of 300 general-information questions: Accuracy of recall, latency of recall and feeling of knowing ratings. *Journal of Verbal Learning and Verbal Behavior, 19,* 338–368.

Newell, A. (1973). Production systems: Models of control structures. In W. G. Chase (Ed.), *Visual Information Processing.* New York, NY: Academic Press.

Nickerson, R. S. (1984). Retrieval inhibition from part-set cuing: A persisting enigma in memory research. *Memory & Cognition, 12,* 531–552.

Nipher, F. E. (1878). On the distribution of errors in numbers written from memory. *Transactions of the Academy of Science of St. Louis, 3,* Pp. ccx–ccxi.

Nisbett, R. E., and Wilson, T. D. (1977). Telling more than we can know: Verbal reports on mental processes. *Psychological Review, 84,* 231–279.

Norman, D. A. (Ed.) (1970). *Models for human memory.* New York: Academic Press.

Norman, D. A., and Rumelhart, D. E. (1975). *Explorations in cognition.* San Francisco, CA: Freeman.

Norman, D. A., and Shallice, T. (1985). Attention to action: Willed and automatic control of behavior. In R. J. Davidson, G. E. Schwartz, and D. Shapiro (Eds.), *Consciousness and self-regulation: Advances in research, Volume 4.* New York, NY: Plenum Press.

O'Connor, N., and Hermelin, B. (1978). *Seeing and hearing and space and time.* London, England: Academic Press.

Ornstein, R. E. (1969). *On the experience of time.* Baltimore, MD: Penguin Books, Inc.

Oscar-Berman, M. (1971). Hypothesis testing and focusing behavior during concept formation by amnesic Korsakoff patients. *Neuropsychologia, 11,* 191–198.

Oscar-Berman, M., Sahakian, B. J., and Wikmark, G. (1976). Spatial probability learning by alcoholic Korsakoff patients. *Journal of Experimental Psychology: Human Learning and Memory, 2,* 215–222.

Osgood, C. E. (1959). The similarity paradox in human learning: A resolution. *Psychological Review, 56,* 132–143.

Ogden, C. K. (1932). *Opposition.* Bloomington, IN: Indiana University Press.

Osier, D. V., and Wozniak, R. H. (1984). *A century of serial publication in psychology, 1850–1950.* Millwood, NY: Kraus.

Paivio, A. (1971). *Imagery and verbal processes.* New York, NY: Holt, Rinehart and Winston.

Paivio, A. (1969). Mental imagery in associative leaning and memory. *Psychological Review, 76,* 241–263.

Parkin, A. J. (1982). Residual learning capability in organic amnesia. *Cortex, 18,* 417–440.

Pavlov, I. P. (1928). *Lectures in conditioned reflexes.* New York, NY: Liveright.

Penney, C. G. (1975). Modality effects in short-term verbal memory. *Psychological Bulletin, 82,* 68–84.

Perfetti, C. A. (1967). A study of denotative similarity with restricted word association. *Journal of Verbal Learning and Verbal Behavior, 6,* 788–795.

Peterson, H. A. (1903). Recall of words, objects and movements. *Psychological Review. Monograph Supplements, 4* (Number 17).

Peterson, J. (1925). *Early conceptions and tests of intelligence.* Chicago, IL: World Book Company.

Peterson, L. R., and Peterson, M. J. (1959). Short-term retention of individual verbal items. *Journal of Experimental Psychology, 58,* 193–198.

Peterson, S. B., and Potts, G. R. (1982). Global and specific components of information integration. *Journal of Verbal Learning and Verbal Behavior, 21,* 403–420.

Pike, R. (1984). Comparison of convolution and matrix distributed memory systems for associative recall and recognition. *Psychological Review, 91,* 281–294.

Plato, (circa 380 B.C./1953). *The Dialogues of Plato.* Translated by B. Jowett. Oxford, England: Clarendon Press.

Pliny, (77 A.D./1952). *Natural History II, Libri III–VII.* Translated by H. Rackhan. *The Loeb Classical Library.* E Page, E. Capps, W. H. D. Rouse, L. A. Post, and E. H. Warmington, (Eds.) London, England: Heinemann.

Plotinus, (circa 300 B.C./1962) *The Enneads.* Translated by S. MacKenna. London, England: Faber and Faber, Ltd.

Posner, M. I. (1966). Components of skilled performance. *Science, 152,* 1712–1718.

Posner, M. I., and Konick, A. F. (1966). On the role of interference in short-term retention. *Journal of Experimental Psychology, 72,* 221–231.

Posner, M. I., and Shulman, G. (1979). Cognitive Science. In E. Hearst (Ed.) *The first century of experimental psychology.* Hillsdale, NJ: Lawrence Erlbaum Associates.

Posner, M. I., and Snyder, C. R. R. (1975). Attention and cognitive control. In R. Solso (Ed.), *Information processing and cognition: The Loyola Symposium.* Hillsdale, NJ: Lawrence Erlbaum Associates.

Postman, L. (1985). Human learning. In G. A. Kimble and K. Schlesinger (Eds.) *Topics in the history of psychology: Volume 1.* Hillsdale, NJ: Lawrence Erlbaum Associates.

Postman, L. (1976). Interference theory revisited. In J. Brown (Ed.), *Recall and recognition,* London, England: John Wiley.

Postman, L. (1973). The experimental analysis of verbal learning and memory: Evolution and Innovation. In C. P. Duncan, L. Sechrest, and A. W. Melton (Eds.) *Human Memory: Festschrift in Honor of Benton J. Underwood.* New York, NY: Appleton-Century-Crofts.

Postman, L. (1968a). Hermann Ebbinghaus. *American Psychologist, 23,* 149–157.

Postman, L. (1968b). Association and performance in the analysis of verbal behavior. In T. R. Dixon and D. L. Horton (Eds.) *Verbal behavior and general behavior theory.* Englewood Cliffs, NJ: Prentice-Hall.

Postman, L. (1962). Repetition and paired-associate learning. *American Journal of Psychology, 75,* 372–389.

Postman, L. (1961). The present status of interference theory. In C. N. Cofer (Ed.) *Verbal learning and verbal behavior*. New York, NY: McGraw-Hill.

Postman, L., Burns, S., and Hasher, L. (1970). Studies of learning to learn: X. Nonspecific transfer effects in free-recall learning. *Journal of Verbal Learning and Verbal Behavior, 9*, 707–715.

Postman, L., Fraser, J., and Burns, S. (1968). Unit-sequence facilitation in recall. *Journal of Verbal Learning and Verbal Behavior, 7*, 127–224.

Postman, L., and Knecht, K. (1983). Encoding variability and retention. *Journal of Verbal Learning and Verbal Behavior, 22*, 133–152.

Postman, L., and Stark, K. (1967). Studies of learning to learn: IV. Transfer from serial to paired-associate learning. *Journal of Verbal Learning and Verbal Behavior, 6*, 339–353.

Postman, L., Stark, K., and Fraser, J. (1968). Temporal changes in interference. *Journal of Verbal Learning and Verbal Behavior, 7*, 672–694.

Potwin, E. B. (1901). Study of early memories. *Psychological Review, 8*, 596–601.

Pressey, L. C. (1926). Proficiency in silent reading. *School and Society, 24*, 589–592.

Pribram, K. H. (1971). *Languages of the brain*. Englewood Cliffs, NJ: Prentice-Hall.

Quantz, J. O. (1897). Problems in the psychology of reading. *Psychological review. Monograph Supplements, 2*, (Number 5).

Quillian, M. R. (1967). Word concepts: A theory and simulation of some basic semantic capabilities. *Behavioral Science, 12*, 410–430.

Quintillian, (96 A.D./1921). *The Institute Oratoria of Quintillian*. Translated by H. E. Butler, *The Loeb Classical Library*. E. Capps, T. E. Page, and W. H. D. Rouse (Eds.) London, England: Heinemann.

Raaijmakers, J. G. W., and Shiffrin, R. M. (1981). Search of associative memory. *Psychological Review, 88*, 93–134.

Rapaport, D. (1974). *The history of the concept of association of ideas*. New York, NY: International Universities Press.

Ratcliff, R. (1981). A theory of order relations in perceptual matching. *Psychological Review, 88*, 552–572.

Ratcliff, R. (1978). A theory of memory retrieval. *Psychological Review, 85*, 59–108.

Reason, J. (1984). Lapses of attention in everyday life. In R. Parasuraman and D. R. Davies (Eds.), *Varieties of attention*. New York, NY: Academic Press.

Reder, L. M. (1987). Strategy selection in question answering. *Cognitive Psychology, 19*, 90–138.

Reder, L. M. (1982). Plausibility judgments vs. fact retrieval: Alternative strategies for sentence verification. *Psychological Review, 89*, 250–280.

Reder, L. M. (1979). The role of elaborations in memory for prose. *Cognitive Psychology, 11*, 221–234.

Reder, L. M. (1976). The role of elaborations in the processing of prose. Doctoral dissertation, University of Michigan. Available through University Microfilms, Ann Arbor, MI.

Reder, L. M., and Anderson, J. R. (1980). A partial resolution of the paradox of interference: The role of integrating knowledge. *Cognitive Psychology, 12*, 447–472.

Reder, L. M., and Wible, C. (1984). Strategy use in question-answering: Memory strength and task constraints on fan effects. *Memory and Cognition, 12*, 411–419.

Reder, L. M., and Ross, B. H. (1983). Integrated knowledge in different tasks: The role of retrieval strategy on fan effects. *Journal of Experimental Psychology: Learning, Memory, and Cognition, 9*, 55–72.

Reddy, R., and Newell, A. (1974). Knowledge and its representation in a speech understanding system. In L. W. Gregg (Ed.), *Knowledge and cognition*. Hillsdale, NJ: Lawrence Erlbaum Associates.

Reid, T. (1785/1969) *Essays on the intellectual powers of man*. Introduction by B. A. Brody. Cambridge, MA: MIT. Press.

Reitman, J. S. (1974). Without surreptitious rehearsal, information in short-term memory decays. *Journal of Verbal Learning and Verbal Behavior, 13*, 365–377.

Restle, F. (1975). *Learning: Animal behavior and human cognition.* New York, NY: McGraw-Hill.

Restle, F. (1970). Theory of serial pattern learning: Structural trees. *Psychological Review, 77,* 481–495.

Reutener, D. B. (1972). Class shift, symbolic shift, and background shift in short-term memory. *Journal of Experimental Psychology, 93,* 90–94.

Richards, R. W. (1981). The ambiguous cue problem: The effect of reduced similarity between trials and the schedule of reinforcement. *Learning and Motivation, 12,* 462–484.

Richardson, J., and Gropper, M. S. (1964). Learning during recall trials. *Psychological Reports, 15,* 551–560.

Rieber, R. W. (Ed.) (1980). *Wilhelm Wundt and the making of a scientific psychology.* New York, NY: Plenum Press.

Rieber, R. W. and Salzinger, K. (Eds), (1977). The roots of American psychology: Historical influences and implications for the future. *Annals of the New York Academy of Sciences, 291,* 56–65.

Riegel, K. F. and Riegel, R. M. (1963). An investigation into denotative aspects of word meaning. *Language and Speech, 6,* 5–21.

Rips, L. J. (1975). Quantification and semantic memory. *Cognitive Psychology, 7,* 307–340.

Rips, L. J., Shoben, E. J., and Smith, E. E. (1973). Semantic distance and the verification of semantic relations. *Journal of Verbal Learning and Verbal Behavior, 12,* 1–20.

Robinson, D. K. (1985). Wundt and Ebbinghaus: What the letters say. *History of Psychology Newsletter, 17,* 46–50.

Robinson, E. S. (1932). *Association theory today.* New York, NY: Century.

Robinson, E. S., and Brown, M. A. (1926). Effect of serial position upon memorization. *American Journal of Psychology, 37,* 538–552.

Rock, I. (1957). The role of repetition in associative learning. *American Journal of Psychology, 70,* 186–193.

Rock, I., and Heimer, W. (1959). Further evidence of one-trial associative learning. *American Journal of Psychology, 72,* 1–16.

Roediger, H. L. (1985). Remembering Ebbinghaus. *Contemporary Psychology, 30,* 519–523.

Roediger, H. L. (1984). Does current evidence from dissociation experiments favor the episodic/semantic distinction? *The Behavioral and Brain Sciences, 7,* 252–254.

Roediger, H. L., (1974). Inhibiting effects of recall. *Memory & Cognition, 2,* 261–269.

Roediger, H. L. (1978). Recall as a self-limiting process. *Memory & Cognition, 6,* 54–63.

Roediger, H. L., and Blaxton, T. A. (1985). Effects of surface features and interval on priming in word fragment completion. Manuscript submitted for publication.

Roediger, H. L., and Payne, D. G. (1982). Hypermnesia: The role of repeated testing. *Journal of Experimental Psychology: Learning, Memory, and Cognition, 8,* 66–72.

Roediger, H. L., and Thorpe, L. A. (1978). The role of recall time in producing hypermnesia. *Memory & Cognition, 6,* 296–305.

Rogers, S. (1805). *The pleasures of memory: In two parts to which are added the pains of memory.* Portland, OR: Daniel Johnson.

Rosenzweig, M. R. (1984). U.S. psychology and world psychology. *American Psychologist, 40,* 877–884.

Ross, J., Herrmann, D. J., Vaughan, J., and Chaffin, R. (1987). Semantic relation comprehension: Components and correlates. ERIC document no. 2774683.

Rozenboom, W. W. (1965). The concept of "memory." *Psychological Record, 15,* 329–368.

Rubin, D. C. (1977). Very long-term memory for prose and verse. *Journal of Verbal Learning and Verbal Behavior, 16,* 611–622.

Rumelhart, D. E., Lindsay, P. H., and Norman, D. A. (1972). A process model for long-term memory. In E. Tulving and W. Donaldson (Eds.), *Organization of Memory.* New York, NY: Academic Press.

Rumelhart, D. E., and Ortony, A. (1977). The representation of knowledge in memory. In R. C.

Anderson, R. J. Spiro, and W. E. Montague (Eds.) *Schooling and the acquisition of knowledge.* Hillsdale, NJ: Lawrence Erlbaum Associates.

Ruoff, H. W. (Ed.) (1910). *Masters of achievement.* Buffalo, NY: Frontier Press.

Ryan, J. (1969). Grouping and short-term memory: Different means and patterns of grouping. *Quarterly Journal of Experimental Psychology, 21,* 137–147.

Sachs, J. D. S. (1967). Recognition memory for syntactic and semantic aspects of connected discourse. *Perception and Psychophysics, 2,* 437–442.

Samuelson, F. (1985). Quoters, questions, and standards for historical research. *American Psychologist, 40,* 243–244.

Sandson, J. and Albert, M. L. (1984). Varieties of perseveration. *Neuropsychologia, 22,* 715–732.

Sarason, S. B. (1981). *Psychology misdirected.* New York, NY: Free Press.

Sarton, G. (1930). *The history of science and the new humanism.* New York, NY: Holt.

Saufley, W. H. Jr., Otaka, S. R., and Baveresco, J. L. (1985). Context effects: Classroom tests and context independence. *Memory & Cognition, 13,* 522–528.

Schacter, D. L. (1982). *Stranger behind the engram: Theories of memory and the psychology of science.* Hillsdale, NJ: Lawrence Erlbaum Associates.

Schacter, D. L. and Tulving, E. (1982). Amnesia and memory research. In L. Cermak, (Ed.), *Human memory and amnesia.* Hillsdale, NJ: Lawrence Erlbaum Associates, 1–32.

Schank, R. C. and Abelson, R. P. (1977). *Scripts, plans, goals and understanding: An inquiry into human knowledge structures.* Hillsdale, NJ: Lawrence Erlbaum Associates.

Schmidt, R., and Vorberg, D. (1979). Multicomponent models for the retention of numbers. *Psychological Research, 40,* 349–366.

Scull, A. (1981). *Madhouses, mad-doctors, and madman.* Philadelphia, PA: University of Pennsylvania Press.

Seashore, C. E., and Kent, G. H. (1905). Periodicity and progressive change in continuous mental work. *Psychological Review. Monograph Supplements, 6,* Number 28, pp. 47–101.

Shakow, D. (1930). Hermann Ebbinghaus. *American Journal of Psychology, 42,* 505–518.

Shallice, T. (1978). The Dominant Action System: An information-processing approach to consciousness. In K. S. Pope and J. L. Singer (Eds.), *The stream of consciousness: Scientific investigations into the flow of experience.* New York, NY: Plenum Press.

Sharp, S. E. (1899). Individual psychology: A study of psychological method. *American Journal of Psychology, 10,* 329–391.

Shaughnessy, J. J., Zimmerman, J., and Underwood, B. J. (1974). The spacing effect in the learning of word pairs and the components of word pairs. *Memory and Cognition, 2,* 742–748.

Shiffrin, R. M. (1970). Memory search. In D. A. Norman (Ed.), *Models of human memory.* New York, NY: Academic Press.

Shiffrin, R. M., and Cook, J. R. (1978). Short-term forgetting of item and order information. *Journal of Verbal Learning and Verbal Behavior, 17,* 189–218.

Shiffrin, R. M., and Schneider, W. (1977a). Controlled and automatic human information processing: I. Detection, search, and attention. *Psychological Review, 84,* 1–66.

Shiffrin, R. M., and Schneider, W. (1977b). Controlled and automatic human information processing, II: Perceptual learning, automatic attending, and a general theory. *Psychological Review, 84,* 127–190.

Shimamura, A. P., and Squire, L. (1984). Paired-associate learning and priming effects in amnesia: A neuropsychological study. *Journal of Experimental Psychology: General, 113,* 556–570.

Sidis, R. (1902). *Psychopathological researches. Studies in mental dissociation.* New York, NY: G. E. Stechert.

Siegel, S., Hinson, R. E., Krank, M. D., and McCully, J. (1982). Heroin "overdose" death: The contribution of drug-associated environmental cues. *Science, 216,* 436–437.

Simon, H. A. (1974). How big is a chunk? *Science, 183,* 482–488.

Slamecka, N. J., (1985). Ebbinghaus: Some associations. *Journal of Experimental Psychology: Learning, Memory, and Cognition, 11,* 414–435.

Slamecka, N. J., and Barlow, W. (1979). The role of semantic and surface features in word repetition effects. *Journal of Verbal Learning and Verbal Behavior, 18,* 617–627.

Slamecka, N. J., and Graf, P. (1978). The generation effect: Delineation of a phenomenon. *Journal of Experimental Psychology: Human Learning and Memory, 4,* 592–604.

Slamecka, N. J., Moore, T., and Carey, S. (1972). Part-to-whole transfer and its relation to organization theory. *Journal of Verbal Learning and Verbal Behavior, 11,* 73–82.

Smedslund, J. (1985). Ebbinghaus, the Illusionist: How Psychology came to look like an Experimental Science. Paper presented at Ebbinghaus Symposium in Passau, West Germany.

Smith, E. E., Adams, N., and Schorr, D. (1978). Fact retrieval and the paradox of interference. *Cognitive Psychology, 10,* 438–464.

Smith, E. E., Shoben, E. J., and Rips, L. J. (1974). Structure and process in semantic memory: A featural model for semantic decisions. *Psychological Review, 81,* 214–241.

Smith, S. M. (1982). Enhancement of recall using multiple environmental contexts during learning. *Memory & Cognition, 10,* 405–412.

Smith, S. M. (1979). Remembering in and out of context. *Journal of Experimental Psychology: Human Learning and Memory, 5,* 460–471.

Smith, T. L. (1896). On muscular memory. *American Journal of Psychology, 7,* 453–490.

Smith, W. G. (1896). The place of repetition in memory. *Psychological Review, 3,* 21–31.

Snodgrass, J. G., and Townsend, J. T. (1980). Comparing parallel and serial models: Theory and implementation. *Journal of Experimental Psychology: Human Perception and Performance, 6,* 330–354.

Snodgrass, J. G., and Vanderwart, M. A. (1980). A standardized set of 260 pictures: Norms for name agreement, image agreement, familiarity, and visual complexity. *Journal of Experimental Psychology: Human Learning and Memory, 6,* 174–215.

Sokal, M. M. (1985). APA publications and the history of psychology. *American Psychologist, 40,* 241–242.

Spaet, T., and Harlow, H. F. (1943). Solution by rhesus monkeys of multiple sign problem utilizing the oddity technique. *Journal of Comparative Psychology, 35,* 119–132.

Sperling, G. (1960). The information available in brief visual presentations. *Psychological Monographs, 74,* No. 11 (Whole No. 498).

Sperling, G., and Speelman, R. G. (1970). Acoustic similarity and auditory short-term memory: Experiments and a model. In D. A. Norman (Ed.), *Models of Human Memory.* New York: Academic Press. Pp. 151–202.

Squire, L. R. (1982a). Comparisons among forms of amnesia: Some deficits are unique to Korsakoff Syndrome. *Journal of Experimental Psychology: Learning, Memory, and Cognition, 8,* 560–571.

Squire, L. R. (1982b). The neuropsychology of human memory. *Annual Review of Neuroscience, 5,* 241–273.

Stasio, T., Herrmann, D. J., and Chaffin, R. (1985). Predictions of relation similarity according to relation definition theory. *Bulletin of the Psychonomic Society,* in press.

Sternberg, S. (1975). Memory scanning: New findings and current controversies. *Quarterly Journal of Experimental Psychology, 27,* 1–32.

Sternberg, S. (1969). Memory-scanning: Mental processes revealed by reaction-time experiments. *American Scientist, 57,* 421–457.

Sternberg, S. (1966). High-speed scanning in human memory. *Science, 133,* 652–654.

Stetson, G. R. (1897). Some memory tests of whites and blacks. *Psychological Review, 4,* 285–289.

Stevens, S. S. (1939). Psychology and the science of science. *Psychological Bulletin, 36,* 221–263.

Stigler, S. M. (1978). Some forgotten work on memory. *Journal of Experimental Psychology: Human Learning and Memory, 4,* 1–4.

Surtees, V. (1971). *The paintings and drawings of Dante Gabriel Rosetti, 1828–1882*. Oxford, England: Oxford University Press.

Sutton, R. S., and Barto, A. G. (1981). Toward a modern theory of adaptive networks: Expectation and prediction. *Psychological Review, 88*, 135–170.

Swift, E. J. (1905). Memory of a complex skillful act. *American Journal of Psychology, 16*, 131–133.

Talbot, E. G. (1897). An attempt to train the visual memory. *American Journal of Psychology, 8*, 414–417.

Taylor, E. (1984). *William James on exceptional mental states*. Amherst, MA: University of Massachusetts Press.

Thios, S. J. (1972). Memory for words in repeated sentences. *Journal of Verbal Learning and Verbal Behavior, 11*, 789–793.

Thomas, D. R., and McKelvie, A. R. (1982). Retrieval of memory in the pigeon by context manipulations. *Animal Learning and Behavior, 10*, 1–6.

Thomson, D. M. and Tulving, E. (1970). Associative encoding and retrieval: Weak and strong cues. *Journal of Experimental Psychology, 86*, 255–262.

Thorndike, E. L. (1931). *Human learning*. New York, NY: Century.

Thorndyke, P. W., and Bower, G. H. (1974). Storage and retrieval processes in sentence memory. *Cognitive Psychology, 5*, 515–543.

Titchener, E. B. (1910). The past decade in experimental psychology. *The American Journal of Psychology, 21*, 404–421.

Titchener, E. B. (1909). *A textbook of psychology*. New York, NY: Macmillan.

Toppino, T. C., and Gracen, T. F. (1985). Lag effect and differential organization theory: Nine failures to replicate. *Journal of Experimental Psychology: Learning, Memory, and Cognition, 11*, 185–191.

Townsend, J. T. (1972). Some results concerning the identifiability of parallel and serial processes. *British Journal of Mathematical and Statistical Psychology, 25*, 168–199.

Townsend, J. T., and Ashby, F. G. (1983). *The stochastic modeling of elementary psychological processes*. Cambridge, MA: Cambridge University Press.

Traxel, W. (1985). Hermann Ebbinghaus: In Memoriam. *History of Psychology Newsletter, 17*, 37–41.

Triesman, A. (1964). Selective attention in man. *British Medical Bulletin, 20*, 12–16.

Tulving, E. (1985a). Ebbinghaus's memory: What did he learn and remember? *Journal of Experimental Psychology: Learning, Memory, and Cognition, 11*, 485–490 (a).

Tulving, E. (1985b). How many memory systems are there? *American Psychologist, 40*, 385–398.

Tulving, E. (1983). *Elements of episodic memory*. New York, NY: Oxford University Press.

Tulving, E. (1974). Cue-dependent forgetting. *American Scientist, 62*, 74–82.

Tulving, E. (1972). Episodic and semantic memory. In E. Tulving, and W. Donaldson (Eds.), *Organization of memory*. New York, NY: Academic Press.

Tulving, E. (1968). Theoretical issues in free recall. In T. R. Dixon and D. L. Horton (Eds.) *Verbal behavior and general behavior theory*. Englewood Cliffs, NJ: Prentice-Hall.

Tulving, E. (1966). Subjective organization and the effects of repetition in multi-trial free recall verbal learning. *Journal of Verbal Learning and Verbal Behavior, 5*, 193–197.

Tulving, E. (1964). Intratrial retention: Notes towards a theory of free recall verbal learning. *Psychological Review, 71*, 219–237.

Tulving, E. (1962). Subjective organization in free recall of ''unrelated'' words. *Psychological Review, 69*, 344–354.

Tulving, E. and Bower, G. H. (1974). The logic of memory representations. In G. H. Bower (Ed.), *The psychology of learning and motivation, Vol. 8*. New York, NY: Academic Press, 265–301.

Tulving, E., and Gold, C. (1963). Stimulus information and contextual information as determinants of tachistoscopic recognition of words. *Journal of Experimental Psychology, 66*, 319–327.

Tulving, E., and Madigan, S. A. (1970). Memory and verbal learning. *Annual Review of Psychology, 21,* 437–484.

Tulving, E., and Osler, S. (1967). Transfer effects in whole-part free-recall learning. *Canadian Journal of Psychology, 21,* 253–263.

Tulving, E. and Pearlstone, Z. (1966). Availability versus accessibility of information in memory for words. *Journal of Verbal Learning and Verbal Behavior, 5,* 381–391.

Tulving, E., Schacter, D. L., and Stark, H. A. (1982). Priming effects in word-fragment completion are independent of recognition memory. *Journal of Experimental Psychology: Learning, Memory, Cognition, 8,* 336–342.

Tulving, E., and Thomson, D. M. (1973). Encoding specificity and retrieval processes in episodic memory. *Psychological Review, 80,* 352–372.

Tulving, E. and Watkins, M. J. (1975). Structure of memory traces. *Psychological Review, 82,* 261–275.

Turvey, M. T., & Egan, J. (1969). Contextual change and release from proactive interference in short-term memory. *Journal of Experimental Psychology, 81,* 396–397.

Tversky, A. (1977). Features of similarity. *Psychological Review, 84,* 214–241.

Twedt, H. M., and Underwood, B. J. (1959). Mixed versus unmixed lists in transfer. *Journal of Experimental Psychology, 58,* 111–116.

Uhlein, H. (1985). Hermann Ebbinghaus as textbook author. *History of Psychology Newsletter, 17,* 51–55.

Underwood, B. J. (1983). *Attributes of memory.* Glenview, IL: Scott, Foresman and Co.

Underwood, B. J. (1972). Are we overloading memory? In A. W. Melton and E. Martin (Eds.), *Coding processes in human memory.* Washington, DC: Winston.

Underwood, B. J. (1969a). Attributes of memory. *Psychological Review, 76,* 559–573.

Underwood, B. J. (1969b). Some correlates of item repetition in free-recall learning. *Journal of Verbal Learning and Verbal Behavior, 8,* 83–94.

Underwood, B. J. (1977). *Temporal codes for memories: Issues and problems.* Hillsdale, NJ: Lawrence Erlbaum Associates.

Underwood, B. J. (1966). Motor-skills learning and verbal learning: Some observations. In E. A. Bilodeau (Ed.), *Acquisition of skill.* New York, NY: Academic Press.

Underwood, B. J., (1965). False recognition produced by implicit verbal responses. *Journal of Experimental Psychology, 70,* 122–129.

Underwood, B. J. (1961). Ten years of massed practice on distributed practice. *Psychological Review, 68,* 229–247.

Underwood, B. J. (1957). Interference and forgetting. *Psychological Review, 64,* 49–60.

Underwood, B. J., Rehula, R., and Keppel, G. (1962). Item selection in paired-associate learning. *American Journal of Psychology, 75,* 353–371.

Underwood, B. J. (1951). Associative transfer in verbal learning as a function of response similarity and degree of first-list learning. *Journal of Experimental Psychology, 42,* 44–53.

Van Hoorn, W. and Verhave, T. (1985). Ebbinghaus, Perception and Memory. Paper presented at the Ebbinghaus Symposium, Passau, West Germany.

Van Hoorn, W. and Verhave, T. (1977). Socioeconomic factors and the roots of American psychology. In R. Rieber and K. Salzinger (Eds.) *The roots of american psychology: Historical influences and implications for the future. Annals of the New York Academy of Sciences, 291,* 203–221.

Verhave, T. (1967). G. W. Leibnitz (1646–1716). on the association of ideas and learning. *Psychological Reports, 20,* 111–116.

Verhave, T., and Van Hoorn, W. (1984). The temporalization of the self. In K. Gergen, and M. Gergen (Eds.) *Historical social psychology.* Hillsdale, NJ: Lawrence Erlbaum Associates.

Von Hartmann, E. (1872). *Das Unbewusste vom Standdpunkte der Physiologie und Descendenztheorie.* Berlin, Germany: Naumbaurg.

Waitz, T. (1849). *Lehrbuch der Phychologie als Naturwissenschaft.* Brunswick, Germany: Vieweg.

Wallace, W. H., Turner, S. H., and Perkins, E. E. (1957). *Preliminary studies of human information storage. Unpublished manuscript.* Signal Corps Projects 1320, University of Pennsylvania Institute for Cooperative Research.

Wallace, W. P. (1969). Clustering in free recall based upon input contiguity. *Psychonomic Science, 14,* 290–292.

Warren, H. C. (1921). *A history of association in psychology.* New York, NY: Scribner's.

Warren, H. C. and Farrand, L. (Eds.) (1895). *Psychological Index, 1,* p. 1.

Warren, H. C. and Shaw, W. J. (1895). Further experiments on memory for square size. *Psychological Review, 2,* 239–244.

Warrington, E. K., and Weiskrantz, L. (1970). Amnesic syndrome: Consolidation or retrieval? *Nature, 228,* 628–630.

Watkins, D. C., and Watkins, M. J. (1977). Serial recall and the modality effect: Effects of word frequency. *Journal of Experimental Psychology: Human Learning and Memory, 3,* 712–718.

Watkins, M. J. (1979). Engrams as cuegrams and forgetting as cue overload: A cueing approach to the structure of memory. In C. R. Puff (Ed.), *Memory organization and structure.* New York, NY: Academic Press, 347–372.

Watkins, M. J. (1977). The intricacy of memory span. *Memory & Cognition, 5,* 529–534.

Watkins, M. J. and Peynircioğlu, Z. F. (1983). Three recency effects at the same time. *Journal of Verbal Learning and Verbal Behavior, 22,* 375–384.

Watkins, M. J. and Peynircioğlu, Z. F. (1983). On the nature of the word recall: Evidence for linguistic specificity. *Journal of Verbal Learning and Verbal Behavior, 22,* 385–394.

Watson, R. I. (1974). *Eminent contributors to psychology,* Vols. 1–2. New York, NY: Springer.

Watson, R. I. (1960). The history of psychology: A neglected area. *American Psychologist, 15,* 251–255.

Waugh, N. C. (1961). Free versus serial recall. *Journal of Experimental Psychology, 62,* 496–502.

Waugh, N. C., and Norman, D. A. (1965). Primary memory. *Psychological Review, 72,* 89–104.

Weber, E. H. (1834/1978). *The sense of touch.* Translated by H. Ross, New York, NY: Academic Press.

Wegman, C. (1979). *Psychoanalyse en cognitieve psychologie.* Meppel, The Netherlands: Krips Repro.

Weimer, W. B. (1973). Psycholinguistics and the paradoxes of the Meno. *American Psychologist, 28,* 15–33.

Weldon, M. S., and Roediger, H. L. (1987). Priming of pictures and words on the word fragment completion test: Reversing the picture superiority effect. Unpublished manuscript.

Welford, A. T. (1984). Between bodily changes and performance: Some possible reasons for slowing with age. *Experimental Aging Research, 10,* 73–88.

Wertheimer, M. (1979). *A brief history of psychology.* New York, NY: Holt, Rinehart & Winston.

Whipple, G. M. (1903). Studies in pitch discrimination. *American Journal of Psychology, 14,* 289–309.

Whipple, G. M. (1902). An analytic study of the memory image and the process of judgment in the discrimination of clangs and tones (concluded). *American Journal of Psychology, 13,* 219–268.

Whipple, G. M. (1901). An analytic study of the memory image and the process of judgment in the discrimination of clangs and tones. *American Journal of Psychology, 12,* 409–457.

Whitehead, L. G. (1896). A study of visual and aural memory processes. *Psychological Review, 3,* 258–269.

Whitten, W. B., and Bjork, R. A. (1972, April). *Test events as learning trials: The importance of being imperfect.* Paper presented at the Midwestern Mathematical Psychology Meeting, Bloomington, IN.

Wickelgren, W. A. (1979). Chunking and consolidation: A theoretical synthesis of semantic networks, configuring in conditioning, S-R versus cognitive learning, normal forgetting, the amnesic syndrome, and the hippocampal arousal system. *Psychological Review, 86,* 44–60.

Wickelgren, W. A. (1969). Context-sensitive coding, associative memory, and serial order in (speech) behaviour. *Psychological Review, 76,* 1–15.

Wickelgren, W. A. (1964). Size of rehearsal group and short-term memory. *Journal of Experimental Psychology, 68,* 413–419.

Wickens, D. D. (1972). Characteristics of word encoding. In A. W. Melton and E. Martin (Eds.) *Coding processes in human memory.* Washington, DC: Winston.

Wickens, D. D. (1970). Encoding categories of words: An empirical approach to meaning. *Psychological Review, 77,* 1–15.

Wickens, D. D., Born, D. G., and Allen, C. K. (1963). Proactive inhibition and item similarity in short-term memory. *Journal of Verbal Learning and Verbal Behavior, 2,* 440–445.

Wickens, D. D., and Cermak, L. S. (1967). Transfer of synonyms and antonyms in mixed and unmixed lists. *Journal of Verbal Learning and Verbal Behavior, 6,* 832–839.

Wickens, D. D., Hall, J., and Reid, L. S. (1949). Associative and retroactive inhibition as a function of the drive stimulus. *Journal of Comparative and Physiological Psychology, 42,* 398–403.

Wickens, D. D., Moody, M. J., and Dow, R. (1981). The nature and timing of the retrieval processes and of interference effects. *Journal of Experimental Psychology: General, 110,* 1–20.

Wickens, C. D., Tuber, D. S., and Wickens, D. D. (1983). Memory for the conditioned response: The proactive effect of preexposure to potential conditioning stimuli and context change. *Journal of Experimental Psychology: General, 112,* 41–57.

Williams, J. P. (1961). A selection artifact in Rock's study of the role of repetition. *Journal of Experimental Psychology, 62,* 627–628.

Winocur, G., and Kinsbourne, M. (1978). Contextual cueing as an aid to Korsakoff amnesia. *Neuropsychologia, 16,* 671–682.

Winograd, T. (1972). *Understanding natural language.* Cambridge, MA: MIT Press.

Winnick, W. A., and Daniel, S. A. (1970). Two kinds of response priming in tachistoscopic recognition. *Journal of Experimental Psychology, 84,* 74–81.

Winston, M. E. and Chaffin, R. (1982). "The semantics of part-whole relationships." Paper presented at the meeting of the American Psychological Association, Washington, DC.

Winston, M. E., Chaffin, R., and Herrmann, D. J. (in press). A taxonomy of part-whole relations. *Cognitive Science.*

Wissler, C. (1901). The correlation of mental and physical tests. *Psychological Review. Monograph Supplements, 3* (Number 16).

Wolfe, H. K. (1886). Untersuchungen uber das Tongedächtnis. *Philosophische Studien, 3,* 534–571.

Wolman, B. B. (Ed.) (1968a). *Historical roots of contemporary psychology* New York, NY: Harper and Row.

Wolman, B. B. (1968b). The historical role of Johann Friedrich Herbart. In B. B. Wolman (Ed.) *Historical roots of contemporary psychology.* New York, NY: Harper and Row.

Wood, G. (1972). Organizational processes and free recall. In E. Tulving and W. Donaldson (Eds.), *Organization of memory.* New York, NY: Academic Press.

Woods, R. T., and Piercy, M. (1974). A similarity between amnesic memory and normal forgetting. *Neuropsychologia, 12,* 437–445.

Woodward, A. E., Jr., Bjork, R. A., and Jongeward, R. H., Jr. (1973). Recall and recognition as a function of primary rehearsal. *Journal of Verbal Learning and Verbal Behavior, 12,* 608–617.

Woodward, W. R. and Ash, M. G. (Eds.). (1982). *The problematic science: Psychology in nineteenth-century thought.* New York, NY: Praeger.

Woodworth, R. S. (1938). *Experimental psychology.* New York, NY: Holt.

Woodworth, R. S. (1909). Hermann Ebbinghaus. *Journal of Philosophy and Scientific Methods, 6,* 253–256.

Wozniak, R. H. (1984). A brief history of serial publication in psychology. In D. V. Osier and R. H. Wozniak, (Eds.) *A century of serial publication in psychology, 1850–1950.* Millwood, NY: Kraus.

Wundt, W. (1873–74). *Grundzüge der physiologischen Psychologie,* Leipzig, Germany: W. Engelmann.

Yates, F. A. (1966). *The art of memory.* London, England: Routledge and Kegan Paul.

Yerkes, R. M. (1911). *Introduction to psychology.* New York, NY: Holt.

Young, D. R., and Bellezza, F. W. (1982). Encoding variability, memory organization, and the repetition effect. *Journal of Experimental Psychology: Learning, Memory, and Cognition, 8,* 545–559.

Young, M. N. (1961). *Bibliography of memory.* Philadelphia, PA: Chilton.

Young, R. K. (1968). Serial learning. In T. R. Dixon and D. L. Horton (Eds.) *Verbal behavior and general behavior theory.* Englewood Cliffs, NJ: Prentice-Hall.

Young, R. M. (1966). Scholarship and the history of the behavioral sciences. *History of Science, 5,* 1–51.

Author Index

Subject Index